With Best
Wishes
Dick Sylvester

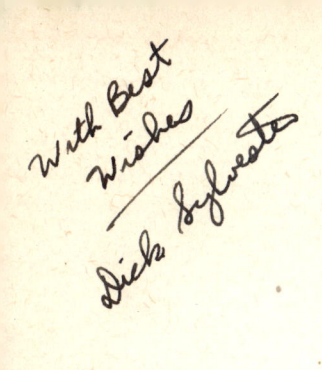

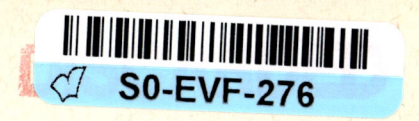

Cavendish: Life of Cardinal Wolsey

EARLY ENGLISH TEXT SOCIETY
No. 243
1959 (for 1957)
PRICE 35s.

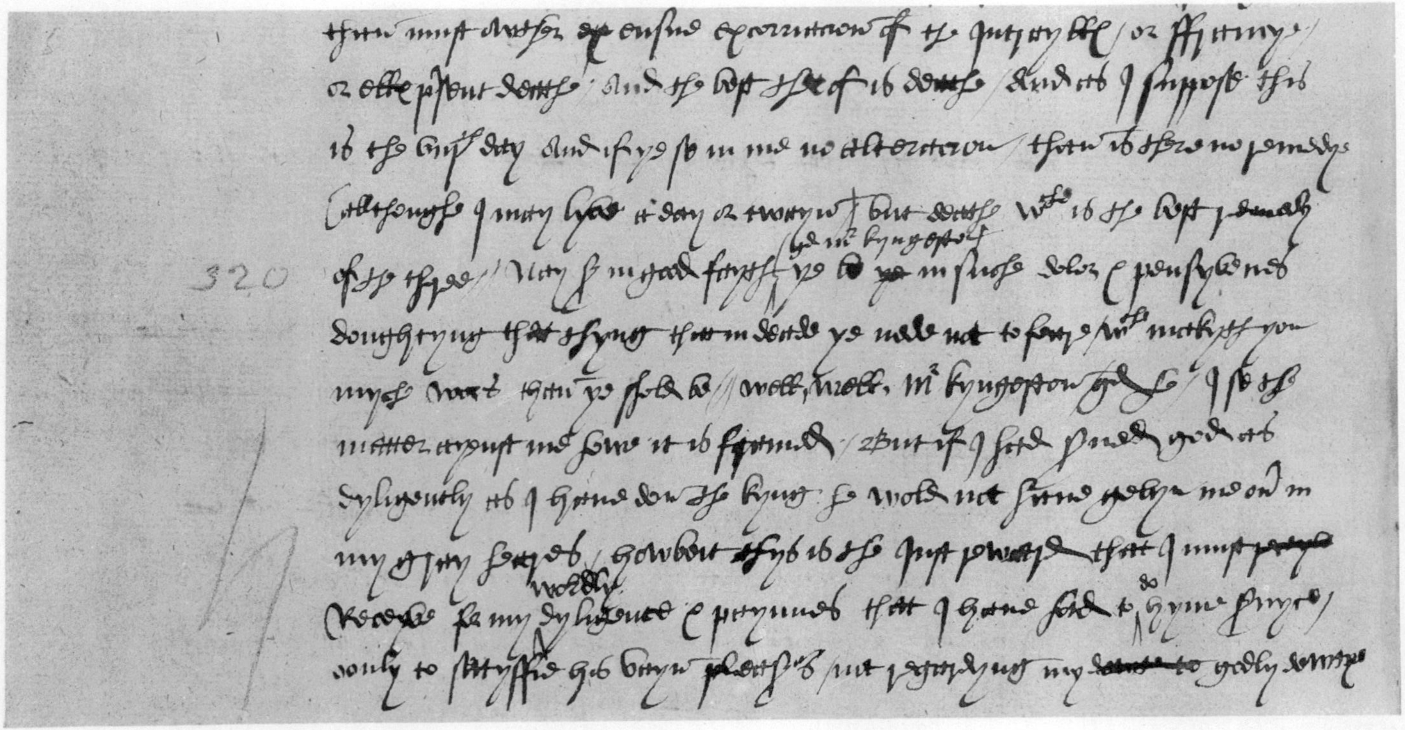

British Museum MS. Egerton 2402, f. 88^{v}
(lower portion)

THE LIFE AND DEATH
of
CARDINAL WOLSEY

by
GEORGE CAVENDISH

EDITED BY
RICHARD S. SYLVESTER

Published for
THE EARLY ENGLISH TEXT SOCIETY
by the
OXFORD UNIVERSITY PRESS
LONDON   NEW YORK   TORONTO
1959

Upsala College
Library
East Orange, N. J.

© Early English Text Society 1959

PRINTED AND BOUND IN GREAT BRITAIN BY
JARROLD AND SONS LTD, NORWICH

PREFACE

I should like to take this opportunity to thank all those who, in their various ways, have helped to make this edition possible. Among many others, I am particularly grateful to the Rev. M. B. McNamee, S.J., of St. Louis University, who, years ago, first aroused my interest in the *Life of Wolsey*; to Professor F. P. Wilson of Oxford University for his whole-hearted encouragement and many helpful suggestions; and to Mr. N. R. Ker, University Reader in Palaeography at Oxford, who first taught me to read Renaissance script and who supervised my transcription of Egerton 2402. I am greatly indebted to the many librarians who have helped me in my search for manuscripts. I wish to thank particularly Dr. R. W. Hunt of the Bodleian Library, the authorities of the British Museum, Mr. H. W. Parke of Trinity College, Dublin, Mr. P. I. King of Lamport Hall, Northampton, Miss Brunskill of the York Minster Library, the Duke of Northumberland (for permission to examine a microfilm copy of his MS. of the *Life*), Dr. Giles E. Dawson of the Folger Shakespeare Library, and the staffs of the Yale and Harvard Libraries for their constant co-operation. Miss Nelly McNeill O'Farrell and Miss Mabel Mills have given me invaluable aid in my work with the London records and Professors Charles T. Prouty and Helge Kökeritz of Yale have supplied me with many helpful hints. I am most deeply grateful to Professor Davis Harding of Yale for his kindly, albeit forceful and searching, criticism and to Dr. C. T. Onions, who helped me to put the glossary in its final form. Finally, I wish to express my thanks to the Honorary Secretary of the Early English Text Society, Mr. R. W. Burchfield, for his patient guidance in all the various stages of editorial work that have preceded this edition, to the members of the Council of the Society for their helpful criticisms, and to my wife for her constant and careful proof-reading of the final manuscript.

R. S. S.

Yale University,
1 *June* 1958

CONTENTS

British Museum MS. Egerton 2402, f. 88ᵛ   *Frontispiece*

PREFACE	v
INTRODUCTION	ix
The Manuscript	ix
Previous Editions	xi
George Cavendish	xiii
Date of Composition	xxvi
Sources	xxviii
Cavendish as Historian	xxxii
The Text	xxxviii
TEXT	3
BIBLIOGRAPHY	189
NOTES	193
APPENDICES	
A. William Forrest's *History of Grisild the Second*	259
B. The Battle of Pavia and the Bohemian Revolt	263
C. The Speeches at the Divorce Trial	268
D. Some Notes on the Later History of the *Life*	270
E. The Secondary Manuscripts	274
GLOSSARY	289
INDEX OF NAMES	301

INTRODUCTION

The Manuscript

The present edition of George Cavendish's *Life and Death of Cardinal Wolsey*[1] is based upon the autograph manuscript, British Museum MS. Egerton 2402. The manuscript is a small paper folio of the sixteenth century, bound in red boards. The pages measure 7 × 11 inches. There are 154 leaves in the manuscript, the *Life* occupying ff. 4 to 93, with f. 4ᵛ blank.[2] The text runs consecutively from f. 5 to f. 93; f. 93ᵛ is blank. Two blank leaves then intervene before Cavendish's poems, which occupy ff. 94 to 151.[3] Ff. 151ᵛ and 152 are blank; on ff. 152ᵛ and 153 a nineteenth-century hand has entered a genealogy of the Cavendish family. F. 153ᵛ is blank; f. 154, the last in the manuscript, contains a list, in a seventeenth-century hand, of eight items that appear to relate to the settlement of an estate in the manor of Exton.[4]

The manuscript is written throughout in a relatively tight and somewhat cramped hand of the early or middle sixteenth century; the ink is a faded, but generally quite legible, light brown. A page of text normally contains from 27 to 32 lines. The left-hand margins average about 1½ inches, but the lines of text often extend to the extreme right-hand edge of the page.[5]

[1] Referred to hereafter as 'the *Life*'.
[2] The first page of the text, which apparently contained about thirty lines of script, has been lost in the autograph manuscript. These lines are reproduced in this edition from Bodleian MS. Douce 363, one of the earliest, as far as it can be ascertained, of the extant secondary manuscripts. See Appendix E on the secondary manuscripts.
[3] The two blank leaves between the *Life* and the poems are not numbered. A sixteenth-century hand (not Cavendish's) originally numbered the *Life* and the poems separately; these numbers have been cancelled and a new hand has numbered the leaves in pencil throughout the manuscript. This later pagination is adopted in the references to the manuscript in this edition.
[4] This list may possibly contain information regarding the owners of the manuscript in the seventeenth century, but I have not been able to discover anything about its compiler.
[5] In some cases the right-hand edge of the page has been frayed away, thus occasioning the loss of a few final letters. These have been supplied in the present edition and their occurrence noted. For a full account of the editorial principles adopted see 'The Text', p. xxxviiiff.

There are no catchwords and no marginal glosses. The author has divided his narrative into sections by spacing large blocks of text a few lines below a preceding section and by heavily shading the first few words of each such section.

There can be little doubt that Egerton 2402 is an autograph. On two pages immediately preceding the text of the *Life* (ff. 2, 2ᵛ) and at the end of both the *Life* and of his poems Cavendish has left ample testimony to his authorship. On f. 2,[1] in the same hand as that in which the text is written, we find the word '⟨I⟩hesu' at the extreme upper edge of the page and beneath it the word 'Cardynall*es*', followed by the lines:

vincit qui patitur// qᵈ G.C.
Maxima vindicta paciencia.

Under this is written 'Cauendyssh de Cauendyss in Com*itatu* Suff*olk* gent' and a little further down the page, 'I begane this booke the 4 day of novemb*er*.' On f. 2ᵛ the initials 'G.C.' are written vertically along the left-hand side of the page and beneath them is the motto of the Cavendish family, 'Concordia res crescunt Cavendo tutus.' F. 3 is blank and on f. 3ᵛ we find the name C. Rossington, followed by an addition apparently in the hand of Mr. Lloyd, who possessed the manuscript in the early nineteenth century, 'i.e. Clement Rossington of Dronfield Gent. whose son Mr James Rossington gave me this MS.' At the bottom of the first page of the text (f. 4) the author has written 'ffinis. qᵈ G.C.' and these words also occur at the end of several of Cavendish's individual poems later in the manuscript. On f. 149, after the 'Lenvoy de Auctour' but before the final epitaph on Queen Mary, occur the lines:

ffinie Et compile le xxiiijᵒʳ Iour de
Iunij aⁱˢ regno*rum* Philippi R*eg*is & Regine
Marie/ iiijᵗᵒ & vᵗᵒ
p*er* le auctor G.C./

[1] f. 1 contains an engraving of a Holbein Henry VIII, pasted in by a later hand. This picture is the same as that reproduced by Singer in his edition of the *Life* (Chiswick, 1825, 2 vols.), ii, 91.

Immediately beneath them is written

> Nouus Rex/ nova lex/ Noua sola Regina
> probz. peur Ruina(?).[1]

The nature of the text itself bears out the evidence of the above passages. Interlineations and cancellations are frequent and occasionally involve changes in the meaning of the text. More often, however, these corrections result from the fact that the author either wrote the same word twice by mistake[2] or overestimated the width of his page. He did not hyphenate words but rather, if he found after beginning a word that he did not have room to complete it at the end of the line, he cancelled the syllables already written (or sometimes the whole word, if it was too cramped to be easily legible) and began the word again on the next line. After a careful study of these cancellations and interlineations, all of which are noted in the present edition, I am inclined to think that Egerton 2402 does not represent Cavendish's first draft of his work or his 'foul papers', but is rather his fair copy.[3] In any event there can be little doubt that the author subjected his book to frequent revision and that he proof-read it with extreme care. As can be seen from the text, the *Life* has required a very small amount of emendation.

Previous Editions

Cavendish's *Life of Wolsey* remained in manuscript from the time of its composition (1554–8) until 1641, when a garbled edition appeared from the press of William Sheares.[4] Meanwhile the work had been widely circulated in manuscript form and large portions of it had been incorporated into the chronicles of Stowe, Holinshed, and Speed.[5] The manuscripts from which the chroniclers worked, though not preserving the

---

[1] The reading is uncertain.

[2] This is the sort of mistake that a writer who is copying one manuscript from another often makes. It is usually less frequent in an original first draft.

[3] This is certainly not true of the poems, where several stanzas are left incomplete.

[4] There was also a pirated edition in the same year. For an account of the editions prior to Singer's, see Appendix D.

[5] There are at least thirty-one extant secondary manuscripts. These are described in Appendix E. The uses to which Cavendish's *Life* was put by later writers are discussed in Appendix D.

Introduction

full text of Egerton 2402, nevertheless contained a great deal more of the *Life* than did the 1641 edition. The autograph manuscript itself was not discovered until the early nineteenth century when S. W. Singer made what has been to this day the only attempt to produce a scholarly edition.[1]

Singer, as he tells us in his preface, had at first decided to edit the *Life* by collating as many of the secondary manuscripts as he could discover. 'Upon naming the design to my friend Mr. Douce, he mentioned to me a very curious copy in the possession of Mr. Lloyd. . . . Upon application to that gentleman, he . . . immediately placed the manuscript in my hands.'[2] Convinced that Mr. Lloyd's manuscript was the autograph, Singer tried to trace back its history and was able, in his second edition, to offer the following note:

> Mr. Hunter informs me that Clement Rossington the elder, who must be here alluded to, died in 1737. He acquired the manor of Dronfield by his marriage with Sarah Burton, sister and co-heir of Ralph Burton, of Dronfield, Esq. who died in 1714. The father of Ralph and Sarah Burton was Francis Burton, also of Dronfield, who was aged twenty-five at the visitation of Derbyshire, 1662, and the mother, Helen, daughter and heir of Cassibelan Burton, son of William Burton the distinguished antiquary and historian of Leicestershire. There is good reason to believe that the Rossingtons were not likely to *purchase* a book of this curiosity, and it is therefore more than probable that it once formed part of the library of William Burton, other books which had been his having descended to them.[3]

I have been unable to add anything to Hunter's theory of the early history of the manuscript.

A good deal of information regarding Singer's edition can be obtained from the loose sheets of paper which Douce inserted into his own copy of the 1825 edition, now in the Bodleian

---

[1] *The Life of Cardinal Wolsey and Metrical Visions* (Cavendish's poems), ed. S. W. Singer, 2 vols., Chiswick, 1825, and 1 vol. (without the poems), London, 1827. Most of the subsequent editions have been based on Singer's text. The two other independent editions, those of William Morris (transcribed by F. S. Ellis) for the Kelmscott Press (Hammersmith, 1893) and that of the Alcuin Press (Chipping Campden, 1930) are 'art' editions. Though both claim to be 'faithfully transcribed' they are in fact, particularly Morris's, shot through with errors. Neither provides any scholarly apparatus.
[2] 1825 ed., I, xv–xvi.   [3] 1827 ed., p. xv, n. 3. Not in the 1825 ed.

Introduction xiii

Library. We there learn that Singer had received Mr. Lloyd's manuscript by 14 May 1821. Douce also records that the autograph was later sold 'at Mr. Lloyd's sale March 1833 for £81. 14 to Thorpe, perhaps for Heber.' The Rev. Thomas Corser either acquired the manuscript through that sale or came to possess it later, for it was from his library that the British Museum purchased it at Manchester on 13 December 1876.[1]

In editing the autograph manuscript, Singer decided, with somewhat unfortunate consequences, to 'take the spelling and pointing into his own hands.'[2] The present edition has been undertaken in an effort to remove from the text many of the errors that crept into it either from Singer's misreadings of the manuscript or from the carelessness of subsequent revisers.[3] The amount of corruption that has overtaken the *Life* since the discovery of the autograph manuscript is, of course, scarcely comparable to that which it underwent in the hands of the sixteenth- and early-seventeenth-century scribes; but it has been sufficiently pervasive to warrant an edition such as the present one, which lays claim to have firmly established the text upon a permanent, scholarly basis.

George Cavendish

It was not until the present century that a good deal of the mystery and legend which had previously surrounded the early

---

[1] According to a pencilled note on the fly leaf of the manuscript. See also the *Catalogue of Additions to the Manuscripts in the British Museum* (1876-81), pp. 282-3.

[2] 1825 ed., I, xxi. He attempted to keep the original spelling and punctuation in the poems, which, however, he did not include in his one-volume edition of 1827. Many of Singer's pencilled glosses are still visible in the autograph manuscript.

[3] The following list of some of Singer's errors will furnish concrete evidence of the degree to which he found Cavendish's manuscript 'difficult' or even 'illegible'. I give Singer's reading, followed by the page number of his first edition, volume I, and then my own reading: things, 3, trouthe; farther, 4, fyrst; there at school with him, 5, at scole there w^t hyme; therby to have appeased, 7, therby to appese; it chanced my said Lord, 7, Yt chaunced the lord; this schoolmaster, 8, The Scole M^r; also to be destitute, 8, to be also destitute; in the present sight, 9, in present sight; was in his head, 9, was pact in his hede; the king one day counselling, 10, the kyng consultyng; of weight and gravity, 10, of waytie gravitie; enterprise and journey, 10, enterpriced Iourney; by ten of the clock, 12, by fore x^{en} of cloke; persons, 26, prisoners; precinct, 28, provynce; opposed, 217, oppressed; forced, 227, fferced (i.e. 'Farced').

history of the Cavendish family began to be removed through the patient efforts of genealogists. Since the descendants of Sir William Cavendish (George's brother) rose to the peerage within two generations of his death,[1] it behoved the pedigree-makers of the seventeenth century to provide them with a Norman ancestry which, passing lightly over the family's Tudor origin, would place its foundations deep in the ancient history of the realm. Thus we are informed that the Cavendishes go back to a certain Ralf de Gernon (d. 1248) and stem directly from the famous Chief Justice of Richard II's reign, Sir John Cavendish.[2] Incidentally, we are told the legendary story of how John Cavendish, the son of the Chief Justice, slew Wat Tyler at Smithfield and how the enraged peasants retaliated by later beheading Sir John himself at Bury St. Edmunds.[3]

The facts of the matter, as they affect the ancestry of Wolsey's biographer and his brother, are by no means so extraordinary. The Cavendish family, so far as it can be ascertained, goes back to a certain 'William atte Watre' of Ewell, Surrey, whose son, Thomas (d. 1348) changed his name to 'Thomas de Cavendish' after that of the London mercer, Walter de Cavendish, whom he served as apprentice from 1304 to 1312.[4] The fourteenth- and fifteenth-century Cavendishes were all mercers and drapers of the city, one of them (Stephen, d. 1372) serving as Lord Mayor. After the death of Stephen's children and those of his brother John (d. 1349), the pedigree shows a gap until we reach William Cavendish, mercer (d. 1433) and his brother Robert, Serjeant-at-law (d. 1439). Not enough data have survived to prove that William and Robert were closely related to the

[1] The Devonshire family obtained its barony in 1605 and its earldom in 1676. The two ducal families of Devonshire and Newcastle both trace their descent from William Cavendish. For a full account, see the Rev. Joseph Hunter's pamphlet, 'Who wrote Cavendish's *Life of Wolsey?*' (1814), reprinted in Singer's edition of the *Life*, II, xiii–lxxii.

[2] This pedigree is given in full detail by Collins. See his *Peerage* (1768), I, 279–83. The best modern account of the family's early history is in J. Horace Round's *Family Origins and other Studies* (London, 1930), pp. 22–32, which forms the basis for the present study.

[3] Wat Tyler was killed on 15 June, 1381 by a certain Ralf Standish; Sir John Cavendish had actually been executed the day before. See Round, pp. 28–30.

[4] Round, p. 26.

Introduction xv

famous Chief Justice; it seems probable that there was some connection between them, for Sir John's daughter-in-law (Alice Neel, d. 1419) made the brothers her executors, but beyond this suggestion we are not able to go.[1] It was this William Cavendish, mercer of London, who was the great grandfather of the author of the *Life of Wolsey*. At his death in 1433 he left one son, Thomas, who died in 1477.[2] Thomas had married Catherine Scudamore, who died on 15 September 1499 and was buried at St. Botolph's, Aldersgate.[3] Catherine and Thomas had one son, also named Thomas, the father of our author and his brother William.[4] We know a good deal more about this Thomas Cavendish (the younger) than we do of his immediate ancestors, for it was apparently he that first brought the family name into governmental work. Some time before 1488[5] he had married Alice, the daughter and

[1] *Ibid.*, pp. 31–32.
[2] Thomas Ruggles, 'Notices of the Manor of Cavendish, in Suffolk, and of the Cavendish family while possessed of that Manor,' *Archaeologia*, XI (1794), 50–62. Ruggles's article is accurate for the fifteenth- and sixteenth-century history of the family but its statements about the earlier Cavendishes need considerable correction.
[3] See the inscription on her tomb in John Weever's *Ancient Funeral Monuments* (London, 1631), Sig. Nnn5. Weever also records the epitaphs of George's mother Alice (12 November 1515) and Margaret, the second wife of his brother William (16 June 1540) from the same church. His inscriptions agree with the three 'hic jacet's' that a nineteenth-century hand has copied into the back of the autograph manuscript. Weever says that he got the epitaphs from 'Robert Treswell, Esquire, Somerset Herald, lately deceased' who had copied them 'about some thirtie seuen yeares since' [i.e. not after 1594]. Few or none of them, he adds, 'are to be found at this present time.' Since the reading of the epitaphs in Egerton 2402 agrees quite closely with Weever's text, it seems impossible to determine whether or not these were copied from Weever or from some other source. The oldest monument now in St. Botolph's, which was rebuilt in 1741, dates only from 1563.
[4] Ruggles, op. cit., says that Thomas Cavendish, George's father, had four sons, one of whom was also named Thomas. I have found no reference to these other two sons, however; there was a sister, Mary Cavendish, who was alive in 1524.
[5] According to the *IPM* taken at his death (R. O., E152/607/13), which refers to him and his wife as married in that year. Reference is also made to Thomas Cavendish's acquisition of the manor of Overhall from '[John Bourgchier Lord Ferrers of Groby, William Chapman, and John Clerke of Cavendish, Suffolk' by a deed of 4 July, 1488. This would seem to be, contrary to Ruggles's statement that the manor belonged to the Cavendishes in the early fifteenth century, the first record of their possession of it. Francis Bickley in his *The Cavendish Family* (London, 1911), p. 7, says that George Cavendish had to defend his inheritance against the claims of Ferrers and Clerke in 1525, but I have found no reference to such claims having been made.

heir of John Smyth the younger of Padbrook Hall, Suffolk, and by this time he was already associated with the Exchequer. He became Clerk of the Pipe under Henry VII and held that office until his death on 13 April 1524. It is more than likely that the elder Cavendish first came into contact with Wolsey while serving in the Exchequer and it may well be that it was through his father's offices that young George Cavendish was placed in the cardinal's service. We can gather a good deal about Thomas's duties from the following description of the work that his position entailed. A 'Clerk of the Pipe' was

> ... an officer in the kings exchequer, who hauing all accounts and debts due to the king delivered and drawne downe out of the Remembrancers offices, chargeth them downe into the great rolle: who also writeth summons to the Shyreeue, to levie the said debts vpon the goods and catels of deptors: and if they haue no goods, then doth he drawe them downe to the L. treasurers remembrancer, to write extreats [i.e. 'estreats', copies of original fines or amercements (*O.E.D.*)] against their lands. The awncient revenew of the Crowne, remaineth in charge afore him, & he seeth the same answered by the fermers & shyreeues to the King. He maketh a charge to al Shyreeues of their summons of the pipe and greenwax, and seeth it answered vpon their accompts. He hath the drawing and ingrossing of all leases of the Kings land.[1]

Thomas Cavendish retained the royal favour under both Henry VII and Henry VIII.[2] He is twice mentioned as a recipient of emoluments from the king,[3] and he gradually

[1] John Cowell, *The Interpreter: or Booke Containing the Signification of Words* (Cambridge, 1607), Sigs. P3–P3v. The 'Clerks of the Pipe' were so called because 'their Records that are registered in their smallest Rolles, are altogether like Organe Pipes.' (Weever, op. cit., Sig. Nnn5v.)

[2] He and his wife are mentioned in Henry VIII's general pardon of 1509 (LP, 2nd ed., revised by R. H. Brodie, I, Part 1, 438). The description of the Cavendishes is as follows: 'Thomas Cavendissh, Caundissh or Candissh, of London, and *Cavendissh*, Suff., g[entleman] of the Exchequer of Henry VII, s[on] and h[eir] of Thomas C., esq; and Alice his wife, d[aughter] and h[eir] of John Smyth, jun., late of Cavendissh, Suff. esq., and kinswoman and h[eir] of John Smyth, senior, of Cavendish, 13 July [1509].'

[3] See the *Letters and Papers Henry VIII*, where he is said to have received £10 'during pleasure' from Henry VII (II, 2736, p. 877) and is mentioned in a royal grant of 8 February, 1520 (III, 644). In May of that year his name appears in an account of 'stuff' used by the Queen (III, 852).

Introduction

acquired a considerable amount of property in his native Suffolk. A subsidy list of April? 1522 for the hundred of Babergh, Suffolk, shows that he owned lands there worth £25 by the year.[1] In 1524 a similar list for Samford describes him as having £6 6s. 8d. in goods in that hundred.[2] His will[3] and the Inquisition Post Mortem taken after his death testify to the relatively comfortable circumstances that he and his family enjoyed.

George Cavendish, the author of the *Life of Wolsey*, was probably the eldest and certainly the eldest surviving son of Thomas and Alice. We cannot precisely determine the date of his birth, but it probably occurred in 1499.[4] His early life and education must remain conjectural, but we know that he was at Cambridge in 1510, at about the age of eleven.[5] He may have remained there for some years, but he left without taking a degree. In 1515, Alice Cavendish died[6] and George's father then married a certain 'Agnes', whose maiden name has not survived in the records.

It could not have been more than a few years after his mother's death that George Cavendish himself married for the first time. Confirmation of this first marriage is based on very late evidence, but there seems to be little reason to question its authenticity. On 16 October 1834, Richard Almack of Melford, Suffolk, wrote to the *Gentleman's Magazine* describing a carving (apparently designed for a mantelpiece) that had been uncovered in excavations near the old site of Cavendish Overhall. The carving showed the Cavendish arms[7] impaling

[1] *Report of the Royal Commission on Historical MSS.*, 'Ancaster MSS.' (1907), p. 495.
[2] 'Suffolk in 1524,' *Suffolk Green Books*, No. x (Woodbridge, 1910), p. 305. The subsidy was paid by 15 February 1524, two months before Thomas's death.
[3] P.C.C. Bodfelde 23. It was made on 13 April 1524, the day of his death, and proved on 22 August. For the *IPM* see above, p. xv. n. 5.
[4] His father's *IPM* shows him to have been twenty-four years old on 18 May 1524, thus fixing his birth between 18 May 1499 and 19 May 1500. Since Alice and Thomas were married by 1488, it is not unlikely that, before George's birth, they may have had other children who did not survive.
[5] *Athenae Cantabrigienses*, ed. C. H. and Thompson Cooper, 2 vols. (1858), I, 217.
[6] See her epitaph in Weever, op. cit. It does not appear that Thomas had any further children by Agnes, who is mentioned as his widow in his will.
[7] 'S. 3 stags' heads cabossed A.' *Athen. Cant.*, I, 218.

those of Spring. The writer continues his description as follows:

> The arms impaled are those used by the Springs of Pakenham, in this county, who became Baronets, and were descended from Thomas Spring of Lavenham, who died 1486. Lavenham is about seven miles from Cavendish, and the Springs were very wealthy clothiers, and intermarried with the De Veres Earls of Oxford.[1]

We do not know which daughter of the Spring family George married, nor can we be certain about the date of the marriage itself. It may have occurred after his entry into Wolsey's service.[2]

Whatever may have been the circumstances of this first marriage, it may safely be conjectured that George's first wife died not long afterwards. For it would appear that he married again in the early 1520s, this time with Margery Kemp, the daughter of William Kemp and Mary Colt of Spains Hall, Essex.[3] Once again the date of his marriage eludes us and we are forced to fall back upon the internal evidence afforded by a somewhat ambiguous passage in the *Life of Wolsey* itself. After his arrest at Cawood in 1530 the cardinal said to his faithful servant:

> ffor nowe/ q^d he/ that I se this gentilman/ (meanyng by me) howe faythefull/ howe diligent/ And howe paynfull, synce the begynneng of my troble/ he hathe serued me/ Abandonyng his owen contrie/ his wyfe & childerne/ his howsse & famelye/ his rest & quyotnes/ only to serue me/ etc.[4]

This passage was cautiously and correctly interpreted by Hunter as indicating that the author of the *Life* 'was married,

---

[1] *Gentleman's Magazine*, New Series, Vol. III, Jan. to June 1835, p. 613. A drawing of the carving is reproduced in Almack's article.
[2] That is, at some time prior to 1522. See below.
[3] See Philip Morant, *The History and Antiquities of Essex* (London, 1768), 2 vols., II, 363. Mary Colt was the sister of Sir Thomas More's first wife Jane, perhaps the younger sister whom More favoured when 'of a certain pity' he married the elder. See the anecdote in Roper's *Life of More*, ed. E. V. Hitchcock (E.E.T.S., o.s. 197, 1935), p. 6. A genealogy of the Colts is given on p. 107.
[4] Below, 159/1–5.

Introduction

and had a family *probably* before he entered into the Cardinal's service, *certainly* while he was engaged in it'.[1] Since there is no record of any children by Cavendish's first marriage and since we know that he had at least a son (William) and a daughter (Jane)[2] in the second, it would appear safe to conclude that it was to his second wife that the cardinal alluded. And if Cavendish had, according to Wolsey, several 'children' while in the cardinal's service, we may probably conclude that his second marriage occurred at some time between 1520 and 1525.

We are on somewhat surer ground when we attempt to establish the date of Cavendish's entry into Wolsey's service. It is not unlikely, as we mentioned previously, that Thomas Cavendish, through his position in the Treasury, was able to procure a post for his son. In the *Life* itself Cavendish speaks as an eye-witness for the first time when he relates the Percy-Anne episode, which occurred in 1522.[3] Thus we can be sure that he was in Wolsey's service by that date and he may have entered the household even earlier. Apart from the evidence which his book furnishes, we have only a reference in the *Chronicle of Calais* to a 'master Caundishe' who was in Wolsey's retinue during the trip to France in 1527.[4] Our author may also be identified with the 'George Cavendish' who was 'escheator' for Bedfordshire and Buckinghamshire during 1528 and 1529, an office which George may have owed to the influence of the cardinal.[5]

The *Life of Wolsey* itself provides us with our best account

---

[1] Hunter, op. cit., p. xli.   [2] See below, p. xxv.
[3] See the historical note to 29/34.
[4] See the note to 44/25–26. Cavendish's name does not appear in the list of the cardinal's servants that attended him on the 1521 embassy to Bruges, but a 'Richard Candyshe' is mentioned there. See MS. Harley 620, f. 41, reprinted in the *Chronicle of Calais*, pp. 97–8. 'Richard' may possibly be an error for 'George', but it is more likely that he is to be identified with a 'Richard Cavendish' who is frequently mentioned in the *Letters and Papers* between 1530 and 1550 as one of Cromwell's agents and as a government official. It is not impossible that this Richard may have been one of the 'four sons' that, according to Ruggles, Thomas Cavendish is supposed to have had. A subsidy roll for Wolsey's household in 1525 (partially calendared in LP, IV, 6185) is also extant, but I have been unable to obtain any additional information about this list,
[5] *Tenth Report of the Deputy Keeper of the Records*, Appendix, ii, 6.

of the nature of Cavendish's duties while in the service of the great cardinal. There we find him entrusted with many tasks, all of them resulting more or less directly from his primary obligation of 'attending personally upon my lord'. He was primarily a messenger, as he shows himself to have been on the French embassy, one who prepared the way for the arrival of the cardinal himself. The servants of the household looked to him for instructions and, in 1527, it was to him that the preparations for the great banquet at Hampton Court were entrusted. The character of Bassiolo in Chapman's comedy *The Gentleman Usher* (1606, written about 1602) embodies a convenient summary of the duties that an office like Cavendish's entailed:

> Lasso: Say, now, Bassiolo, you on whom relies
> The general disposition of my house
> In this our preparation for the Duke,
> Are all our officers at large instructed
> For fit discharge of their peculiar places?
> Bas: At large, my lord, instructed.
> Las: Are all our chambers hung? Think you our house
> Amply capacious to lodge all the train?
> Bas: Amply capacious, I am passing glad.
> And now, then, to our mirth and musical show,
> Which, after supper, we intend t'endure,
> Welcome's chief dainties; for choice cates at home
> Ever attend on princes, mirth abroad.[1]

We may note here the rather remarkable circumstance that no evidence, except for his marriage with Margery Kemp, has survived to connect George Cavendish with the circle of Sir Thomas More. Margery was More's niece by marriage and it seems likely that Cavendish would have known the Lord Chancellor with some intimacy. Moreover, he would have seen More frequently in his days as Wolsey's servant. Yet not only is there nothing in the records to testify to contacts between Cavendish and More's relatives, but the *Life*

---

[1] George Chapman, 'The Gentleman Usher', in *The Plays and Poems of George Chapman*, ed. T. M. Parrott, 2 vols. (London, 1910), II, 242.

of Wolsey itself makes no mention of Sir Thomas.[1] The only explanation for these omissions would seem to rest on the fact that More, Harpsfield, and Roper were all extremely hostile to Wolsey and his policies. More himself had delivered a scathing speech against the cardinal at the opening of Parliament in 1529[2] and, in the *Lives* of Harpsfield and Roper, Wolsey is accused of instigating the divorce and thus setting in motion the series of events that estranged England from Rome. Cavendish, who manifests a deep sympathy for Wolsey, would not have agreed with such an interpretation of the cardinal's character. And, in the middle 1550s, when not only the *Life of Wolsey* but also the biographies of Harpsfield and Roper were being written and the great edition of More's *Works* was going through the press, the former gentleman-usher would have stood almost alone in his balanced attitude towards his old master. Pro-Catholic though he was, Cavendish may have thought it better to omit all mention of More in the interests of friendship than to attack the opinions of a man to whom he was related.

George Cavendish left the service of the great for ever in 1530 when, after Wolsey's death, he refused the king's offer of a post in the royal household. He returned 'to his country' and probably remained at Cavendish Overhall, living the life of a country gentleman, until shortly before the end of his life. Thomas Cavendish had died in 1524 and George, who was appointed overseer of the will, inherited all his father's estate except for his 'lands in Kent',[3] which were given to George's step-mother Agnes 'to sell for herself'. £40 was put aside for Mary's (George's sister) wedding portion, but we cannot tell if she was ever able to put it to use. Agnes was still alive on

[1] In one place at least Cavendish seems to have deliberately suppressed More's name. See 79/30–33, where he describes Fisher's martyrdom (22 June, 1535), which occurred only a few weeks before More's own on 6 July. We might have expected Cavendish to mention the fact that More succeeded Wolsey as Lord Chancellor. But the only possible reference to More in the *Life* may occur in the speech of the anonymous council member (131/3–20 and n.).
[2] Reported by Hall in his *Chronicle* (1809 reprint), p. 764.
[3] These 'lands' would probably have included the alienation of rent in Canterbury which Thomas Cavendish and others received in a grant o 22 October 1512. See LP (2nd ed., revised by R. H. Brodie), I, 1463g. (27).

24 December 1531, when she is mentioned in a grant as holding 'a tenement called the White Bere, in the parishes of St. Mary Magdalene and All Saints, in Westcheap and Bread Street, London'.[1]

When George Cavendish retired to Suffolk, disillusioned by his experiences in the service of princes, his brother William (1505?–57) was just beginning a career which, through his own endeavours and the happy fortune of two wealthy marriages, was eventually to lead him to the office of Treasurer in the king's household. The story of William's rise in the royal favour is available elsewhere[2] and its stages can be verified in the numerous references to him in the *Letters and Papers* after 1530. He became an agent for Cromwell in the dissolution of the monasteries and somehow managed to escape unscathed when his master was executed in 1540. We may note that it was perhaps through the offices of his brother that William was first introduced to Cromwell;[3] George Cavendish, as the *Life of Wolsey* shows us, knew the cardinal's secretary extremely well. The two brothers seem to have maintained some contact with each other, but George refused to profit from the sale of monastic lands, a process through which William, like so many men of the period, built himself a sizeable fortune.

Of George himself, in the years between his retirement from court and his death, we know relatively little. His name occurs occasionally in the *Letters and Papers* and some idea of his activities from 1530 until 1558 can be gleaned from the references there. Thus we find him listed as one of the commissioners for Bedfordshire who were making inquiries into the Tenths of Spiritualities in 1535;[4] and on 24 August of the following year he sat on a commission that was conducting an investigation of certain 'articles' supposed to have been spoken against Cromwell by 'Dan Aswell', the Test Prior of St. Albans.[5] These

[1] LP, V, 606.
[2] For example, in the *D.N.B.* or in Hunter's article. A portrait of Sir William at the age of forty-four (formerly in the collection of the Duke of Devonshire) is reproduced in A. S. Turberville's *History of Welbeck Abbey*, 2 vols. (London, 1938–9), I, 20.
[3] Bickley's suggestion, op. cit., p. 11.
[4] LP, VIII, 1535; the grant is dated 30 January.
[5] LP, XI, 354, ii.

Introduction xxiii

commissions no doubt involved Cavendish in official duties that, as a country gentleman, he could not avoid when they were imposed upon him. His service on two of Cromwell's committees would seem to indicate that, even if he did not approve of the government's policies, he went along with the tide, at least temporarily. Neither commission involved any extended service and, after 1536, we no longer find him serving in any public capacity. In October 1541, he participated in a conveyance of lands that his brother William had arranged in preparation for his third marriage, this time with Elizabeth Paris, later Countess of Shrewsbury.[1]

It was about 1543 that George's son William married a certain Anne Coxe, the daughter of John Coxe, and it was apparently as a part of the marriage settlement that George 'levied a fine' on his manors of Overhall and Netherhall.[2] The resultant agreement between John Coxe and Cavendish stipulated that the former should pay a sum of £400 (the marriage portion) in return for which Cavendish would put his manor in trust for his son William and Anne, William's wife. Such a method of alienating land was a common practice in the sixteenth century although, strictly speaking, a licence to alienate should first have been obtained. A pardon for alienation without licence was granted to Cavendish in 1545. The Coxes, in any event, were taking no chances on the manors slipping out of their family's hands after the marriage. That the properties were fairly rich

[1] Patent Roll, 33 Hen. VIII, p. 4, m. 26, calendared in LP, XVI, 1308 (34). They were married on 3 November 1541.
[2] The legal procedure involved here is explained as follows by the *O.E.D.*: A fine was 'the compromise of a fictitious or collusive suit for the possession of lands: formerly in use as a mode of conveyance in cases where the ordinary modes were not available or equally efficacious. . . . The person to whom the land was to be conveyed sued the holder for wrongfully keeping him out of possession; the defendant (hence called the cognizor [in this case, George Cavendish]) acknowledged the right of the plaintiff (or cognizee [here John Coxe and a certain John Seymour]); the compromise was entered on the records of the court; and the particulars of it were set forth in a document called the *foot of the fine*.' This device was often used by married women, who could alienate land only in this manner, and to bar entails. The 'cognizor' was said to have 'acknowledged' or 'levied' the fine. The relevant documents for Cavendish's fine are the Feet of Fines for Suffolk, Trinity Term, 35 Hen. VIII (R. O.) and a Patent Roll (P. 17, m. 21) of 37 Hen. VIII, the latter calendared in LP, XX, Part II, 910 (82), 6 November 1545.

ones at this date is shown by the text of the fine, which lists the following items:

> the manors of Overhall and Netherhall and 3 messuages, 10 cottages, one watermill, 300 acres of land, 20 acres of meadow, 100 acres of pasture, 12 acres of woods, 100 acres of heath and furze, and 40s. rent in Overhall, Netherhall, and Cavendish.

Whether George continued to live at Glemsford after this settlement cannot be shown with certainty; but, if he can be identified with the 'George Cavendysshe' who, in 1546, is described as holding tenure in some tenements near Dunstable, Bedfordshire, then it would seem that he had already given up his manor to his son.[1] Certainly the agreement of 1543 prepared the way for his final enfeoffment of his property to William in 1557. It may also be noted that, in 1546, George and an 'Anthony Stubbinge' are mentioned in a royal 'book of orders' as owing £32 10s. to the crown.[2] The debt, however, was not large and there seems to be no indication that Cavendish was in any sort of financial distress. We know from his book that life as a Catholic in these times was often bitter for him, but he seems to have enjoyed a modest competence during his later years.

Whatever may have been George's whereabouts between 1546 and 1557, it was on 1 October of the latter year that he made a permanent grant of Overhall and Netherhall to his son. The indenture notes that William had already paid a competent sum for the manors (presumably in addition to the £400 of 1543) and had released to George a yearly payment of twenty marks. As a final settlement, the contract stipulates that William shall pay George £40 per year for life, the payments to begin on 25 March, 1558, and to be paid 'at the Scite of the manor of Spaines Hall with in the parishe of Finchingfeld', Essex.[3] George Cavendish acknowledged the indenture on 16 January 1558; one year later, on 15 January 1559 we find William named in Elizabeth's general pardon of that date and

---
[1] See Patent Roll, 37 Hen. VIII, P. 16, m. 25, calendared in LP, XX, Part II, 1068 (46).
[2] LP, XXI, Part I, 1280, fol. 43, 30 May 1546.
[3] Close Roll, 3 & 4 Philip and Mary, Part I (R. O., C54/525).

Introduction

described as 'of Glemysforde, co. Suffolk, *alias* of Cavendyshe, co. Suffolk'.[1]

Spains Hall belonged to Robert Kemp, the son of William Kemp and the brother of George's wife, Margery. It was apparently at Spains Hall that George put the finishing touches to his *Life* of the cardinal and his *Poems*, completing his manuscript on 24 June 1558. He was certainly alive six months or so later when he wrote his epitaph on Queen Mary and added a postscript prophesying 'ruin' for England under its new government.

There seems to be no certain evidence regarding the date of George's death. Ruggles[2] conjectured that it occurred in 1561 or 1562, but the only evidence he could cite was the fact that William Cavendish was in possession of Overhall in 1562. Since George's son, as we have seen, already possessed the manor in 1559, the latter date is of little importance. But George was almost certainly dead by 28 June 1562 when his brother-in-law, Arthur Kemp, made his will.[3] Arthur specifically mentions 'my sister Cauvendish' and 'Jane her daughter' but does not refer to George. William himself seems to have died between 1562 and 1565; his son (also named William) was a London mercer, back at the trade of his fifteenth-century forebears. In 1569 he sold the manor outright to William Downes of Sudbury, Suffolk; after that date, the family's connections with Cavendish Overhall cease altogether.[4]

Thus there is good reason to believe that the former gentleman-usher had ample opportunity to put into practice the maxim that he affixed to the opening pages of his *Life of Wolsey*—'Vincit qui patitur, Maxima vindicta paciencia'.[5] The last thirty years of Cavendish's life must indeed have been years of patience, years in which he had ample time to meditate upon the vagaries of Fortune, 'wherof for my part', he tells us,

[1] Calendar of Patent Rolls Elizabeth, 1558–1560, p. 162.
[2] Ruggles, op. cit.; see also W. A. Copinger, *The Manors of Suffolk*, 7 vols. (London, 1905–11), I, 62.
[3] P.C.C. Streat 25, proved 13 October 1562. George Cavendish himself appears to have died intestate. I have found no record of his making a will; nor, apparently, was there an inquisition held at his death.
[4] For these later transactions, see Ruggles, p. 59.
[5] The expression was a proverbial one, occurring in Chaucer and Langland. See Skeat's note (v. 388) to 'The Franklin's Tale,' l. 771.

'I haue tasted of thexperience' (10/26–7). The triumph that his patience achieved was not a material one; on this side of the grave it rests upon the literary excellence of the biography which he wrote in his old age, the *Life* of the great cardinal whom he had served as a young man.

Date of Composition

When we turn from the somewhat scattered facts that comprise what we know of the life of George Cavendish to a consideration of his book itself, a good deal more information becomes available. His own statements provide us with some knowledge of when he wrote his *Life of Cardinal Wolsey* and these statements can be supplemented from internal evidence. According to the autograph manuscript, Cavendish finished his manuscript on 24 June 1558;[1] at the beginning of the *Life* (f. 2) he tells us that he began his book on the fourth day of November, but he does not give the year. We are thus provided with a satisfactory *terminus ad quem* for the *Life*,[2] but Cavendish's statement about the day on which he began his manuscript presents us with a problem that is not so easily solved.

There are only two references in the text that enable us to fix the date of composition more exactly.[3] In the early part of his narrative (21/22–4) Cavendish speaks of 'themprour Charles the 5 that nowe reygnyth and nowe ffather vnto kyng Phillipe our Soueravn lord'. This passage has a double signifi-

[1] See above, p. x. The manuscript must have remained in Cavendish's hands until after 17 November 1558, for at some time after that date he composed his epitaph on Queen Mary and added his final note on the 'ruin' which was likely to ensue now that Elizabeth was on the throne. When he introduced this poem on Mary's death into his book, he seems to have disturbed its binding. Thus the poems, as we have them today, are not in their original order. For a full discussion of the binding of the manuscript see E. P. Hammond's edition of selections from the poems in *English Verse between Chaucer and Surrey* (Durham, North Carolina, 1927), pp. 366–70.

[2] It seems impossible to determine precisely how long before 24 June 1558 Cavendish began work on his poems. Judging by the order in which they appear in the manuscript they would seem to have been composed after the *Life*, presumably, let us say, in 1557–8. On the basis of the internal evidence, there is no reason to suppose that any portion of the *Life* itself, except perhaps for final revisions, was written after 1557.

[3] The allusion to 'the frenche kynges second Sonne ... at this present kyng of ffraunce' (62/12–13) merely indicates a date between 1546 and 1559, the years of Henry II's reign.

Introduction xxvii

cance, for we know that Philip did not become emperor until his father abdicated in January 1556. It would thus seem that this portion of the text was written after July 1554, but before the news of Charles's retirement had reached England in 1556. Cavendish's 'fourth of November' must then refer to either 1554 or 1555. Further evidence is provided by the author's reference to 'mr Ratclyfe Sonne & heyer to the lord ffitzwalter and after Erle of Sussex' (61/17–18). The Rev. Joseph Hunter, who first proved conclusively that George Cavendish and not his brother William was the author of the *Life*,[1] argued from the evidence of this passage that the *Life* must have been written before 17 February 1557, the date of Henry Radcliffe's death. Hunter, however, used one of the secondary manuscripts in which the passage read 'and *now* Earl of Sussex' instead of Cavendish's 'and *after* Earl of Sussex'. On the basis of the autograph manuscript it appears that this part of the text must have been composed after February 1557.

In the absence of any other conclusive data, it may well be doubted if we can go any further towards determining when Cavendish began his book. Since both the passages just cited occur in the early part of the *Life*, the period of time that elapsed between them should probably be narrowed as much as possible, thus making 4 November 1555 the more likely date. Even if that date is accepted, it might still seem somewhat unusual that Cavendish spent at least a year and a half on the first third of his work and then crammed the second two-thirds of it, not to mention his poems, into a period of about the same length.[2] As the matter stands, we can scarcely be more exact in our attempts to date the composition of the work and must be content to rest with the knowledge that the *Life of Wolsey* was written between 4 November 1554 and 24 June 1558.[3]

[1] In his pamphlet, 'Who Wrote Cavendish's *Life of Wolsey*?', cited above, p. xiv, n. 1.
[2] There is, of course, always the possibility that Cavendish did not hear of Charles's abdication until some time after it took place, or that he was simply careless in his reference to it.
[3] In this connection, perhaps attention should be called to the inexact dates which the *O.E.D.* gives in its references to Cavendish. Most of its citations from the *Life* are assigned to '*a*. 1562', the presumed date of his death.

Sources

If it were possible to be as certain about the sources from which Cavendish drew some of the materials that went into his *Life of Wolsey* as we can be about the date of its composition, a number of problems which the *Life* raises might be cleared up. We should like to know, for example, if he obtained any of his information from printed sources which were available to him and, if he did make use of such materials, how he developed or modified what he found there. Cavendish himself is fairly explicit about the matter. He tells us, at the opening of the *Life*, that he intends

> to wryt heare some parte of the procedings of the said Legat & Cardynall Wolsey Archebysshope of yorke . . . wherof some parte shalbe of myn owen knowlege And some of other persons Informacion/ etc. (3/27–32)

There can scarcely be any doubt that the major portion of his book is the product of his own direct experience. All of the second half of the *Life*, which concentrates on the last year of Wolsey's career when Cavendish was with him constantly, and much of the first half are presented as eye-witness accounts with Cavendish himself, as gentleman-usher, taking a part in the scenes that are related. Nevertheless, his statement about 'other persons' information' indicates that a certain amount of his material, at any rate, was not drawn directly from his own recollection of events.

An attempt to discover the identity of these 'other persons' and the extent to which Cavendish used them raises immediately the whole question of Cavendish's reliability as a reporter. Since much of the action which takes place in the *Life* is directly concerned with matters of state and public personalities, we are frequently able, by using the *State Papers* and the *Letters and Papers Henry VIII*,[1] to keep a close check on

---

[1] No previous edition of Cavendish has attempted to make anything like a full use of this material. John Holmes, whose notes are included in Wordsworth's fourth edition (1853) as well as in his own edition of 1852, had access to the *State Papers* but not to the *Letters and Papers*. While often helpful to the reader, his annotations do not attempt to check Cavendish's historical accuracy.

Introduction xxix

Cavendish's accuracy. If he can be shown to have been exact in those passages where his account can be confirmed, then the credibility of his narrative where he himself is our only witness should carry a considerably greater weight. On the other hand, if errors do occur, we should like to know if there is a possibility that they may be put down to his having relied not 'on his own knowledge' but rather 'on other persons' information', whoever they may have been.

It is apparent from the *Life* itself that one of Cavendish's principal informants for Wolsey's early career, where a good many of the historical errors in the work occur, was the cardinal himself. After describing Wolsey's speedy journey to France when he was a royal chaplain to Henry VII, Cavendish tells us (10/29–30) that he received this tale 'of his [Wolsey's] owen mowthe and report/ after his ffall lyeng at that tyme in the great parke of Richemond'. How much else the cardinal may have told his usher during those dark days of 1530 is a matter for speculation, but we do know that they had several conversations of this nature together, two of which are reported later in the *Life*.[1] After the second of these garden talks between servant and master, Cavendish tells us (138/3–4) that 'we had myche more talke', but he does not tell us what he and the cardinal discussed. Such words force an editor of the *Life* into conjecture, but there is at least the possibility that a good part of Cavendish's book resulted from these conversations.

The *Life* tells us little more about Cavendish's other possible informants.[2] That he did rely chiefly on some such oral information when he was not writing from his own memory seems probable from the manner in which he refers to the printed histories that he had seen. He began his book, he informs us in

---

[1] See the text, pp. 127 ff. and pp. 135 ff. The first conversation took place at Richmond and the second at Sir William Fitzwilliam's house at Milton Manor, Northampton.

[2] There are occasional references to conversations or stories that Cavendish 'heard reported from other persons'. Thus he tells us that he relied on the report of 'them that wayted vppon the kyng at dynner' for his account of the conversation between Anne and Henry at Grafton (94/33–4). Earlier he says that he 'hard his chapleyn say' that Wolsey always said his office completely through before going to bed (22/36).

his prologue, in order to tell the truth about the cardinal; furthermore, the truth could not be learned from books for

> I have harde & also sene sett forthe in divers printed bookes some vntrue imaginations after the death of divers parsons ... that weare inventyd rather to bringe there honest names into infamie & perpetuall slander of the common mvltitude then otherwyse.

These were the writers who 'with there blasphemous trompe' had 'spred abrode innvmerable lyes ... where in there is notheng more vntrwe'. Writing as a Catholic in the reign of Mary, Cavendish is determined to correct those distortions of history which he must have considered to have been the Protestant propaganda of the previous two reigns, particularly as they related to the cardinal and the events of his life.

Later on in the first part of the *Life*[1] we find him referring to 'historygraffers of Cronycles of prynces' (11/8), to 'the writers of Cronycles' (43/10) and to the 'Cronycles of Englond' (50/33). In each case he carefully distinguishes his own biography from the narratives of the historians. He is not describing coronations or relating opinions of governmental policy, but instead is concerned with building up a picture of the life of one man. What is important for our purposes here is that Cavendish shows a considerable familiarity with the chronicles that had appeared before Mary's reign. What were these chronicles and what might they have contributed to the *Life of Wolsey*?

The one historical work published prior to 1554–8 that contains any detailed account of Wolsey's activities was Hall's *Chronicle*,[2] a book notoriously Protestant in its bias and famed for the defence which it makes of the policies of Henry VIII.

---

[1] It is interesting to observe that every reference which Cavendish makes to printed books or to other writers occurs in the first portion of his narrative. All but two of them, in fact, come in the first fifty pages and these two (pp. 73 and 78) simply compare his own descriptions with what one might read elsewhere in 'histories or chronicles.' The other references occur on pp. 3, 11, 13, 43, and 50.

[2] Edward Hall, *The Vnion of the Two Noble and Illustre Famelies of Lancastre & York*, London, 1542, 1548, 1550. No complete copy of the 1542 edition is now extant. I use the reprint of 1809. Cavendish may very well have read the chronicles of Fabyan (1516, 1533, etc.) and Hardyng (1543, with Grafton's continuation) but these supply little detailed information

Introduction xxxi

It would perhaps be going too far to assert that it was the publication of Hall's work which first prompted Cavendish to begin his *Life*, but there is ample reason to believe both that he knew the *Chronicle* well and that he may have taken some of his material from it. This is not the place to set down the correspondences between Hall and the *Life*, which are cited in detail in the historical notes, but on the basis of the evidence there provided it is possible to generalize on the nature of Cavendish's debt.

While it must be emphasized that Cavendish wrote to correct such versions of history as may be found in Hall, it seems equally true that, as he worked at the *Life*, he was turning over the pages of the historian, refreshing his memory at the same time that he was firing his indignation. The verbal parallels between the two works are often quite close.[1] Thus, for example, the items in Cavendish's list of the presents which the citizens of London gave to the French embassy of 1527 all appear in a similar but more detailed list in Hall.[2] So too Hall's description of Wolsey at Canterbury, in which he tells us how the cardinal directed the litany to be recited,[3] parallels Cavendish's 'Sancta maria ora pro papa nostro Clemente And so pervsed the litteny

about Wolsey and the reign of Henry VIII. He seems also to have known the *Cronicles of Englonde* which Wynkyn de Worde edited in 1515 and 1528 (STC 9987 and 10002; see the note to 50/33). It seems unlikely that Cavendish would have had access to other chronicles like the *Chronicle of Calais* or Wriothesley's *Chronicle*, which remained in manuscript until the nineteenth century.

It is not, of course, impossible that Cavendish had seen the third edition (1555) of Polydore Vergil's *Anglica Historia*, which contains a highly prejudiced account of the cardinal. Polydore's first two editions (1534 and 1546), the first of which was certainly used by Hall, carry the story down only so far as 1509. I have not been able to discover any close resemblances between Polydore's narrative and Cavendish's.

It should perhaps also be noted that when Cavendish speaks of the slanders against Wolsey he may be thinking of the verse satires of Skelton, Roy, and Barlowe, or of the anti-Catholic tracts of Barnes, Fish, and Tyndale. For these works, see the article by P. L. Wiley, 'Renaissance Exploitation of Cavendish's *Life of Wolsey*,' *SP*, XLIII (1946), 121–46. In none of these works do we find any close correspondences with Cavendish's narrative, but they undoubtedly contributed to the general atmosphere of dislike for the cardinal against which the gentleman-usher writes.

[1] See Appendix C for the speeches, too long to be given here, at the divorce trial as reported by Hall and Cavendish.
[2] See the historical notes to p. 66.
[3] p. 728, 'S. Maria, ora pro Clemente papa. S. Petre ora pro Clemente papa. & so furthe al yᵉ letany.'

thoroughe'. Much more often than not, however, Cavendish, as we might expect, either omits details given by Hall or amplifies Hall's descriptions in order to present a more favourable account of Wolsey.[1] Thus where Hall describes in detail the pomp that the cardinal intended to display at his installation in York cathedral, Cavendish emphasizes the modest ceremonies that were to have taken place and reinforces his account with the statement 'The trowthe wherof I perfectly knowe/ for I was made pryvye to the same/ And sent to yorke to forse all thyng' (148/11–12).

Such parallel or contrasted passages, which can be followed in detail in the notes to the present edition, will not prove that Cavendish actually copied any of Hall's narrative into his own pages in the same manner as the later sixteenth-century historians were to transpose both Hall and Cavendish into theirs;[2] nor, indeed, are they offered as showing conclusively that Cavendish knew and used Hall's work. They should indicate, however, that of all the writers whom Cavendish may have had in mind when he spoke of the 'Cronycles of prynces', Hall comes closest to satisfying his description. In any event, it seems evident that the words with which Hall concludes his summary of the cardinal's character—'To write the life and doynges of this Cardinal, it were a great worke'—could not have failed, had Cavendish read them, to have inspired the *Life of Cardinal Wolsey*.

Cavendish as Historian

The problem of the sources which Cavendish may have used when he came to compose his *Life of Wolsey* leads directly to the more important question of his own accuracy as a chronicler of events. While it is probable, as has been seen, that he relied to some extent on 'other persons' information', which may have included such 'information' as he could have found in Hall, it

---

[1] Among other instances, see especially the words put into Suffolk's mouth at the trial scene (90/26–7) and the account of Wolsey's words when arrested by Northumberland (155).

[2] At times, as in Cavendish's garbled account of the battle of Pavia, one almost wishes that the source of his errors could be found in Hall. For the vexed question of this battle see Appendix B and, for the uses which later writers made of Cavendish, Appendix D.

Introduction xxxiii

is nevertheless true that his book has claimed the attention of historians principally because of its value as an eye-witness account in its own right. This has been the case, so far as we can determine, from the very first. The compiler of the materials for a life of Bishop Fisher, who at some time before 1576 copied passages from Cavendish into his manuscript collections,[1] did so in the belief that he was thus preserving a first-hand version of the bishop's words at the divorce trial of 1529. Subsequent Elizabethan historians, who take over much of Cavendish's narrative directly from manuscript, or from Stowe, who first printed portions of it in 1580, accept, with or without acknowledgement, the *Life of Wolsey* as a faithful account of the cardinal's life and times. Even Cavendish's first editor, the Puritan propagandist who published the *Life* in 1641 to demonstrate the parallel between Wolsey's career and Archbishop Laud's, did not, with one exception,[2] change or attempt to criticize any of Cavendish's statements.

While the historians continue to make use of Cavendish's narrative, it is not until after the Restoration that they begin to question his accuracy. Burnet, whose *History of the Reformation* appeared between 1670 and 1715, was apparently the first historian to comment adversely upon Cavendish's account of the battle of Pavia.[3] His strictures were amplified by Wolsey's eighteenth-century apologist, Richard Fiddes, who nevertheless gives us an evaluation of Cavendish's worth as an historian that has been generally accepted down to the present day:

> ... a Man of Probity, who lived under a Sense of Religion, and spake from the Heart. If he had not all the great Talents, requisite in a Historian, he is yet much to be valued for those Qualities. His Fidelity may be depended upon concerning Things, which

[1] These are now in British Museum MS. Arundel 152. The *Life of Fisher* was edited by Franciscus Van Ortroy in *Analecta Bollandiana*, x (1891), 121–365 and xii (1893), 97–287. Van Ortroy notes that the author, in compiling his materials, 'ne néglige aucun moyen de contrôle et n'affirme rien à la légère' (x, 139).
[2] He did introduce the words 'at which time it was apparent that he had poisoned himself' into the narrative of Wolsey's last illness. Otherwise, the 1641 edition merely compresses and summarizes Cavendish's work; the distortions it contains result principally from omission, not commission.
[3] Gilbert Burnet, *The History of the Reformation of the Church of England*, ed. Nicholas Pocock (7 vols., Oxford, 1865), i, 31.

he relates upon his personal Knowledge, or which fell more directly within the Compass of his own Observation. His Stile is clear, and, for the Time wherein he lived, significant and polite enough. He writes with the free and negligent Air of a Gentleman, which much becomes him; and he is sometimes happy, without appearing to have any such design, in addressing himself to the Imagination and Passions. There are some Passages in him, whereby a Reader who has any true Taste, will find himself agreeably moved. He writes with great Impartiality, and tho' he had an Honour and Esteem for his Master, he does not conceal or dissemble his Failures, nor fly out into any indecent Heats or Expressions, against those, who used him very ill.[1]

A similar opinion was voiced in 1810 by a reviewer of Wordsworth's *Ecclesiastical Biography*, in the first volume of which the *Life of Wolsey* was printed for the first time in anything like its full form.[2] Cavendish, he notes, 'was not one of those unobserving men, who seem never to apprehend that what is familiar to themselves will become curious to posterity. He saw with an exact and discriminating eye, and what he beheld he was able to describe'.[3] This was also the judgement of Van Ortroy,[4] whose considered evaluation of Cavendish's accuracy we shall have occasion to discuss later.

But it was left for a great modern historian, A. F. Pollard,[5] to incorporate the historical evidence which Cavendish preserves into a brilliant biography of Wolsey. As the notes to the present edition will illustrate, a considerable part of the present editor's historical work has already been done for him in this masterly study. For Pollard, Cavendish 'gives us the classic example of history as it appears to a gentleman-usher'.[6] The

---

[1] Richard Fiddes, *The Life of Cardinal Wolsey* (London, 1724). This passage occurs in Fiddes's 'Collections' of documents, which form the second part of his volume (p. 242).

[2] Singer (I, xxiv–xxv) says that Joseph Grove, who had reprinted a large part of the 1641 edition of Cavendish in the footnotes to his *Life and Times of Cardinal Wolsey* (4 vols., London, 1742–44), later came across one of the better secondary manuscripts and in 1761 'printed off a small impression with a preface and notes'. I have not been able to discover a copy of this volume, which was said by Singer to be 'one of the rarest of English books.'

[3] *Quarterly Review*, iv (1810), 97.

[4] Van Ortroy, op. cit., x, 354, note 2. See below, p. xxxvi.

[5] A. F. Pollard, *Wolsey* (London, 1929).

[6] *Ibid.*, p. 2.

Introduction xxxv

gentle irony of his remark by no means indicates that Pollard fails to give Cavendish the fullest possible credit as an observer of events; it does point up the fact that he measures Cavendish's narrative by a far more stringent standard of historical accuracy than had been applied to it by previous biographers of the cardinal who had made use of the *Life of Wolsey*. On the other hand, Pollard's real appreciation of Cavendish's literary achievement[1] enhances the value of those passages in his own biography where he makes most use of Cavendish's narrative.[2] From his book and from a comparison with contemporary documents of those portions of Cavendish which he does not analyse, certain points emerge concerning the reliability of the *Life* as history.

The first problem that such a study confronts is the question of Cavendish's memory, the state of affairs in that 'gross old head' when, nearly thirty years after the major events which the *Life* describes, he began to set down the results of his meditations. Time, which may mellow literary perceptions and give them strength, is singularly unkind to the historian. It destroys records and blurs the factual surface of events. Although Cavendish can at times assert that he is certain about the truth of his account, there are several places in the *Life* where he expresses doubt about his ability to recall the exact circumstances of the events he describes. The gifts to that French embassy in 1527, for instance, 'w^{che} I cannot nowe call to my remembraunce' (75/19); or the details of Wolsey's dinner, when the cardinal's cross fell on Doctor Bonner, which 'I wyll (god wyllyng) declare ... accordyng to my symple remembraunce' (149/34–150/1). And what of those other passages where Cavendish is relating not his own observations but those things which the cardinal, himself recollecting events that happened twenty years before,

[1] Historians have, in general, been much more ready to take cognizance of Cavendish's artistic ability than have the literary critics upon whose shoulders that task would seem most naturally to devolve. Mattingly's remark (*Catherine of Aragon*, Boston, 1941, p. 459) is typical: 'Direct quotations [in his account of the divorce trial] are from Cavendish, not because I am sure he got the speeches verbatim, but because the temptation to steal Cavendish's language when one can is irresistible.'

[2] Note, for example, how his fifth chapter (pp. 165 ff.) is organized around Cavendish's dramatic scene between Wolsey and the Duke of Norfolk (below, pp. 114 ff.).

told him when they conversed in the garden at Richmond? In the light of these statements it would not seem at all remarkable if Cavendish should have turned to the pages of Hall in an effort to restore a certain freshness to the events which he had once lived through.

There are a number of factual errors in the *Life*. Some of these, perhaps the majority of them, can be safely attributed to Cavendish's occasionally faulty memory. In order to get a proper perspective on the *Life*, however, it is necessary to consider the several classes into which these 'errors' fall. At least three separate types can be distinguished:

I. *Errors of fact*

These include the misnaming of personages, as Richard Wiltshire for John Wiltshire (45/16), and mistakes in geographical distances, as in the statement that Cawood is seven miles from York (144/10-11). Most of Cavendish's minor errors, in so far as they can be demonstrated, are of this sort. They are usually fairly easy to correct and probably were committed through simple carelessness.

II. *Errors in the sequence of events*

Van Ortroy, in analysing the uses which the author of the anonymous *Life of Fisher* made of Cavendish, remarks shrewdly that

> Les documents contemporains, mis au jour dans ces derniers temps, ont considérablement réhabilité l'autorité de Cavendish pour l'exactitude des faits, mais non pour l'ordre chronologique dans lequel ils se sont passés. Je suis donc porté à admettre son témoignage, quand il n'est pas contredit par ailleurs ou par des invraisemblances manifestes.[1]

This class of mistake is by far the most frequent in the *Life*. Thus Cavendish places the appeal to the universities for opinions on the divorce before and not after the trial itself; he represents the cardinal as calling the bishops together after and not before the trip to France in 1527; and he gives a thoroughly confused account of Wolsey's indictment for praemunire after

[1] Van Ortroy, op. cit., x, 354, note 2.

his fall.[1] This sort of error can sometimes be assigned to a failure of memory, but, as I shall presently suggest, there is good reason to believe that Cavendish at times deliberately disregards the exigencies of chronology in the interests of the total artistic structure of his biography.

III. *Omissions*

It is evident to anyone who is familiar with the events of Wolsey's life that many things about which Cavendish, unless he was blinder than he elsewhere shows himself to be, must have known, are omitted from his narrative. He tells us almost nothing of Wolsey's personal life; there is no mention, for example, of Wolsey's mistress or of his illegitimate son, Thomas Winter. Furthermore, when Cavendish repeats criticisms that he had heard made against the cardinal, he does so to deny them, never to offer confirmatory evidence. He himself criticizes, it is true, but he does not accept the criticisms of others. Sometimes we are able to show that he deliberately suppressed material that was known to him. The most striking instance of this is a passage from his poems relating to Wolsey's activities after his fall:

> To forrayn potentates [I] wrott my letters playn,
> Desireng their ayd, to restore me to favor againe.
> (Singer, II, 15)

But we learn nothing at all of these intrigues from the *Life* itself.

Historians may well deplore the limitation which such 'faults' as these place upon the value of the *Life of Wolsey* as a factual record of the cardinal's rise and fall. On the other hand, the literary critic may surmise that Cavendish's mistakes are not always to be explained as simple lapses of a hazy memory. Wolsey as he was in himself appears only partially in Cavendish's *Life*, but the artistic idea which his gentleman-usher formed of him is given to us in the full. Yet, when due allowance has been made for Cavendish's slips of memory and the exigencies of his

[1] His recollection, says Pollard (p. 262), 'when he wrote in 1557, of what had happened in 1529 was so confused that he gives the failure of the "bill" in the house of commons in December as the reason for Wolsey's indictment for praemunire in the king's bench on the preceding 4 October'.

sense of form, we can nevertheless affirm that in many passages the factual accuracy of his book is astonishing. Whether or not Cavendish kept a record of events as they occurred cannot now be determined. He was, most assuredly, no Boswell, constructing a monument to a great man from an ever-increasing accumulation of memoranda, even if he may have had no small part of Boswell's talent for organizing conversations into set dramatic pieces. But he has a Renaissance eye for details of splendid clothing and for scenes of pomp and luxury. His sense of colour is almost as good as his ear for voices and he can remember a detail like the three steps ('gresis') on Wolsey's traverse at Amiens (54/3 and n.). He may be wrong about the colour of the French king's coat but another contemporary account shows him to have been right about the material with which it was lined (52/25–6 and n.). Sometimes we are even able to confirm the very words which he puts into the mouths of those he is writing about (84/13–4, 127/5–6 and notes, Appendix C). Through all of his work runs a tireless curiosity, a quality in himself which Cavendish reveals directly when he tells us that he accepted an invitation to visit 'Chastell de Crykkey' because he 'was allwayes desirous to se and be acquaynted w^t strayngers inespecyall w^t men in honour and Auctorytie' (55/1–3). And it is the cardinal himself, the greatest, for Cavendish, of those in 'honour and Auctorytie', who lives for us in the vivid pages of the *Life of Wolsey*.

The Text

Believing that an edition of a sixteenth-century manuscript should be as faithful as possible to the original and, at the same time, intelligible to modern readers, I have adopted an apparatus which, it is hoped, will prove satisfactory on both counts.

The first page of the text is reproduced from Bodleian MS. Douce 363 to replace the missing first page of Egerton 2402. The Douce MS. (transcribed in 1578) has few abbreviations and presents no major difficulties for the editor. MS. Egerton 2402, on the other hand, is written in a frequently difficult script which is characterized by a highly irregular system of spelling,

Introduction xxxix

capitalization, and punctuation. Cavendish's spelling is here reproduced exactly, including his superscript letters, some of which also function as abbreviations. Thus w^t (with), w^{che} (whiche), yor (your), ma^{tie} (maiestie), $instrume^t$ (instrument), etc. So too with Cavendish's numbers, which are usually written in Roman numerals, e.g. vjj^{en} (seven), $viij^{th}$ (eighth), etc. The superscript ^{li} is an abbreviation for *libra* (pound); the symbol $xiiij^{xx}$ (68/30) means 'fourteen score' (280).

In addition to these superscript letters, Cavendish uses ten true marks of abbreviation. All of these, as listed below, have been silently expanded in the present text.

1. The mark standing for *us*. E.g. *oblivyous* 5/28.
2. The mark standing for *ur*. E.g. *fauour* 4/25. When this mark follows No. 9 (below) the combination has been expanded as *sure* (cf. *displeasure* in full, 171/26). See Frontispiece, line 12 *pleasures*.
3. Superior *a*. Expanded as *a* or as *au*, depending on the spelling of the word in which it occurs. In words like *plesaunt* Cavendish uses it as simply a superior *a*; but, when *m, n*, or *u* precedes the *a*, the superior *a* is employed as an abbreviation for *au*. Thus Cavendish writes *chaunced, demaunded, dauncyng*, etc., in full, spelling them almost always[1] with *au*, no doubt to avoid writing six or seven minims in succession. The only exception to this rule is the word *quarter* (52/16, etc.) where the superior *a* is equivalent to *ua*.
4. ⁀ Expanded as *m* or *n* (*commyttyng, incontynent*) except in the word *sperytuall*[2] (MS. *spu̯all*) which is written in full as *Sperytuall* at 10/18. *Cŏenly, cŏenwell*, etc., are expanded as *comenly* and *comenwell* in view of the fact that Cavendish has *comenly* in full at least four times (11/29, 22/34, 61/35, 74/14). If the expanded forms did not occur in the text one would be inclined to print *commenly, commenwell*, etc., since the ⁀ abbreviation in these words is based on that for the Latin *commune* (*cŏe*).

[1] The only two exceptions I have found are *gouernance* (35/31) and *ordynance* (172/12).
[2] But cf. *sprituall* (MS. *spriu̯all*) 17/23, perhaps a pronunciation spelling.

5. The looped abbreviation, which occurs only as a suffix, is expanded as *es*. See Frontispiece, line 1 *Intraylles*.
6. p with a curly stroke through it. Expanded as *pro*, e.g. *prospered* 4/33, etc.
7. p with a straight stroke through it. Expanded as *per* whenever this spelling is possible (*person* 5/1, etc.), or as *par* (*departyng* 5/16, etc.).
8. The mark standing for *er* (except when it occurs above p). E.g. *euer, Douer, mercy*. The mark above p has been expanded as *re* or *ri*, according to the spelling required, e.g. *preferment*; *privye* 7/11 (*pryvy* in full, 22/34).
9. Long s with a back stroke through it. Expanded as *ser* (*serued*); as *sir*, when it stands alone (cf. *Syr* in full, 26/30); when followed by No. 2 (above), as *sur* in the prefix *sur-* (17/15, etc.) and as *sure* at the end of a word (cf. No. 2, above). See Frontispiece, line 8 *serued*, line 5 *sir*, line 12 *pleasures*.
10. A horizontal stroke through an ascender is expanded as (a) *sub-* (MS. sb̄ 11/20, etc.), (b) *iesu* (MS. iħu 10/36, etc.), (c) *syngular* (MS. syngl̄r 33/25, etc.). Cavendish does not write either *syngular* or *synglar* in full and an editor's judgement must be arbitrary in this case.

As the manuscript is an autograph, the textual footnotes have been made as full as possible. They record the interlineated and cancelled readings in the manuscript as well as the editor's emendations. The latter are relatively few in number and are usually concerned with slight revisions of Cavendish's punctuation. An indecipherable, cancelled letter within a word in the manuscript is represented in the present edition by a point (.); single indecipherable letters are described as such in the notes. Expanded abbreviations are italicized in the footnotes when the reading is relevant to an emendation: thus, 4/25, honours] *MS.* hono*ur*rs.

Cavendish capitalizes words without any apparent system and I have tried to follow the vagaries of his script exactly. This causes no difficulty where the lower and upper case forms are markedly different, but when small and capital letters can be distinguished only by their size, the editor's choice must be

Introduction   xli

somewhat arbitrary. I have not noted any significant distinctions of form or size in Cavendish's *h*, *k*, or *l* and these are all reproduced in lower case. The letters *a*, *v*, *w*, and *y* can occasionally be distinguished by their size and *a* by its shape as well. All other letters have separate upper and lower case forms. The heavily shaded letters with which Cavendish begins paragraphs or speeches are here reproduced in bold face type. The folio numbers of the manuscript are placed within square brackets in the text.

Cavendish's punctuation is equally irregular and has occasioned a number of editorial emendations. He uses a virgule (/) to mark most pauses and sometimes doubles or triples the bar for a more emphatic stop.[1] Where a pause seems absolutely necessary to the sense and no punctuation is given in the manuscript, I have supplied the virgule. The only other mark of punctuation which Cavendish uses is an occasional comma and this normally occurs in items in a sequence, as *wyne, Suger, waxe*, etc., 66/5. The parentheses in the text are Cavendish's own; he employs them for asides and to indicate a foreign phrase or a word used in an unusual sense (e.g. (*boye*), 5/1). Occasionally there are parentheses within parentheses (e.g. 130/7–8).

The word division of the manuscript has been retained in the text: thus *a mong* (among) 17/4, and *a ray* (array) 52/17–18.[2]

[1] Note how the characterization of Anne Boleyn as *the nyght Crowe* (137/19) is followed by four virgules.

[2] For a full discussion of Cavendish's literary achievement (cf. above, p. xxxv ff.) see my article, 'Cavendish's *Life of Wolsey*: The Artistry of a Tudor Biographer,' which is to appear in a forthcoming (1959) issue of *Studies in Philology*.

Thomas Wolsey late Cardinall,
his lyffe and deathe,
Written by
George Cauendishe,
his gentleman Vsshar.

To write the life and doynges of this Cardinal,
it were a great worke.

(Hall, *Chronicle*)

THE PROLOGE

Me Semes it Were no Wisdom to creadit every light tale, blazed by the blasphemous mowthes of rude commonalty, for we dayly here how with there blasphemous trompe they spred abrode innvmerable lyes, without ether shame or honestye (which prima facie) sheweth forth a vysage of trwthe, as thowghe it weare a perfet veritie, & matter in deede. where in there is notheng more vntrwe, And amonge the wyse sorte so it is esteemed, with whome these bablinges be of small force & effect/ fforsothe I have redd thexclamations of divers woorthy & notable authors made agaynste suche false Rumors & fonde opinions of the fantasticall comonaltye, who delytith notheng more then to here strainge thinges, And to see new alterations of authorites, reioyseng somtyme in suche new fantises wch afterwarde geveth them more occasion of repentans then of Ioyfulnes. Thus maye all men of wisdom & discretion vnderstande the temerous madnes of the rvde commonaltye & not geveng to them to hastie credite of every sodayne rumor, vntill the trwthe bee perfetly knowene by the reporte of some approved & credible person, y^t owght to have there of trwe intelligence/

I have harde & also sene sett forthe in divers printed bookes some vntrue imaginations after the death of divers parsons, wch in there lyffe, were of great estimation, that weare inventyd rather to bringe there honest names into infamie & perpetuall slander of the common mvltitude then otherwyse/

The occasyon thereof y^t maketh me to rehersse all these thinges, is this, That for az miche az I intende God willing, to wryt heare some parte of the procedings of the said [Egerton 2402, f. 4] Legat & Cardynall Wolsey Archebysshope of yorke/ and of hys assendyng & dissendyng/ to & frome honorous estate/ wherof some parte shalbe of myn owen knowlege And some of other persons Informacion/ fforsothe this Cardynall was my

30 honorous estate *canc. after* frome

lord & m^r whome in his lyve I seruyd/ and so remayned w^t
hyme/ after hys fall contynually duryng the terme of all his
troble vntill he died/ as well in the Sowthe as in the Northe
parties/ And noted all hys demeanor & vsage in all that tyme/
5 As also in his welthy tryhumphe & gloryous estate/ And synce
his deathe/ I haue hard dyuers sondry surmysis & Imagyned tales
made of his procedynges & doynges w^che I my selfe haue
perfightly knowen/ to be most vntrewe vnto the w^che I cowld
haue sufficyently answered accordyng to the trouthe/ but as me
10 semyth than/ it was myche better for me to suffer and dissimull
the matter and the same to remayn styll as lyes/ than to replie
ayenst ther vntrouthe of whome I myght for my boldnes soner
haue kyndeled a great flame of displeasures than to quenche
oon sparke of ther malycious ontrowthe/ Therfore I commyt the
15 treuthe to hyme that knowyth all trouthe/ ffor what so euer/
any man hath conceyved in hyme whan he lyued or synce his
dethe/ thus myche I dare be bold to say w^tout displeasure to
any person or of affeccion/ that in my Iugeme^t I neuer sawe thys
realme/ in better order quyotnes & obedyence/ than it was in
20 the tyme of his auctoryte & Rule/ ne Iustice better mynestred
w^t indifferencye/ As I could euydently prove/ If I shold not be
accused of to myche affeccion or elles that I setforthe more than
trouthe/ I wyll therfore here desist to speke any more in his
commendacion/ And proced fyrst to his orygynall begynnyng
25 assendyng by fortunes fauour to highe honours/ dignyties/
promocions/ and riches//

ffinis. q^d. G. C.

[f. 5] **Trewthe it ys**/ Cardynall wolsey somtyme Archebisshope/
of york/ was an honest poore mans Sonne borne in Ipsewiche
30 w^t in the Countie of Suffolk/ And beyng but a child was very
Apte to learnyng/ by means wherof his parentes or his good
ffrendes and maysters conveyed hyme to the vnyuersitie of
Oxford/ where he prospered so in learnyng that (As he told me

---

1 lord *canc. before* lord; lord *interl.*; r *of* m^r *no longer visible*   7 self
canc. before selfe   8 cowld *canc. before* cowld   12 past *canc.*
after my   25 v *canc. before* to; honours] *MS.* honourrs   31 of
canc. before or; or *interl.*

Life of Cardinal Wolsey 5

his owen person) he was called the (boye) bacheler for as myche
as he was made bacheler of art at xv^en yeres of age/ w^che was a
rare thyng And seldome seen/

Thus prosperyng And encreasyng in learnyng, was made fellowe
of Magdaleyn Collage/ And after appoynted (for his learnyng) 5
to be Schole M^r there// At w^che tyme the lord Marques Dorsett
had iij^re of his sonnes At scole there w^t hyme/ Commyttyng
As well vnto hyme there vertuous Educasion as ther Instruccion
and learnyng/ Yt pleased the seyd Marques Ayenst A Cristmas
season to send as well for the Scole m^r As for his childerne home 10
to hys howsse for ther recreacion in that pleasaunt & honorable
feast/ They beyng then there/ My lord ther ffather perceyved
them to be right well employed in learnyng for ther tyme w^che
contentyd hyme so well/ that he haueng a benefice in his gyft
beyng at that tyme voyde/ gave the same to the Scole M^r in 15
reward for hys diligence/ At his departyng after Cristmas vppon
his retourne to the vnyuersitie/ And havyng the presentacion
therof repayred to the Ordynarie for his Institucion And
Induccion/ than beyng fully ffurnysshed of all necessarie
Instrume^tes at the Ordinaris handes for his preferment/ made 20
spede w^tout any fferther delay to the [f. 5^v] seyd benefice to take
therof possession/ And beyng there for that entent Oon sir Amys
Pawlett knyght dwelling in that Contrie there Abought toke an
occasion of displeasure Ayenst hyme/ Vppon what ground I
knowe not/ But sir by yor leave he was so bold to sett the Scole 25
M^r by the feete duryng hys pleasure/ The w^che was afterward
nother forgotten ne forgevyn ffor whan the Scole M^r mountyd
the dignytie to be Chauncelour of Englond he was not oblivyous
of the old displeasure mynystred vnto hyme by Mr Pawlett/ but
sent for hyme And after many sharpe & heynous wordes enioyned 30
hyme to attend vppon the Councell vntill he ware by them
dismyssed/ And not to departe w^tout licence vppon an vrgent
payn & forfiture/ So that he contynued w^tin the Middell temple
the space of .v. or vj yeres or more/ whos logyng there was in
the Gathowsse next the strett/ the w^che he reedefied very 35
sumptiously garnysshyng the same on the owtsyde therof w^t

8 vertuous *interl.*   12 thus *canc. before* there   18 ord *canc. before*
Institucion; Institucion] *MS.* Instituticion   26 w^che *interl.*   28 to be
interl.; Chauncelour] *MS.* of Chauncelour

Cardynalles hattes And Armez bagges And Cognysaunces of the Cardynalles w^t dyuers other devisis in so gloryous a sort that he thought therby to appese his old onkynd displeasure/

Nowe may thys be a good example And precedent to men in
5 Auctoritie/ (w^{che} woll sometyme worke ther wyll w^{t}out wytt) to remember in ther Auctoritie/ howe Auctoritye may dekaye/ And whome they punysshe of wyll more than of Iustice may after be Advaunced in the publyke wele to highe dignytes And gouernaunce/ And they based as lowe/ who wyll than seke the
10 means to be revenged of old wronges susteyned wrongfully byfore/ who wold haue thought than that whan sir Amys Pawlett punysshed this poor Scoler that euer he shold haue attayned to be Chauncelour of Englond consideryng his basenes in euery condicion/ Thes be wonderfull workes of god And
15 ffortune/ Therfore I wold wysshe All men in Auctorytie & dignytie to knowe and feare god in all ther tryhumphes & glory consideryng [f. 6] in all ther doynges that Auctorytes be not permanent but may slide And vanyssh as pryncs pleasures do Alter & chaynge/

20 **Than as all** lyvyng thynges must of very necessitie pay the dewe dett of natur w^{che} no earthely creature can resist Yt chaunced the lord Marques to depart owt of this present lyfe/ After whos deathe/ The Scole M^r consideryng than w^t hym self to be but a small beneficed man/ And to haue lost his ffelowe-
25 shype in the College (ffor as I vnderstand if a fellowe of that College be oons promoted to a benyfice he shall by the Rewles of the howsse be dismyssed of his ffellowshipe)/ And perseyvyng hyme self to be also destitute of his syngular good lord/ thought not to be long onprovided of some other Socours or stafe to
30 defend hyme frome all suche Stormes as he lately susteyned/ And in hys travell there Abought/ he fill in acquayntaunce w^t oon sir Iohn Nanfant A very grave & auncyaunt knyght who had a great rome in Calice vnder kyng herre the vijth/ This knyght he serued & behaued hym so discretly and Iustly that he
35 opteyned thespecyall fauour of his seyd M^r/ in so myche that for his wytt, gravite & Iust behauour/ he commytted all the

1 armez *canc. before* Armez; and *canc. after* Armez   7 of wyll *canc. before* than   15 did *canc. after* &   31 in] *written over* as

Life of Cardinal Wolsey

charge of his office vnto his Chapleyn/ And as I vnderstand the Office was the Treasorshipe of Calice/ who was in Consideracion of his great age discharged of his chargeable Rome/ And retorned agayn in to England entendyng to lyve at more quyett/ And thoroughe his Instant labor And especyall fauor his chapleyn was promoted to the kynges seruyce and made his Chapleyn/ And whan he had oons cast anker in the port of promocion [f. 6ᵛ] howe he wrought I shall somewhat declare/ he hauyng than a Iust occasion to be in present sight of the kyng daylye by reason he attendyd and seyd Masse byfore his grace in his privye closett/ And that done he spent not the day forthe in vayn Idelnes but gave his attendaunce vppon thos whome he thought to bere most rewle in the Councell and to be most in fauour wᵗ the kyng/ the wᶜʰᵉ at that tyme ware Doctor ffoxe bysshope of wynchester than Secretory and lord privye Seale/ And also sir Thomas lovell knyght a very sage Councellour & witty beyng Mʳ of the kynges wardes and Constable of the Tower/ Thes auncyent and grave Councellours in processe of tyme after often resort perceyved this Chapleyn to haue a very ffyne wytt/ And what wysdome was pact in his hede thought a mete & an apte person to be preferred to wytty affayers/ Yt chaunced at a certyn season that the kyng had an vrgent Occasion to send an ambassette vnto the Emprour Maxymylian/ who lay at that present in the lowe Contrie of fflaunders not ferre from Calice/ The bysshope of wynchester and sir Thomas lovell/ whome the kyng most highly estemed as cheaffe among his Councellours/ the kyng consultyng and debatyng wᵗ them vppon this ambassett/ Sawe that they hade a convenyent occasion to preferre the kynges Chapleyn/ Whos excellent wytt Eloquence and learnyng they highly commendyd to the kyng/ The kyng gevyng eare vnto theme/ And beyng a prynce of an excellent Iugemeᵗ And Modestie/ commaundyd to bryng his Chapleyn (whome they so myche commendyd) byfore his grace presence to prove the wytt of his chapleyn/ At whos repayer the kyng fill in Commynycacion wᵗ hyme in matters of waytie gravitie/ And perceyvyng his wytt to be very fynne/ thought hyme sufficient

11 he *canc. before* he 15 chefe *interl. and canc. before* Secretory
21 affayers/ Yt] *MS.* affayers Yt 31 prince *canc. before* prynce
34 his *canc. after* prove

to be put in auctorytie & trust w⁺ this ambassett commaundyd hyme there vppon to prepare hyme self to this enterpriced Iourney/ And for his depeche to repayer to his grace and his trusty Councellours aforseyd/ [f. 7] Of whome he shold receyve
5 his commyssion and Instruccions by means wherof he had than a dewe occasion to repayer frome tyme to tyme in to the kynges presence/ Who perceyved hyme more & more to be a very wyse man and of good entendemeᵗ/

And havyng his depeche toke his leave of the kyng at Riche-
10 mond abought none and so came to london w⁺ spede where than the Barge of Graveshend was redy to launche forthe bothe w⁺ a prosperous tyde and wynd/ wᵗout any further abode he entred the barge and so passed forthe/ his happye spede was suche that he arryved at Gravesend wᵗin littill more than iijʳᵉ howers/
15 where he taried no lenger than his post horssis ware providyd And travellyng so spedely w⁺ post horssys that he came to Dover the next mornyng erely where as the passengers ware redy vnder sayle displayed to sayle to Calice/ In to wᶜʰᵉ passenger wᵗout any ferther aboode he entred and sayeled forthe w⁺ them that he
20 arryved at Calice wᵗin iijʳᵉ howers & havyng there post horsis in a redynes departyd Incontynent makyng suche hasty spede that he was that nyght w⁺ the Emprour/ who hauyng vnderstandyng of the Commyng of the kynges of Englondes Ambassitor wold in no wyse deferre the tyme but sent incontynent for hyme (his
25 affeccion vnto kyng herry the vijᵗʰ was suche that he reioysed whan he had an occasion to showe hyme pleasure) The ambassitor hauyng opportunyte disclosed the Somme of his ambassett vnto the Emprour/ of whome he desired spedy expedycion/ the wᶜʰᵉ was grauntyd So that the next day he was
30 clearely dispeched w⁺ all the kynges requestes fully accom-plesshed/ at wᶜʰᵉ tyme he made no further taryaunce but w⁺ post horsis rood incontynent that nyght toward Calice agayn/ conducted thether w⁺ suche nomber of horsmen as themprour had appoynted and at the opynyng of the Gattes there [f. 7ᵛ]
35 where the passengers ware as redy to retourne into Englond as they ware byfore in his avauncyng in so myche that he arryved

9 to *canc. before* toke; toke *interl.*   15 horsyse *canc. before* horssis
30 dis *canc. before* accomplesshed   32-33 agayn/ conducted] *MS.* agayn/ (conducted   36 avauncyng] *MS.* avauauncyng; he *interl.*

at Dover by fore x^{en} of cloke byfore none/ And hauyng post
horsis in a redynes came to the Court at Richemond that nyght
where he takyng his rest for that tyme vntill the mornyng/ at
w^{che} tyme after he was redy repayred to the kyng at his first
commyng owt of his graces bedchamber toward his closett to here 5
masse/ Whome whan he sawe chekked hyme for that he was not
past on hys Iourney/ Sir q^d he if it may stand w^t yor highnes
pleasure I haue all redy byn w^t themprour And dispeched yor
affayers (I trust) to yor graces contentacione/ And w^t that
delyuerd vnto the kyng themprours letters of credence/ The 10
kyng beyng in a great confuse & wonder of his hasty spede/ w^t
redy furnyture of all hys procedynges/ Dissymbled all his
Imagynacion & wonder in that matter And demaundyd of hyme
whether he encountered w^t his purseuaunt the w^{che} he sent vnto
hyme (supposyng hyme not to be skantly owt of london) w^t 15
letters concernyng a very necessary cause neclected in his commyssion & Instruccions/ the w^{che} the kyng Coueted myche to be
sped/ yes forsothe sir/ q^d he/ I encounterd hyme yester day by
the way/ And hauyng vnderstandyng by yor graces letters of
yor pleasure therin/ haue notw^tstandyng byn so bold vppon myn 20
owen discression (perceyveyng that matter to be very necessarye
in that behalf) to dispeche the same/ And for as myche as I haue
excedyd yor graces commyssion I most humbly requyer yor
gracious remyssion & pardon/ The kyng Reioysyng inwardly
not a littill sayd agayn/ we do not oonly pardon you therof but 25
also geve you our pryncely thankes bothe for the procedyng
therin and also for yor good spedy exployt/ commaundyng hyme
for that tyme to take hys rest and to repayer agayn after dyner for
the ferther relacion of his ambassett/

[f. 8] The kyng than went to masse/ And after at convenyent tyme 30
he went to dynner/ it is not to be doughted but that this
ambassitor hathe byn synce hys retourne w^t his great ffrendes
the bysshope of wynchester And sir Thomas lovell to whome he
hathe declared theffect of all his spedy progresse/ Nor yet what
Ioy they conceyved therof/ And after his departure frome the 35
kyng in the mornyng his highnes sent for the bysshope and sir

4 he was *canc. before* he   11 his *interl.*   16 in *canc. before* in
18 sped/yes] *MS.* sped yes   27 spedy *canc. before* spedy   31 dyn*er*
interl. and canc. before went; to dynner *interl.*

10   Life of Cardinal Wolsey

Thomas lovell to whome he declared the wonderfull expedicion of his ambassitor commendyng therw^t his excellent wytt/ and in especyall the Invencion and avauncyng of the matter left owt of hys commyssion and Instruccions/ the kynges wordes reioysed
5 thes worthy councellours not a littill/ ffor as myche as he was of ther preferment///

Than whan/ this ambassitor remembred the kynges Commaundeme^t and sawe the tyme drawe fast on of his repayer before the kyng and his councell/ prepared hyme in a redynes
10 and resorted vnto the place assigned by the kyng/ to declare his ambassett/ w^tout all dowght he reported theffect of all his affayers and procedynges so exactly w^t suche gravitie and eloquence/ that all the Councell that hard hyme cowld do no lesse but commend hyme estemyng his expedicion to be
15 allmost by yond the Capacitie of man/ the kyng of his mere mocion and gracious concideracion gave hyme at that tyme for his diligent & faythfull seruyce the Deanry of lyncolne w^{che} at that tyme was oon of the worthiest Sperytuall promocions that he gave vnder the degree/ [f. 8^v] of a bysshoperyke and thus
20 frome thence forward he grewe more & more in to estimacion And auctorytie and after promoted by the kyng to be his almener/ **Here may** all men/ note the chaunces of ffortune/ that folowyth/ some/ whome she lystithe to promote/ And evyn so to Somme hyr fauour is contrary thoughe they shold travell
25 neuer so myche w^t vrgent diligence/ & paynfull studye that they could device or Imagyn/ wherof for my part I haue tasted of thexperience **Nowe ye** shall vnderstand that all this tale that I haue declared of his good expedicion in the kynges Ambassett/ I receyved it of his owen mowthe and report/ after his ffall lyeng
30 at that tyme in the great parke of Richemond I beyng than there attendyng vppon hyme takyng an occasion vppon dyuers commynycacions to tell me this Iourney w^t all the Circumstaunce as I haue here byfore rehersed///

Whan deathe that favoryth non Estate kyng or Cayser, had
35 taken that prudent prynce kyng herre the vijth owt of this present lyfe (on whos sowle Iesu haue mercy) who for his

3 of *canc. before* and   5 he *interl. and canc. after* myche; he *interl.*
16 that *canc. before* that   18 was *interl.*   25 est *canc. after*
paynfull; that *interl.*   36 sowle *interl.*

Life of Cardinal Wolsey

inestymable wysdome was noted and called in euery Cristian Region the Second Salomon what practysis, Invencions, and compass ware than vsed abought that yong Prynce kyng herre the viijth his oonly Sonne/ And the great provicion made for the ffuneralles of theon/ And the costly devisis for the Coronacions of thother w^t that vertuous Quene katheren than the kynges wyfe newely maried/ I Omyt and leave the circumstaunce therof to historygraffers of Cronycles of pryncyes/ the w^{che} is no part myn entendement// After all thes Solempnytes and Costly tryhumphes fynesshed/ And that our naturall yong, lusty, And Coragious prynce/ And [f. 9] soueraym lord kyng herre the viijth entreng in to the flower of pleasaunt youthe had taken vppon hyme the Regall Septour and themperyall Dyademe of this fertill and plentifull Realme of Englond/ w^{che} at that tyme florysshed in all aboundaunce of welthe & Riches/ wherof he was inestymably garnysshid & furnyshed/ called than the golden world/ suche grace of plenty Raygned than w^t in this Realme

Nowe lett vs retorne agayn vnto the Almosyner (of whome I haue taken vppon me to wright) whos hed was full of subtyll wytt and pollecy/ perceyveng a playn pathe to walke in towardes promocion handelled hyme self so politykly that he found the means to be oon of the kynges Councell and to growe in good estymacion & favour w^t the kyng to whome the kyng gave an howsse at Bridwell in fflet strett sometyme sir Richard Emsons where he kepte howsse for his ffamely/ And he dayly attendyd vppon the kyng in the Court beyng in his especyall grace & fauour/ who had than great sewte made vnto hyme as Councellours most comenly haue that be in fauour/ his Sentences and wytty perswasions in the Councell chamber was allwayes so pithye that they allwayes as occasion moved them/ assigned hym for his filed tong and ornat eloquence to be ther expositer vnto the kynges ma^{tie} in all ther procedynges/ In whome the kyng conceyved suche a lovyng fantzy/ especyally for that he was most earnest and Redyest among all the Councell to avaunce

15 & *interl.*; t *canc. before* he   16 had *canc. before* was; the *canc. before* the   21 in *interl.*   24 gave *interl.*   27 grace & *interl.*   31 t *canc. before* hym; hym] y *written over* e   32 tong *canc. before* tong   33 procedynges/ In] *MS.* procedynges In

the kynges oonly wyll & pleasure w^{t}out any respect to the Case/
The kyng therfore perceyved hyme to be a mete Instrume^t for
the accomplyssheme^t of his devysed wyll & pleasure called
hyme more nere vnto hyme and estemed hyme so highly that
5 his estymacion and fauour put all other auncyent councellours
owt of ther accustumed fauour that they ware in byfore/ In so
myche as the kyng commytted all his [f. 9^v] wyll & pleasure vnto
his disposicion and order/ who wrought so all his matters that
all his endevour was oonly to satisfie the kynges mynd/ knowyng
10 rightwell that it was the very vayn and right Cours to bryng
hyme to highe promocion/ The kyng was yong and lusty,
disposed all to myrthe & pleasure and to followe his desier &
appetyte no thyng myndyng to travell in the busy affayers of
this Realme/ the w^{che} the Almosyner perseyved very well/ toke
15 vppon hyme therfore to disborden the kyng of so waytie a
charge & troblesome busynes puttyng the kyng in Comfort that
he shall not nede to spare any tyme of his pleasure for any busynes
that shold necessary happen in the Councell as long as he beyng
there hauyng the kynges auctorytie & commaundeme^t doughted
20 not to se all thynges sufficiently furnysshed & perfected the
w^{che} wold first make the kyng privye of all suche matters (as
shold passe thoroughe ther handes) byfore he wold procede to
the fynyssheng or determynyng of the same/ whos mynd &
pleasure/ he wold fullfyll & folowe to the vttermost wherw^t the
25 kyng was wonderly pleased/ And where as thother Auncyent
Councellours wold (accordyng to the office of good Councellers)
dyuers tymes perswade the kyng to haue sometyme an entercours in to the Councell/ there to here what was don in waytye
matters the w^{che} pleased the kyng no thyng at all for he loved no
30 thyng worse than to be constrayned to do any thyng contrary
to his Royall wyll & pleasure/ And that knewe the Almosyner
very well hauyng a secrett Intellygence of the kynges naturall
Inclynacion/ And so fast as thother Councellers advised the
kyng to leave hys pleasure/ and to attend to the affayers of his
35 Realme/ So busylie did the Almosyner perswade hyme to the
Contrary w^{che} delyghted hyme myche and caused hyme to haue

3 his *and* & *interl.*   4 more *interl.*   16 kyng *interl.*   21 & *canc.*
after kyng   24 he wold *canc. before* fullfyll   26 wold] *M.S.*
(wold   30 than *interl.*   34 take *canc. before* leave; the *canc. before* hys

Life of Cardinal Wolsey 13

the greatter affeccion and love to the Almosyner/ Thus the
Almosyner rewled all them that byfore rewled hyme/ suche did
his pollecy and wytt bryng to passe/ **Who was** nowe [f. 10] in
highe favoure but m^r Almosyner/ who had all the Sewte but m^r
Almosyner And who ruled all vnder the kyng but m^r Almosyner/ 5
Thus he perceuered still in fauour/ at last in came presentes,
gyftes, and rewardes so plentifully that (I dare sey) he lakked no
thyng that myght other please his fantzy or enriche his Coffers/
ffortune smyled so vppon hyme/ but to what end she brought
hyme/ ye shall here after/ Therfore lett all men to whome 10
ffortune extendythe hir grace not to trust to myche to hir fikkyll
fauor and plesaunt promysis vnder Colour wherof she Cariethe
venemous galle/ ffor whan she seyth hir seruaunt in most
highest Auctorytie And that he assuryth hyme self most
assuredly in hir fauour/ than tournythe she hir visage And 15
plesaunt countenaunce vnto a frownyng chere And vtterly
forsakyth hyme/ suche assuraunce is in hir inconstaunt fauour
and Sewgerd promyse/ whos disseytfull behauour hathe not byn
hyd among the wyse sort of famous Clarkes that hathe exclamed
hir And written vehemently ayenst hir dissymulacion and 20
fayned fauour warnyng all men therby the lesse to regard hir/
And to haue hir in small estymacion of any trust or ffaythfulnes/
Thys/ Almosyner/ clymmyng thus hastely vppe fortunes whele
that no man was of that estymacion w^t the kyng as he was for his
Wysdome And other witty qualites/ he hade a specyall gyft of 25
naturall eloquence w^t a fyled tong to pronunce the same that he
was able w^t the same to perswade/ And allure all men to his
purpose/ **Procedyng** thus in ffortunes blysfulnes/ Yt chaunced
that the warres bytwen the Realmes of Englond & ffraunce to be
opyn but vppon what occasion I knowe not/ In so myche as the 30
kyng beyng fully perswaded and resolued in his most Royall
person to envade his forrayn ennemyes [f. 10^v] w^t a peusaunt
Army to delay ther hault bragges w^t in ther owen terretory
Wherfore it was thought very necessary that this Royall enterprice shold be spedely provyded and plentifully ffurnysshed in 35

4 Als *canc. before* Almosyner   6 perceuered *canc. before* perceuered
11 grace *canc. before* grace   14 f *canc. before* Auctorytie   16 countenaunce *canc. before* countenaunce   17 in constancie in hir *canc. before* in
26 the *canc. before* he   28 in *interl.*   30 what *interl.*

euery degree of thynges apte and convenyent for the same/
Thexpedycion wherof the kynges highnes thought no oon mans
wytt so mete for pollecy and paynfull travayll as his welbeloved
Almosyner was/ To whome therfore he commytted his hole
5 affiaunce and trust ther in/ And he beyng no thyng Scripulous
in any thyng that the kyng would commaund hyme to do/ and
althoughe it semyd to other very deficyll/ yet toke he vppon
hyme the hole charge & bourden of all this busynes/ And
procedyd so ther in that he brought all thynges to a good passe
10 & purpose in a right decent order as of all maner of victualles,
provisions, and other necessaryes convenyent for so nobyll a
voyage & pieusaunt Armye/
All thynges beyng by hym perfected and furnesshed/ The kyng
not myndyng to delay or neclecte the tyme appoynted/ but w^t
15 noble and valyaunt Corage avaunced to his Royall enterprice/
passed the sees bytwen Douer and Calice/ where he prosper-
ously arryved and after some abode there of his grace as well
for the arryvall of his pieusaunt Army Royall, provision and
Munycions/ as to consult abought his pryncely affayers,
20 Marched forward in good order of battayll thoroweghe the lowe
Contrie vntill he came to the strong towen of Teurwyn/ to the
w^{che} he layed his assault/ and assaylled it so fercely w^t contynuall
assultes that w^{t}in short space/ he caused them w^t in to yeld the
towen/ Vnto w^{che} place the Emprour Maximylian repayred vnto
25 the king our Souerayn lord/ w^t a pieusaunt army lyke a myghty
& frendly prynce/ takyng of the kyng his graces wages as well
for his owen person as for his retynewe/ The w^{che} ys a rare thyng
seldome seen, hard, or red that an Emprour to [f. 11] take wages
and to fight vnder a kynges banner/ Thus after the kyng had
30 opteyned the possession of this pieusaunt fort and sett all
thynges in dewe order for the defence & preseruacion of the
same to his highnes vse/ he departed frome thence and marched
toward the Citie of Tourney and there agayn layed his sege/ to
the w^{che} he gave so ferce and sharpe assaultes that they w^t in

2 oon *interl.*   4 Th *canc. before* To   15–16 enterprice/ passed] *MS*.
enterprice passed   18 provision] *MS.* provisicion   19 as *canc.*
before as   22 that *canc. before* w^t 25 whos wages *canc. before* w^t;
a *interl. before* pieusaunt   31 of *canc. after* defence   34 they] y
written over r

Life of Cardinal Wolsey   15

ware constrayned of fynforce to yeld vppe the Town vnto his
victoryous maiestie/ At w^{che} tyme he gave the Almosyner the
bysshopryke of the same see/ for some part of recommpence of
his paynnes susteyned in that Iourney/ And whan the kyng had
establysshed all thynges there aggreable to his pryncely pleasure/ 5
And furnysshed the same w^t noble valyaunt Capteynnes and
men of warre for the savegard of the town ayenst his ennemyes/
he retourned agayn in to Englond taking w^t hyme dyuers worthy
prisoners of the peeres of fraunce As the Duke of longvyle/ the
Countie Clermount and dyuers other taken there in asskyr- 10
mouche most victoryously/ After whos retourne Immedyatly
the See of lyncolne fyll voyde by the dethe of Doctour Smythe
late bysshope of that dignytie/ the w^{che} Benefice & promocion
his grace gave vnto his Almosyner/ bysshope elect of Tourney/
Who was not neclygent to take possession therof And made all the 15
spede he cowld for his consecracion/ the Solempnyzacion wherof
endyd he found the means to gett the possession of all his predicessors gooddes in to his handes wherof I haue seen dyuers
tymes some part therof furnyshe his howsse/ Yt was not long after
that Doctor Baynbryge/ Archebysshope of yorke dyed at Roome 20
beyng ther the kynges ambassitor vnto pope Iulius/ vnto w^{che}
benyfice the kyng presented his newe bysshope of lyncolne So
that he had iij^{re} bysshoprykes in oon yere gevyn hyme/ [f. 11^v]
Than prepared he agayn of newe As fast for his translacion
from the See of lyncolne vnto the see of yorke/ After w^{che} 25
Solempnyzacion don and he beyng in possession of the Arche-
bisshoprike of yorke/ And/ primas Anglie/ thought hyme
sufficient to compare w^t Caunterburye/ And there vppon erected
his crosse in the Court and in euery other place as well in the
presence of the bysshope of Caunterbury and in the precyncte of 30
his Iurysdiccon as elles where/ And for as myche as Caunterbury
claymyth superyorytie & obedyence of yorke as he dothe of all
other bysshoppes w^tin this realme/ for as myche as he is primas
tocius anglie/ And therfore claymyth as a tokyn of an Auncient

2 he *interl.*   4 Iourney/ And] *MS.* Iourney And   12 dethe of
interl.   18 haue *interl.*   19 ther of *interl.*   20 to *canc. before*
dyed   21 the *canc. before* pope   26 possion *canc. before* possession
30 presence *canc. before* presence; the bysshope of *interl.*   31 where/
And] *MS.* where And

obedyence of yorke to abate the avauncyng of hys crosse in the presence of the Crosse of Caunterbury Notw^{t}standyng yorke no thyng myndyng to desist frome beryng of his crosse in maner as is seyd before/ Caused his Crosse to be auaunced and borne byfore hym/ as well in the presence of Caunterbury as elles where/ Wherfore Caunterbure beyng moved therw^t gave yorke a certyn cheke for his presumcyon/ by reason wherof there engendred some grudge bytwen Caunterburye & yorke/ And yorke perceyveng the obedyence that Caunterbury claymed to haue of yorke entendyd to provyde some suche means that he wold rather be superiour in dignytie to Caunterbury than to be other obedient or equall to hyme/ Wherfore he opteyned first to be made preest Cardynall and legatus de latere vnto whome the Pope sent a Cardynalles hatt w^t certyn bulles for his auctorytie in that behalf/ **Yet by** the way of Commynycacion/ ye shall vnderstand that the Pope sent this hatt as a worthy Ioyell of his honor, dygnitie, and auctorytie the w^{che} was conveyed hether in a verlettes bugett/ who semyd to all men to be but a person of small estymacion/ Wherof yorke beyng aduertised of the bassnes of the messanger and of the peoples oppynyon and rumor/ thought it for his honour/ mete/ that so highe a Ioyell shold not be conveyed by so symple a messenger/ Wherfore he caused hyme to be stayed by the way Immedyatly after his arryvall in Englond/ where he was newely furnysshed [f. 12] in all maner of apparell w^t all kynd of costly sylkes w^{che} semyd decent for suche an highe ambassitor/ And that don he was encountred vppon blakhethe And there receyved w^t a great assemble of prelattes & lusty gallaunt gentilmen/ And frome thence conducted and conveyed thoroughe london w^t great tryhumphe/ Than was great and spedy provision & preparacion made in Westminster Abbey for the confirmacion of his highe dignytie/ the w^{che} was executed by all the bisshopes and Abbottes nyghe or abought london in riche myters And Coopes and other costly ornamentes/ w^{che} was don in so solompne a wyse as I haue not seen the lyke oonless it had byn at the coronacion of a myghti prynce or kyng///

16 as a *interl*. humphe Than
23 be *interl*.
30 great *canc. before* great
29–30 tryhumphe/ Than] *MS*. tryhumphe Than
32 the *canc. after* by

Life of Cardinal Wolsey 17

Opptaynyng/ thys/ dygnyte/ thought hyme self mete to
encounter w^t Caunterbury in his highe Iurysdiccion byfore
expressed And that also he was as mete to beare auctoryte
among the temporall powers as a mong the sperytuall Iurisdiccions wherfore remembryng/ as well the tauntes & chekkes 5
byfore susteyned of Caunterbury (w^{che} he entendyd to redresse)
hauyng a respecte to the auauncemet of worldly honour,
promocion, And great benefites/ ffound the means w^t the kyng
that he was made Chauncelour of Englond/ And Caunterbury
therof dismyssed/ who had contynued in that honorable rome 10
and office synce long byfore the deathe of kyng herry the vijth/
Nowe he beyng in possession of the Chauncellourshipe
endowed w^t the promocion of an archebysshop and Cardynall/
legatte allso de latere/ thought hyme self fully furnysshed w^t
suche auctoryties And dygnyties that he was able to surmount 15
Caunterbury in all ecclesiasticall Iurysdiccions havyng power
to convocatt Caunterbury and other bysshopes w^{t}in his provynce
to assemble at his convocacion in any place w^t in this realme
where he wold assigne/ takyng vppon hyme the Coreccion of
all matters in euery [f. 12^v] Dyoces hauyng there thorough all 20
the realme all maner of sperytuall mynysters As commyssaryes,
Scribbes, Apparitours, And all other officers to furnysshe his
Courtes/ visited also all sprituall howsis/ and presentyd by
prevencyon whome he listed to ther benyfices/ And to the
avauncyng of hys legantyn honour & Iurisdiccion he had 25
maysters of his ffaculties/ and maysters Cerimoniarum and
suche other lyke officers to the gloryfieng of his dygnyte/ Than
hade he ij great Crossis of Syluer where of oon of them was for
his archebysshopriche/ And the other for his legacye/ borne
alwayes byfore hyme whether so euer he went or rode/ by ij of 30
the most tallest and comlyest prestes that he cowld gett w^{t}in all
this realme/ And to thencreas of his gaynnes he had also the
bysshopryche of Duresme And the Abbey of seynt Albons in
Commendam/ howbeit after whan bysshope ffoxe of wyncester

1 hyme *interl.*   6 by *canc. after* susteyned; of *interl.*   17 provynce]
ce *written over* s   18 in *interl. and canc. after* w^t; h *canc. before*
in this   20–21 all the *interl.*   23 all *canc. before* all; pre *canc.*
before by   27 dygnyte/ Than] *MS.* dygnyte Than   31 tallest *canc.*
before tallest; persons *canc. before* prestes   32 he had *canc. before* the

18   *Life of Cardinal Wolsey*

dyed he Surrendred Duresme in to the kynges handes/ and in lieu therof toke the bysshopriche of wynchester/ Than he had also as it ware in ferme/ bothe bathe, & worcester and hereford bycause thencombentes therof ware Strayngers borne owt of
5 thys realme contynuyng allwayes be yond the sees in ther owen natife Contries or elles at Rome frome whence they ware sent by the pope in legacion in to Englond to the kyng And for ther reward at ther departure the prudent kyng herre the vijth thought it better to reward them w^t that thyng he hyme self
10 could not kepe than to defray or disburse any thyng of his treasure/ And than they beyng but Strayngers thought it more mete for ther assuraunce And to haue ther Iurisdiccions conserued and Iustly vsed to permyt the Cardynall to haue ther benyfices for a convenyent yerely Somme of mony to be payed them by
15 eschaunce in ther Contries/ than to be trobled or burdened w^t the conveyaunce therof vnto them/ So that all ther sperytuall promocyons and Iurysdiccions of ther bysshopperiches ware clearely in his demayns & disposicion to preferre or promote whome he listed vnto them/ he hade also a great nomber dayly
20 attendyng vppon hyme bothe of noble men and worthy [f. 13] gentilmen of great estymacion and possessions w^t no small nomber of the tallest yomen that he Could gett in all this Realme/ In so myche that well was that noble man or gentilman that myght preferre any tall & comly yoman vnto his
25 seruyce/

Nowe to speke of the order of his howsse & officers/ I thynke it necessarie heare to be remembred/ ffirst ye shall vnderstand that he had in his hall dayly iij^{re} especyall tables furnesshed w^t iij^{re} pryncypall officers that is to sey A Steward/ w^{che} was
30 allwayes a Docter or a preste/ A Treasorer a knyght/ A Controller a esquyer/ w^{che} bare allwayes w^{t}in his house ther whight Staves/ Than hade he a Cofferer/ iij^{re} Marshalles/ ij yomen Vsshers/ ij Gromes and an Almosyner/ he hade also in the hall kytchen ij Clarkes of his kytchen/ A Clarke Controller/ A
35 surveyour of the Dressor/ A Clarke of his Spicery/ Also there in

1 surrendred *canc. after* he   2 had *interl.*   3 & *canc. after* bathe,   7 b *canc. before* in legacion   10 dispurse *canc. before* disburse   14 them *interl.*   18 creal *canc. before* clearely   23 or] *written over* &   32 Marshalles/ ij] *MS.* Marshalles ij

his hall kytchen he hade ij Mr Cookes/ And xij^th of other
laborers & childern as theye called theme/ A Yoman of his
Scollery/ w^t ij other in his syluer Scollery/ ij yomen of his pastery,
and ij Groomes/ Nowe in his privy kytchen he had a Mr Cooke
who went dayly in Dammaske, Satten or velvett w^t a chayn of
gold abought his nekke/ And ij Gromes w^t vj laborers &
childerne to serue in that place/ In the larder there a yoman and
a Grome/ In the Skaldyng howsse a yoman & ij Gromes/ In the
Scollery there ij persons/ In the Buttery ij yomen and ij Gromes
w^t ij other pages/ In the pantrie ij yomen/ ij Gromes and ij pages/
And in the Ewrie lykewyse/ in the seller iiij yomen ij Gromes &
ij pages/ besides a gentilman for the monthe/ In the Chaundrye
iij persons/ In the wafery ij/ In his Garderobbe of Beddes a m^r
and x^en other persons/ in the laundry a yoman a Grome and iiij
pages/ Of purvyours ij and oon Grome/ In the bakhowsse
[f. 13^v] a yoman & ij Gromes/ In the woodyerd a yoman & a
Grome/ In the Garner j In the Garden a yoman & ij laborers/
Nowe at the Gate he had of porters ij tall yomen and ij Gromes/
a yoman of his Barge// In the Stabyll/ he hade a m^r of his
horsses/ A Clarke of the Stable/ A yoman of the same/ A Sadler/
A fferrour/ A yoman of his Charyot/ A Sompter man/ A yoman
of his Stirrope/ A Mewlytor/ xvj^en Gromes of hys stable euery
of them kepyng iiij^or great Geldynges/ In the Almosory a
yoman & a Grome//

Nowe wyll I declare to you the Officers of his Chappell and
Syngyng men of the same/ ffirst he hade there A Dean who was
allwayes a great clarke & a devyn/ A Subdean/ A Repetor of the
Quyer/ A Gospeller/ A Pystoler/ And xij Syngyng prestes/ Of
seculers he had first a M^r of his childern/ xij syngyng Childerne/
xvj^en syngyng men/ a seruaunt to attend vppon the seyd
Childerne/ In the revestrie a yoman & ij Gromes/ Than ware
there dyuers Reteynours of connyng syngyng men that came at
dyuers sondrie pryncypall feastes/ **But to** speke of the ffurnyture
of his Chappell/ passithe my Capasitie to declare the nomber of
the costly ornamentes And riche Ioyelles that ware occupied in
the same contynually/ I haue seen there in a procession worne

11 lykewyse/ in] *MS.* lykewyse in   15 p *canc. after* the   18 of
porters *interl.*   23 Geldynges/ In] *MS.* Geldynge*s* In   26 men *interl.*
27 a *interl. before* devyn   31 the *interl. before* revestrie

xliiij^{ti} Coopes of oon sewte very riche besides the Somptious Crossis, Candyllstykes, and other necessary orname^{tes} to the comly furnature of the same/ **Nowe** shall ye vnderstand that he had ij Crosberers & ij Pillers berers/ And in his chamber/ All thes persons that is to sey/ his highe Chamberlayn/ his Vice-Chamberlayn/ xij Gentilmen vsshers dayly wayters, beside ij in his privye Chamber/ And of Gentillmen wayters in his privye chamber he had vjth/ And also he had of lordes ix^{en} or x^{en}/ who had eche of them allowed ij seruauntes/ And the Erle of Derby had allowed v^{e} men/ Than had he of gentilmen/ As Cupberers/ kervers/ Sewers/ And gentilmen dayley wayters xl^{ti} persons/ Of yomen vsshers he had vj/ Of Gromes in his chamber he had viijth/ Of yomen of his chamber he had xlvj^{ti} dayly to attend vppon his person/ he had also a prest there [f. 14] w^{che} was his Almosyner to attend vppon his tabell/ at dynner/ Of doctors & chapplens attendyng in his Closett to sey dayly masse byfore hyme/ he had xvj^{en} persons/ A Clarke/ of his Closett/ Also he had ij Secretorys/ And ij Clarkes of his signett/ And iiij^{or} Councellours learned in the lawes of this realme/ And for as myche as he was Chauncelor of England yt was necessary for hyme to haue dyuers Officers of the Chauncery to attend dayly vppon hyme for the better ffurnyture of the same/ that is to say/ he had a Clarke of the Crowne/ A ridyng Clarke/ A Clarke of the hamper/ A Chaffer of waxe/ Than had he A Clarke of the Chekke as well to chekke his Chappleyns as hys yomen of the Chamber/ he had also iiij^{or} ffootmen w^{che} ware apparelled in riche Runnyng Cootes whan so euer he rode any Iourney/ Than had he an harrold at Armez/ Also a Seriaunt at Armez/ A Phisicion/ A Pottecarye/ iiij^{or} Mynstrelles/ A keper of his Tentes/ An Armorer/ And Instructer of his wardes/ ij yomen in his Garderobbes/ And a keper of his Chamber in the Court/ he had also dayly in his howsse the Surveyour of yorke/ And a Clarke of the Grean clothe/ and an Audytor All this nomber of

6 ij *canc. before* xij   9 allowed] *MS.* alloweed   11 gentilma *canc. before* gentilmen   12 vj/ Of] *MS.* vj Of   13 in his *canc. before first* chamber   16 Closed *canc. before* Closett   17 persons *canc. before* persons   19 of *canc. before* learned   21 for hyme *interl.* 22 aly *canc. before* dayly; dayly *interl.*   29 Mynstrelles] *MS.* Mynstelles 30 his *interl.*   31 *first* his *interl.*; Garderobbes] *MS.* Gardebobbes   33 and an Audytor *interl.*

persons ware daylye attendaunt vppon hyme in hys howsse,
down lyeng And vppe risyng/ And at meales/ There was contynually in his chamber a bord kept for his Chamberlayns and
gentilmen vsshers/ hauyng w^t theme a messe of the yong lordes
And an other for gentilmen/ besides all this there was neuer an
officer and gentilman or any other worthye person in his howesse
but he was allowed some iij some ij seruauntes And all other
(oon) at the least w^{che} amounted to a great nomber of persons//

Nowe haue I shewed you the order of his howsse/ And what
officers & seruauntes he had accordyng to his Chekker Rolle
attendyng dayly vppon hyme besides hys reteynors and other
persons beyng Sewters that most Comenly ware fedde in his
hall And whan so euer we shall se any more suche Subiectes
w^{t}in thys realme that shall maynteyn any suche estat & howshold
I ame content he be auaunced above hyme in honour & estymacion therfore here I make [f. 14^v] an end of his howsshold/
wherof the nomber ware abought the Somme of fyve hundred
parsons accordyng to his chekker rolle//

Yow have hard of the order & Officers of his howsse/ nowe do
I entend to proced forthe vnto other of his procedynges/ ffor
after he was thus ffurnysshid in maner as I haue byfore rehersed
vnto you he was twyse sent in Ambassett vnto themprour
Charles the 5 that nowe reygnyth and nowe ffather vnto kyng
Phillipe our Souerayn lord/ for as myche as the old Emprour
Maximylian was deade/ And for dyuers vrgent causys touchyng
the kynges ma^{tie} yt was thought good that in so waytie a matter/
And to so noble a prince that the Cardynall was most meate to
be sent on so worthy an Ambassett/ wherfore he beyng redy to
take vppon hyme the charge therof/ was ffurnysshed in all
degrees and purposys most lykest A great prynce w^{che} was
myche to the highe honour of the kynges ma^{tie} and of this
realme/ ffor first in his procedyng he was furnysshed lyke a
Cardynall of highe estimacion/ havyng all thyng therto correspondent & agreable/ his gentilmen beyng in nomber very many
clothed in lyuere Coottes of Crymmosyn velvett of the most

3 in his chamber *interl.*   10 the *canc. before* his   14 howsheld
canc. after &   16 th *canc. before* therfore   17 wherof *interl.*;
nomber] *MS.* nomber of; his persons wherof *canc. before* ware   23 vnto
kyng *canc. after* kyng   32 realme/ ffor] *MS.* realme ffor

purest Colour that myght be Invented/ w^t chaynnes of gold
abought ther nekkes/ And all his yomen And other mean officers
ware in Cottes of ffynne Skarlett garded w^t blake velvett an hand
brode/ he beyng thus furnysshid in thys maner was twyse sent
5 vnto themprour in to fflaunders Themprour lyeng than in
Brugges who entertayned our Ambassitor very highly/ dischargyng hyme and all his trayn of ther charges/ ffor ther was
no howsse w^{t}in all bruges wherin any gentilman of the lord
ambassitors lay or had recourse/ but that the owners of the
10 howses ware commaunded by themprours officers that they
vppon payn of ther lyves shold take no mony for any thyng that
the Cardynalles seruauntes shold take or dispend in victualles/
ne allthoughe they ware disposed to make any costly bankettes/
fferthermore commaundyng ther seyd hostes to se that they
15 lakked no suche thynges as they desired or requyred to haue for
ther pleasures [f. 15] Also themperours Officers euery nyght
went thoroughe the towen frome howsse to howsse where as any
Englysshemen lay & resorted/ And there serued lyueres for all
nyght w^{che} was don after this maner// **ffirste**/ the Emprors
20 Officers brought in to the howsse a Cast of fynne manchett
brede/ ij great Siluer pottes w^t wynne and a pound of fynne
Sewger/ Whight lightes And yelowe/ A bolle or goblett of Syluer
to drynke in And euery nyght a staffe torche/ this was thorder
of ther lyueres euery nyght/ And than in the mornyng whan the
25 Officers came to fetche a way ther stuffe than wold they
Accompte w^t the host for the gentillmens costes spent in that
nyght & day byfore/ Thus themprerour entertayned the
Cardynall & all hys trayn for the tyme of his Ambassett there/
And that don he retourned home agayn in to Englond w^t great
30 tryhumphe beyng no lesse in estymacion w^t the kyng than he
was byfore but rather myche more///
Now wyll I declare vnto you his order in goyng to westmynster
hall dayly in the tearme season/ ffirst byfore hys commyng owt of
hys pryvy chamber he hard most comenly euery day ij massis
35 in his privye closett/ And there than seyd his dayly seruyce w^t
his chapleyn (And as I hard his chapleyn say beyng a man of

1 be *interl*.   10 *A single indecipherable letter canc. before* by   28 amb
canc. before Ambassett   36 as *canc. before* as

credence/ and of excellent learnyng) that the Cardynall what
busynes or waytie matters so euer he had in the day he neuer
went to his bed w^t any part of his devyn seruyce onsayd/ yea not
so myche as oon Collect/ wherin I dought not but he disseyved
the oppynyon of dyuers persons/ And after masse he wold
retourne in his privye chameber agayn and beyng aduertised of
the furnyture of his chambers w^{t}out w^t noble men and gentil-
men/ w^t other persons wold issue owt in to theme apparelled
all in red in the habytt of a Cardynall w^{che} was other of fynne
skarlett or elles of crymmosyn Satten/ Taffeta Dammaske/ or
Caffa/ the best that he could gett for mony/ and vppon hys hed a
round pyllion w^t a nekke [f. 15^v] of blake velvett set to the same
in the Inner side/ he had also a tippett of fynne Sables a bought
his nekke/ holdyng in his hand a very fayer Orrynge wherof the
mete or substaunce w^t in was taken owt and fylled vppe agayn
w^t the part of a Sponge wherin was vyneger and other confeccions agaynst the pestylente Ayers to the w^{che} he most
commenly smelt vnto/ passyng among the prease or elles whan
he was pesterd w^t many Sewters/ There was also borne byfore
hyme first the great Seale of Englond/ And than his Cardynalles
hatt by a noble man or some worthy Gentilman right Solemply
barehedyd/ And as Sone as he was entered in to hys chamber of
presence where was attendyng his Commyng to awayt vppon
hyme to westminster hall as welle noble men and other worthy
gentilmen/ as noble men & gentilmen of his owen famely/ thus
passyng forthe w^t ij great Crossis of Syluer borne byfore hyme
w^t also ij great pillers of syluer/ And his seriaunt at Armez w^t a
great mase of syluer gylt/ Than his gentilmen vsshers cried and
sayd/ on my lordes & maysters/ make way for my lordes grace/
thus passed he down frome his chambers thoroughe the hall/
And whan he came to the hall doore ther was attendaunt for
hyme his mewle trapped all to gether in Crymmosyn velvett and
gylt Stirroppes/ whan he was mounted/ w^t his crosse berers/
and Piller berers also/ vppon great horsis trapped w^t red skarlett

1 of *interl*.   6 bed *canc. before* privye; privye *interl*.   9 habit of *canc. after* the   12 set to] *MS*. setto   13 of *canc. before* he   15 of *canc. before* or *canc. before* many and; and *interl*.   17 ayer *canc. after* confeccions; to *interl*.   19 any   22 as he *canc. before* as he   24 as *canc. before* before w^t; w^t *interl*.   29 sayd/ on] *MS*. sayd on   33 and *canc*.

Than marched he forward w^t his trayn & furnyture in maner as I haue declared/ hauyng abought hyme iiij^{or} footmen w^t gylt pollaxes in ther handes/ And thus he went vntill he came to westminster hall doore/ And there lighted and went after this maner vppe thoroughe the hall in to the Chauncery/ howebeit he wold most commynly stay a while at a barre made for hyme a littill benethe the chauncery And there Commyn some tyme w^t the Iuges and somtyme w^t other persons/ And that don he wold repayer in to the Chauncery/ And sittyng there vntill xj^{en} of the clocke heryng Sewters and determynyng of dyuers matters/ And frome thence he wold dyuers tymes goo in to the sterrechamber as occasion dyd serue/ where he spared nother highe nor lowe but Iuged euery estate accordyng to ther merites and desertes/ he vsed euery Sonday to repayer to the Court beyng than for the [f. 16] most part at Grenwyche in the terme/ w^t all his former order takyng his barge at his pryvy stayers furnyished w^t tall yomen standyng vppon the baylles And all gentilmen beyng w^tin w^t hyme/ And londed at the Crane in the vyntrie And frome thence he rode vppon hys mule w^t his Crossis/ his pillers/ his hatt/ And the great Seale, thoroughe temmes strette vntill he came to Byllyngesgate or there aboughtes And there toke his barge agayn and rowed to Grenwyche/ where he was noblly receyved of the lordes and cheafe officers of the kynges howsse/ As the Treasorer and Controllers w^t other and conveyed vnto the kynges Chamber/ his Crosses commonly standyng (for the tyme of hys aboode in the Court) on the oon syde of the kynges clothe of estate/ he beyng thus in the Court/ yt was wonderly furnysshed w^t noble men and gentilmen myche otherwyse than it was byfore hys commyng/ And after Dynner among the lordes hauyng some consultacion w^t the kyng or w^t the councell he wold departe homeward w^t lyke sorte/ And thys order he vsed contynually as opportunyte dyd serue//

Thus in greate honour/ tryhumphe & glorye he raygned a long season Rewlyng all thyng w^t in thys Realme appurteynyng vnto

2 hyme *interl.*   3 on *canc. before* went; went *interl.*   6 at *canc. after* stay; made *interl.*   11 tymes *interl.*   18 hy *canc. before* w^t   26 of *interl.*   30 the *canc. after* among; the *interl. before* lordes

Life of Cardinal Wolsey

the kyng by his wysdome/ And also all other waytie matters of
fforrayn Regions w^t whome the kyng & this Realme had any
occasion to entermeddell/ All Ambassitors of fforrayn potentates
ware allway dispeched by hys discression/ to whome they had
allwayes accesse for ther dispeche/ his howsse was also allwayes
resorted and furnesshed w^t noble men/ gentilmen, & other
persons w^t goyng & commyng in and owt/ ffeastyng & bankatyng
all Ambassitors dyuers tymes and other Strayngers right nobly/
And whan it pleased the kynges ma^{tie} for his recreacion to
repayer vnto the Cardynalles howsse (as he dyd dyuers tymes
in the yere) at w^{che} tyme there wanted no preparacions or
goodly furnyture w^t vyaundes of the fynnest Sort that myght be
provided for mony or frendshippe/ Suche pleasures ware than
devysed for the kynges comfort & consolacion as myght be
Invented or by mans wytt Imagyned/ the bankettes ware sett
forthe w^t [f. 16^v] Maskes and Mumerreys in so gorges a sort
and Costly maner that it was an hevyn to behold/ ther wanted
no dames or damselles meate or apte to daunce w^t the maskers
or to garnysshe the place for the tyme/ w^t other goodly disportes/
than was there all kynd of musyke and armonye setforthe w^t
excellent voyces bothe of men and Childerne/ **I haue** seen the
kyng sodenly come in thether in a maske w^t a dosyn of other
maskars all in garmentes lyke Shepherdes made of fynne
Clothe of gold and fyn Crymosyn Satten paned and Cappes
of the same w^t visors of good proporcion of visonamy, ther
heares & beardes other of fynne gold wyers or elles of syluer/
And Some beyng of blake sylke/ havyng xvj^{en} torches berers
besides Dromes And other persons attendyng vppon them w^t
visors & clothed all in Satten of the same Colours/ and at his
commyng & byfore he came in to the hall ye shall vnderstand
that he came by water to the water gate w^{t}out any noys where
ayenst his commyng was layed charged many chambers/ At whos
londyng they ware all Shot of w^{che} made suche a Romble in the
Ayer that it was lyke thonder it made all the noble men ladys
& gentilwomen to muse what it shold mean commyng so
sodenly they syttyng quyotly at a solempne bankett vnder this

8 straynger *canc. before* Strayngers 16 sort *canc. before* sort 22 of
interl. 33 a *interl.* 36 solempne *interl.*

sort/ ffirst ye shall perceyve that the tables ware sett in the
Chamber of presence/ Bankett wyse couered/ my lord Cardynall
syttyng vnder the clothe of estat/ And there hauyng all his
seruyce all alone/ And than was there sett a lady and an noble
5 man or a gentilman and a gentilwoman thorougheowt all the
tables in the Chamber on the oon syde w^{che} was made & Ioyned
as it ware but oon table/ All w^{che} order & device was don and
devysed by the lord Sandes lord Chamberlayn w^t the kyng/ And
also by sir herry Gwyldford controller w^t the kyng/ Than
10 Immedyatly after this great shott of Gonnes/ the Cardynall
desired the seyd lord Chamberleyn & Controller to loke what
this soden shot shold mean (As thoughe he knewe no thyng of
the matter) They thervppon lokyng owt of the wyndowe in to
Temmes retorned agayn & shewed hyme that it Semed to them
15 that there shold be some noble men & strayngers arryved at his
brygge As Ambassitors frome some fforrayn prynce/ W^t that q^d
the Cardynall/ I shall desier you bycause ye can speke ffrenche
to take the paynnes to goo down in to the hall to encounter and
to receyve them accordyng to [f. 17] ther estates And to con-
20 ducte them in to thys Chamber/ where they shall se vs and all
thes noble personages syttyng merely at our Bankett desyryng
them to sitt down w^t vs and to take part of our fare & pastyme/
They went incontynent down in to the hall/ where they receyved
them w^t xx^{ti} newe torches And conveyed theme vppe in to the
25 Chamber w^t suche a nomber of Dromes and fyves as I haue
seldome seen together at oon tyme in any Maske/ At ther
aryvall in to the chamber ij & ij together they went directly
byfore the Cardynall where he satt/ Salutyng hyme very
reuerently to whome the lord Chamberlayn (for them) sayd/
30 Syr for as myche as they be strayngers And can speke no
Englysshe thay haue desired me to declare vnto yor grace thus/
They havyng vnderstandyng of thys yor tryhumphant bankett
where was assembled suche nomber of excellent fayer dames/
cowld do no lesse vnder the supportacion of yor grace but to

5 a *interl. after* or   9 also *interl.*; also *canc. before* w^t   15 they
canc. before there; there *and* some *interl.*   16 ambassitours *canc. after* As
17 speke can ffenche *canc. after* ye *with* can *interl.*   18 them *canc. before*
and   19 to ther] *MS.* to/ ther   20 *a single indecipherable letter canc.
before* in   24 theme *interl.*   27 to the *canc. before* together; they
interl.   31 thay *interl.*   31–32 Th *canc. before* | They; /[They] *MS.* They

repayer hether to vewe as well ther incomperable beawtie as for
to accompany them at Mume chaunce And than After to daunce
w^t them/ And so to haue of them acquayntaunce And sir they
furthermore requyer of yor grace lycence to accomplesshe the
cause of ther repayer/ to whome the Cardynall answered that
he was very well contentyd they shold so do/ Then the Maskars
went first and saluted all the Dames as they sat and than
retorned to the most worthyest and there opyned a Cuppe full
of gold w^t Crowns & other peces of coyn to whome they sett
dyuers peces to cast at/ thus in this maner pervsyng all the
ladys & gentilwomen/ And to some they lost And of some they
won/ And this don they retourned vnto the Cardynall w^t great
reuerence poryng down all the Crownes in the Cuppe w^{che} was
abought ij^C Crownes/ at all q^d the Cardynall and so cast the
dyse And wane them all at a Cast/ where at was great Ioy made/
Than q^d the Cardynall to my lord Chamberlayn/ I pray you q^d
he shewe them that it semys me howe there shold be among
theme some noble man/ whome I suppose to be myche more
worthy of honor to sitt and occupie this rome & place than I/ to
whome I wold most gladly [f. 17^v] (yf I knewe hyme) surrender
my place accordyng to my dewtie/ than spake my lord Chamberlayn vnto them in ffrenche declaryng my lorde cardynalles
mynd And they Roundyng hyme agayn in the eare/ my lord
Chamberlayn seyd to my lord Cardynall/ Sir they confesse q^d
he that among them there is suche a noble personage/ Among
whome if yor grace can appoynt hyme frome the other he is
contented to discloos hyme self And to accepte yor place most
worthely/ w^t that the Cardynall takyng a good advyseme^t among
them/ at the last/ q^d he/ me Semys the gentilman w^t the blake
beard shold be evyn he/ And w^t that he arrose owt of hys
chayer and offered the same to the gentilman in the blake beard
(w^t his Cappe in his hand) The person to whome he offered than
his Chayer/ was sir Edward Neveyll A comly knyght of a
goodly personage that myche more resembled the kynges person
in that Maske than any other/ The kyng heryng & perceyvyng

2 them *interl.*   12 this] *MS.* thus   17 that *canc. before* howe;
howe *interl.*   19 and] *MS.* an   21 dewtie/ than] *MS.* dewtie
than   22 frenche *canc. before* ffrenche   23 eare *canc. after* the
28 ad *canc. before* among

the Cardynall so disseyved in his estymacion and choys cowld not forbeare lawyng/ but plukked down his visare & m^r Neveylles & dasht owt w^t suche a pleasaunt Countenaunce & cheare/ that all noble estates there assembled seyng the kyng to be there
5 amoong them reioysed very myche/ the Cardynall eftsons desired hys highnes to take the place of estate/ to whome the kyng answered that he wold goo first & shyfte hys apparell and so departed/ and went strayt to my lordes bed Chamber where was a great fier made & prepared for hyme/ And there newe
10 apparelled hyme w^t riche & pryncely garmentes/ And in the tyme of the kynges absence/ the disshes of the bankett ware clean taken vppe and the table spred agayn w^t newe & swett perfumed clothes euery man syttyng still vntill the kyng & his maskers came in among theme agayn euery man beyng newly
15 apparelled/ Than the kyng toke his seate vnder the clothe of estate comaundyng no man to remove but sit still as they dyd byfore/ Than/ In came a newe bankett byfore the kynges ma^tie and to all the rest thorough the tables/ wherin I suppose was serued ij^cc disshes or above of wonderouse costly meates &
20 devysys subtilly devysed/ thus passed [f. 18] they fforthe the hole nyght w^t banketyng, dauncyng & other tryhumphant devyses to the great comfort of the kyng and plesaunt regard of the nobylitie there assembled// All this matter I haue declared at large bycause ye shall vnderstand what Ioy & delight the
25 Cardynall had to se his prynce and souerayn lord in his howsse so nobley entertayned and pleased w^che was Allwayes his oonly study to devise thynges to his commfort not passyng of the charges or expences/ yt delighted hyme so myche the kynges plesaunt pryncely presence/ that no thyng was to hyme more
30 delectable than to cheare his souerayn lord to whome he owght so myche obedyence and loyaltie/ as reason requyred no lesse/ All thynges well considered/

Thus/ passed the Cardynall hys lyfe & tyme frome day to day And yere to yere in suche great welthe, Ioy tryhumphe/ & glory
35 hauyng allwayes on his syde the kynges especyall fauour/ vntill ffortune (of whos fauour no man is lenger assured than she is

6 the place *canc. before* estate   10 w^t] *MS.* w^che   15 se *canc.*
after his   20 substam *canc. before* subtilly; they *interl.*   21 de *canc.*
before tryhumphant   34 & *canc. before* tryhumphe

Life of Cardinal Wolsey

dysposed) began to wexe some thyng wrothe w^t his prosperous estate// thought she wold devyse a mean to abate his hyghe port wherfor she procured Venus the Insaciat goddesse to be hir Instrument to worke hir purpose/ She brought the kyng in love w^t a gentillwoman that after she perceyved and felt the kynges good wyll towardes hir And howe dilygent he was bothe to please hir And to graunt all hir requestes she wrought the Cardynall myche displeasure as hereafter shalbe more at large declared/ This gentilwoman the doughter of sir Thomas Bolayn beyng at that tyme but oonly a bacheler knyght the w^{che} after for the love of his dowghter was promoted to higher dignytes/ he bare at dyuers seuerall tymes for the most part all the Romes of estimacion in the kynges howsse as/ controller/ Treasorer/ vice Chamberleyn/ and lord Chamberlayn/ than was he made Viscount Rocheford/ And at the last created Erle of wyltshere/ & knyght of the noble order of the Garter/ And for his more encrease of gayn & honour he was made lord pryvye seale and most chefest of the kynges privye Councell/ Contynuyng therin vntill his Sonne & doughter did encurre the kynges Indignacion and displeasure/ The kyng fantazed so myche his doughter Anne that allmost euery thyng began to growe owt of fframe & good order/ [f. 18^v]

To tell you/ howe the kynges love began to take place/ And what folowed therof/ I will do evyn as myche as in me lyeth declare you/ This gentillwoman Mrs Anne Boleyn beyng very yong was sent in to the realme of ffraunce/ And there made oon of the ffrenche Quens women contynuyng there vntill the ffrenche Quene dyed/ And than was she sent for home agayn/ And beyng agayn w^t hir ffather he made suche means that she was admytted to be oon of Quene katheryns maydes/ Among whome for hir excellent gesture & behauour dyd excell all other in so myche/ As the kyng began to kyndell the brond of Amours/ w^{che} was not knowen to any person ne skantly to hir owen person/ In so myche my lord Percye the Sonne & heyer of the Erle of Northumberland who than attendyd vppon the lord

5 a *interl.*   12 for *interl.*   15 at *interl.*   18 seale/ *canc. after* privye; Contynuyng] *MS.* Contynyng   20 and *interl.*; displeasure/ The] *MS.* displeas*ur*e The   27 women] *MS.* woman   28 was *canc. before* was   32 Amours] *MS.* Amo*ur*rs

Cardynall/ And was allso hys seruyture/ And whan it chaunced the lord Cardynall at any tyme to repayer to the Courte/ The lord Percye wold than resort for his pastyme vnto the Quens chamber/ And there wold fall in dalyaunce among the quens
5 maydens beyng at the last more conuersaunt w^t Mrs Anne Bolleyn than w^t any other so that there grewe suche a secrett love bytwen them/ that at lengthe they ware ensured together entendyng to marye/ the w^{che} thyng came to the kynges knowlege/ who was than myche offendyd/ wherfore he cowld hyde no
10 lenger his secrett affeccion but revealed his secrett entendement vnto my lord Cardynall in that behalf/ And consultyd w^t hyme to enfrynge the precontracte bytwen them/ In so myche that after my lord Cardynall was departyd frome the Court & retourned home vnto his place at westminster/ not forgetyng the kynges
15 request & Councell/ beyng in his Gallery/ called there byfore hyme the seyd lord Percye/ vnto his presence/ And byfore vs his seruauntes of his chamber sayeng thus vnto hyme/ **I mervell** not a littill/ q^d he/ of thy pevysshe follye that thou woldest tangle and ensuer thy self w^t a folysshe gyrlle yonder in the
20 Court/ I mean Anne Bolloyn/ dost thou not consider thestate that god hathe called the vnto in this world/ ffor after the deathe of thy noble ffather thou art most lyke to enherite & possesse oon of the most worthyest Erldomes of thys Realme/ therfore it had byn most meate & convenyent for the to haue sewed for the
25 concent of thy ffather/ [f. 19] in that behalfe And to haue also made the kynges highnes privye therto requeryng than his pryncely favor submyttyng all thy hole procedyng in all suche matters vnto his highnes/ who wold not oonly accepte thankfully yor submyssion/ but wold I assure the/ provyde so for yor
30 purpose therin that he wold auaunce you myche more nobly And haue matched you accordyng to yor estat & honour/ wherby ye myght haue growen so by yor wysdome & honorable behauour in to the kynges highe estymacion that it shold haue byn myche to yor encrease of honor/ But nowe behold what ye
35 haue don thorowghe yor wyllfullnes/ ye haue not oonly offendyd yor naturall father but also yor most gracious souerayn

3 Qune *canc. before* Quens   4 he *canc. before* fall   12 precontract *canc. after* the   25 to *canc. before* to   27 all *interl. before* thy   30 auaunce] *MS.* auunced

Life of Cardinal Wolsey

lord And matched yor selfe w^t oon suche as nother the kyng ne yet yor ffather wilbe agreable w^t the matter/ And herof I put you owt of dought/ that I wolle send for yor ffather/ And at his Commyng he shall other breke this onadvysed contracte or elles disinherit the for euer/ The kynges ma^{tie} hyme self woll complayn to thy ffather on the/ And requyer no lesse at his handes than I haue seyd/ whos highnes entendyd to haue preferred hir/ vnto an other person/ w^t whome the kyng hathe travelled allredye/ and beyng allmost at a poynt w^t the same person (allthoughe she knowyth it not) yet hathe the kyng most lyke a polityke & a prudent prynce/ conveyed the matter in suche sort that she vppon the kynges mocyon wilbe (I dought not) right glad & agreable to the same/ **Syr**/ q^d the lord Percye (all wepyng) I knewe no thyng of the kynges pleasure therin (for whos displeasure I ame very sory) I considered that I was of good yeres and thought my selfe sufficient to provyd me of a convenyent wyfe where as my ffantzy serued me best (not doughtyng) but that my lord my father wold haue byn right well perswadyd/ And thoughe she be a symple mayde & hauyng but a knyght to hir father yet is she dissendyd of right noble parentage/ as by hyr mother she [f. 19^v] is nyghe of the Norffolk bloode/ And of hyr ffather side lynyally dissendyd of the Erle of Ormond he beyng oon of the Erles heyers generall/ wye shold I than (sir) be any thyng scrypolous to matche w^t hir whos estate of dissent is equyvolent w^t myn/ whan I shalbe in most dygnytie/ Therfore I most humbly requyer yor grace of yor especyall fauour herin/ And also to entret the kynges most royall ma^{tie} most lowly on my behalf for his pryncely benyvolence in thys matter the w^{che} I cannot deny or forsake// **Loo sirs**/ q^d the Cardynall ye may se what conformytie or wysdome is in this wylfull boys hed/ I thought that whan thou hardest me declare the kynges entendyd pleasure & travell herein thou woldest haue relented and holy submytted thy self and all thy wyllfull and onadvysed fact to the kynges Royall wyll & prudent pleasure to be fully disposed & ordered by his graces disposicion as his highnes shold seme good

2 yo *canc. before* you; you *interl.*   3 ffaher *canc. after* yor   5 disinherite *canc. after* elles   6 no le *canc. before* at   10 the *interl.*   13 right] *MS.* be right *with* be *interl.*   25 equylol *canc. before* equyvolent; in *interl.*

Sir so I wold q^d the lord Percye/ but in this matter I haue goon so ferre byfore so many worthy witnesses that I knowe not howe to avoyde my self nor to discharge my Concyence/ **Wye** thynkest thou q^d the Cardynall/ that the kyng And I/ knowe not what we
5 haue to do in as waytie a matter As this/ yes q^d he/ I warraunt the/ howbeit I can se in the no submyssion to the purpose/ **ffor sothe** my lord/ q^d my lord Percye if it please yor grace I wyll submytt my self holy to the kynges ma^tie & grace in thys matter my consience beyng discharged of the waytie burden of
10 my precontract/ Well than q^d the Cardynall/ I wyll send for yor ffather owt of the Northe parties/ And he and we shall take suche order for the avoydyng of thys thy hasty folly as shalbe by the kyng thought most expedyent/ And in the mean season/ I charge the & in the kynges name commaund the that thou
15 presume not oons to resort in to hir Company as thou entendest to avoyde the kynges highe indygnacion/ And this sayed he roose vppe & went in to his Chamber/
Than was/ the Erle of Norhumberland sent for in all hast in the kynges name/ who vppon knowlege of the kynges pleasure made
20 quyke spede to the Court/ And at his first Commyng owt of the Northe he made his first [f. 20] repayer vnto my lord Cardynall/ at whos mouthe he was advertysed in the cause of his hasty sendyng for/ beyng in my lorde Cardynalles gallerye w^t hyme in secrett commynycacion a long whyle/ And after ther long talke
25 my lord Cardynall Called for a Cuppe w^t wynne/ And drynkyng together they brake vppe/ and so departed the Erle vppon whome we ware commaunded to wayte & to convey hyme to hys seruauntes/ And in his goyng a way whan he came to the Galleryes ende he satt hyme down vppon a fforme/ that stode there
30 for the wayters some tyme to take ther ease/ And beyng there sett/ Called hys Sonne the lord Percye vnto hyme And sayed in our presence/ thus in effect/ **Sone** q^d **he**/ thou hast allwayes byn a prowde, presumpcious, disdaynfull, And a very onthryfte waster/ And evyn so hast thou nowe declared thy self/ Therfore

3 d. *canc. before* avoyde   5 this/ yes] *MS.* this yes   6 .e *canc. before* in   7 q^d *canc. before* my lord   13 season *canc. after* mean
15 in to *interl.*; vnto *canc. before* hir   19 know *canc. before* knowlege
27 wayed *canc. before* wayte; wayte *interl.*; vppon hyme *canc. after* wayte; convey] *MS.* contey   28 seruauntes/ And] *MS.* seruauntes And
31 vnto & *canc. before* in   34 So *canc. before* And

Life of Cardinal Wolsey 33

what Ioy,/ what Comfort,/ what pleasure/ or solace shold I
conceyve in the/ that thus w^tout discression & advisement hast
mysused thy self/ havyng no maner of regard to me thy naturall
father ne inespecyall vnto thy souerayn lord/ to whome all
honest And loyall subiectes berythe faythfull & humble 5
obedyence/ ne yet to the welthe of thyn owen estate But hathe
so onadvysedly ensured thy self to hir for whome thou hast
purchased the/ the kynges displeasure intollerable for any
subiecte to susteyn/ but that his grace of his mere wysdome
dothe consider the lightnes of thy hed and wilfull qualites of 10
thy person/ his displeasure and Indignacion ware sufficient to
cast me and all my posterytie in to vtter subuercion & dysso-
lacion/ but he beyng my especyall & syngular good lord and
fauorable prynce/ And my lord Cardynall my good lord/ hathe
and dothe clearely excuse me in thy lowd facte/ And dothe 15
Rather lament thy lightnes, than malyng the same/ And hathe
devysed an order to be taken for the/ to whome bothe thou & I
be more bound than we be able well to consider/ I pray to god
that this may be to the a sufficient monycion & warnyng to vse
thy self more wittier hereafter for thus I assure the yf thou dost 20
not amend thy prodigalitie thou wylt be the last Erle of our
howsse/ ffor of thy naturall Inclynacion thou art disposed
[f. 20^v] to be wastfull prodegall And to consume all that thy
progenytors hathe w^t great travell gathered to gether And kept
w^t honour/ But hauyng the kynges ma^{tie} my syngular good & 25
gracious lord I entend (god wyllyng) so to dispose my succession
that ye shall consume therof but a littill/ for I do not purpose
(I assure the) to make the myn heyer (ffor prayses be to god)
I haue more choyes of Boyes who I trust wyll prove them selfes
myche better And vse them more lyke vnto nobilitie/ among 30
whome I woll chos & take the best & most lykelyest to succed
me/ Nowe maysters & good gentilmen q^d he vnto vs/ yt may be
yor chaunces herafter whan I ame deade to se the prove of thes

3 mys mysused *canc. before* mysused *with* mys *interl.*; mysused *interl.*
7 advysed *canc. before* onadvysedly; onadvysedly] *MS.* on advysedly   9 of
canc. before grace   12 in *interl.*   20 thus] s *frayed away at edge
of page*   21 last] st *frayed away at edge of page*   22 disposed]
d *frayed away at edge of page*   23 that *interl.*   25 good *interl.*; lord
canc. before &   29 more] *MS.* more more   30 vnto noblytye//
canc. before vnto

thynges that I haue spoken to my Sonne prove as true as I haue spoken them/ yeat in the mean season I desier you all to be his frend and to tell hyme hys fault whan he dothe amys wherein ye shall shewe yor selfes to be myche his frendes/ And w^t that
5 he toke hys leave of vs/ And sayed to his sonne thus/ goo yor wayes And attend vppon my lordes grace yor mayster/ And se that you do yor dewtie/ And so departyd and went his ways down thoroughe the hall in to his barge/ Than after long debatyng and consultacion vppon the lorde Percyes assuraunce/
10 yt was devysed that the same shold be enfrynged and dissolued/ And that the lord Percye shold mary w^t oon of the Erle of Shrewesburyes doughters/ As he dyd after/ By means whereof the former contracte was clearely ondon/ wherew^t m^{rs} Anne Bolloyn was greatly offendyd/ Sayeng that if it lay euer in hir
15 power she wold worke the Cardynall as myche displeasure (As she dyd in dede after) And yet was he nothyng to blame/ ffor he practised no thyng in that matter but it was the kynges oonly devyse/ And evyn as my lord Percye was commaundyd to avoyd hir Company/ Evyn so was she commaundyd to avoyde the
20 Court/ And she sent home agayn to hir ffather for a season/ where at she smoked for all this while she knewe no thyng of the kynges entendyd purpose/ **But ye**/ may se whan ffortune begynnythe to lower howe she can compasse a matter to worke displeasure by a farre fetche/ **ffor nowe** marke good reder the
25 grudge howe it began that in processe burst owt to the vtter ondoyng of the Cardynall/ **O lord** what a god art thou that workest thy secrettes so wondersly w^{che} be not [f. 21] perceyved vntill they be brought to passe and ffynysshed/ marke thys history folowyng/ good reder/ And note euery circumstaunce/
30 And thou shall espie at thyn eye the wonderfull workes of god agaynst suche persons as forgettithe god and his great benefites/ Marke I say/ marke them well/
After that all thes troblesome matters of my lord Percys was brougthe to a good staye/ And all thynges ffynesshed that was
35 byfore devysed/ Mrs Anne Bolloyn was revoked vnto the Court where she florisshed after in great estimacion And ffauour/

10 be *interl.*   16 he *interl. before* nothyng   17 it] t *written over* s; was *interl.*   20 father *canc. before* ffather   25 h *canc. before* it   29 esto *canc. before* history

Life of Cardinal Wolsey 35

havyng allwayes a privye Indygnacion vnto the Cardynall for
brekyng of the precontract made bytwen my lord Percye & hir
supposyng that it had byn his owen devyse & wyll and non
other/ not yet beyng privye to the kynges secrett mynd allthoughe that he hade a great affeccion vnto hir/ howbeit after 5
she knewe the kynges pleasure and the great love that he bare hir
in the bottome of his stomake/ Than began she to loke very
hault and stowt hauyng all maner of Ioyelles or riche apparell
that myght be gotten w^t mony/ yt was therfore Iuged by and by
thoroughe all the Court of euery man that she beyng in suche 10
fauour w^t the kyng myght worke maystres w^t the kyng And
opteyn any sewte of hyme for hir ffrend/ And all this while she
beyng in this estymacion in all places/ yt is no dought but good
Quen katheren hauyng this gentillwoman dayly attendyng vppon
hir/ bothe hard by report/ And perceyved byfore hir eyes the 15
matter howe it framed ayenst hir (good lady) allthoughe she
shewed (to m^{rs} Anne/ ne vnto the kyng) any sparke or kynd of
grudge or displeasure/ but toke and accepted all thynges in good
part And w^t wysdome and great pacience dissimuled the same/
hauyng Mrs Anne in more estymacion for the kynges sake than 20
she had byfore/ declaryng hir self therby to be a perfect
Grysheld/ as hir pacient actes shall hereafter more evidently to
all men be declared/ The kyng waxed so ferre in amours w^t this
gentilwoman/ that he knewe not howe myche he might avaunce
hir/ This perceyveng the great lordes of the Councell beryng a 25
secrett grudge ayenst the Cardynall because that they could not
rewle in the Comenwell (for hyme) as they wold/ who kept them
lowe and rewled theme as well as other meane subiectes/ where
at they caught an occasion [f. 21^v] to Invent a mean to bryng
hyme owt of the kynges highe fauour and them in to more 30
auctorytie of Rewle & Cyvell gouernance/ after long and secrett
consultacion among them selfes howe to bryng ther malice to
effect ayenst the Cardynall/ They knewe right well that it was
very deficyll for them to do any thyng directly of them selfes

3 hys *canc. before* his   9 wha *canc. before* was   10 thoug *canc. before* thoroughe; the *canc. before* that   12 while *interl.*   18 *a single indecipherable letter canc. before* or   25 hir/ This] *MS.* hir This; beryng] *MS.* berying   26 not *interl.*   27 Comenwell] *MS.* Coen well. *See n.*   31 Cyvell *canc. before* Cyvell   34 thyng *interl.*

Life of Cardinal Wolsey

wherfore they perceyvyng the great affeccion that the kyng bare lovyngly vnto Mrs Anne Bolleyn ffantazyng in ther heddes that she shold be for them a suffycyent & an Apte Instrument to bryng ther maliciouse purpose to passe/ w^t whome they often
5 consulted in this matter/ And she hauyng bothe a very good wytt and also an Inward desier to be revenged of the Cardynall/ was as aggreable to ther requestes as they ware them selfes/ wherfore ther was no more to do but oonly to Imagyn some pretenced circumstaunce to Induce ther malicious accusacion/
10 In so myche that there was Imagyned & Invented among them dyuers Imagynacions and subtill devysis howe this matter shold be brought aboughт/ the enterprice therof was so dayngerous that thoughe they wold fayn haue often attempted the matter w^t the kyng/ yet they durst not/ for they knewe the great lovyng
15 affeccion and thespecyall fauour that the kyng bare to the Cardynall/ And also they feared the wonder wytt of the Cardynall/ for thys they vnderstode very well/ that if ther matter that they shold propone ayenst hyme ware not grounded vppon a Iust and an vrgent cause the kynges fauor beyng suche
20 towardes hyme and his wytt suche that he wold w^t pollecye vanquyshe all ther purpose & travayll and than lye in a waytte to worke them an vtter distruccion and subuercion wherfore they ware compelled all thynges considered to forbere ther enterprice vntill they myght espie a more convenyent tyme & occasion/
25 And yet the Cardynall espieng the great zeale that the kyng had conceyved in this Gentill woman/ Ordered hym self to please as well the kyng as hyr/ Dissimulyng the matter that laye hyd in his brest/ And prepared great Bankettes And solempne feastes to entertayn them bothe/ at his owen howsse/ And thus the world
30 began to growe in to wonderfull Invencions not hard of byfore in this Realme/ the love bytwen the kyng & this gorgious lady grewe to suche a perfeccion that dyuers Imagynacions ware Imagyned/ wherof I leve to speke vntill I come to the place where I may haue more occasion/ [f. 22]

2 /hyme my lady *canc. after* vnto; M^rs *interl.*   9 circumstaunce] *MS.* circumstaɑunce   12 aboughт/ the] *MS.* aboughт the   13 of *canc. before* often   17 vn *canc. before* they   18 matt *canc. before* matter; pp shold *canc. after* they *with* shold *interl.*; hyme *interl.*   19 an *canc. before* and; and an *interl.*; cause the] *MS.* cause (the   24 p . . . *canc. before* occasion   32 grewe *interl.*

Than began/ a Certeyn Grodge to arise betwen the ffrenche kyng and the Duke of Burbon/ in so myche as the Duke beyng vassayll to the howsse of ffraunce was constrayned for the savegard of his person to ffle his domynion and to forsake his terretory & Contrie dowghtyng the kynges great malice and Indignacion/ The Cardynall havyng therof Intelligence/ Compased in his hed that if the kyng our souerayn lord (havyng an occasion of warres w^t the Realme of ffraunce) myght Retayn the Duke to be his generall in his warres there in as myche as the Duke was ffled vnto the Emprour to Invyte hyme also to stere warres ayenst the ffrenche kyng/ The Cardynall hauyng all this Imagynacion in his hed/ thought it good to move the kyng in this matter And after the kyng was oons aduertised herof/ And conceyved the Cardynalles Imagynacion & Invencion/ he dremed of this matter more & more vntill at the last it came in question among the Councell in consultacion So that it was there fynally concludyd that an Ambassett shold be sent to the Emprour abought this matter/ w^t whome it was concludyd that the kyng and the Emperour shold Ioyn in thes warres ayenst the ffrenche kyng And that the Duke of Burbon shold be our Souerayn lordes Champion & generall in the feld/ who had appoynted hyme a great nomber of good Souldiors ouer & besides the Emperours army w^{che} was not small/ and led by oon of his owen noble men/ and also that the kyng shold pay the Duke his wages & his retynewe monthly/ In so myche as sir Iohn Russell (w^{che} was after Erle of Beddford) lay contynually by yond the sees in a secrett place assigned bothe for to receyve the kynges mony and to paye the same monthly to the Duke/ So that the Duke began fierce warre w^t the ffrenche kyng in his owen terretory & Dukdome/ w^{che} the ffrenche kyng had confiscatt and seased in to his handes/ yet not knowen to the dukes ennemyes that he had any Ayed of the kyng our souerayn lord/ And thus he wrought the ffrenche kyng moche troble & displeasure/ In so myche as the ffrenche kyng was compelled of

3 a *canc. before* vassayll   11 ffrenhe/ *canc. before* ffrenche   13 aduerty *canc. before* aduertised *and* of the *before* herof   15 matter *canc. before* matter   24 pay *interl.*   25 s *canc. after* Duke; *first* his *interl.*; wages *canc. before* wages *and* monthely *before* monthly; monthly/ *interl.*   28 the *interl. before* Duke   30 owen *interl.*   31 confiskatt *canc. before* confiscatt

fyne force to put harnoys on his bake & to prepare a pieusaunt army Royall and in his own person to auaunce to defend and resist the Dukes power and malice/ the duke hauyng vnderstandyng [f. 22ᵛ] of the kynges avauncemeᵗ was compelled of
5 force to take Pavya a strong town in Itally wᵗ his host for ther securitie where as the kyng beseged hyme & encamped hyme wonderouse strongly entendyng to enclose the Duke wᵗ in thys towen that he shold not Issewe/ yet notwᵗstandyng the Duke wold & did many tymes Issewe and escramoche wᵗ the kynges
10 army/ **Nowe** lett vs leave the kyng in his Campe byfore Pavya And retourne to the lord Cardynall/ who Semed to be more ffrenche than Emperyall/ but howe it came to passe I cannot declare you/ but the kyng lyeng in hys Campe sent secretly in to Englond a pryvy person a very wytty to treatte of a peace
15 bytwen hyme and the kyng our souerayn lord whos name was Iohn Iokyn/ he was kept as secrett as myght be that no man had Intelligence of his repayer for he was no ffrenche man but an Itallion borne a man byfore of no estymacyon in ffraunce/ or knowen to be in fauour wᵗ hys mʳ, but to be a merchaunt, and for
20 his subtill wytt elected to entreat of suche affayers as the kyng had Commaundyd hyme by ambassett/ This Iokyn after his arryvall here in England was secrettly conveyed vnto the kynges manour of Richemond and there remayned vntill wytsontyd at wᶜʰᵉ tyme the Cardynall resortyd thether and kept there the seyd
25 feast very Solomply/ In wᶜʰᵉ season my lord Caused thys Ioken dyuers tymes to dyne wᵗ hyme/ whos talke & behauour semed to be wytty, sober & wonderouse discrett who contynued in Englond long after vntyll he had (as it semed) brought his purposed ambassett to passe wᶜʰᵉ he had in commyssion// ffor
30 after this there was sent owt Immedyatly a restraynt vnto sir Iohn Russell in to thos parties where he made his abydyng by yond the sees that he shold retayne and kepe bake that monythe wages still in hys handes wᶜʰᵉ shold haue byn payed vnto the Duke of Burbon (vntyll the kynges pleasure ware to hyme
35 further knowen) ffor want of wᶜʰᵉ mony at the day appoynted of

15 called *canc. before* was; was *interl.*   17 borne *canc. before* but
21 comaay *canc. before* Commaundyd   24 his *canc. after* there   25 of *canc. before* very   27 se *canc. after* be   30 Immedyatly] t *written over* l

Life of Cardinal Wolsey

payment/ The Duke & his retynewe ware greatly dismayd and sore disapoynted/ And whan they sawe that ther mony was not brought vnto them as it was wont to be/ And beyng in so dayngerous a case for want of victualles w^che was wonderouse skant & deare there was many Imagynacions what shold be the cause of the lett therof/ Some sayd this & some sayd they wyst neuer what/ So that they mystrusted no [f. 23] thyng lesse than the very Cause therof/ In so myche at the last what for want of victuall and other necessaryes w^che could not be gotten w^t in the town The Capteyns & Sowldiours began to grudge and Mutter And at the last for lake of victuall ware lyke all to perysshe/ they beyng in this extremytie came byfore the Duke of Burbon ther Capteyn/ And sayd/ Sir we must be of very force and necessitie compelled to yeld vs in to the daynger of our ennemyes and better it ware for vs so to do then here to sterve lyke dogges/ whan the Duke hard ther lamentacions and vnderstode the extremytie that they ware brought vnto for lake of mony (sayd agayn) vnto theme/ Sirs q^d he ye are bothe valyaunt men and of noble Corage who hathe seruyd here vnder me right worthely and for yor necessitie wherof I ame particypant I do not a littill lament/ howbeit I shall desier you as you are noble in hartes and Corage so to take pacience for a day or twayn/ And if Socoure come not than frome the kyng of Englond (as I dought no thyng) that he wyll dissayve vs/ I woll well agree that we shall all put our selfes and all our lyfes vnto the mercy of our ennemyes/ wher w^t they ware all agreable And expectyng the Commyng of the kynges mony the space of iij^re dayes (the w^che dayes past) the Duke seyng no remedye/ called his noble men & Capteyns And Sowldiours byfore hyme/ And all wepyng sayd/ O ye noble Capteyns and valyaunt men, my gentill Companyons/ I se no remedye in this necessitie but other we must yeld vs vnto our ennemyes or elles ffamysshe/ And to yeld the town and our selfes I knowe not the mercye of our ennemyes/ And as for my part I passe not of ther Cruelties/ ffor I knowe very well that I shall suffer most cruell deathe if I come oons in to ther handes/

5 wh *canc. before* shold   6 therof/ Some] *MS.* therof Some   7 thynke lesse *canc. before* thyng   16 r *of* vnderstode *interl.*   20 wherof] *MS.* (wherof   29 sayeng *canc. before* all; all *interl.*   32 ffamysshe/ And] *MS.* ffamysshe And; to *interl.*; yeld *canc. after* to   35 most *interl.*

yt is not for my selfe therfore that I do lame^t but it is for yor
sakes, yt is for yor lyfes/ yt is also for the saluegard of yor persons
ffor so that ye myght escape the daynger of yor ennemyes handes
I wold most gladly suffer deathe/ Therfore good Companyons
and noble Sowldyours I shall requyer yow all/ consideryng the
dayngerous mysery and Calamytie/ that we stand in at this
present to sell our lyves most derely rather then to be murdered
lyke beastes/ yf ye wyll folowe my Councel we woll take vppon
vs this nyght to geve our ennemyes an assault to ther Campe and
by [f. 23^v] that means we may other escape or elles geve them
an ouerthrowe/ And thus it ware better to dye in the feld lyke
men than to lyve in captivytie and mysery as prisoners/ To the
w^che they all agreed/ Then q^d the Duke/ ye perceyve that our
ennemyes hathe encamped vs w^t a strong Campe And that there
is no way to enter but oon w^che is so plantyd w^t great ordynaunce
And force of men that it is not possible to enter that wayes to
fight w^t our ennemyes w^tout great daynger/ And also ye se that
nowe of late they haue hade small dought of vs In so myche as
they haue kepte but slender watche/ therfore my pollecye &
devyse shall be this/ that abought the deade tyme of the nyght
whan our ennemyes be most quyot at rest/ shall Issue frome vs a
nomber of the most delyuerest sowldyours to assault ther
Campe who shall geve the assaulte right fercely evyn dyrectly
ayenst the entre of the Campe w^che is all most Invyncyble/ yor
ferce & sharpe assault shalbe to them in the Campe so doughtfull that they shalbe compelled to torne the strengthe of ther
entre that lyethe ouer ayenst yor assault to beate you frome the
assaulte than wyll I issue owt at the posterne and come to the
place of ther strenthe newlie torned And there or they beware
woll I entere and fight w^t them at the same place where ther
gonnes & strengthe lay byfore And so come to the rescue of you
of the sault/ And wynnyng ther ordynaunce w^che they haue
torned And beat them w^t ther owen peces/ And than we
Ioynyng together in the feld I trust we shall haue a fayer hand
of theme/ This devyse pleased them wonderouse well/ than

8 yf *interl.*   10 that *canc. before* that   12 prisoners/ To] *MS.*
prisoners To   22 sowldyours *interl.*   27 beate y *canc. before* beate
29 of ther strenthe *interl.*; b *canc. before* beware   30 place *interl.*
31 b *canc. before* byfore   34 to *canc. after* trust; we shall *interl.*

Life of Cardinal Wolsey 41

prepared they all that day for the purposed devyse And kept
them secrett & cloose w^tout Any noyse or shott of peces w^tin
the town w^{che} gave ther ennemyes the lesse feare of any troble
that nyght but euery man went to ther rest/ w^tin ther Tentes &
lodgynges quyotly no thyng mystrustyng that after ensued/ 5
Then whan all the kynges host was at rest/ the assaylauntes
issued owt of the town w^t owt any noyce accordyng to the
former appoyntme^t And gave a ferce & cruell assault at the
place appoynted/ that they w^t in the Campe had as myche a do to
defend as was possible to resist/ And evyn as the Duke had 10
byfore declared to his sowldyours [f. 24] they w^tin ware compelled to torne ther shott that lay at ther entre ayenst the
assayllauntes/ w^t that Issued the duke and w^t hyme abought
xv^{en} or xvj^{en} thousand men or more/ And secrettly in the nyght
his ennemyes beyng not privey of his Commyng vntill he was 15
entred the fyld and at his first entre he was m^r of all the
ordynaunce that lay there and slewe the gonners and charged
the seyd peces & bent them ayenst his ennemyes whome he
slewe wondersly a great number/ he Cut down Tentes and
Pavylions and murdred them w^t in them or they wyst of ther 20
Commyng/ Suspectyng/ no thyng lesse than The dukes entre/
So that he whan the feld or euer the kyng could aryse to the
rescue/ who was taken in hys lodgyng or euer he was armed/
And whan the Duke had opteyned the fyld & the ffrenche kyng
taken prisoner, his men slayn And his tentes Robbed & spoyled 25
w^{che} was wonderous Riche And in the spoyle sercheng of the
kynges treasour in his Coffers/ there was found among them
the leage newely concludyd bytwen the kyng of Englond & the
ffrenche kyng vnder the great seale of Englond/ w^{che} oons by
hyme perceyved he began to smell the Impedyme^t of his mony 30
w^{che} shold haue come to hyme frome the kyng/ havyng (vppon
dewe serche of this matter) further Intellygence that all this
matter & his vtter vndoyng was concludyd & devysed by the
Cardynall of Englond/ And the Duke conceyvyng suche an

3 lesse *interl.*   5–6 ensued/ Then] *MS.* ensued Then   6 host *canc.*
before kynges   7 owt *interl. after* w^t   13 assayllauntes/ w^t] *MS.*
assayll*au*ntes w_t   16 the *canc. before* all   17 er *canc. between the two* n's
of gonners   20 wyst *canc. after* they; ware *canc. before* wyst; wyst *interl.*
21 no thyng *canc. after* Suspectyng   25 spoyled *canc. before* spoyled

Indygnacion herevppon ayenst the Cardynall/ that after he hade establysshed all thynges there in good order & securitie/ he went Incontynent vnto Rome entendyng ther to sakke the town And to haue taken the Pope prisoner/ where at his first assault of the walles he was the first man that was there slayn (yet notw^tstandyng) his Capteyns contynued there the assault And in conclusion wane the town And the Pope fled vnto Castell Ayngell/ where he contynued long after in great Calamyte/ **I have** writtyn thus thys history at large bycause it was thought that the Cardynall gave the chefe occasion of all thys myschefe/ ye may perceyve what thyng so euer a man purposithe [f. 24^v] be he prynce or prelate yet notw^tstandyng god disposithe all thynges at his wyll & pleasure/ wherfore it is great foly for any wyse man to take any waytie enterprice of hyme self trustyng all together to his owen wyll not callyng for grace to assist hyme in all his procedynges/ I haue knowen & seen in my dayes that prynces And great men wold other assemble at any Parliament or in any other great busynes first wold most reuerently call to god for his gracious assistaunce therin And nowe I se the contrary/ wherfore me semys that they trust more in ther owen wisdomes & Imagynacions than they do to goddes helpe & disposicion And therfore often they spede therafter and ther matters take suche successe/ Therfore not oonly in this history but in dyuers others ye may perceyve right evydent examples And yet I se no man in auctorytie or highe estate Allmost regard or haue any respect to the same (the greatter is the pitie and the more to be lamented/ Nowe wyll I desist frome this matter/ and procede to other)

Vppon the takyng of the ffrenche kyng many Consultacions And dyuers oppynyons ware than in argument among the Councell here in England/ wherof Some hild oppynyon/ that if the kyng wold Invade the realme of ffraunce in propir person w^t a pieusaunt Army Royall he myght easely conquere the same consideryng that the ffrenche kyng and the most part of the noble pieers of ffraunce ware than prisoners w^t the Emproure/

2 there *interl.*   4 a *canc. before* assault   11 th *canc. before* so
12 kyng *canc. before* prelate   13 at *canc. before* at   15 vppon *canc. before* for   18 wold *interl.*   27 I *interl.*   35 Emproure] *MS.* Emprou*r*re

Some agayn sayed/ howe that ware no honour for the kyng our
souerayn lord (the kyng beyng in Captiuyte) But some sayed that
the ffrenche kyng owght by the lawe of Armez to be the kynges
prisoner/ for as myche as he was taken by the kynges Capteyn
Generall (the Duke of Burbon) and not by the Emprours so that
some moved the kyng to take warre thervppon w^t the Emprour/
onles he wold delyuer the ffrenche kyng owt of his handes and
possession/ w^t dyuers many other Imagynacions and Invencions
evyn as euery mans ffantazys seruyd theme to long here to be
rehersed the w^{che} I leave to the writers of Cronycles/ Thus
contynuyng [f. 25] long in debatyng vppon this matter/ And
euery man in the Court had there talke as wyll w^{t}out wyt led
ther fantazis/ At the last it was devysed by means of dyuers
ambassettes sent in to Englond owt of the Realme of ffraunce
desyryng the kyng our souerayn lord to take order w^t the
Emprour for the ffrenche kynges delyuere as his Royall wysdome
shold seme good/ wherin the Cardynall bare the stroke/ So that
After long delyberacion And Advyse taken in this matter it was
thought good by the Cardynall that the Emprour shold
redelyuer owt of his ward the ffrenche kyng vppon sufficyent
pledges/ And that the kynges too Sonnes (that is to say) the
Dolphyn and the Duke of Orlyaunce shold be delyuerd in hos-
tage for the kyng ther ffather w^{che} was in conclusion brought to
passe/ Than after the kynges delyuere owtt frome themprours
vse & the kynges our souerayn lordes securitie for the recompence of all suche demaundes and restitucions as shold be
demaundyd of the ffrenche kyng/ The Cardynall lamentyng the
ffrenche kynges Calamytie/ And the Popes great aduersitie
(w^{che} yet remayned in Castell ayngell) owther as a prisoner or
elles for his defence & savegard (I cannot tell whether) Travelled
all that he could w^t the kyng & his Councell to take order as well
for the delyuere of the oon, as for the quyotnes of thother/ At
last as ye haue hard here tofore/ howe dyuers of the great
estates/ & lordes of the Councell lay in a wayt w^t my lady Anne

1 howe *interl.*; the kyng *interl.*   3 the *interl. before* kynges
5 Ge *canc. before* Generall   6 thervppon *interl.*   10 Cronycles]
MS. Cronyclers   11 in *canc. after* contynuyng   18 taken *canc.*
before taken   25–26 the recompence of *interl.*   34 estes estates
canc. before estates

Bulloyn to espie a convenyent tyme & occasion to take the Cardynall in a brake/ thought it than that nowe is the tyme come that we haue expected supposyng it best to cause hyme to take vppon hyme the kynges Commyssion and to travell by yond the
5 sees in this matter/ Sayeng (to encorage hyme therto) that it ware more mete for his highe discression, wytt & auctorytie to compasse & bryng to passe a perfight peace among thes great & most myghty prynces of the world than any other w^t in this Realme or elles where/ Ther ententes & purpose was oonly but
10 to gett hyme owt of the kynges dayly presence/ And to convey hyme owt of the Realme that they myght haue convenyent laysor and opportunytie to Aduenture ther long desired enterprice/ And by the ayde of ther Cheafe m^{rs} (my lady Anne) to deprave hyme so vnto the kyng in his absence that he shold
15 be rather in his hyghe displeasure than in his accustumed fauour/ or at the lest to be in lesse estymacion w^t his ma^{tie}/ well what wyll you haue more/ [f. 25^v] Thys matter was so handeled that the Cardynall was commaundyd to prepare hymself to this Iourney the w^{che} he was fayn to take vppon hyme/ but wether
20 it was w^t his good wyll or no I ame not well able to tell you/ but this I knewe that he made a short abode after the determynat resolucyon therof but caused all thynges to be prepared onward toward his Iourney And euery oon of his seruauntes ware appoynted that shold attend vppon hyme in the same/
25 **Whan all thynges** was fully concludyd And for thys noble ambassett provyded and furnysshed than was no lett but auaunce forwardes in the name of good/ my lord Cardynall had w^t hyme suche of the lordes & bysshopes and other worthy persons as ware not privye of the Conspiracye/ Than marched
30 he forward owt of his owen howsse at westminster passyng thoroughe all london ouer london brydge/ hauyng byfore hyme of gentillmen a great nomber iij^{re} in a ranke in blake veluett lyuere Cottes and the most part of them w^t great chayns of gold
35 aboughte ther neckes/ And all his yomen w^t noble men & gentilmens seruauntes folowyng hyme in ffrenche tauny lyuere Coottes hauyng enbrodered vppon ther bakes & brestes of the

3 it *interl.*   9 or any other *canc. before* or   15 & *canc. before* than; than *and* accustumed *interl.*   17 whyll *canc. before* wyll

Life of Cardinal Wolsey

same Coottes thes letters/ T & C/ vnder the Cardynalles hatte/ his Sompter Mewlles w^che ware xx^tl in nomber & moore w^t his Cartes & other Cariages of his trayn ware passed on by fore/ conducted & garded w^t a great number of bowes & speres/ he Roode lyke a Cardynall very soumptiously on a mewle/ trapped w^t Crymmesyn veluett vppon veluett and his stirropes of Copper & gylt And his spare mewle folowyng hyme w^t lyke apparrell/ And byfore hyme he hade his ij great Crossys of siluer/ ij great pillers of Syluer/ the great seale of England/ his Cardynalles hatt/ And a gentilman that Caried his valaunce otherwyse called a clooke bage w^che was made all to gether of ffynne Scarlett clothe enbrodered ouer & ouer w^t clothe of gold very richely hauyng in hit a Clooke of fynne Scarlett/ thus passed he thoroughe london and all the way of his Iourney/ hauyng his harbergers passyng byfore to provyde lodgynges for his trayn/ The first Iourney he made to Dertford in kent vnto sir Richard wyltchers howsse w^che is too myles beyond Dertford where all his trayn ware lodged that nyght & in the Contrie there abought/ The next day he roode to Rochester and lodged in the bysshopes palice there and the rest of his trayn in the Cytie & in Strode on this side the bryge [f. 26] The iij^de day/ he Rode frome thence to ffeuersham/ And there was lodged in the Abbey and his trayn in the town and some in the Contrie/ there aboughtes/ The iiij^th day he Rode to Caunterbury where he was encountered w^t the worshipfullest of the town and Contrye and loged in the Abbey of Crystes churche in the Prours lodgyng/ And all his trayn in the Citie/ where he contynued iij^re or iiij^or dayes in w^che tyme ther was the great Iubely And a fayer in honour of the feast of Seynt Thomas ther patrone/ In w^che day of the seyd feast w^tin the abbey there was made a Solompne procession and my lord Cardynall presently in the same Appareled in his legantyn ornamentes w^t his Cardynalles hatt on hys hed/ who commaundyd the monkes and all ther quyer to syng the littany after thys sort Sancta maria ora pro papa nostro Clemente And so pervsed the litteny

2 ware *interl.* 4 bylles & *canc. before* bowes 13 cloke *canc. before* Clooke 14 harbergers *canc. before* harbergers 15 pro *canc. before* provyde 18 abought/ The] *MS.* abought The 20 stro *canc. before* Strode 23 aboughtes/ The] *MS.* aboughtes The 26 loging *canc. before* lodgyng 27 tyme *interl.* 31 same *canc. before* same

thoroughe/ my lord Cardynall knelyng at the quyer doore at a
forme couered w^t Carpettes and Cusshons The monkes & all
the quyer standyng all that while in the myddes of the bodye of
the chirche/ At w^{che} tyme I sawe the Cardynall wepe very
tenderly w^{che} was as we supposed for hevynes that the pope was
at that present in suche Calamytie & great daynger of the
launceknyghtes/ The next day I was sent w^t letters frome my
lord Cardynall vnto Calice by emposte In so myche as I was that
same nyght in Calice/ And at my landyng I found standyng
vppon the peere w^{t}out lanterne Gate all the Councell of the
towne to whome I delyuerd and dispeched my message &
letters or euer I entred the town/ where as I lay ij dayes after or
my lord came thether/ who arryved in the havyn there ij day
aftyr my commyng abought viijth of the Cloke in the mornyng/
where he was receyved in procession w^t all the worshipfullest
persons of the town in most Solomplest wyse And in the lantern
gate was sett for hyme a forme w^t Carpettes & Cusshons/ where
att he kneled & made hys prayers byfore his entre any further in
the town and there he was senced w^t ij great Sencers of Syluer
and sprynkylled w^t halewater/ That don he arrose vppe &
passed on w^t all that assemble byfore hyme syngeng vnto Seynt
Maris churche/ where he standyng at the highe Aulter tornyng
hyme self to the people gave them his benediccion & clean
remyssion/ And than they conducted hyme frome thence vnto
an [f. 26^v] howsse called the Chekker/ where he lay & kepte his
howse as long as he abode in the town (goyng Immedyatly to his
naked bed by cause he was somewat trobled w^t syknes in his
passage vppon the Sees that nyght) vnto this place of the
Chekker resorted to hyme Monsur de Bees Captayn of Bolloyn
w^t a number of gallaunt gentilmen, who dyned w^t hyme/ And
after some consultacion w^t the Cardynall/ he w^t the rest of the
gentilmen departid agayn to Bolloyn Thus the Cardynall was
dayly visited w^t oon or other of the ffrenche nobilitie/ Than whan
all his trayn & Cariages ware londed at Calice And euery thyng
prepared in a redynes for his Iourney/ he called byfore hyme all

13 came *canc. before* came 16 Solomplest] e *written over* y 20 Thi
canc. before That 21 hyng *canc. after* byfore; hyme *interl.*; the *canc.*
before Seynt 28 sees *canc. before* Sees; nyght)] *MS.* nyght/
32 w^t *canc. before* Thus 33 nobilitie/ Than] *MS.* nobilitie Than

Life of Cardinal Wolsey

his noble men and gentilmen in to his privye chamber/ where
they beyng assembled sayd vnto them in thys wyse in effect/
I haue (q^d he) called you hether to thys entent to declare vnto
you/ that I consideryng the dyligence that ye mynyster vnto me/
And the good wyll that I bere you agayn for the same entendyng
to remember yor dyligent seruyce here after in place where ye
shall receyve condygn thankes & rewardes/ And also I wold shewe
you ferther what Auctorytie I haue receyved directly frome the
kynges highnes/ And to enstruct you somwhat of the nature of
the ffrenche men/ And then to enforme you what reuerence ye
shall vse vnto me for the highe honour of the kynges ma^{tie}/ And
also howe ye shall entertayn the ffrenchemen whan so euer ye
shall mete at any tyme/ **ffyrste**/ ye shall vnderstand that the
kynges ma^{tie} vppon certyn waytie consideracions hathe for the
more avauncemet of his Royall dignytie assigned me in this
Iourney to be his lieutenaunt generall/ And what reuerence
belongythe to the same I wyll tell you/ That for my part I must
by vertue of my commyssion of leutenauntshipe Assume & take
vppon me in all honour and degrees to haue all suche seruyce &
reuerence as to his hyghnes presence is mete & dewe/ And
nothyng therof to be neclected or omytted by me that to his
Royall estat is appurtenaunt/ And for my part ye shall se me that
I will not omyt oon Iote/ therof/ Therfore bycause ye shall not
be Ignoraunt in that behalf/ ys oon of thespecyall causis of this
yor assemble wyllyng and commaund you as ye entend my
fauour/ not to forgett the same in tyme & place but euery of you
do obserue thys enformacion & Instruccion/ as ye woll at my
retorne avoyd the kynges Indignacion but to opteyn his highnes
thankes the w^{che} I wyll further for you as ye shall deserue
[f. 27] Nowe to the poynt of the frenche mens nature/ ye shall
vnderstand that ther disposicion is suche/ that they wylbe at the
first metyng as ffamylier w^t you as they had byn acquayntyd w^t
you long byfore and commyn w^t you in the frenche tong as
thoughe ye vnderstode euery word they spoke/ therfore in lyke
maner/ and be ye as famylier w^t them agayn as they be w^t you/
yf they speke to you in the ffrenche tong speke you to them in the

15 his *interl.*; hathe *canc. before* assigned 21 me *with* e *written over* y *canc. before* me 21-22 that to his *canc. before* Royall 23 I will not *interl.* 29 shall *interl.* 35 ye *interl.*

Englysshe tong for if you vnderstand not them/ they shall no
more vnderstand you/ And my lord spekyng merely to oon of the
gentilmen there (beyng a welsheman) sayd Rice/ q^d he/ speke
thou welshe to hyme/ And I ame well assured that thy welshe
5 shall be more defuse to hyme/ than his frenche shall be to the/
And than/ q^d he agayn to vs all/ lett all yor entertaynme^t &
behauor be accordyng to all gentilnes & humanytie/ that it may
be reportyd after yor departure frome thence/ that ye be
gentilmen of right good hauour And of myche gentilnes/ And
10 that ye be men that knowyth yor dewtie to yor souerayn lord
& to yor mayster/ Allowyng myche yor great Reuerence/ Thus
shall ye nott oonly optayn to yor selfes great commendacion &
prayce for the same/ but also auaunce the honour of yor prynce
& contrie/ Nowe goo yor wayes admonysshed of all thes poyntes/
15 And prepare yor selfes ayenst to morowe/ ffor than we entend
(god wyllyng) to sett forward/ And thus we beyng by hyme
Instructed & enformed departed to our lodgynges makyng all
thynges in a redynes ayenst the next day/ to avaunce forthe w^t
my lord/

20 **The next morowe** beyng Marie Magdalens day all thynges
beyng ffurnysshed my lord Cardynall Roode owt of Calice w^t
suche a nomber of blake veluett Coottes as hathe not byn seen
w^t an Ambassitor/ All the speres of Calice, Gynnes, and hamnes
ware there attendyng vppon hyme in this Iourney in blake
25 veluett Cootes many great & massy Chaynnes of gold ware
worne there/ thus passed he forthe w^t iij^{re} Gentilmen in a ranke
w^{che} occupied the lengthe of iij^{re} quarters of a myle or more/
hauyng all his accustumed and [f. 27^v] gloryous furnyture caried
byfore hyme evyn as I before haue rehersed excepte the brode
30 seale the w^{che} was left w^t doctor Tayllour in Calice than M^r of
the Rolles vntill his retorne/ passyng thus on his way And beyng
skant a myle of his Iourney it began to rayn so vehemently that
I haue not seen the lyke for the tyme/ that endured vntill we
came to Bulloyn/ And or we came to Sandyngfeld/ the Cardynall

---

5 be *canc. before* be to   5–6 the/ And] *MS.* the And   6 all/ lett]
MS. all lett   10 of *canc. before* that knowyth   16 forward/And] *MS.*
forward And; beyng *canc. before* beyng   24 the *canc. before* hyme
28 and] a *written over* g   30 m^r *canc. before* doctor   33 w^{che}
was *canc. before* vntill   34 Bulloyn *canc. before* Bulloyn

of lorrayn a goodly yong gentilman encountered my lord And receyved hyme w^t great reuerence & Ioy And so passed forthe together vntill they came to Sandyngfeld w^che is a place of Religion standyng bytwen the frenche Englyshe & themprors domynyons beyng newter holdyng of nether of theme/ And beyng come thether/ met w^t hyme there le Countie Brian Capteyn of Pykardy w^t a great nomber of men of Armez as Stradiates and Arbanoys w^t other standyng in array in a great pece of Oates all in harnoys vppon light horsis passyng w^t my lord as it ware in a wyng all his Iourney thoroughe Pykkardy/ ffor my lord Somewhat doughted the Emprour lest he wold lay an Ambusshe to betray hyme/ ffor w^che cause the frenche kyng commaundyd theme to awayte vppon my lord for the Assuraunce of hys person owt of the daynger of his ennemyes/ Thus Roode he accompanyd vntill he came to the town of Bolleyn/ where he was encountered w^tin a myle therof w^t the worshypfullest Citezyns of the Town hauyng among them a learned man that made to hyme an Oracion in latten/ vnto the w^che my lord made answere semblably in latten/ And that don Monsur de Bees Capteyn of Bolloyn w^t the Retynewe there of gentilmen mett hyme on horsebake w^che conveyed hyme in to the towen w^t all this assemble vntill he came to the Abbey gate where he lighted and went directly in to the Churche and made hys prayers byfore the Image of our lady to whome he made his offeryng/ And that don he gave there his blessyng to the people w^t certyn dayes of pardon/ than went he in to the abbey where he was lodged and hys trayn ware lodged in the highe & basse towns// [f. 28] **The next mornyng**/ after he hard masse he rode vnto Muterell sur la mere where he was encountered in lyke case as he was the day byfore w^t the worshypfullest of the town all in oon lyuere hauyng oon learned that made an oracion byfore hyme in laten whome he answered in lyke maner in laten And as he entred in to the town there was a Canapie of sylke enbrodred w^t the letters & hatte that was on ther seruauntes Cottes borne ouer hyme w^t the most persons of estymacion w^t

10 Ioy *canc. before* Iourney   14 person *canc. before* ennemyes   15 w^t *canc. before* vntill   22 town *canc. before* towen   24–25 made his offeryng *interl.*; offered *canc. after* offeryng   26 he in *canc. before* he   27 b. d *canc. after* trayn   35 persons *interl.*

Life of Cardinal Wolsey

in the town/ And whan he was alighted his footmen seased the same as a ffee dewe to ther office/ nowe was there made dyuers paiauntes for Ioy of hys Commyng/ who was called there and in all other places w^t in the Realme of ffraunce as he travelled/ (le
5 Cardynall pacyfike) And in laten (Cardynallis pacificus) who was accompaned all that nyght w^t dyuers worthy gentilmen of the Contrie there abought/ The next day he Roode towardes Abvyle/ where he was encountred w^t dyuers gentilmen of the Town & Contrie And so conveyed vnto the town where he was
10 most honorably receyved w^t paiauntes of dyuers kyndes wyttely & Costly Invented standyng in euery Corner of the strettes as he roode thoroughe the town/ hauyng a lyke Cannapie borne ouer hyme beyng of more richer sort than the other at Mutterell or at bolleyn was/ They brought hyme to hys
15 lodgyng w^che was as it semed a very fayer howsse newly bylt w^t brykke/ At w^che howsse kyng lowice maried my lady mary kyng herre the viij^th Sister w^che was after maried to the Duke of Suffolk Charles Brandon/ And beyng w^tin yt was in maner of a Gallery/ yet notw^tstandyng it was very necessary/ In thys
20 howsse my lord remayned other viij^th or x^en dayes/ to whome resorted daly dyuers of the Councell of ffraunce/ feastyng theme & other noble men & gentilmen that accompaned the Councell bothe at Dyners and Soppers/ Than whan the tyme came that he shuld depart frome thence he roode to a Castell beyond the
25 water of Somme called Pynkney castell adioynyng vnto the seyd watter standyng vppon a great rokke or hyll w^tin the w^che was a goodly Collage of prestes [f. 28^v] the Cituacion wherof was most lyke vnto the Castell of wyndesore in Englond And there he was receyved w^t a Solompne procession conveyng hyme fyrst in to
30 the Chirche/ And after vnto his logyng w^tin the Castell/

At thys castell kyng Edward the iiij^th met w^t the ffrenche kyng vppon the bryge that goyth ouer the water of Somme/ as ye may red in the Cronycles of Englond/ whan my lord was settilled w^tin his logyng/ it was reported vnto me that the ffrenche kyng
35 shold come that day in to Amyens w^che was w^tin vj^th Englysshe

4 he *canc. before* (le In] *MS.* necessary In   19 very *canc. before* very; very *interl.*; necessary/   25 le chatu *canc. before* Pynkney   33 Cro *canc. before* Cronycles; Englond/ whan] *MS.* Englond whan; lord was *interl.*   35 come *interl.*

Life of Cardinal Wolsey 51

myles of Pynkkney Castell/ And beyng desirous to se his first commyng in to the town Axed licence And toke w^t me oon or too gentilmen of my lordes And rood in contynent thether/ As well to provyde me of a necessary lodgyng as to se the kyng/ And whan we came thether beyng but strayngers toke vppe our Inne (for the tyme) at the signe of the Ayngell dyrectly ayenst the west doore of the Cathederall Churche de notre dame saynt Marye/ And after we had dyned there and tarieng vntill iij^{re} or iiij^{or} of cloke expectyng the kynges Commyng/ In came Madame Regent (the kynges mother) Ridyng in a very riche Charyott and in the same w^t hir was hir doughter the Quene of Naver furnysshed w^t an Cth ladys or gentilwomen or more folowyng/ ridyng vppon whight Palfrayes ouer & besides dyuers other ladys & gentillwomen that roode some in riche chariottes and Some in horsse litters/ who lighted at the west doore w^t all this trayn accompaned w^t many other noble men & gentilmen besides hir gard w^{che} was not small in nomber/ than w^t in ij howers after the kyng came in to the town w^t a great shott of Gonnys/ And dyuers paiauntes made for the nons at the kynges (byen venewe) hauyng abought his person bothe byfore hyme and byhynd hyme/ beside the wonderfull nomber of nobyll men & gentilmen iij^{re} great Gardes dyuersly apparelled/ the first was of Souches and Burgonyons/ w^t Gonnes & halfe hakkes/ The second was of ffrenche men some w^t bowes and Arrowes/ and some w^t bylles/ The iij^{de} Gard was pur le corps w^{che} was of tall Scottes myche moore comlier persons than all the rest/ The ffrenche gard & the Scottes had all oon lyuere w^{che} ware riche Coottes of fynne wyght clothe w^t a gard of Syluer bullyons enbrodred an handfull brode/ [f. 29] The kyng Came Ridyng vppon a goodly Genett/ And lighted at the west doore of the sayd Chirche and so conveyed in to the Chirche vppe to the highe Aulter where he made his prayers vppon his knees And than conveyed in to the bysshoppes palleyes where he was lodged and also his mother/ The next mornyng I roode agayn to Pynkney to attend vppon my lord at w^{che} tyme my lord was redy to take hys mule towardes Amyens/ And passyng on his

9 Royall *canc. after* came   12 *first* or] *written over* &   21 men *interl.*
23 hakkes/ The] *MS.* hakkes The   28 syluer *canc. before* a   34 Pyk *canc. after* to

Iourney thetherward he was encontered frome place to place w^t dyuers noble & worthy personages makyng to hyme dyuers oracions in latten/ to whome he made answere agayn ex tempore/ At whos excellent learnyng & pregnant witt they wondred very
5 myche///
Than was word brought my lord that the kyng was commyng to encounter hyme/ w^t that he hauyng none other shifte was compelled to allyght in an old Chappell (that stode by the highe way) and there newly apparelled hyme in to more
10 Richer apparell/ And than mounted vppon a newe Mewle very richely trapped w^t a foote clothe & trapper of Crymmesyn veluett vppon veluett pirld w^t gold and ffrynged abought w^t a depe frynge of gold very costly his stirropes of siluer and gylt the bosses & chekes of his brydell of the same/ And be that tyme
15 that he was mounted agayn after this most gorgious sort/ the kyng was come very nere/ w^t in lesse than a quarter of a myle englysshe/ mustryng vppon an hill side his gard standyng in a ray along the same/ expectyng my lordes Commyng/ To whome my lord made as myche hast as convenyently it became hyme
20 vntill he came w^t in a payer of butt lengthes/ And there he stayed a whyle/ the kyng perceyvyng that stoode still & hauyng ij worthy gentilmen yong & lusty beyng bothe brethern and brethern to the Duke of lorrayn & to the Cardynall of lorrayn/ wherof oon of theme was called monsur de Gwees and thother
25 monsur Vademount/ they ware bothe apparelled lyke the kyng in [f. 29^v] Purpull veluett lyned w^t clothe of Syluer and ther Cottes cutt/ the kyng caused mounsur vademount to issue frome hyme And to ride vnto my lord to knowe the cause of his tractyng who roode vppon a fayer Courser takyng his race in a
30 full gallope evyn vntill he came vnto my lord And there cawsed his horsse to come a loft oons or twyse so nye my lordes mewle that he was in dowght of his horsse/ And w^t that he lighted frome his Courser And doyng his message to my lord w^t humble reuerence/ w^che don he mounted agayn And caused his
35 horsse to do the same at his departyng As he did byfore And so repayred agayn to the kyng/ And after his answere made/ the

11 *two indecipherable letters canc. before* trapped; Crymmesyn *MS.* Crynmesyn
15 sort *canc. before* sort   16 w^t *interl.*   21 t *canc. after* that
27 ca *canc. before* caused   36 endyd *canc. before* made; made *interl.*

Life of Cardinal Wolsey

kyng auaunced forward/ that seyng my lord did the lyke/ And in the mydway they mett enbracyng eche other on horsbake w^t most amyable countenaunce entertaynyng eche other right nobly/ then drewe in to the place all noble men & gentilmen on bothe sides w^t wonderfull chere made oon to an other as they had byn of an old acquayntaunce/ the prece was suche and thyke that dyuers had ther legges hurt w^t horsysse/ Than the kynges officers cried/ marche/ marche devaunt/ Ale devaunt/ And the kyng & my lord Cardynall (on his right hand) Roode together to Amyens euery Englysshe gentilman accompanyd w^t an other of ffraunce/ The trayn of ffrenche & Englysshe endured ij long myles/ that is to sey/ frome the place of ther encounter vnto Amyens/ where they ware very nobly receyved w^t shott of Gonnes and Costly paiauntes vntill the kyng had brought my lord to his logyng and there departed a sonder for that nyght/ the kyng beyng lodged in the bysshoppes palice/ The next day after dynner my lord w^t a great trayn of noble men & gentillmen of Englond rode vnto the kynges Court at w^{che} tyme the kyng kept his bed beyng somwhat disseased/ yet notw^{t}standyng my lord came in to his bed Chamber/ where satt on theon side of his bed his mother madam Regent/ And on thother sid the Cardynall of lorrayn w^t dyuers other noblemen of ffraunce/ And after a short commynycacion and drynkyng of a Cuppe of wyn w^t the kynges mother/ my lord departed agayn to hys lodgyng accompanyd w^t dyuers gentilmen & noble men of ffraunce who supped w^t hyme/ Thus contynued the kyng & my lord in Amyens the space of ij wekes & more consultyng & feastyng eche other dyuers tymes [f. 30] And in the feast of the Assumpcion of our ladye my lord Roose betymes & went to the Cathederall chirche/ de noster dame/ and there byfore my lady regent and the quen of Naver in our lady chappell he sayd his seruyce & masse and after masse he hymself mynystred the Sacreme^t vnto bothe my lady Regent & to the quene of Naver/ And that don the kyng resortyd vnto the chirche and was

3 entennyng *canc. before* entertaynyng; entertaynyng *interl.*   6 acquayntaunce] *MS.* acquaytaunce   7 horsysse/ Than] *MS.* horsysse Than
9 hade *canc. before* hand   13 Amyens] s *written over* ce   18 rode *interl.*
19 somwhat disseased *interl.*; syke *canc. before* / yet   23 ffraunce] *MS.* ffraaunce   28 dyuers] *MS.* dyuer   32 hymself *interl.*

54   *Life of Cardinal Wolsey*

conveyed in to a riche Travers At the highe Aulters end and
dyrectly ayenst hyme on the other side of the Aulter sat my lord
Cardynall in an other Riche trauers iij^{re} gresis hyer than the
kynges And At the aulter byfore theme bothe a bysshope sang
5 hye masse And at the ffraccion of the host the same bysshope
devyded the Sacrame^t bytwen the kyng and the Cardynall for
the performance of the peace concludyd bytwen theme/ w^{che}
masse was song solompnly by the kynges Chappell hauyng
among theme Cornettes and Sakbuttes And after masse was
10 don the Troppeters blewe in the Roodeloft vntill the kyng was
past inward to his lodgyng owt of the chirche And at his
commyng in to the bysshoppes palice where he entendyd to dyne
w^t my lord Cardynall/ there satt w^t in a Closter aboughte ij^c
parsons deseased w^t the kynges evyll (vppon ther knees) And
15 the kyng or euer he went to dynner pervsed euery of theme w^t
robbyng and blessyng them w^t his bare handes beyng barehedyd
all the while/ after whome folowed his Almosyner distributyng of
mony vnto the persons disseased/ & that done he sayd certyn
prayers ouer theme and than whasht his handes & so came vppe
20 into his Chamber to dynner/ where as my lord dyned w^t hyme///
Than yt was determyned that the kyng and my lord shold
remove owt of Amyens/ And so they did to a towne or Citie
called Compygne w^{che} was more than xx^{ti} Englisshe myles
frome thence/ vnto w^{che} towen I was sent to prepare my lordes
25 lodgyng/ And so as I rode on my Iourney beyng vppon a ffriday
my horse chaunced to cast a shoo in a littill village where stode
a fayer Castell/ and as it chaunced ther dwelte a smythe to
whome I commaundyd my seruaunt to carry my horsse to shoo
and standyng by hyme while my horsse was a shoyng there
30 came to me [f. 30^v] oon of the seruauntes of the Castell perceyvyng me to be the Cardynalles seruaunt and an Englysheman/
who requyred me to goo w^t hyme in to the Castell to my lord
his m^r/ whome he thought wold be very glad of my commyng

2 ayenst *interl.*; byfore *canc. before* hyme   3 Cardynall] *final* l *frayed away at edge of page*   8 Chapley *canc. before* Chappell; have *canc. after* Chappell; hauyng *interl.*   11 h *canc. before* lodgyng   13 second w^t *interl.*   14 desea *canc. before* deseased   16 ha *canc. before* bare   18 disseased *interl.*; disseased *canc. after* disseased   25 lodgeng *canc. before* lodgyng   27 where in dwellt *with* in *interl. canc. before* and

& company/ to whose request I grauntyd by cause that I was allwayes desirous to se and be acquaynted w^t strayngers inespecyall w^t men in honour and Auctorytie/ So I went w^t hyme/ who conducted me vnto the Castell And beyng entred in the first ward/ the watchemen of that ward beyng very honest tall men came & saluted me most reuerently/ And knowyng the cause of my commyng/ desired me to stay a littill while vntill they had aduertised my lord ther m^r/ of my beyng there/ And so I dyd/ And incontynent the lord of the Castell came owt to me/ who was called monsur Creekey a noble man borne and very nyghe of bloode to kyng lowice the last kyng that raygned byfore this kyng ffraunces/ And at his first commyng he enbraced me/ Sayeng that I was right hartely welcome/ And thanked me that I so gently wold visit hyme & his Castell/ sayeng furthermore that he was preparyng to encounter the kyng & my lord to desier them most humbly the next day to take his castell in the way/ if he could so entret theme And trewe it is that he was redy to ride in a Coote of veluett w^t a payer of veluett Armyng shoos on his ffeete and a payer of gilt sporres on his heles/ Than he toke me by the hand and most gentlye led me in to his Castell thoroughe an other ward/ And beyng oons entred in to the base Court of the Castell I sawe all his ffamely and howshold seruauntes standyng in goodly order in blake Cootes and Gownnes lyke morners who led me in to the hall w^{che} was hanged w^t handgonnes as thyke as oon cowld hang by an other vppon the walles/ And in the hall stode also an haukes perke wheron stode iij^{re} or iiij^{or} fayer goshalkes/ than went we in to the parlour w^{che} was hanged w^t fynne old Arras/ And beyng there but a while commonyng together of my lorde of Suffolk howe he was there to haue beseged the same/ his seruauntes brought to hyme brede & wynne of dyuers sortes/ wherof he caused me to drynke/ And after/ q^d he/ I will shewe you the strengthe of my howsse howe herd it wold haue byn for my lord of Suffolk to haue wonne it/ than led he me vppon [f. 31] the walles w^{che} was very strong more than xv^{en} foote thyke/ And as well garnysshed w^t batere peces

1 company/ to] *MS.* company to 3 Auctorytie/ So] *MS.* Auctorytie So 11 *of canc. before* nyghe; of *interl.*; the *canc. after* of 17 he *canc. after* is; was *canc. before* that 31 sortes *canc. before* sortes; he *canc. after* after 35 as *interl.*

of ordynaunce redy charged to shoot of/ ayenst the kyng and my lordes Commyng/ whan he had shewed me all the walles & bulwarkes Abought the Castell/ he dissendyd frome the walles and came down in to a fayer Inner Court where his Genyt
5 stoode for to mount vppon w^t xijth other Genettes the most fayrest bestes that euer I sawe/ And in especyall his owen w^{che} was a mare genett/ he shewed me that he myght haue had for hir iiij^C Crownnes/ but vppon the other xijth genettes ware mounted xij goodly yong gentilmen called pages of honor all bare hedyd
10 in Coottes of Clothe of gold & blake veluett clokked and on ther legges bootes of red Spaynysshe lether And spurres parcell gylt/ Then he toke his leave of me commaundyng his Steward & other his gentilmen to attend vppon me/ And conducte me vnto my lady his wyfe to dynner/ And that don he mounted
15 vppon his genett/ And toke his Iourney forthe owt of his castell And than the Steward w^t the rest of the gentilmen led me vppe in to a tower in the gathowsse where than my lady ther mastresse lay for the tyme that the kyng & my lord shold tary there/ I beyng in A fayer great dynyng chamber where the table
20 was Couered to dynner/ And there I attendyng my lades Commyng/ And after she came thether owt of hir owen chamber she receyved me most gently lyke an noble estate hauyng a trayn of xij gentilwomen/ And whan she w^t hir trayn came all owt/ she sayd to me/ ffor as myche/ q^d she/ as ye be an Englysshe
25 man whos Custume^t is in yor Contrie to kys all ladyes and gentilwomen w^{t}out offence/ And althoughe it be not so here in this Realme/ yet woll I be so bold to kys you & so shall all my maydens/ by means wherof I kyst my lady & all hir women/ then went she to hir dynner beyng as nobly serued/ as I haue seen
30 any of hir estat here in Englond/ hauyng all the dynner tyme w^t me pleasaunt commynycacion w^{che} was of the vsage & behauour of our gentilwomen & gentilmen of Englond/ And comendyd myche the behauour of them right [f. 31^v] excellently/ ffor she was w^t the kyng at Arde when the great
35 encounter & meatyng was betwen the ffrenche kyng & the kyng

6 bestes *canc. before* bestes 17 to *canc. before* to 21 owt *canc. before* thether 23 came *interl.* 25 Cu *canc. before* Custume^t
27 real *canc. before* Realme; do *canc. before* all 28 wherof *interl.* 31 ple *canc. before* pleasaunt 32 of *canc. before* & 34 A *canc. before* Arde

our souerayn lord at w^che tyme she was bothe for hir person &
goodly hauour appoynted to company w^t the ladys of Englond/
And to be short after dynner/ pausyng a littill I toke my leave
of hir & so departed & roode on my Iourney//

I passyd so forthe/ on my Iourney/ by reason of my tractyng of
tyme in Chastell de Crykkey that I was constrayned that nyght
to lye in a town by the way called Montdedyer/ the Suburbes
wherof my lord of Suffolk hade lately burnd/ And in the next
mornyng I toke my Iourney and came to Compign vppon the
Saturday than beyng there the markett day/ And at my first
Commyng I toke my Inne in the myddes of the market place
and beyng there sett at dynner in a fayer Chamber that had a
fayer wyndowe lokyng in to the streett I hard a great Rumour
and clatteryng of bylles/ w^t that I loked owt in to the strett/ And
there I espied where the officers of the town brought a prysoner
to execucion/ whos hed they strak of w^t a sword/ And whan I
demaunded the cause of his offence/ yt was answered me/ that
it was for kyllyng of a rede dere in the fforrest thereby the
punyshement wherof is but deathe/ Incontynent they had sett
vppe the poore mans hed vppon a pole in the markett place
bytwen the stagges hornes/ and his quarters in iiij^or partes of the
fforrest/ Than went I abought to prepare my lordes lodgyng &
to se it furnysshed w^che was there in the great Castell of the
town/ wherof to my lord was assigned theon halfe and thether
half was reserued for the kyng/ and in lyke wyse there was a long
Gallery devyded bytwen theme/ wherin was made in the
myddes therof a strong wall w^t a doore & wyndowe/ And there
the kyng & my lord wold many tymes mete at the same wyndowe
and secretly talke togethers & dyuers tymes they wold goo
theon to the tother at the seyd doore/ Nowe was there lodged
also madame Regent the kynges mother and all hir trayn of
ladys & gentillwomen/ vnto w^che place the Chauncelor of
ffraunce came (a very witty man) w^t all the kynges grave

6 my *canc. before* tyme; that *interl. before* I   7 to lye *interl.*   9 mornyng
interl.   10 than *interl.*; the *interl.*; than *canc. before* markett   11 n *canc.*
after my   13 Ret . . . or *canc. after* great   17 demaunded]
MS. demaund; ar *canc. before* answered   21 hed *canc. after* stagges
27 therof *canc. before* therof   28 secretly *canc. before* mete   29 take
canc. before secretly; wold *interl.*   30 *a single indecipherable letter canc.*
before the tother   31 also *canc. before* also

councellers/ who toke great paynnes dayly in Consultacion/ In so myche as I hard my lord Cardynall fall owt w^t the Chauncelor layeng vnto his charge that he went abought [f. 32] to hynder the leage w^{che} my sayd lord Cardynall hade byfore his commyng
5 concludyd bytwen the king our souerayn lord & the ffrenche kyng his m^r In so myche that my lord stomaked the matter very stoutly/ And told hyme that it shold not lie in his power to dissolue the amyable ffidelitie bytwen them/ And if his mayster the kyng beyng there present forsake his promyse & followe his
10 Councell he shold not fayle/ after his retourne in to Englond/ to feale the smarte/ and what a thyng it is to breake promys w^t the kyng of Englond/ wherof he shold be well assured/ and ther w^t all he arose & went in to his owen lodgyng wondersly offendyd/ So that his stowte Countenaunce and bold wordes made them all
15 in dowght howe to pacyefie hys despleasure & revoke hyme agayn to the Councell who was then departyd in a furye/ there was sendyng/ there was commyng/ there was also entreatyng/ And there was great submyssion made to hyme to reduce hyme to his former frendly commynycacion/ who wold in no wyse
20 relent/ vntill madame Regent came hir self/ who handelled the matter so discretly & wittely that she reconsild hyme to his former commynycacion/ And by that means he brought ther matters to passe that byfore he cowld not atteyne nor cause the Councell to graunt/ w^{che} was more for feare than for any
25 affeccion to the matter/ he hade the hedes of all the Councell so vnder his gyrdell that he myght ruell them all there as well as he myght the Councell of Englond/ the next mornyng after this conflycte he roose earely in the mornyng abought iiij^{or} of the Clocke/ syttyng down to wright letters in to England vnto the
30 kyng commaundyng oon of his Chapleyns to prepare hyme to masse/ in so myche that his seyd chapleyn stode reuested vntill iiij^{or} of the Clocke at after none/ All w^{che} season my lorde neuer roose oons to pis/ ne yet to eate any meate but contynually wrott his letters w^t his owen handes/ hauyng all that tyme his nyght

4 hade byfore] *MS.* hade/ byfore   10–11 to *interl. before* feale   11 and *interl.*   17 was commyng] *MS.* was/ commyng; was also *interl.*   18 *first* hyme *interl.*   19 hys *canc. before* his   23 vi *canc. before* nor   31 er *canc. between the* u *and* e *of* reuested   33 contynually] *MS.* contynally

Life of Cardinal Wolsey 59

Cappe & keuerchefe on his hed/ And abought iiij^{or} of the Clocke at after none he made an end of writtyng Commaundyng oon Cristofer Gonner the kynges seruaunt to prepare hyme w^tout delay to ride empost in to Englond w^t his letters/ whome he dispeched a way or euer he [f. 32^v] dranke/ And that don he went 5
to masse/ and sayd his other dyvyn seruyce w^t his Chappelleyn as he was accustumed to do/ and than went strayt in to a garden/ and after he had walked the space of an hower or more And there sayed his evyn song/ he went to dynner & Sopper all at oons/ And makyng a small repast/ he went to his bed to take his 10
rest for that nyght/ The next nyght folowyng he caused a great Supper to be provyded for madame Regent and the quen of Naverne and other great estates of ladyes & noble women/ there was also madam Reigne/ oon of the doughters of kyng lewyce whos Syster kyng ffraunces had maried (latly deade) thes sisters 15
ware by ther mother enheritrices of the duchye of Bryttayn/ And for as myche as the kyng had maried oon of the Systers by whome he had the moytie of the sayd Duchie And to attayn thother moytie/ And to be lord of the hole/ he kepte the sayd lady Reygnye w^tout mariage entendyng that she hauyng non 20
Issue that the hole duchye myght dissend to hyme or to his succession after hir deathe for want of yssue of hir body/ But nowe lett vs retorne agayn to the Supper or rather a Solompne bankett/ where all thes nobyll persons ware hyghly feasted/ And in the myddes of ther tryhumphe the ffrenche kyng w^t the kyng 25
of Naverne came sodenly in vppon them onknowen/ who toke ther places at the nether end of the table/ there was not oonly plenty of ffynne meates/ but also myche myrthe and Solace/ as well in commynycacion as in instrumentes of musyke setforthe w^t my lordes mynstrelles/ who played there so Connyngly & 30
dulce all that nyght that the kyng toke therin great pleasure/ In so myche that he desired my lord to lend theme vnto hyme the next nyght/ And after Supper & bankett ffynysshed the ladys & gentilwomen went to dauncyng/ Among whome oon madame ffountayn a mayd had the price/ And thus passed they the nyght 35

7 to d *canc. before* in   12 be *interl.*   13 noble *canc. before*
ladyes; women/ there] *MS.* women there   15 kyng *canc. before* whos
19 so *canc. before* to   21 that *interl.*   24 feasted] *MS.* feaster
28 plenty *interl.*

in plesaunt myrthe & Ioye/ the next day the kyng toke my lordes mynstrelles and Roode vnto a noble mans howsse where was some goodly Image that he had avowed a Pilgrymage vnto/ to performe his devocion whan he came there he daunced &
5 other w^t hyme the most part of that nyght my lordes mynstrelles played there so excellently all that nyght that the Shalme (whether it ware w^t extreme labor of blowyng or w^t poysonyng (as some Iuged) by cause they ware more commendyd & accepted w^t the kyng than his owen) I cannot tell but he that
10 played the Shalme (an excellent man in that art) died w^t in a day or twayn after [f. 33]

Then the kyng Retorned agayn vnto Compigne/ And caused a wyld boore to be lodgyd for hyme in the fforrest/ there whether my lord Roode w^t the kyng to the huntyng of the wyld Swyne
15 w^{t}in a Toyle where the lady Regent stode in Charyottes or waggans lokyng ouer the toylle on the owtsyde therof accompanyd w^t many ladyes & dameselles/ among whome my lord stode by the lady Regent to regard & behold the pastyme/ & maner of huntyng/ there was w^{t}in the toyle dyuers goodly
20 gentillmen w^t the kyng redy garnysshed to this hyghe enterprice and dayngerous huntyng of the perellous wylld Swyne/ the kyng beyng in his dublett & hosyn oonly w^{t}out any other garme^{tes} all of shepes Colour clothe his hosyn frome the kne vppward was alltogether thrommed w^t sylke very thyke of the
25 same Colour havyng in a slipe a fayer brace of grette wyhight greyhoundes Armed as the maner is to arme ther greyhoundes frome the violence of the boores tuskes/ And all the rest of the kynges gentilmen beyng appoynted to hunt this boore ware lykewyse in ther dublettes & hosyn holdyng eche of them in ther
30 handes a very sharpe boores spere/ the kyng beyng thus furnesshed commaunded the huntes to oncouche the boore/ And that euery other person shold goo to a standyng/ among whome ware dyuers gentilmen & yomen of Englond/ And incontynent the boore issued owt of his denne/ chaced w^t an hound in to the
35 playn/ And beyng there/ stalled a while gasyng vppon the

3 some *interl.*; some *canc. after* avowed; a *interl.* devocion; vowed *canc. before* whan nyght that   7 poysonyng *canc. after* or 33 Englond/ And] *MS.* Englond And   4 he *canc. after* 6 he *interl. and canc. after* 27 k *canc. after* rest of

Life of Cardinal Wolsey

people/ And incontynent/ beyng forced by the hound he espied
a littill busse standyng vppon a banke ouer a diche vnder the
w^{che} lay ij gentilmen of ffraunce/ And thether fleed the boore to
defend hyme thrustyng his hede snoffyng in to the same bushe
where thes ij gentilmen lay/ who fled w^t suche spede as men do
frome the daynger of deathe/ Than was the boore by violence &
pursewt of the hound & huntes dryvyn frome thence And ran
strayt to oon of my lordes footmen a very comly person & an
hardy who hild in his hand an Englysshe Iavelen w^t the w^{che} he
was fayn to defend hymeself frome the fierce assault of the
boore/ who foyned at hyme contynually w^t his great tuskes/
wherby he was compelled at the last to pytche his Iavelen/ [f. 33^v]
in the Grownd bytwen hyme & the boore/ the w^{che} the boore
breke w^t his force of foynyng/ And w^t that the yoman drewe his
sword And stode at defence/ And w^t that the huntes came to the
rescue/ And put hyme oons agayn to flight/ w^t that he fled & ran
to an other yong gentylman of England Called m^r Ratclyfe
Sonne & heyer to the lord ffitzwalter and after Erle of Sussex/
who by chaunce had borowed of a ffrenche gentilman a fynne
boore spere very sharpe/ vppon whome (the boore beyng sore
chaffed) began to assault very egerly/ And the yong gentilman
delyuerly Avoyded his strokkes and in tornyng abought/ he
stroke the boore w^t suche violence w^t the same speere (that he
had borowed) vppon the howghes/ that he cutt the Senowes of
bothe his legges at oon stroke that the boore was constrayned to
sitt down vppon his haunches and defend hyme self for he
cowld goo no more/ thys gentilman perceyvyng than his most
aduauntage/ thrust his speere in to the boore vnder the sholder
vppe to the hart/ And thus he slewe the great boore/
wherfore among the noble men of ffraunce it was reputed to be
oon of the noblest enterprices that a man myght do/ (As
thoughe he had slayn a man of Armez)/ And thus our m^r
Ratclyfe bare than a way the price of that feacte of huntyng this
dayngerous & Royall pastyme in kyllyng of the wyld boore/
whoos tuskes the ffrenche men dothe most comenly dowght

2 littill *interl.* 6 deathe/ Than] *MS.* deathe Than 8 co *canc. before* comly 11 .rul *canc. before* great 13 bo *canc. after* & the 24 be *canc. after* cutt 30 it was reputed *interl.* 33 t *canc. before* than 34 h *canc. before* pastyme

above all other dayngers as it semed to vs englyshe men than beyng present/

In thys tyme of my lordes beyng in ffraunce ouer & besides his noble entertaynment w^t the kyng & nobles/ he susteyned
5 dyuers displeasures of the ffrenche slaves/ that devised a certyn boke w^{che} was setforthe in dyuers articles vppon the causis of my lordes beyng there/ w^{che} shold be as they surmysed/ that my lord was come thether to conclude too mariages/ theon bytwen the kyng our souerayn lord And madame Reygne of whome I
10 spake hertofore/ And an other bytwen the pryncs than of England (Nowe beyng quene of this reallme my lady marye/ the kynges doughter/) And the frenche kynges second Sonne the duke of Orlyaunce who ys at this present kyng [f. 34] of ffraunce/ w^t dyuers other conclusions and agrementes touchyng the same/
15 of thes bokes many ware Imprynted & conveyed in to Englond vnknowen to my lord beyng than in fraunce/ to the great slaunder of the Realme of Englond & of my lord Cardynall/ but whether they ware devysed of pollecy to pacefie the mutteryng of the people w^{che} had dyuers Commynycacions and
20 Imagynacions of my lordes beyng there/ or whether it ware devysed of some malicious person as the disposicion of the Comen people are accustumed to do vppon suche secrett consultacions I knowe not/ but what so euer the occasion or cause was the Auctor hathe settforthe suche bokes/ this I ame well
25 assured that after my lord was therof aduertised/ And had pervsed oon of the same bokes/ he was not a littill offendyd/ And assembled all the pryvye Councell of ffraunce together to whome he spake hys mynd thus/ sayeng that it was not oonly a suspecyon in them but also a great rebuke and a diffamacion to
30 the kynges honour to se & knowe any suche sedicius ontrewthe opynly devoulged and setforthe by any malicious & subtyll traytor of this Realme/ sayeng furthermore that if the lyke had byn attempted w^tin the realme of Englond he doughted not but to se it punysshed accordyng to the trayterous demeanour &
35 desertes/ Notw^tstandyng I sawe but small redresse/ So this was

4 entertaynment] *MS.* entertayment   8 p peace *canc. before* too; too *interl.*   9 lord *canc. after* souerayn   10 than *interl.*   11 Nowe *interl.*
15 ware *interl.*   16 beyng] *MS.* byng   17 / & to *canc. after* Realme   22–23 C *canc. before* consultacions   28 it] t *written over* s

oon of the displeasures that the ffrenche men shewed hyme for
all his paynnes and travell that he toke for qualefieng of ther
kynges Raumsome/ **Allso another** displeasure was this/ there
was no place where he was lodged after he entred the terretorye
of ffraunce but that he was robbed in his privye chamber other
of oon thynge or other/ And at Compigne he lost his standysshe
of Syluer & gylt/ And there it was espied & the partie taken
w^{che} was but a littill boy of xijth or xiij^{en} yere of age a ruffians
page of Paris w^{che} haunted my lordes lodgyng w^{t}out any suspicion vntill he was taken lyeng vnder my lordes privye stayers/
vppon w^{che} occasion he was apprehendyd and examyned And
incontynent confessed all thynges that was myst w^{che} he stale
and brought to his m^r the ruffian who receyved the same &
procured [f. 34^v] hyme so to do/ After the spyall of thys boye/
my lord revelled the same vnto the Councell/ by means wherof
the Ruffian/ the boys master was apprehendyd/ and set on the
pillorye/ in the myddest of the markett place (A goodly recompence for suche an haynous offence) Also an other displeasure
was/ Some lewd person (who so euer it was) had engraved in
the great Chamber wyndowe where my lord lay vppon the
leanyng stone there a Cardynalles hatte w^t a payer of Galhowsse
ouer it in derision of my lord w^t dyuers other onkynd de-
meanors/ the w^{che} I leave heare to wright they be matters so
slaunderous//

Thus/ passyng dyuers dayes in consultacion expectyng the
retourne of Crystopher Gunner w^{che} was sent in to Englond w^t
letters vnto the kyng as it is rehersed hertofore by empost/ who
at last retorned agayn w^t other letters/ vppon receypt wherof my
lord Cardynall mad hast to retorne in to Englond/ In the
mornyng that my lord shold depart And remove beyng than at
masse in his Closett he consecrated the Chauncelour of ffraunce
A Cardynall And put vppon hyme the habyt dewe to that order/
And than toke his Iourney in to Englond ward makyng suche
necessary expedycion that he came to Gwynnes where he was
nobley receyved of my lord Sandes Capteyn there w^t all the

8 age] *MS.* ages   13 it *canc. before* to   16 on] o *written*
over v   30 lord *interl.*   31 masse] sse *written over a single*
final s   33 than] n *written over* t   35 receyved *canc. after*
nobley

retynewe therof/ And frome thence he roode to Calice/ where he taried the shyppyng of his stuffe, horsses, & trayn And in the mean tyme he establysshed there a marte to be kept for all nacions (but howe long indewred and in what sort it was vsed
5 I knowe not) for I neuer hard of any great good that it dide/ or of any worthie assemble there of marchauntes or marchantdice/ that was brought thether for the furnyture of so waytie a matter/ Thes thynges fynysshed and others for the weale of the town/ he toke shippyng And Arryved at Douer/ ffrome wence he
10 roode to the kyng (beyng than in his progresse at sir harre wyates howsse in kent) supposyd among vs his seruauntes that he shold be Ioyfully receyved at his home Commyng as well of the kyng as of all other noble men but we ware dissayved in our expectacion/ notw^{t}standyng he went Immedyatly after his Com-
15 myng to the kyng w^t whome he had long talke and contynued there in the Court ij or iij^{re} dayes and than retorned to hys howsse at Westminster where he remayned [f. 35] vntill myhelmas terme w^{che} was w^t in a fourthnyght after/ And vsyng his Rome of Chauncellorshipe as he was wont to do/ At w^{che}
20 tyme he caused an assemble to be made in the starre Chamber of all the noble men, Iuges, and Iustices of the peace of euery shere that was at that present in westminster hall/ And there made to theme a long Oracion declaryng vnto them the cause of his ambassett in to ffraunce And of his procedynges there/
25 Among the w^{che} he sayd that he had concludyd suche an amytie And ffrendshipe as neuer was hard of in this Realme in our tyme byfore/ As well bytwen the Emprour and vs as bytwen the ffrenche kyng and our souerayn lord concludyng a perpetuall peace w^{che} shall be confirmed in writyng alternatly sealed w^t the
30 broode seales of bothe the Realmes graved in fynne gold/ Affirmyng ferthermore that the kyng shold receyve yerely his tribute (by that name) for the Duchye of Normandye w^t all

1 therof *interl.*; there *canc. after* therof   2 shyppyng of his *interl.*; stuffyng of *canc. before* stuffe; horsses] h *written over* v   6 therof *canc. before* there   8 weale of *canc. before* weale   9 douer *canc. before* Douer; wence] *final* e *written over* s   14 expectacion/] *MS.* expectacion   18 in *interl.*   19 do/ At] *MS.* do At   20 an *canc. before* an; an *interl.*   21 of *interl. before* all   26 *a single indecipherable letter canc. before* hard   31 after *canc. before* ferthermore; that the kyng *canc. before* shold; shold] *MS.* sheld

Life of Cardinal Wolsey

other costes w^{che} he hathe susteyned in the warres And where there was a restraynt made in fraunce of the ffrenche quens dower (whome the Duke of Suffolk had maried) for dyuers yeres/ dewryng the warres/ yt ys fully concludyd that she shall not oonly receyve the same yerely agayn but also the arrerages beyng onpayed duryng the restraynt/ All w^{che} thynges sholld be perfected at the commyng of the great ambassett owt of ffraunce/ in the w^{che} shalbe a great nomber of noble men and gentilmen for the conclusion of the same/ as hathe not byn seen repayer hether owt of oon Realme in an Ambassett/ This peace thus concludyd there shalbe suche an Amytie bytwen gentilmen of eche realme/ And entercourse of marchauntes w^t marchandyse, that it shall seme to all men the terretorys to be but oon monarche/ Gentillmen may travell quyotly frome oon contrie to an other for ther recreacion and pastyme/ And marchauntes beyng arryved in eche contrie shalbe assured to travell abought ther affayers in peace & tranquylite So that this Realme shall Ioy & prospere for euer/ wherfore it shalbe well don for all trewe Englisshemen to auaunce & setforthe this perpetuall peace/ bothe in Countenaunce & gesture w^t suche entertaynme^t as it may be a Iust occasion vnto the ffrenche men to accept the same in good part/ And also to vse you w^t the semblable/ And make of the same an noble report in ther contries [f. 35^v] Nowe good my lordes & gentilmen/ I most entierly requyer you in the kynges behalfe that ye wyll shewe yor selfes herin very lovyng & obedyent subiectes wher in the kyng woll myche reioyce yor towardnes and geve to euery man his pryncely thankes for suche liberalitie & gentilnes as ye or any of you shall mynester/ vnto theme/ And here he endyd his perswacion and so departyd in to the dynyng chamber there and dyned among the lordes of the Councell///

Thys greate ambassett/ long loked for was nowe come ouer w^{che} ware in nomber above iiij^{xx} persons of the most noblest & worthiest gentilmen in all the Court of ffraunce/ who ware right honorably receyved frome place to place after ther

1 costes *interl.*   2 fraunce] *MS.* fraaunce   7 i. *canc. before* at; at *interl.*   10 thus *interl.*   14 men *of* Gentillmen *interl.*
29 Oracio *canc. before* perswacion   30 the *canc. before* the dynyng
31 Co *canc. before* Councell

arryvall/ And so conveyed thoroughe london vnto the bysshoppes
palice in powlles chirche yerd/ where they ware lodged/ To
whome dyuers noble men resortyd/ And gave theme dyuers
goodly presentes/ And in especyall the mayer & Citie of london/
5 As wyne, Suger, waxe, Capons, wyldfowle, beafes, mottons, and
other necessaries in great aboundaunce for the expences of ther
howsse/ Then the next Sonday after ther resort to london they
repayred to the Court at Grenwyche/ And there by the kynges
ma^{tie} most highely receyved & entertayned/ they had a specyall
10 commyssion to creat & stalle the kynges ma^{tie} in the Royall
order of ffraunce/ ffor w^{che} purposely they brought w^t theme a
Colour of fyne gold of the order w^t a myhell hankyng ther at and
Robbes to the same appurtenaunt the w^{che} was wonderous
costly & comly of purpull veluet richely embrodered/ I sawe the
15 kyng in all this apparell & habytt passyng thoroughe the chamber
of presence vnto his Closett & offered in the same habytt at
masse benethe in the Chappell/ And to gratefie the ffrenche kyng
w^t lyke honour sent incontynent vnto the frenche kyng the lyke
order of Englond by an noble man (the Erle of wyltshere)
20 purposly for that entent to Creat hyme oon of the same order
of England/ accompaned w^t Garter the harold/ w^t all robys Garter
& other abyllmentes to the same belongeng as Costly in euery
degree as thother was of the ffrenche kynges the w^{che} was don
byfore the retourne of the great ambassett and for the perform-
25 aunce of this noble & perpetuall peace/ it was concludyd & determyned that a Solompne masse shold be song in the Cathederall
chirche of powlles by the Cardynall/ ayenst w^{che} tyme there was
prepared a Gallerye [f. 36] made frome the west doore of the
Chirche of powlles vnto the quyer doore Raylled on euery syde
30 vppon the w^{che} stode vessels full of Parfeumes bornyng/ Then
the kyng & my lord Cardynall & all the ffrenche w^t all other
noble men & gentilmen ware conveyed vppon this Gallery vnto
the highe Aulter in to ther trauersys/ than my lord Cardynall
prepared hymeself to masse assocyatted w^t xxiiij^{tl} myters of
35 bysshoppes and Abbottes attendyng vppon hyme & to serue

3 the *canc. after* whome   10 kynges] *MS.* kyng   13 to
interl.   20 establysshe *canc. before* Creat   30 stode vessels
full] *MS.* stode full; bornyng/ Then] *MS.* bornyng Then

hyme in suche ceromynyes as to hyme (by vertue of his
legantyn prerogatyfe) was dewe/ And after the last Agnus the
kyng Roose owt of his trauers And kneled vppon a Cusshon &
carpett at the highe Aulter/ And the Graund m^r of ffraunce the
cheafe Ambassitore that represented the kyng his m^{r}s person
kneled by the kynges ma^{tie}/ bytwen whome my lord devydyd the
sacrame^t as a firme oathe & assuraunce of this perpetuall peace/
that don the kyng resortyd agayn vnto his trauers And the
graund m^r in lyke wyse to his/ this masse fynysshed (w^{che} was
song w^t the kynges chapell & the quyer of powles) my lord
Cardynall toke the Instrument of this perpetuall peace &
amytie And rede the same opynly byfore the kyng and the
assemble bothe of Englisshe & frenche/ to the w^{che} the kyng
subscribed w^t hys owen hand and the Graund m^r for the frenche
kyng in lyke wyse/ the w^{che} was sealed w^t seales of fynne gold
engraven and delyuerd to eche other as ther firme deades/ And
all thys don & fynysshed they departed/ the kyng rode home to
the Cardynalles howse at westminster to dynner w^t whome
dyned all the ffrenche men/ passyng all day after in Consultacion
in waytie matters touchyng the conclusion of thys peace &
amytie// that don the kyng went agayn by water to Grenw^{che}/
at whos departyng it was determyned by the kynges devyse that
the ffrenche gentilmen shold resort vnto Richemond to hunt
there in euery of the parkes/ And frome thence to hampton
Court And there in lyke wyse to hunt/ And there my lord
Cardynall to make for theme a Supper & lodge theme there that
nyght/ And frome thence they shold ride to wyndesore/ And
there to hunt/ And after ther retourne to london they shold
resort to the Court where as the kyng wold bankett theme/ And
this perfectly determyned the kyng & the frenche departyd////
[f. 36^v]
Then was there no moore to do but to make provysion at
hampton Court for thys assemble/ ayenst the day appoynted/
my lord called for his pryncypall officers of hys howsse as his

1 hyme *interl. before* in; (*canc. before* as   2-3 the kyng *interl.*
5 m^{r}s] *MS.* m^r; person] *MS.* persons *interl. with final* s *written over* e
10 ther *canc. before* of   13 of *interl.*   14 his *canc.*
before w^t 17 in *canc. before* to; to *interl.*   18 kyng *canc. before*
Cardynalles   19 *first* all *interl.*   22 devyse *canc. before* devyse
33 t all *canc. before* thys

68 *Life of Cardinal Wolsey*

steward/ Controller And the Clarkes of his kytchen whome he
commaundyd to prepare for this bankett at hampton Court And
nother to spare for expences or travell to make them suche
tryhumphant chere as they may not oonly wonder at hit here
but also make a gloryous report in ther Contrie to the kynges
honour & of this Realme/ his pleasure oons knowen to accomplysshe his commaundeme^t they sent forthe all ther Cators/
purveyours & other persons to prepare of the fynnest vyandes
that they cowld gett other for mony or frendshyppe among my
lordes frendes/ Also they sent for all the expertest Cookes
besydes my lordes that they could gett in all Englond where they
myght be gotten to serue to garnysshe this feast/ The purvyours brought and sent In suche plenty of Costly provysion as
ye wold wonder at the same/ The Cookes wrought bothe nyght
& day in dyuers subtiltes and many crafty devisis/ where lakked
nother gold, Syluer ne any other costly thyng meate for ther
purpose/ The yomen And Gromes of the ward Robbes ware
busied in hangyng of the Chambers w^t costly hangynges And
furnysshyng the same w^t Beddes of sylke and other furnyture
apte for the same in euery degree/ Than my lord Cardynall sent
me beyng gentilman vssher w^t ij other of my ffellowes to
hampton Court to fforsee all thynges touchyng our Romes/ to be
noblely garnysshed accordyngly/ ower paynnes ware not small
or lyght/ but travellyng dayly frome Chamber to Chamber/ Than
the Carpenters, the Ioynors, the Masons, the paynters, And all
other Artificers necessary to glorefie the howsse & feast ware
sett a worke/ there was cariage & recariage of plate, stuffe, and
other riche Impleme^{tes}/ So that there was no thyng lakkyng or
to be Imagyned or devysed for the purpose/ There was also
xiiij^{xx} beddes providyd and furnysshed w^t all maner of ffurnyture to them belongyng to long partuculerly here to reherse/ but
to all wysmen it suffisithe to Imagyn that knowyth what

4 chere *canc. before* tryhumphant; hit] h *written over* y   6 accom *canc. before* accomplysshe   11 gett *interl.*   14 same/ The] *MS.* same The   16 meate *canc. after* thyng   18 hank *canc. before* hangyng   19 Beddes *canc. before* Beddes   21 *a single indecipherable letter canc. before* ij   24 light *canc. before* lyght   27–28 stuffe, and other] *MS.* stuffe, other   29 purpose *canc. before* purpose   32 to all *canc. before* to all; and *canc. before* that; that *interl.*; he *canc. before* knowyth

Life of Cardinal Wolsey

belongythe to the ffurnyture of suche a tryhumphant feast or bankett/// [f. 37]

The day was come/ that to the ffrenchemen was assigned and they redy assembled at hampton Court (some thyng byfore the hower of ther appoyntment)/ wherfore the Officers caused them to Ride to hanworthe a place & parke of the kynges w^{t}in ij or iij^{re} mylles there to hunt & spend the tyme vntill nyght/ At w^{che} tyme they retorned agayn to hampton Court/ And euery of them conveyed to hys Chamber seuerally havyng in them great fiers and wynne redy to refresshe theme remaynyng there vntill ther Supper was redy And the Chambers where they shold suppe ware ordered in dewe forme/ The first waytyng chamber was hanged w^t fynne Arras And so was all the rest oon better than an other furnysshed w^t talle yomen/ there was sett tables round aboughte the Chamber bankett wyse all couered w^t fynne clothes of dyaper/ A Cup bord w^t plate of parcell gylt/ havyng also in the same chamber to geve the more lyght iiij^{or} plates of syluer sett w^t lightes vppon them/ a great fier in the Chymney/ The next chamber beyng the Chamber of presence hanged w^t very riche arras/ wherin was a gorgious & a precyous clothe of estate hanged vppe/ replenysshed w^t many goodly gentilmen redy to serue/ the bordes ware sett as thother bordes ware in the other chamber byfore/ save that the highe table was sett & removed benethe the clothe of estate towardes the myddes of the chamber couered w^t fynne lynnen clothes of dammaske worke swetly perfumed/ there was a Cupboard made (for the tyme) in lengthe of the bredthe of the nether end of the same chamber of vjth deskes highe/ full of gilt plate very somptious & of the most newest facions/ and vppon the nether most deske garnysshed all w^t plate of clean gold hauyng ij great Candylstykes of syluer & gylt most Curiously wrought the worke manshype wherof w^t the syluer cost iij^C markes and lightes of waxe as bygge as torches burnyng vppon the same/ this Cupbord was barred in round aboughte that no man myght come nyghe it/ ffor there

1 therof *canc. before* of; of] *MS*. /// of; suche a tryhumphant] *MS*. suche tryhumphant   3 that *interl*; was *interl. after* ffrenchemen   12 wa *interl. and canc. before* waytyng; waytyng *interl*.   20 sett *canc. after* was; a *interl. after* &   21 may *canc. before* many   32 cost *canc. before* w^t

was none of the same plate occupied or sterred duryng this feast for ther was sufficient besides// the plattes that hong on the walles to geve lightes in the chamber ware of syluer & gylt w^t lightes burnyng in them and a great fier in the chymney/ And all
5 other thynges necessary for the furnyture of so noble a feast///
[f. 37^v]
Nowe was all thinges in a redynes and Supper tyme at hand/ My lordes Officers caused the Truppettes to blowe to warne to Supper And the seyd Officers went right discretly in dewe
10 order And conducted thes nobyll personages frome ther Chambers vnto the Chamber of presence where they shold Suppe/ And they beyng there caused them to sytt down/ ther seruyce was brought vppe in suche order & Aboundaunce bothe Costly & full of subtilties w^t suche a pleasaunt noyce of dyuers
15 Instrumentes of musyke/ that the ffrenche men (as it semyd) ware rapte in to an hevynly paradice/ ye must vnderstand that my lord was not there ne yet come/ but they beyng mery and plesaunt w^t ther fare/ devysyng and wonderyng vppon the subtilties/ byfore the second Course/ my lord Cardynall came In
20 among them, booted & sporred (all sodenly) And bad them proface/ At whos commyng they wold haue risyn & gyve place/ w^t myche Ioye/ whome my lord commaundyd to sitt still & kepe ther Romes/ And strayt way (beyng not shifted of his ridyng apparell) called for a Chayer/ And satt hyme self down in the
25 myddes of the table/ lawghyng & beyng as mery as euer I sawe hyme in all my lyfe/ Anon came vppe the Second Course w^t so many disshes, subtilties, & curious devysis w^{che} ware above an Cth in nomber of so goodly proporcion and Costly/ that I suppose the ffrenchemen neuer sawe the lyke/ the wonder was no
30 lesse than it was worthy in deade/ there ware Castelles w^t Images in the same/ powlles Chirche & steple in proporcion for the quantitie as well counte^{r}feited as the paynter shold haue paynted it vppon a clothe or wall/ There ware, beastes, byrdes, fowles of dyuers kyndes And personages most lyvely made &
35 counterfet in dysshes/ some fightyng (as it ware) w^t swordes/ some w^t Gonnes and Crosebowes/ Some vaughtyng & leapyng/

4 them and a] *MS.* them a 5 other *interl.* 7 was *canc.*
before in; hand *canc. before* hand 27 curious *interl.*; bove *of* above
interl.; bove *canc. before* an

Life of Cardinal Wolsey

Some dauncyng w^t ladyes/ Some in complett harnes Iustyng w^t speres/ And w^t many more devysis than I ame able w^t my wytt to discribbe/ Among all oon I noted/ there was a Chesse bord subtilly made of spiced plate/ [f. 38] w^t men to the same/ And for the good proporcyon bycause that frenche men be very 5 experte in that play/ my lord gave the same to a gentilman of fraunce commaundyng that a Case shold be made for the same/ in all hast to preserue it frome perysshyng in the conveyaunce therof in to hys Contrie/ Then my lord toke a boll of gold (w^{che} was estemed at the valewe of .V^{Cth} markes) And fillyd w^t 10 Ipocras (wherof there was plentie) putyng of his Cappe sayed/ I drynke to the kyng my souerayn lord & m^r/ and the kyng yor mayster/ And ther w^t dranke a good draught/ And whan he had don, he desired the graund m^r to plege hyme cuppe & all/ the w^{che} Cuppe he gave hyme/ And so caused all thother lordes & 15 gentilmen in other Cuppes to plege thes ij Royall prynces/ then went Cuppes meryly aboughte that many of the ffrenche men were fayn to be led to ther beddes/ Than went my lord (levyng theme syttyng still) in to hys privye Chamber to shyft hyme And makyng there a very short sopper or rather a small repast 20 retorned Agayn among theme in to the chamber of presence/ vsing them so nobly w^t so lovyng & famylier Countenaunce & entertaynment that they cowld not commend hyme to myche/ And whillest they ware in Commynycacion And other pastymes/ all ther lyueres ware serued to ther chambers/ Euery chamber 25 had a bason & an yewer of siluer & some clean gylt & some parcell gylt and some ij great pottes of siluere in lyke maner And oon pott at the least w^t wyne & beare/ A boll or Coblett/ And a siluer pott to drynk bere/ a siluer kandyllstyke or ij/ bothe w^t whight lyghtes & yelewe lightes of iij^{re} Cisis of waxe/ and a 30 staffe torche/ a fynne maynchett & a cheete love of brede/ thus

2–3 wytt to discribbe] *MS.* wytt discribbe 8 fr *canc. before* in the; conveyaunce] *MS.* conyeyaaunce 10 to *canc. before* And *and* be *before* fillyd; And *interl.* 12 dynke *canc. before* drynke; drynke *interl.* 16 theme *canc. before* thes 17 mery *canc. before* meryly; meryly *interl.* 25 chambers/ Euery] *MS.* chambers Euery 26 ewer *canc. after* an; yewer *interl.*; some clean *interl. with* Clean *interl. and canc. before* clean 27 great *interl.* 29 drynk] k *written over* g 30 lightes of iij^{re}] *MS.* lightes iij^{re} 31 brede/] *MS.* brede; and yet not *canc. before* thus

was euery chamber ffurnysshed thoroughe owt the howsse And yet the ij Cupbordes in the too bankettyng Chambers not oons towched/ Than beyng past mydnyght as tyme serued they ware conveyed to ther lodgynges to take ther rest for that nyght/ In
5 the mornyng of the next day (not early) they rose & hard masse & dyned w^t my lord/ And so departed [f. 38^v] toward wyndesore and there hunted delightyng myche of the Castell & Collage and in the order of the Garter/ they beyng departed frome hampton Court/ my lord retourned agayn to westminster bycause it was
10 in the myddes of the terme/ **Yt is not** to be doughted but that the kyng was privye of all this worthy feast/ who entendyd ferre to exced the same/ whome I leave vntill the retourne of the frenche men who gave a specyall commaundement to all his Officers to devyse a farre Sumptioser bankett for thes strayngers
15 otherwyse than they had at hampton Court w^{che} was not neclectyd but most spedely put in execucion w^t great delygence//

After the retorne of thes Strayngers frome wyndesore/ w^{che} place w^t the goodly order therof/ they myche Commendyd/ The day Approched that they ware invited to the Court at Grenw^{che}/
20 where first they dyned/ And after long consultacion of the Sagest w^t our Councellours/ dauncyng of the rest & other pastyme the tyme of Supper came on/ Than was the bankettyng Chamber in the Tyltyerd furnysshed for thentertaynme^t of thes estraynegers/ to the w^{che} place they ware conveyed by the noblest
25 persones beyng than in the Court/ where they bothe Supped & banketted/ But to discrybe the disshes, the subtylltes, the many straynge devysis/ & order in the same/ I do bothe lake wytt in my grosse old hed & Cunnyng in my bowelles to declare the wonderfull and Curious Imagynacions in the same Inventyd &
30 devysed/ yet this ye shall vnderstand that allthoughe it was at hampton Court marvelous Sumptious/ yet dyd thys bankett ferre exced the same as fynne gold dothe siluer/ in waytt & valewe/ And for my part I must nedes confesse (w^{che} sawe them bothe) that I neuer sawe the lyke or rede in any story

1 of *canc. after* owt   3 as tyme serued *interl.*   7 they *canc. before* there; there *and* myche *interl.*   12 retourne] *MS.* retournee
15 not *interl.*   21 day daunced *canc. before* dauncyng   29 wondeff *canc. before* wonderfull   30 hau *canc. after* shall   34 l *canc. before* lyke

or cronycle of any suche feast// In the myddes of this bankett
ther was tornyng at the barriers (evyn in the Chamber) w^t lusty
gentilmen in gorgious complett harnoys on foote/ Than was
there the lyke on horssebake/ And after all this there was the
most goodlyest disguysyng or enterlude made in latten & 5
frenche/ whos apparell was of suche excedyng riches that it
passithe my capacitie to expound/ this don than came in suche a
nomber of fayer ladys & gentilwomen that bare any brute or fame
of beawtie in all this realme/ in the most richest apparell and
devysied in dyuers goodly facions that all the connyngest 10
tayllours could devyse to shape or Cut to sett forthe ther
beawtie, geesture, & the goodly proporcion of ther bodyes/ who
semyd to all men more Ayngelyke than yerthely made of flesshe
& bone/ [f. 39] (Sewerly to me Symple sowle) it semyd
Inestymable to be discribed/ And so I thynke it was to other of a 15
more higher Iugeme^t/ w^t whome thes Gentilmen of ffraunce
daunced vntill an other maske cam In of noble Gentilmen/ who
daunced & masked w^t thes fayer ladyes & gentillwomen euery
man as hys ffantazy serued theme/ this don and the maskers
departed/ there came in an other maske of ladyes so gorgiously 20
apparelled in costly garmentes that I dare not presume to take
vppon me to make therof any declaracion lest I shold retther
deface than beawtifie them therfore I leave it ontouched/ Thes
ladys maskeresses toke eche of theme a frenche gentilman/ to
daunce & maske w^t theme/ ye shall vnderstand that thes lady 25
maskers spake good ffrenche w^{che} delighted myche thes gentilmen to here thes ladyes speke to theme in ther owen tong/ thus
was thys nyght occupied & consumed frome .v. of the cloke vntill
ij or iij after mydnyght at w^{che} tyme it was convenyent for all
estattes to drawe to ther rest/ And thus euery man departed/ 30
whether as they had most releave//

Than as nothyng/ other helthe wealthe or pleasure can
allwayes endure So endyd this tryhumphant bankett/ the w^{che}

1 or cronycle *interl.* 3 foote/ Than] *MS.* foote Than 4 after
and second the *interl.* 10 dyuers goodly *interl.* 11 forthe] *MS.*
for 13 yerthely] *first* y *written over* e 21 apparell *canc.*
before apparelled; apparelled *interl.*; presume to *interl.* 23 it *canc.*
before them; them *interl.* 24 maskeresses] *second* e *written over* s
25 thes *interl.* 29 co *canc. before* convenyent 31 as
interl.

in the next mornyng semyd to all the beholders but as a ffantasticall dreame/ After all this solompne chere at a day appoynted they prepared them to retourne w^t bagg & baggage/ than as to the office of all honorable persons dothe appurteyn/ they
5 resorted in good order to the Court to take ther leave of the kyng and other noble men than beyng there/ to whome the kyng commytted his prynycely commendacions to the kyng ther m^r/ And thanked theme of ther paynnes & travell And after long commynycacion w^t the most honorable of that ambassett/ he
10 bad theme adewe/ who was assigned by the Councell to repayer vnto my lord Cardynall for to receyve the kynges most noble reward/ wherfore they repayred to my lord & takyng of ther leave/ they receyved euery man the kynges reward/ after this sort euery honorable person in estymacion had most comenly
15 plate to the valewe of iij^{re} or iiij^{cli} & some more & some lesse besides other great gyftes receyved at the kynges handes byfore/ as riche gownes, horsses or goodly geldynges/ of great valewe & goodnes/ and some had waytie chaynnes of fynne gold w^t dyuers other gyftes w^{che} I cannot nowe call to my remembraunce/ but
20 this I knowe that the lest of [f. 39^v] them all had a Somme of Crownes of gold/ the worst page among them had xx^{ti} Crownnes for his part/ and thus they (nobley rewardyd) departed And my lord after humble commendacions had to the ffrenche kyng he bade them a dewe/ And the next day they conveyed all ther
25 stuffe & furnyture vnto the sees side/ accompanied w^t lusty yong gentilmen of Englond/ but what prayse or commendacions they made in ther Countrie at ther retorne in good faythe I cannot tell you for I neuer hard any thyng therof

Than began other matters to brewe & take place/ that occupied
30 all mens hedes w^t dyuers Imagynacions/ whos stomakes ware therw^t fulfilled w^{t}out any perfect disgestion/ The long hyd & secrett love bytwen the kyng and m^{rs} Anne Boloyn began to breke owt in to euery mans eares/ the matter was than by the kyng disclosed to my lord Cardenall/ whos perswasion to the

1 next *interl.*; it *canc. before* semyd   3 as *interl.*   4 persons dothe appurteyn/] *MS.* persons/ dothe appurteyn *with* dothe appurteyn *interl.*   5 toke *canc. before* resorted   10 theme *canc. before* theme
11 Cardynall; ll *frayed away at edge of page*   17 riche *interl.*   21 gold/ the] *MS.* gold the   22 the *canc. before* my   33 in *interl.*; by *canc. before* by

contrarie made to the kyng vppon his knees cowld not effect/ the kyng was so amorously affeccionate/ that wyll bare place/ and highe discression banysshed for the tyme/ My lord provoked by the kyng to declare his wyse oppynyon in thys matter for the furtheraunce of his desired affecte/ who thought it not mete for hyme alone to wade to ferre to geve his hasty Iugeme^t or advyse in so waytie a matter desiered of the kyng licence to axe the Councell of men of Auncyent study & of ffamous learnyng bothe in the lawes dyvyn & Civell (that opteyned) he by his legantyne Auctorytie sent owt his commyssion vnto all the bysshoppes of this realme and for other that was exactly owther learned in any of the seyd lawes/ or elles had in any estymacion for ther prudent Councell & Iugeme^t in pryncely affayers of long experyence/ Than assembled these prelattes byfore my lord Cardynall at his place in westminster w^t many other famous & notable Clarkes of bothe the vnyuersites/ Oxford & Cambryge/ and also owt of dyuers Colleges & cathederall chirches of this realme renommed & allowed learned & of wytty discression in the determynacion of doughtfull questions// Than was the matter of the kynges Case debated, reasonyd & Argued Consultyng frome day to day & tyme to tyme/ that it was to men learned a goodly heryng/ but in Conclusion it semyd me by the departure of the Auncyent fathers of the lawes/ that they departed w^t oon Iugement contrary to thexpectacion of the princypall parties/ I hard the oppynyon of Somme of the most famous persons among that sort report/ that the kynges case was so obscure & doughtfull for any learned man to [f. 40] discus/ the poyntes therin ware so darke to be credyttyd that it was very hard to haue any true vnderstandyng or Intellygence/ And therfore they departed w^{t}out any resolucion or Iugeme^t/ Than in this assemble of bysshoppes it was thought most expedyent that the kyng shold fyrst send owt his commyssioners in to all the vnyuersites of Cristendome/ As well here in Englond as in to fforreyn Contries and regions/ to haue among them his

1 not *canc. after* cowld; not] t *written over* n   5 not *interl.*
10 al *canc. before* the   11 other le exactly *with* exactly *interl. canc. after* was; exactly *interl.*   16 vy *canc. before* vnyuersites   17 owt of *interl.*
18 & *interl. before* of; f *canc. before* wytty   22 a goodly heryng *canc. after* heryng; that *canc. before* by   23 auncyent *canc. before* Auncyent
28 poytes *canc. before* poyntes

graces case Argued substancyally And to bryng w^t them frome thence the very defynycion of ther oppynyoons in the same/ vnder the sealles of euery seuerall vnyuersitie/ thus was ther determynacion for thys tyme/ And thervppon agreed that
5 Commyssioners ware Incontynent appoynted and sent forthe abought this matter in to seuerall vnyuersites/ as some to Oxford Some to Cambryge/ some to lovayn/ Some to Paris/ Some to Orlyaunce/ some to bononye/ And some to Padwaye/ And some to other/ Allthough thes Commyssioners had the
10 traveylle/ yet was the charges the kynges the w^che was no small sommes of mony/ And all went owt of the kynges Coffers in to fforrayn Regions/ ffor as I hard it reported of credyble persons (as it semed in dead) that besides the great charges of the Commyssioners ther was in estimable Sommes of mony gevyn
15 to the ffamous Clarkes to choke theme/ and in especyall to suche as hade the gouernaunce & custody of ther vnyuersite sealles/ In so myche as they agreed not oonly in oppynyons but also opteyned of theme the vnyuersites sealles (the w^che atteyned) they retourned home agayn furnesshed for ther purpose at whos
20 retorne ther was no small Ioy made of the pryncypall parties/ In so myche as the Commyssioners ware not oonly euer in great estymacion but also most liberally auaunced & rewardyd/ fferre beyond ther worthy desertes/ Notw^tstandyng they prospered/ And the matter went still forward/ hauyng than as they thought
25 a sewer foundacion to ground them vppon/ thes procedynges beyng oons declared to my lord Cardynall/ Sent agayn for all the bysshoppes whome he made privye of thexpedicion of the commyssioners and for the very profe therof he shewed theme the oppynyons of the seuerall vnyuersites in writyng vnder ther
30 vnyuersities sealles/ Thes matters beyng thus brought to passe/ they went oons agayn to consultacion/ howe thes matters shold be ordered/ [f. 40^v] to the purpose/ Yt was than thought good & concludyd by the Advyse of them all that the kyng shold (to avoyd all ambyguyties) send vnto the pope a legacion w^t the

9 Allthough] g *canc. between g and* h; *uncanc.* g *written over* h   10 no *canc. after* w^che   16 vnyuersite] *MS.* vnyersite   18 vnyere *canc. before* vnyuersites   23 desertes/ Notw^tstandyng] *MS.* desertes Notw^tstanding   25 staffe *canc. after* sewer; foundacion *interl.*   29 r *canc. before* oppynyons; of the seuerall vnyuersites *interl.*

Instrume^t declaryng the oppynyons of the vnyuersites vnder ther sealles To the w^che it was thought good that all thes prelattes in this assemble shold Ioyn w^t the kyng in thys legacion makyng intersession & sewte to the pope for advyse & Iugement in this great & waytie matter/ And if the pope wold not dyrectly 5 consent to the same request that than the Ambassitors shold further requyer of hyme a Commyssion to be dirrected vnder leade/ to establysshe a court Iudicyall in England (ac vice tantum) directed to my lord Cardynall & vnto the Cardynall Campagious w^che was than bysshope of Bathe/ (Althoughe he 10 ware a straynger) w^che the kyng gave hyme at suche tyme as he was the Popes ambassitorie here in Englond/ to here & determyn accordyng to the Iust Iugementes of ther concyence/ The w^che after long & great sewt they oppteyned of the pope his commysson/ this don and atchyved they made retorne in to Englond 15 makeng report vnto the kyng of ther expedicion/ trustyng that hys graces pleasure & purpose shold nowe perfectly be brought to passe/ consideryng the estate of the Iuges who ware the Cardynall of Englond & of Campagious beyng bothe hys hignes subiectes in effecte/ 20

Long was the desier & greatter was the hoppe/ on all sides expectyng the Commyng of the lagacion & Commyssion frome Rome yet at lengthe yt came/ And after the arryvall of the legat Campasious (w^t thys solompne commyssion) in England/ he beyng sore vexed w^t the gowtte was constrayned by force 25 therof to make a long Iourney or euer he came to london/ who shold haue byn most solompnly receyved at Blak hethe/ And so w^t great tryhumphe conveyed to london but his glory was suche/ that he wold in no wyse be entertayned w^t any suche pompe or vaynglory/ who suddenly came by water in a wyry to his owen 30 howsse w^tout Temple barre called than Bathe place w^che was furnysshed for hyme w^t all maner of Stuffe & Impleme^tes of my lordes provysion/ where he contynued & lodged duryng his abode here in Englond/ Than after some delyberacion/ his commyssion [f. 41] vnderstandyd, rede, & perceyved/ yt was by the councell 35

5 dyrectly *interl.*   12 do *canc. after* to   14 to whome *canc. after* pope
14–15 his commysson *interl. with the virgule placed before* his   15 the *canc. before* and   17 be *canc. before* perfectly   19 es *canc. after* Cardynall
21 r *canc. after* greatter was the   34 rede *canc. after* commyssion

determyned that the kyng & the Quene his wyfe shold be lodged at Bridewell/ And that in the blake ffriers a certyn place shold be appoynted where as the kyng & the Quene myght most convenyently repaire to the Court there to be erected & kepte for the disputacion & determynacion of the kynges case/ where as thes ij legattes sat In Iugeme^t as notable Iuges/ byfore whome the kyng & the Quene ware dewly Cited and Sommoned to appere/ **W^{che} was** the strayngest & newest sight & devyse that euer was rede or hard in any history or Cronycle in any Region/ That a kyng and a quene/ to be convented and constrayned by processe compellatory to appere in any Court (as comen persons) w^t in ther owen Realme or domynyon to abyde the Iugeme^t & decrees of ther owen subiectes/ havyng the dyadem & prerogatyfe therof **Ys it not** a world to consider the desier of wylfull prynces whan they fully be bent and Inclyned to fullfyll ther voluptious Appetytes/ Ayenst the w^{che} no reasonable perswasions wyll suffice/ littill or no thyng wayeng or regardyng the dayngerous sequelles that dothe ensue as well to them selfes as to ther Realme & subiectes/ And Above all thynges ther is no oon thyng that causithe theme to be more wylfull than Carnall desier & voluptious affeccion of folyshe love/ thexperyence is playn in this case bothe manyfest & evydent/ ffor what surmysed Invencions hathe byn Invented/, what lawes hathe byn enacted/, what noble and auncyent monastorys ouerthrowen & defaced/ what dyuersites of religious oppynyons hathe rissyn/ what execucions hathe byn commytted/ howe many famous & notable Clarkes hathe suffered deathe/ what charitable foundacions ware peruertyd frome the releafe of the poore vnto prophan vsis/ And what alteracions of good and holsome auncyent lawes & custumes hathe byn tossed by wyll & wyllfull desier of the prynce/ almost to the subuercyon and desolacion of this noble Realme/ all men may vnderstand what hathe chaunced to this reegion/ The prove ther of hathe taught all vs Englisshemen a comen experyence/ the more is the pitie/ & to all good

---

1 wyfe *canc. before* wyfe   7 assi *canc. before* dewly; dewly *interl.*   10 *two indecipherable letters canc. after* kyng   11 comen] *MS.* coen   20 to be *interl.*   22 bothe *interl.*; & *canc. before* &   24 hathe byn *canc. before* ouerthrowen   26 of *canc. before* hathe *and* what *before* howe   30 la *canc. before* auncyent   34 comen] *MS.* coen

Life of Cardinal Wolsey

men very lamentable to be considered/ yf eyes be not blynd men may se/ if eares be not stopped they may here/ And if pitie be not exiled they may lament/ the sequell of this pernycious and inordynat/ [f. 41ᵛ] Carnall love/ the plage wherof is not seased (allthoughe this love lasted but a whyle) wᶜʰᵉ our lord quenche/ And take frome vs his Indygnacion/ Quia peccauimus cum patribus nostris et Iniuste egimus/ &ᶜᵉ/

Ye shall vnderstand/ As I sayd before/ that there was a Courte erected in the blake ffriers in london/ where thes ij Cardynalles satt for Iuges/ Nowe wyll I set you owte the maner & order of the Court there/ ffirst there was a Court placed wᵗ tabylles, benches, & barres, lyke a consistory a place Iudicyall for the Iuges to sytt on/ there was also a clothe of estate vnder the wᶜʰᵉ sate the kyng/ & the Quene sat some distaunce benethe the kyng/ vnder the Iuges feet sat the officers of the Court/ the chefe Scribbe there/ was than Doctor Stephens (wᶜʰᵉ was after bysshope of wynchester) the apparitor was oon Cooke (most comenly called Cooke of wynchester) Than satt there wᵗ in the seyd Court directly byfore the kyng & Iuges/ the Archebisshope of Caunterbure (Doctor warham) and all the other bysshoppes/ than At bothe thendes wᵗ a barre made for them/ the councelles on bothe sydes/ the doctors for the kyng was Doctor Sampson wᶜʰᵉ was after bysshope of Chichester/ And Doctor Bell wᶜʰᵉ after was bysshope of worcetor/ wᵗ dyuers other/ the proctors on the kynges part was doctor Peter/ wᶜʰᵉ was after made the kynges chefe secretory/ And Doctor Tregonell/ And dyuers other/ Nowe on thother side stode the Councell for the quene/ Doctor ffissher Bisshope of Rochester/ And Doctor Standysshe Sometyme a gray ffreer and than bysshope of Saynt Assaᵖʰ in wales/ ij notable Clarkes in dyvynytie and in especyall the bysshoppe of Rochester/ a very godly man and a devout person/ who after sufferd deathe at Tower hyll the wᶜʰᵉ was greatly lamented thoroughe all the forrayn vnyuersites of cristendom/ ther was also an other auncyent doctor called (as I do remember) doctor

---

14 kyng/ & the Quene sat] *MS.* kyng & the Quene/ sat   17 wynchester)] *MS.* wynchester/   18 comenly] *MS.* co*m*nly   22 sydes] y *written over* e   29 Assaᵖʰ] a *written over* e   32 of *canc. before* at; at *interl.*   33 among *canc. before* thoroughe; thoroughe *interl.*; cristendom/ ther] *MS.* cristendom ther

Life of Cardinal Wolsey

Rydley a very small person in stature/ but sewerly a great & an excellent Clarke in dyvynytie/ The Court beyng thus ffurnysshed & ordered/ The Iuges commaundyd the Crier to commaund Scylence/ than was the Iuges Commyssion w^{che} they had of the
5 pope publysshed & red opynly byfore all the Audyence there assembled/ that don/ the Crier called the kyng by the name of kyng herre of Englond come in to the Court/ &^{ce}/ w^t that the kyng answered & sayd (here my lordes) than he called also the quene/ by the name of katheren quen of Englond come in to the
10 Court/ &^{ce}/ who made no answere to the same/ but rose vppe incontynent [f. 42] owt of hir chayer where as she satt/ And bycause she cowld not come dyrectly to the kyng/ for the distaunce w^{che} seuered theme/ she toke payn to goo abought vnto the kyng knelyng down at his feete/ in the sight of all the
15 Courte & assemble/ To whome she sayd in effect/ in broken Englysshe as folowyth/

Syr/ q^d she/ I beseche you for all the loves that hathe byn bytwen vs And for the love of god/ lett me haue Iustice & right/ take of me some pitie & compassion/ for I ame a poore woman
20 and a Straynger borne owte of yor domynyon/ I haue here no assured frendes/ And muche lesse Indifferent Councell/ I flee to you as to the hed of Iustice w^t in thys realme/ Alas sir where In haue I offendyd you/ or what occasion of displeasure haue I deserued ayenst yor wyll or pleasure/ entendyng (as I perceyve)
25 to put me frome you/ I take god & all the world to wytnes that I haue byn to you a trewe humble and obedyent wyfe/ euer confirmable to yor wyll and pleasure that neuer sayed or dyd any thyng to the contrarye therof/ beyng allwayes well pleased & contented w^t all thynges wherin ye had any delight or
30 dalyaunce/ whether it ware in littill or myche/ I neuer grudged in word or countenaunce or shewed a vysage or sparke of discontentacion/ I loued all thos whome ye loued/ oonly for yor sake/ whether I had cause or no/ and whether they ware my ffrendes or my ennemyes/ this xx^{ti} yeres I haue byn yor true

---

3 &] *written over* or; Crier *canc. before* Crier   8 also *interl.*   8-9 the *canc. before* quene   14 C *canc. after* all   23 In haue] *MS*. In/ haue   25 to put yo *canc. before first* to   26 an hun *canc. before* a; a *interl.*   31 the *canc. after* shewed; a *interl.*   32 discontentacion] *MS*. discontacion

wyfe (or more) and by me ye haue had dyuers childerne/
Allthoughe it hathe pleased god to call theme owt of this
world/ w^{che} hathe byn no default in me/ And whan ye had me
at the ffirst (I take god to be my Iuge) I was a true mayed w^towt
touche of man/ And whether it be true or no I put it to yor
concyence/ Yf there be any Iust cause by the lawe that ye can
allegge ayenst me other of dishonestie or any other Impedyme^t
to banysshe & put me frome you/ I ame well content to departe
to my great shame & dishonour/ And if there be none/ than here
I most lowly beseche you lett me remayn in my former estate
And to receyve Iustice at yor pryncely handes/ The kyng yor
ffather was in the tyme of his [f. 42^v] Reyn of suche estymacion
thoroughe the world for his excellent wysdome that he was
accompted and called of all men/ the second Salamon/ And my
ffather fferdynando kyng of spayn who was estemed to be oon
of the wyttiest Pryncies that Reygned in Spayn many yeres
byfore/ Who ware bothe wyse & excellent kynges in wysdome &
pryncely behauour/ yt is not therfore to be doughted but that
they elected & gathered as wyse Councellers abought theme as
to ther highe discressions was thought mete/ Also as me semyth
ther was in thos dayes/ as wyse, as well learned men/ And men
of as good Iugeme^t as be at this present in bothe Realmes/ Who
thought than the mariage bytwen you And me good & lawfull/
Therfore it is a wonder to me/ what newe Invencions are nowe
Invented ayenst me/ that neuer entendyd but honestie/ And
cause me to stand to the order & Iugeme^t of this newe Court/
wherin ye may do me myche wrong if ye entend any Cruel-
tie/ ffor ye may condempne me for lake of sufficyent Answere/
hauyng no Indifferent Councell/ but suche as be assigned me/
w^t whos wysdome & learnyng I ame not acquaynted/ ye must
Consider that they cannot be Indifferent councellers for my
parte/ w^{che} be yor subiectes & taken owt of yor owen councell
byfore wherin they be made pryvye/ And dare not for yor
displeasure disobey yor wyll & entent/ beyng oons made privye

1 had *interl*.   10 I *interl*.   11 & haue *canc. before* And; to *interl*.
13 excellent *interl*.   15 ffurdyna *canc. before* fferdynando   18 pryncell
canc. before pryncely; is *interl*.   26 C *canc. before* newe   27 d *canc.
before* may; *a single indecipherable letter canc. before* if   29 Indifferent]
MS. Indifferen; assi *canc. before* assigned   30 w^t *interl*.   32 owen
nterl.

ther to/ ther for I most humbly requyer you in the way of
charitie and for the love of god (who is the Iuste Iuge) to spare
thextremytye of thys newe Court vntill I may be aduertised
what way & order my frendes in Spayn woll advyse me to take/
5 And if ye wyll not extend to me so myche Indifferent ffauour/
your pleasure than be fullfilled/ And to god I commyt my case/
And evyn w^t that she rose vppe makyng lowe curtosye to the
kyng/ And so departed frome thence/ Supposed that she wold
haue resortyd agayn to hir former place/ but she toke hir direct
10 way owt of the howsse/ leanyng (as she was wont allwayes to
do/) vppon the arme of hir Generall receyvour called m^r
Griffithe/ And the kyng beyng aduertysed of hir departure
commaundyd the Crier to call hir agayn/ who called hir by the
name of katheren quen of Englond come in to the Court// &^{ce}/
15 w^t that q^d Gryffyth/ madame ye be called agayn/ on on/ q^d she/ it
[f. 43] makes no matter/ for it is no Indifferent Court for me/
therfore I wyll not tary/ goo on yor wayes/ And thus she
departyd owt of that Court w^t out any further Answere at that
tyme or at any other nor wold neuer appere in any Court after/
20 **The kyng perceyveng**/ that she was departed in suche sort
callyng to his graces memory all hir lamentable wordes that she
had pronuncyd byfore hyme & all the Audyence/ sayd thus in
effect/ **ffor as myche**/ q^d he/ as the quen is goon I wyll in hir
absence/ declare vnto you all my lordes here presently assembled/
25 She hathe byne to me as true obedyent & as confirmable a wyfe
as I cowld in my fantzy wyshe or desier/ She hathe all the
vertuouse qualities that owght to be in a woman of hir dignytie
or in any other of basser estate/ Sewerly/ she is also a noble
woman borne/ if nothyng ware in hir but oonly hir condicyons
30 woll well declare the same/ w^t that q^d my lord Cardynall sir I
most humbly beseche yor highnes to declare me byfore all this
Audyence/ whether I haue byn the cheafe Inventor or first
mover of this matter vnto yor maiestie/ for I ame greatly suspected of all men herein// My lord Cardynall/ q^d the kyng/ I can
35 well excuse you herin/ mary indeade ye haue byn rather ayenst

2 of *interl.*   3 Cr *canc. before* newe   7 *a single indecipherable
letter canc. before* she   9 to hir] r *written over* s   14 co *canc.
before* come   17 tary/ goo] *MS.* tary goo   21 lamentable] *MS.*
lament   32 Audyence *canc. before* Audyence   35 you *interl.*

me in attemptyng or settyngforthe ther of/ And to put you all
owt of dought I wyll declare vnto you thespecyall cause that
moved me herevnto/ yt was a certyn Scripulositie that prykked
my concyence vppon dyuers wordes that ware spoken at a
certyn tyme by the Bysshope of Biean the frenche kynges 5
Ambassitor/ who had lyen here long vppon the debatyng for the
conclusion of a mariage to be concludyd bytwen the pryncess our
doughter Marye/ and the yong duke of Orlyaunce the ffrenche
kynges second Sonne/ And vppon the resolucyon & determynacion therof he desired respight to aduertise the kyng his 10
m^r therof/ whether our doughter Marie shold be legittimate/ in
respect of the mariage w^{che} was somtyme bytwen the Quene here
& my brother late prynce Arthure/ thes wordes ware so conceyved w^t in my scripulous concyence/ that it brede a doughtfull
prike w^t in my brest w^{che} dought prykked vexed & trobled so 15
my mynd [f. 43^v] And so disquyoted me that I was in great
dowght of goddes Indignacion (w^{che} as semyd me) appered right
well/ myche the rather for that he hathe not sent me any Issue
male/ ffor all suche issue males as I haue receyved of the
quene died incontynent after they ware borne/ so that I dought 20
the punysshement of god in that behalf/ Thus/ beyng trobled in
waves of a scripulos concience/ And partly in dispayer of any
Issue male by hir/ it drave me at last to consider thestate of this
Realme/ And the daynger it stode in for lake of Issue male/ to
succed me in this Emperyall dignyte/ I thought it good therfore 25
in the releafe of the waytie borden of scrypulous concience/ And
the quyet estate of this noble Realme/ to attempte the lawe ther
in And wether I myght take an other wyfe/ in case that my first
copulacion w^t this gentilwoman ware not lawfull/ w^{che} I entend
not for any carnall concupisence, ne for any displeasure or 30
myslyke of the quens person or age/ w^t whome I could be as well
content to contynewe duryng my lyfe/ if our mariage may stand
w^t godes lawes as w^t any woman alyve/ in w^{che} poynt consistithe
all this dought that we goo nowe abought to trie by the learned

6 of *canc. before* for; for *interl.*   13 p *canc. before* late   14 doughtfull
interl.   15 of concyence *canc. before* w^t; prykked *interl.*   23 consult
canc. before consider; consider *interl.*   25 En *canc. before* Emperyall
27 the *interl. before* lawe   28 the f *canc. after* case   31 displeasure
canc. before person

wysdome & Iugeme^tes of you our prelates & pastures of this
realme here assembled for that purpose to whos concyence and
Iugemet/ I haue commytted the charge accordyng to the w^che
(god wyllyng) we will be Right well contentyd to submyt our
5 selfe to obbey the same for my part/ wherin after I oons perceyved my concyence wondyd w^t the doughtfull case herin/ I
moved first this matter in confession to you my lord of lyncolne
(my gostly father)/ And for as myche as than your self ware in
some dought to geve me councell/ moved me to axe ferther
10 councell of all you my lordes/ wherin I moved you first my lord
of Caunterbury axyng yor lycence (for as myche as you ware our
Metropolytan) to put this matter in question/ And so I dyd of all
you my lordes/ to the w^che ye haue all graunted by writyng vnder
all yor seales/ the w^che I haue here to be shewed/ That is truthe
15 yf it please yor highnes (q^d the bysshope of Caunterbury) I
dought not but all my bretherne here present woll affirme the
same/ No sir not I/ q^d the bysshoppe of Rochester ye haue not
my consent therto/ no hathe/ q^d the kyng/ loke here vppon this
is not this yor hand & seale/ and shewed hyme the Instrument/
20 [f. 44] w^t Sealles/ No forsothe sir q^d the bysshope of Rochester
it is not my hand nor seale/ to that q^d the kyng to my lord of
Canterbury/ Sir howe say ye/ is it not his hand & seale/ yes sir
q^d he/ that is not so q^d the bysshope of Rochester/ for in dead
you ware in hand w^t me/ to haue bothe my hand & seale/ as other
25 of my lordes hathe all redy don/ but than I sayed to you that I
wold neuer consent to no suche acte for it ware myche agaynst
my concyence nor my hand & seale shold neuer be seen at any
suche Instrument (god wyllyng) w^t myche more matter touchyng
the same commynycacion bytwen vs/ you say truthe/ q^d the
30 bysshope of Canterbury suche wordes ye had vnto me/ but at the
last ye ware fully perswadid that I shold for you subscribe yor

1 of *canc. before* of this   3 Iugeme^t *interl.*; concyence *canc. after*
Iugeme^t; & Iugement *canc. before* accordyng; I wyll *canc. after* w^che   4 we
will be *interl.*; be *canc. before* contentyd   5 sef *canc. before* selfe; I *canc.
before* after   7 you *interl.*   8 my lord of lyncoln *canc. before* ware
9 co *canc. before* councell   11 myche as you] *MS*. myche you   12 que
canc. after in   13 vnder *canc. before* by   17 so sir/ *with* sir/*interl*.
canc. before q^d   18–19 this *interl. before* is   19 Instrument] *MS.*
Instrment   20 sea *canc. after* w^t   21 is *interl.*   23 the *canc.
before* he; Rog *canc. before* Rochester   31 resolued & *canc. before* perswadid;
perswadid *interl.*; put yor seale *canc. before* subscribe; subscribe yor *interl.*

name and put to a seale my selfe and ye wold allowe the same/
all w^che wordes & matter q^d the bysshope of Rochester vnder
yor correccion my lord & supportacion of this noble audyence/
ther is no thyng more ontrewe// well well/ q^d the kyng it shall
make no matter we woll not stand w^t you in argume^t here in for 5
you are but oon man/ And w^t that the Court was aiourned vntill
the next day of ther Session/

The next court day the Cardynalles satte there agayn/ At w^che
tyme the Councelles on bothe sydes ware there present/ The
kynges Councell alledged the mariage not good frome the 10
begynnyng by cause of the Carnall knowlege commytted
bytwen prynce Arthure hir first hosbond the kynges brother/
and hir/ thys matter beyng very sore touched & mayntened by
the kynges Councell/ and the contrary defendyd by suche as
toke vppon them to be on that other part w^t the good quene/ 15
And to prove the same carnall copulacion they alleged many
colored reasons and symulitudes of trouthe/ it was answered
agayn negatifely on the other side by w^che it semed that all ther
former allegacions to be very doughtfull to be tried/ so that it
was sayd that no man cowld knowe the trowthe/ yes q^d the 20
bysshope of Rochester/ Ego nosco veritatem howe knowe ye the
trouthe/ q^d my lord Cardynall/ for sothe/ q^d he/ Ego sum
professor veritatis/ I knowe that god is truthe it self nor he neuer
spake but truthe/ w^che sayd/ Q^d deus coniunxit homo non
separet/ And for as myche as this mariage/ [f. 44^v] was mad and 25
Ioyned by god to a good entent I say that I knowe the trouthe/
the w^che cannot be broken or losed by the power of man vppon
no on fayned occasyon/ So myche dothe all faythfull men
knowe/ q^d my lord Cardynall/ as well as you/ yet this reason is
not sufficent in this case/ ffor the kynges Councell dothe allege 30
dyuers presumcyons to prove the mariage not good at the
begynnyng/ ergo/ say they/ it was not Ioyned by god at the

10 alledged *canc. before* alledged   11 bri *canc. before* begynnyng
12 and *canc. before* the   16 carnall *interl.*   17 colored
interl.   18 w *canc. before* by   20 knew *canc. before* cowld
21 veritatem *interl.*; veryt verytatem *canc. before* howe   22 q^d my lord
canc. after trouthe *and* yes *after* Cardynall/; *first* q^d *interl.*; the *canc. before* he
23 therfore *canc. before* I   25 was *interl.*   26-27 w^che falcefied by
god/ *canc. after* trouthe/ the   27 broked *canc. after* be; broken *interl.*; *a single
indecipherable letter canc. before* power   28 on *interl.*; Iust *canc. after* on;
fayned *interl.*; that god hathe made *canc. after* occasyon

begynnyng & therfore it is not lawfull/ for god ordynyth nor Ioynyth nothyng wtout a Iust order therfore it is not to be doughted but that ther presumcyons must be treu as yt playnly apperys/ And no thyng can be more true/ in case ther allagacions cannot be avoyded/ therfore to say that the matremony was Ioyned of god/ ye must prove it ferther than by that texte wche ye haue alleged for yor matter/ for ye muste first avoyd ther presumcyons/ Than qd oon doctor Rydley/ Yt is a shame & a great dishonor to this honorable persons that any suche presumpcyons shold be alledged in this opyn Court wche be to all good & honest men most detestable to be rehersed/ what qd my lord Cardynall/ Domine Doctor/ Magis reuerenter/ no no my lord/ qd he/ ther belongyth no reuerence to be gevyn to this abhomynable presumcyons ffor an vnreuerent tale wold be onreuerently answered/ And there they left & procedyd no further at that tyme/

Thus thys court/ passed frome Cession to Session and day to day/ In so myche that a certyn day the kyng sent for my lord at the brekyng vppe oon day of the Court to come to hyme in to Brydwell/ And to accomplysshe his commaundemet he went vnto hyme/ And beyng there wt hyme in commynycacion/ in his graces privye chamber frome xjen vnto xijth of the cloke and past at none/ my lord came owte & departed frome the kyng and toke his barge at the blake ffriers steyers and so went to hys howisse at westminster/ the bysshope of Carelyle beyng wt hyme in his barge sayd vnto hyme wypyng the swett frome his face/ sir qd he it is a very hot day/ yea qd my lord Cardynall/ yf ye had byn as well chaffed as I haue byn wtin this hower/ ye wold say it ware very hott/ And asson as he came home to his howesse at westminster/ he went incontynent to his naked bed where he

1 not *canc. before* nor; nor *interl.*   3 as *and* playnly *interl.*   4 apperys *canc. before* apperys; yet *canc. before* And; And *and* can be *interl.*   6 it *interl. and canc. before* prove; it *and* by *interl.*   7 if *canc. before* second for; second for *interl.* prove wyll *canc. before* muste; muste first *interl* 11 be *interl.* rehersed/ what] *MS.* rehersed what   13 the *interl. and. canc. before* this; this *interl.*   14 matter *canc. before* presumcyons *and* vnreuerent *before* vnreuerent; presumcyons *interl.*; have *canc. before* be 15 answered/ And] *MS.* answered And   17 passed *interl.*   23 & *canc. before* came; at *canc. before* and; and *interl.*   25 westminster/ the] *MS.* westminster the; of Carelyle *interl.*   26 of *canc. before* the; the swett frome *interl.*   27 wt swett/ *canc. before* sir; is *interl.*

had not lyen ffully the space of ij howers but that my lord of
wyltchere came to speke w^t hyme of a messwage frome the
kyng/ my lord hauyng vnderstandyng of his commyng caused
hyme to be brought [f. 45] vnto his beddes side/ And he beyng
there shewed that the kynges pleasure was that he shold
incontynent (accompaned w^t thother Cardynall) repayer vnto
the quene at Bridwell in to hir chamber/ to perswade hir by ther
wysdomes Advysyng hir to surrender the hole matter in to the
kynges handes by hir owen wyll & consent w^{che} shold be myche
better to hyr honor/ than to stand to the triall of the lawe/ and to
be condempned w^{che} shold be myche to hir slaunder & de-
famacion/ To fullfyll the kynges pleasure/ q^d my lord he was
redy and wold prepare hyme to goo thether owt of hand/ sayeng
further to my lord of wyltshere/ ye and other of my lordes of the
Councell w^{che} be nere vnto the kyng/ are not a littill to blame &
mysadvysed to put any suche ffantazis in to his hed wherby ye
are the causers of great troble to all this realme/ And at lengthe
gett you but small thankes owther of god or of the world/ w^t
many other vehemet wordes & sentences that was lyke to ensewe
of thys matter/ w^{che} wordes caused my lord of wyltshere to
water his eyes knelyng all this while bye my lordes beddes syde
and in conclusion departed/ And than my lord Roose vppe &
made hyme redy takyng his barge And went strayt to bathe
place to the other Cardynall And so went to gether vnto
Bridwell/ dyrectly to the quenes lodgyng/ And they beyng in
hir Chamber of presence/ shewed to the gentilman vssher that
they came to speke w^t the quenes grace/ the gentilman vssher
Aduertised the quene ther of/ Incontynent w^t that she came
owt of hir privye Chamber w^t a skayn of whight thred abought
hir neke in to the chamber of presence/ where the Cardynalles
ware gevyng of attendaunce vppon hir Commyng/ At whos
commyng/ q^d she/ Alake my lordes I ame sory to cause you to
attend vppon me/ what is yor pleasure w^t me/ if it please you/
q^d my lord Cardynall/ to goo in to yor chamber/ we woll shewe

1 ffor *canc. before* ffully   7 vnto *canc. before* in; in to *interl.*; hir
chamber] r *of* hir *written over* s   8 to *canc. after* hir   15–16 mysadvy
canc. after &   18 ne *canc. before* or; or *interl.*   22 Roose *canc.
before* Roose   28 of/ Incontynent] *MS.* of Incontynent   33 me/
what] *MS.* me what   34 cause you *canc. before* shewe

you the cause of our Commyng/ my lord/ q^d she/ Yf ye haue any thyng to say speke it opynly byfore all thes folkes ffor I feare no thyng that ye can sey or allege ayenst me/ but that I wold all the world shold bothe here & se it/ therfor I pray you
5 speke yor mynd opynly/ Than began my lord to speake/ to hir in latten// Nay good my lord/ q^d she/ speke to me in Englysshe I beseche you/ allthoughe I vnderstand latten/ ffor sothe than/ q^d my lord/ Madame if it please yor grace we come bothe to [f. 45^v] knowe yor mynd howe ye be disposed to do in thys
10 matter bytwen the kyng & you and also to declare secretly our oppynyons & our Councell vnto w^{che} we haue entendyd of very zele/ and obedyence that we beare to yor grace/ My lordes I thanke you than q^d she/ of yor good wylles/ but to make answare to yor request/ I cannot so sodenly for I was sett among
15 my maydens at worke thynkyng full littill of any suche matter/ wherin there nedyth a lenger deliberacion and a better hed than myn to make answere to so noble wyse men as ye be/ I had nede of good Councell in this case w^{che} touchethe me so nere/ And for any Councell or frendshype that I can fynd in England are
20 nothyng to my purpose or profette/ thynke you (I pray you my lordes) wyll any Englishe man councell or be frendly vnto me ayenst the kynges pleasure they beyng his subiectes (nay for sothe my lordes)/ And for my councell in whome I do entend to put my trust be not here/ they be in Spayn in my natife
25 Countrie/ Alas my lordes I ame a poore woman lakkyng bothe wytt & vnderstandyng sufficyently to answere suche approved wyse men as ye be bothe in so waytie a matter/ I pray you to extend yor good & indifferent myndes in yor auctorytie/ vnto me for I ame a symple woman destitut & barrayn of frendshype and
30 Councell here in a forreyn Region/ And as for yor Councell I woll not refuse but be glad to here/ And w^t that she toke my lord by the hand and led hyme in to hyr privye chamber w^t thother Cardynall/ where they ware in long Commynycacion/ we in the other Chamber myght some tyme here the quene speke

6 q^d she] *MS.* q^d/ she   7 latten/ ffor] *MS.* latten ffor   12 u *canc. after* yor 13 to *interl.*   16 n *canc. before* nedyth
20 to my *interl.*; my lordes *canc. before* (I   20–21 my lordes *interl.*
23 to *canc. before* in; in *interl.*   25 Countrie/ Alas] *MS.* Countrie Alas
27 ye *interl.*   28 me *interl.*   29 a *interl.*   30 as *interl.*
31 here/ And] *MS.* here And

Life of Cardinal Wolsey

very lowde but what it was we could not vnderstand/ Ther
Commynycacion endyd the Cardynalles departed and went
directly to the kyng makyng to hyme relacion of ther talke w^t
the quene/ And after resortyd home to ther howsses to supper//
Thus went thys straynge Case forward frome Court day to
Court day/ vntill it came to Iugeme^t/ So that euery man expected
the Iugeme^t to be gevyn vppon the case at the next Court day/
At w^{che} day the kyng came thether and sat w^t in a gallery ayenst
the doore of the same that loked vnto the Iuges where they satt
whome he myght se & here speke/ to here what Iugement they
woold geve/ in his sewte/ At w^{che} tyme all ther procedynges ware
first opynly red in latten/ And that don the kynges learned
Councell [f. 46] At the barre called fast for Iugeme^t/ w^t that q^d
the Cardynall Campagious I wyll geve no Iugement herin vntill
I haue made relacion vnto the Pope of all our procedynges/
whos Councell & commaundeme^t in thys highe case I wyll
obserue/ the case is to hyghe (& notable knowen thoroughe all
the world) for vs to geve any hasty Iugeme^t/ consideryng the
highenes of the persons and the doughtfull allegacions/ And
also whos Commyssioners we be/ vnder whos auctorytie we sitt
here/ yt ware therfore reason that we shold make our cheafe hed
a councell in the same byfore we procede in to Iugeme^t defyny-
tyfe/ I come not so ferre to please any man for ffere, mede, or
fauour/ be he kyng or any other potentate/ I haue no suche
respect to the persons that I woll offend my consience/ I woll
not for fauour or displeasure of any highe estat or myghty prynce/
do that thyng that shold be ayenst the lawe of god/ I ame an old
man bothe syke & Impotent lokyng dayly for deathe/ what shold
it than avaylle me to put my sowlle in the daynger of goddes
displeasure to my vtter dampnacion for the fauour of any prynce
or hyghe estate in this world/ my commyng & beyng here is
oonly to se Iustice mynystred accordyng to my Concyence/ As
I thoughte therby the matter other good or bade/ And for as
myche as I do vnderstand and hauyng perceueraunce/ by the

7 Court] t *written over* d   15 of *canc. before* vnto   17 case
interl. thought thoroughly// *canc. before* knowen   22 defyn-
ytyve *canc. before* defynytyfe   26 prynce] y *written over* ei   31 world/
my] *MS.* world my   32 if *canc. before* As; As *interl.*   33 &
canc. after good

allegacions And negacions in this matter layed for bothe the parties that the truthe in this Case is very doughtfull to be knowen/ and also that the partye defendaunt woll make no answere ther vnto/ dothe rather Appell frome vs supposyng that
5 we be not Indifferent/ consideryng the kynges highe dignytie And Auctorytie w^t in thys his owen realme/ w^{che} he hathe ouer hys owen subiectes And we beyng his subiectes and hauyng our lyvynges & dignytes in the same/ she thynkythe that we cannot mynester true & Indifferent Iustice for feare of his displeasure/
10 Therfore to avoyd all thes Ambyguytes and obscure doughtes I entend not to dampne my sowle for no prynce or potentate alyfe/ I wold therfore (god wyllyng) wade no further in this matter onles I haue the Iust oppynyon & Iugement w^t the assent of the Pope/ And suche other of his councell as hathe
15 more experyence And better learnyng in suche doughtfull lawes than I haue/ [f. 46^v] Wherfore I woll adiourne this Court for this tyme accordyng to the order of the Court in Rome frome whence this Court & Iurisdiccon is derevyed/ And if we shold goo further than our commyssion dothe warraunt vs it ware folly
20 & vayn And myche to our slaunder & blames and myght be for the same accompted brekers of the orders of the hygher Court frome whence we haue (as I sayd) our orygynall Auctorytes/ w^t that the Court was desolued/ And no more plee holden/ **w^t that/** stept forthe the Duke of Suffolk frome the kyng And by his
25 commaundeme^t spake thes wordes w^t a stought & hault countenaunce/ Yt was neuer (q^d he) mery in Englond whilest we had Cardynalles among vs w^{che} wordes ware setforthe w^t suche a vehement Countenaunce that all men marvelled what he entendyd/ to whome no man made Answere/ The Duke
30 agayn spake thos wordes in great dispight/ to the w^{che} wordes my lord Cardynall (perceyvyng his vehemency) soberly made answere And sayd Sir of all men w^{t}in this Realme ye haue lest cause to disprase or be offendyd w^t Cardynalles/ ffor if I symple Cardynall had not byn/ ye shold haue had at this present no hed
35 vppon yor sholders wherin ye shold haue a tong to make any suche report in dispight of vs who entendyd you no maner of

[3 the *interl*.   8 lyvynges] v *written over* u   23 hild *canc.*
after more; plee holden] *MS.* plee/ holden; holden *interl.*   25 & *interl.*
31 es *canc. after* lord

Life of Cardinal Wolsey 91

displeasure nor we haue geven you any occasion w^t suche dispight to be revenged w^t yor hault wordes/ I wold ye knewe it my lord that I and my brother here entendyd the kyng and his realme as myche honour welthe & quyotnes as ye or any other of what estat or degree so euer he be w^t in this realme/ And wold as gladly accomplysshe his lawfull desier As the poorest subiect he hathe// But my lord I pray shewe me/ what wold ye do if ye ware the kynges Commyssioner in a fforrayn Region/ hauyng a waytie matter to treate vppon And the conclusion beyng doughtfull therof wold ye not Aduertise the kynges ma^{tie} or euer ye went thoroughe w^t the same/ yes, yes, my lord I dought not/ Therfor I wold ye shold banysshe yor hastie malice & dispight owt of yor hart/ And consider that we be but commyssioners for a tyme/ And can ne may not bye vertue of our commyssion procede to Iugeme^t w^{t}out the knowlege & concent of the chefe hed of our auctoritie/ [f. 47] & havyng his concent to the same w^{che} is the pope/ therfore we do no lesse ne other wyse than our warraunt wyll beare vs/ And if any man wyll be offendyd w^t vs therfor he is an vnwyse man/ wherfore my lord hold yor peace/ and pacefie yor self and frame yor tong lyke a man of honour & of wysdome/ And not to speke so quykly or so reprochefully by yor frendes ffor ye knowe best what frendshype ye haue receyved at my handes/ the w^{che} yet I neuer reveled to no person alyve byfore nowe/ nowther to my glory ne to yor dishonour/ And therw^t the Duke gave ouer the matter w^{t}out any wordes to replie and so departed and folowed after the kyng w^{che} was goon In to Bridwell at the begynnyng of the Dukes first wordes//

Thys matter contynued long thus/ And my lord Cardynall was in displeasure w^t the kyng for that the matter in his sewte toke no better Successe/ the fault wherof was ascribed myche to my lord/ notw^{t}standyng my lord excused hyme allwayes by his Commyssion w^{che} gave hyme no fferther auctoryte to proced in Iugeme^t w^{t}out knowlege of the pope/ who reserued the same to

---

3 nor *canc. after* I; and *interl. after* I; & *canc. before* the *canc. before* other   5 estat or *interl.*   9 And *interl. after* not   12 b *canc. before* ye *and* you *before* yor therfore] *MS.* pope therfore; lesse *canc. before* lesse *canc. before* at   31 as *canc. before* was

4 other 10 be *canc.* 17 pope/ 27 at the by

hyme self/ At the last they ware aduertised by ther post that the pope wold take delyberacion in respeyght of Iugeme^t/ vntill his Courtes ware opyned/ w^{che} shold not be a fore Bartholmewetyd next/ The kyng consideryng the tyme to be very long or the matter shold be determyned thought it good to send an newe ambassett to the pope to perswade hyme to shewe suche honorable favoure vnto his grace that the matter myght be soner endyd than it was lykly to be/ or elles at the next Court in Rome to ruell the matter ouer accordyng to the kynges request/ To this ambassett was appoynted Doctor Stephyns than Secretory that after was made Bysshope of wynchester/ who went thether and there taried vntill the latter end of Sommer/ as ye shall here after/ The kyng commaundyd the Quene to be removed owt of the Court And sent vnto an other place/ and his hyghnes roode in his progresse w^t Mrs Anne Boleyn in his company all the grece season/ Yt was so that the Cardynall Campagious made Sewte to be discharged that he [f. 47^v] myght retourne agayn to Rome/ And yt chaunced that the Secretory w^{che} was the kynges Ambassitor to the Pope was retorned frome Rome/ wheruppon it was determyned that the Cardynall Campagious shold resort to the kyng at Grafton in Northamton shere and that my lord Cardynall shold accompanye hyme thether/ where Campagious shold take hys leave of the kyng/ And so they toke ther Iourney thether ward frome the More and came to Grafton vppon the Sonday in the mornyng/ byfore whos commyng ther rose in the Court dyuers oppynyons that the kyng wold not speke w^t my lord Cardynall and ther vppon ware layed many great wagers/ Thes ij prelattes beyng come to the Gattes of the Court where they alyghted frome ther horssys/ Supposyng that they shold haue byn receyved by the hed officers of the howsse (as they ware wont to be) yet for as myche as Cardynall Campagious was but a straynger in effect/ the seyd Officers receyved them and conveyed hyme to a lodgyng w^{t}in the Court w^{che} was prepared for hyme oonly/ And after my lord had brought hyme thus to his lodgyng/ he left hyme ther & departed supposyng to haue

4 next/ The] *MS.* next The   5 be *canc. after* shold   6 to shewe *canc. after* hyme   13 after/ The] *MS.* after The   15 M^{rs}] *MS.* M^r 17 be d *canc. before* be; be *interl.*   21 the *canc. after* that   26 not *interl.*   30 offic *canc. before* hed

Life of Cardinal Wolsey 93

goon directly lyke wyse to his Chamber (as he was accustumed
to do) and by the way as he was goyng it was told hyme that he
had no lodgyng appoynted for hyme in the Court and beyng ther
w^t astonyed/ Sir herre Norreys grome of the stole w^t the kyng
came vnto hyme (but wether it was by the kynges commaunde- 5
me^t or no I knowe not) and most humbly offered hyme hys
Chamber for the tyme vntill an other myght some where be
provyded for hyme/ ffor sir I assure you (q^d he) here is very
littill Rome in this howsse skantly sufficient for the kyng/ therfor
I beseche yor grace to accept myn for the season/ whome my 10
lord thanked for his gentill offer/ And went strayt to his
chamber/ where as my lord shyfted his ridyng apparell/ And
beyng thus in this Chamber/ dyuers noble persons & gentilmen
beyng his lovyng ffrendes came to visit hyme and to wellcome
hyme to the Court/ by whome my hed was aduertised of all 15
thynges touchyng the kynges displeasure towardes hyme w^{che}
dyd hyme no small pleasure/ & caused hyme to be the more
redyly provyded of sufficyent excusys for his defence/ Than was
my lord aduertysed by Mr Norres that he shold [f. 48] prepare
hyme self to geve attendaunce in the Chamber of presence ayenst 20
the kynges commyng thether/ who was disposed there to talke
w^t hyme and w^t the other Cardynall/ who came to my lordes
Chamber and they to gether went in to the seyd Chamber of
presence where the lordes of the Councell stode in a Rowe/ in
order a long the Chamber/ my lord puttyng of his Cappe to 25
euery of theme most gently/ And so did they no lesse to hyme/
at w^{che} tyme the Chamber was so ffurnysshed w^t noble men,
gentilmen, and other worthy persons that oonly expected the
meatyng & the countenaunce of the kyng & hyme/ & what
entertaynme^t the kyng made hyme/ Than Immedyatly after 30
came the kyng in to the Chamber/ and standyng there vnder the
Clothe of estate/ my lord kneled down byfore hyme who toke
my lord by the hand (and so he dyd the other Cardynall) than he

4 grome *canc. after* Norreys   6 or no *interl.*   9 littill *canc.*
before littill; littill *interl.*; sufficyently *canc. before* sufficient   13 of
canc. after dyuers   16 touchyng] *MS.* touchyng*es*   17 riply
canc. before the   17–18 the more redyly *interl.*   18 excusys] *final* s
written over d   19 he *interl.*   22 the other Cardynall ca *canc.*
before who   29 at the meatyng *canc. before* & what   32 me *canc.*
after who; toke *interl.*   33 toke *canc. before* by

toke my lord vppe by bothe Armez & caused hyme to stand vppe/ whome the kyng receyved w^t as amyable a chere as euer he dyd/ & called hyme a side and led hyme by the hand to a great wyndowe where he talked w^t hyme And caused hyme to
5 be Couered/ Than to behold the countenaunce of thos that had made ther wagers to the contrarye/ yt wold haue made you to smyle and thus ware they all dyssayved (as well worthy for ther presumpcyon) the kyng was in long and ernest commynycacion w^t hyme In so myche as I hard the kyng say/ howe can that be/
10 is not this yor owen hand/ and plukked owt frome hys bosome a letter or writyng and shewed hyme the same/ and as I perceyved that it was answerd so by my lord that the kyng had no more to say/ in that matter but sayd to hyme/ my lord goo to yor dynner and all my lordes here wyll kepe you company/ And after dynner
15 I wyll resort to you agayn/ and than we woll commen further w^t you in this matter/ and so departed/ the kyng dynned that same day w^t m^rs Anne Boleyn in hir chamber (who kept there an estate more lyke a quen than a symple mayd) than was a table sett vppe in the chamber of presence for my lord & other lordes
20 of the Councell where they all dyned together/ and sittyng thus at dynner commenyng of dyuers [f. 48^v] matters/ q^d my lord/ it ware well don if the kyng wold send his chaplayns and bysshoppes to ther Cures and benyfices/ yea mary q^d my lord of Norffolk/ ye say very well/ And so it ware for you to/ I cowld be contentyd
25 therw^t very well/ q^d my lord/ if it ware the kynges pleasure to graunt me lycence w^t his fauour to goo to my benefice of Wynchester/ Nay q^d my lord of Norffolk/ to yor benefice of yorke where consistithe your greattest honour and charge/ Evyn as it shall please the kyng/ q^d my lord/ and so fill in to other
30 commynycacion/ ffor the lordes ware very lothe to haue hyme planted so nyghe the kyng as to be at wynchester/ Immedyatly after dynner they fill in secrett talke vntill the wayters had dynned/ And as I hard it reported by them that waytedd vppon the kyng at dynner that Mrs Anne Bolleyn was myche offendyd

2 kyng receyved w^t] *MS.* kyng w^t; as *interl. before* amyable   3 & *interl.*   7 specyally thos *canc. before* thus; all *interl.*   13 in that matter *interl.*; hyme/ my] *MS.* hyme my   17 (wh *canc. after* chamber   18 lyke *canc. before* more   23 C. *canc. after* ther   31 ph *canc. before* planted

w^t the kyng/ as ferre as she durst/ that he so gentilly entertayned
my lord/ sayeng as she satt w^t the kyng at dynner in commynycacion of hyme/ Sir/ q^d she/ is it not a marvelous thyng to
consider what debt & daynger the Cardynall hathe brought you
in w^t all yor subiectes/ howe so swett hart/ q^d the kyng/ ffor sothe/ 5
sir/ q^d she/ there is not a man w^t in all yor realme worthe .v^{li}
but he hathe endettyd you vnto hyme by hys means (meanyng
by a lone that the kyng had but late of hys subiectes) well, well,
q^d the kyng/ as for that ther is in hyme no blame/ ffor I knowe
that matter better than you or any other/ Nay sir/ q^d she/ besides 10
all that what thynges hathe he wrought w^{t}in this realme to yor
great slaunder & dishonor/ there is neuer an noble man w^t in
this realme that if he had don but half so myche as he hathe don
but he ware well worthy to lease his hed/ Yf my lord of Norffolk/
my lord of Suffolk/ my lord my father/ or any other noble person 15
w^t in yor realme had don myche lesse than he but they shold haue
lost ther hedes or thys/ whye than I perceyve/ q^d the kyng ye are
not the Cardynalles frend/ fforsothe sir than/ q^d she/ I haue no
cause nor any other man that lovythe yor grace/ no more haue
yor grace if ye consider well his doynges// at thys tyme the 20
wayters had taken vppe the table And so they endyd ther
commynycacion

Nowe ye may perceyve the old malice begynnyth to breake
owt and newely to kyndell the brand that after proved to a great
ffier/ w^{che} was as myche procured by his secrett ennemyes 25
(touched some thyng byfore) as of hir self/ After all this commynycacion the dynner thus endyd/ the kyng Rose vppe & went
Incontynent in to the Chamber of presence where as my lord
& other of the lordes ware attendyng his commyng/ to whome
he called my lord/ in to the great [f. 49] wyndowe/ and talked 30
w^t hyme there a while very secretly/ And at the last the kyng
toke my lord by the hand and led hyme in to his privye Chamber
syttyng there in Consultacion w^t hyme all a lone/ w^{t}out any other
of the lordes of the Councell vntill it was nyght/ the w^{che} blanked
hys ennemyes very sore/ And made them to stere the Coles 35

2 they fill *canc. before* in 4 brought you *interl.* 5 yor
subiectes/] *MS.* yor/ subiectes *with* subiectes *interl.* 20 be *canc. before*
at; at *interl.* 21 taken *interl.*; dynned *canc. after* taken 29 sat at
dynner *canc. before* ware 30 vnto hyme *canc. after* lord

beyng in dowght what this matter wold growe onto/ havyng
nowe non other refuge to trust to/ but to Mrs Anne in whome
was all ther hole & firme trust/ and affiaunce/ w^{t}out whome they
doughted all ther enterprice but frustrate & voyde/ Nowe/ was
I fayn beyng warned that my lord had no lodgyng in the Court/
to ride in to the contrie to provyde for my lord a lodgyng/ So
that I provyded a lodgyng for hyme at an howsse of m^r Empsons
Called Eston iij^{re} myles frome Grafton/ whether my lord came
by torche lyght/ it was so late or the kyng & he departyd at whos
departyng the kyng commaundyd hyme to resort agayn erley
in the mornyng to thentent they myght fynysshe ther talke w^{che}
they had than begon & not concludyd/ After ther departyng my
lord cam to the seyd howsse at Eston to his lodgyng/ where he
had to supper w^t hyme dyuers of his ffrendes of the Court/ And
syttyng at Supper in came to hyme Doctor Stephyns the
Secretory late Ambassiter vnto Rome (but to what entent he
came I knowe not) howebeit my lord toke it that he came bothe
to dissembell a certyn obedyence & love towardes hyme or elles
to espie hys behauor and to here his Commynycacion at Supper/
Not w^{t}standyng my lord bad hyme wellcome/ And commaundyd
hyme to sytt down at the table to supper/ w^t whome my lord had
thys commynycacion w^t hyme vnder thys maner/ Mr Secretory
q^d my lord ye be welcome home owt of Itally whan came ye
frome Rome/ fforsothe/ q^d he/ I came home allmost a monethe
agoo/ and where/ q^d my lord/ hathe ye byn euer sence/ fforsothe/
q^d he/ folowyng the Court this progresse/ Than haue ye hunted
& had good game/ & pastyme/ fforsothe sir/ q^d he/ and so I haue/
I thanke the kynges ma^{tie}// what good greyhoundes haue ye q^d
my lord/ I haue some sir/ q^d he/ And thus in huntyng & lyke
[f. 49^v] disportes passed they all ther commynycacion at Supper/
And after Supper my lord and he talked Secretly together vntill
it was mydnyght or they departed/ The next mornyng my lord
Rose earely And rode strayt to the Court At whos commyng the
kyng was redy to ride wyllyng my lord to resort to the councell
w^t the lordes in his absence And seyd he cowld not tary w^t hyme

2 trust to *canc. before* but   5 to *canc. before* beyng   7 howsse *canc. after* an   8 as *canc. before* my   18 an *canc. before* a; hyme *interl.*   25 agoo/ and] *MS.* agoo and   29 in *canc. after* & 34 to *canc. after* resort; to *interl. before* the

Life of Cardinal Wolsey 97

commaundyng hyme to retorne w^t Cardynall Campagious who
hade taken hys leave of the kyng/ where vppon my lord was
constrayned to take hys leave also of the kyng/ w^t whome the
kyng departyd amyably in the syght of all men/ the kynges
soden departyng in the mornyng was bye the specyall labor of
m^{rs} Anne/ who rode w^t hyme oonly to leade hyme abought
bycause he shold not retorne vntill the Cardynalles ware goon
the w^{che} departyd after dynner retornyng agayn towardes the
more/ the kyng Rode that mornyng to vewe a ground for a
newe parke w^{che} is calld at thys day hartwell parke where m^{rs}
Anne had made provysion for the kynges dynner fearyng his
retorne or the Cardynalles ware goon/ Than rode my lord &
thother Cardynall after dynner on ther way homward/ And so
came to the monastory of Seynt Albons/ wherof he hyme self
was Commendatory/ And there lay oon hole day/ And the next
day they rode to the More/ And frome thence the Cardynall
Campagious toke his Iourney towardes Rome w^t the kynges
reward (what it was I ame incerteyn)/ Neuerthelesse after his
departure the kyng was enformed that he Caried w^t hyme great
treasures of my lordes conveyed in great Tonnes notable
Sommes of gold & syluer to Rome/ whether they Surmysed my
lord wold secretly convey hyme self owt of thys realme// In so
myche that a post was sent spedely after the Cardynall to serche
hyme/ whome they ouertoke at Calice/ where he was stayed
vntill serche was made/ there was not so myche mony found as
he receyved of the kynges reward/ And so he was dismyssed
And went his way [f. 50]

After cardynall/ Campagious was thus departed And goon/
Mihelmas terme drewe nere Ayenst the w^{che} my lord retourned
vnto hys howsse at Westminster And whan the terme began he
went to the hall in suche lyke sort and Iesture As he was wont
most comenly to do/ And sat in the Chauncery beyng chaun-
celour/ After w^{che} day he neuer sat there more/ the next day he
taried at home expectyng the commyng of the ij Dukes of

---

2 where *interl.*   10 parke *canc. after* newe; day] *MS.* day (; harwell
parke *canc. before* hartwell parke   13 w *canc. before* homward
14 the *canc. before* to   19 had *canc. before* Caried   22 of thys
canc. before realme   32 to do *canc. before* most   32–33 chauncelour/
After] *MS.* chauncelour After   34 of *interl. after* Dukes

Suffolk & Norffolk w^{che} came not that day/ but the next day they Came vnto hyme to whome they declared/ how the kynges pleasure was that he shold surrender and delyuer vppe the great Seale in to ther handes And to depart symplely vnto Assher
5 an howsse (cytuat nyghe hampton Court) belongyng to the bysshope of wynchester/ my lord vnderstandyng ther messwage demaundyd of them what commyssion they haue to geve hyme any suche commaundeme^t who answered hyme agayn/ that they ware sufficyent commyssioners in that behalf hauyng the kynges
10 commaundeme^t by his mouthe so to do/ yet/ q^d he/ that is not sufficyent for me/ w^tout a ferther commaundeme^t of the kynges pleasure/ for the great seale of Englond was delyuerd me by the kynges owen person to enioy dewryng my lyfe w^t the mynystracion of the office & highe Roome of Chauncellershype of
15 England ffor my sewertie wherof/ I haue the kynges letters patentes to shewe/ w^{che} matter was greatly debated bytwen the Dukes & hyme/ w^t many stowt wordes bytwen them/ whos wordes & chekkes he toke in pacience for the tyme/ In so myche that the Dukes ware fayn to departe agayn w^tout ther purpose
20 at that present And retorned agayn vnto wyndesore to the kyng/ And what report they made I cannot tell howbeit the next day they came agayn frome the kyng bryngyng w^t theme the kynges letters/ After the receypte & redyng of the same/ by my lord w^{che} was don w^t myche reuerence/ he delyuerd vnto them the
25 great Sealle/ contentyd to obey the kynges highe commaundeme^t/ And seyng that the kynges pleasure was to take hys howsse w^t the contentes/ was well pleased symplely to depart to Assher takyng no thyng but only some provysion for his howsse/ And after long talke bytwen the Dukes & hyme/ they departed w^t
30 the great Seale/ of Englond to wyndesore vnto the kyng/
[f. 50^v] Than went my lord and Called all officers in euery office in his howsse byfore hyme to take accompte of all suche stuffe as they had in charge/ And in his Gallery there was sett dyuers tables where vppon a great nomber of Riche stuffe of sylke in

8 or *canc. before* who 9 fo *canc. after* commyssioners 10 commaundeme^t] t *frayed away at edge of page* 11 by *canc. before* of; of *interl.* 15 my *interl.* 18 toke *canc. before* toke 28 only *interl. and canc. after* but; oon *canc. before* only; only *interl.* 31 Tha *canc. before* Than 32 take *interl.*

hole peces of all Colours/ as veluett/ Satten/ Damaske/ Caffa/ Taffata/ Grograyn/ Sarcenet/ And of other not in my remembraunce/ Also there lay a M¹ peces of fynne holand Clothe/ wherof as I hard hyme say after ward ther was V^{Cth} peces therof conveyed bothe frome the kyng & hyme/ ffurthermore ther was also the walles of the gallery hanged w^t clothes of gold & tissue of dyuers makynges and clothe of syluer in lykewyse/ on bothe the sydes and riche clothes of Baudkyn of dyuers Colours/ ther hong also the richest Sewtes of Coopes of his owen provysion w^{che} he caused to be made for his Colleges of Oxford & Ipsew^{che}/ that euer I sawe in Englond/ Than had he in ij Chambers adioynyng to the Gallery/ thoon called the gylt Chamber/ and thother called most Comenly the Councell chamber/ wherin ware sett in eche ij brode & long tables vppon trestelles where vppon was sett suche a nomber of plate of all sortes/ as ware all most Incredyble/ In the gylt Chamber was sett owt vppon the tables nothyng but all gylt plate/ And vppon a Cupbord standyng vnder a wyndowe/ was garnysshed all holy w^t plate of cleane gold wherof Somme was sett w^t peerle & riche stones/ And in the Councell chamber was sett all wyght plate & parcell gylt/ And vnder the tables in bothe the Chambers ware sett baskettes w^t old plate w^{che} was not estemed but for broken plate & old not worthy to be occupied/ And bokes conteynyng the valewe & wayte of euery parcell layed by them/ redy to be sen/ And so was also bokes sett by all maner of Stuffe conteynyng the contentes of euery thynge/ Thus euery thyng beyng brought in good order & furnysshed he gave the charge of the delyuere therof (vnto the kyng) to euery officer w^t in his office/ of suche stuffe as they had byfore in charge/ by Indenture/ of euery parcell/ ffor the order of his howsse was suche as that euery Officer was charged by Indenture w^t all suche parcelles as belonged to ther office
[f. 51]
Than all thyng/ beyng ordered as it is byfore rehersed my lord prepared hyme to depart by water/ And byfore his departyng

1 Colours] *MS.* Colourrs   5 hyme/ ffurthermore] *MS.* hyme ffurthermore   11 sawe *canc. before* sawe   14 sir *canc. before* was
18 all *interl. and canc. before* w^t   23 conteyned *canc. before* conteynyng; conteynyng] *MS.* conteyng   26 thynge] g *written over* k; beyng *interl.*
31 of *canc. before* w^t; w^t *interl.*

he commaundyd sir w^m Gascoyn his treasorer to se thos thynges byfore remembred delyuerd savely to the kyng at his repayer/ that don the seyd sir willam seyd vnto my lord/ Sir I ame sory for yor grace/ for I vnderstand ye shall goo strayt way to the tower// Ys this the good Comfort and councell q^d my lord/ that ye can geve yor m^r in aduersitie/ yt hathe byn allwayes yor naturall Inclynacion to be very light of Credytt and myche more lighter in reportyng of falce newes/ I wold ye shold knowe sir w^m and all other suche blasfemers that it is no thyng more falce than that/ ffor I neuer (thankes be to god) deserued by no wayes to come there/ vnder any arrest/ allthoughe it hathe pleased the kyng to take my howse redy furnysshed for his pleasure at this tyme/ I wold all the world knewe and so I confesse to haue no thyng other riches, honour, or dignyty that hathe not growen of hyme & by hyme therfore it is my very dewtie to surrender the same to hyme agayn as his very owen w^t all my hart/ or elles I ware an onkynd seruaunt/ therfore goo yor wayes & geve good attendaunce vnto your charge that no thyng be embeselled/ And therw^tall he made hyme redy to departe w^t all his gentilmen & yomen w^{che} was no small nombre/ And toke his barge at his privye stayers And so went by water vnto Putney where all his horsys wayted his Commyng/ And at the takyng of his barge ther was no lesse than a M^l bottes full of men & women of the Citie of london waffetyng vppe & down in temmes expectyng my lordes departyng/ supposyng that he shold haue goon directly frome thence to the tower/ where at they reioysed/ And I dare be bold to sey that the most part neuer receyved dammage at his handes// **O waueryng**/ and newfangled multitude ys it not a wonder to consider the inconstant mutabilitie/ of thys oncertyn world/ the comen peple allwayes desireng alteracions & newelties of thynges for the strayngenes of the case/ [f. 51^v] w^{che} after tournyth them to small profett & commodytie/ ffor if the sequell of this matter be well considered & digested ye shall vnderstand that they had small cause to tryhumphe at his fall/ what hathe

1 take *canc. after* to   4 ye shall shall *canc. before* ye   5 ye can *canc. before* q^d   8 of *canc. before* in   10 by *interl.*   13 tha *canc. before* and *and* me *before* to   15 is *interl.*   17 an *interl.* 18 therw^t *canc. after* And   19 the *canc. after* all; his *interl.*   22 at *interl.*   29 se the *canc. before* consider   30 comen] *MS.* coen; desireng] *MS.* desirenges   31 for *canc. before* of thynges

succedyd all wyse men dothe knowe/ And the Comen sort of them hathe felt/ Therfore to grudge or wonder at it/ suerly ware but folly/ To study a redresse/ I se not howe it can be holpen/ ffor the Inclynacion and the naturall disposicion of Englisshemen/ is & hathe allways ben to desier alteracion of officers w^{che} hathe byn thorougly fed w^t long contynuaunce in ther romes/ w^t sufficyent riches & possessions/ And they beyng putt owt/ than commythe an other hongery and a leane officer in his place that byttythe nerer the bone than the old/ So the pepill be euer pild & pold w^t hongery dogges/ thoroughe ther owen desier of chaynge of newe officers/ nature hathe so wrought in the people that it woll not be redressed/ wherfore I cannot se but allways men in auctorytie be disdayned w^t the comen sort of men/ And suche most of all/ that Iustly mynestrethe equytie to all men Indifferently/ ffor where they please some oon w^{che} receyveth the benefit of the lawe at his handes accordyng to Iustice/ there dothe they In lykewyse displease the contrary partie who supposith to sustayn great wrong/ where they haue equyte & right/ Thus all good Iusticers be allwayes in contempte w^t some/ for executyng of Indifferentcye/ and yet suche mynysters must be/ ffor if there shold be no mynysters of Iustice/ the world shold rone full of error and Abhomynacion and no good order kept ne quyotnes among the people/ there is no good man but he wyll commend suche Iusticers as dealyth vpp rightly in ther romes and reioyse at ther contynuaunce & not at ther fall/ And whether this be true or no/ I put me to the Iugeme^t of all discret persons// nowe lett vs leave & begyn agayn where we left//

Whan he was/ w^t all his trayn arryved & londed at Putnethe he toke his mewle and euery man his horsse/ And settyng forthe not past the lengthe of a payer of Garden buttes he aspied a man come ridyng empost down the hyll in Putnethe town/ demaundyng of his ffootmen who they thought it shold be/ And they answered agayn and sayd/ that they supposed it shold be sir herre Norres/ [f. 52] And by & by he came to my lord &

1 succedyd *canc. before* succedyd *and*/all *before* all; Comen] *MS*. Coen   5 & offices w^{che} hathe *canc. after* officers   6 lon *canc. after* long   8 an other *interl.*; offi *canc. before* and   9 So they .eu *canc. after* old/   13 comen] *MS*. coen   15 where *interl.*; there *interl. and canc. after* where   23 o *of* quyotnes *interl.*   24 righely *canc. before* rightly; rightly *interl.*   30 a pay *canc. before* the   32 shold *canc. before* shold   34 No *canc. before* Norres

salutyd hyme and sayd that the kynges ma^tie had hyme commendyd to his grace/ and willyd hyme in any wyse to be of good
chere/ for he was as myche in his highenes fauor as euer he was/
And so shalbe/ and in tokyn therof/ he delyuerd hyme a ryng of
gold w^t a riche stone w^che ryng he knewe very well for it was
allwayes the prevye tokyn bytwen the kyng & hyme whan so
euer the kyng wold haue any specyall matter dispatched At his
handes/ And seyd ferthermore that the kyng commaundyd hyme
to be of good chere & take no thought for he shold not lake/ And
allthoughe the kyng hathe delt w^t you onkyndly as ye supposse/
he saythe that it is for no displeasure that he beryth you/ but
oonly to sattysfie more the myndes of some (w^che he knowyth be
not yor frendes)/ than for any indygnacion/ And also ye knowe
right well that he is able to recompence you w^t twyse as myche
as yor goodes amountithe vnto/ and all this he bad me that I
shold shewe you/ therfore sir take pacience/ And for my part
I trust to se you in better estate than euer ye ware/ But whan he
hard m^r Norres reherce all the good & comfortable wordes of the
kyng/ he quykly lyghted frome hys mewle/ all alone as thoughe
he had byn the yongest person among vs/ And in contynent
kneled down in the dyrte/ vppon bothe his knes holdyng vppe
his handes for Ioye/ Mr Norres perceyvyng hyme so quykly
frome his mewle vppon the ground mused & was astoned
therw^t and therw^t he allyghted also and kneled by hyme enbracyng hyme in his armez & axed hyme howe he dyd callyng
vppon hyme to Credyt his messwage/ Mr Norres/ q^d he/ whan
I consider yor comfortable & Ioyfull newes I can do no lesse
than to reioyse/ ffor the sodden Ioy surmounted my memory
haueng no respect nowther to the place or tyme/ but thought it
my very bounden dewtie to render thankes to god my maker
and to the kyng my souerayn lord & m^r/ who hathe sent me
suche comfort/ in the very place where I receyved the same/ and
talkyng w^t m^r Norres vppon his knees in the myer/ he wold haue
pulled of his vnder Cappe of veluett but he cowld not [f. 52^v]

1 the] *MS.* the/; kynges had hyme to *canc. before* kynges   5 the *canc.
after* was   11 it *interl.*   16 you *interl.*   19 ri *canc.
after* quykly; horsse *canc. before* mewle   21 dust dirr *canc. before* dyrte
23 mys *canc. before* &   24 allyghted *canc. before* allyghted; allyghted
interl.   34 vnder *interl.*

vndo the knott vnder his chyne/ wherfore w^t violence/ he rent
the laces & pulled it frome his hed and so kneled barehedyd/
And that don he couered agayn his hed and aroose & wold haue
mounted his mewle but he cowld not mount agayn w^t suche
agilitie as he lighted byfore where his footmen had as myche a
do to sett hyme in his saddell as they could haue/ Than roode he
forthe vppe the hill in the town talkyng w^t m^r Norres/ And
whane he came vppon Putnethe hethe/ Mr Norres toke hys
leave & wold haue departed/ than/ q^d my lord/ vnto hyme/
Gentill Norres if I ware lord of a realme thoon half therof ware
insufficient a reward to geve you for yor paynnes and good
comfortable newes/ But good Mr Norres consider w^t me that
I haue no thyng left me but my clothes on my baccke/ therfore
I desier you to take this small reward of my handes (the w^che was
a littyll chayn of gold made lyke a bottell chayn) w^t a crosse of
gold hangyng there at/ wherin was a pece of the holy crosse
(w^che he ware contynually aboughte hys necke next his skyn) And
sayd further more/ I assure you m^r Norres/ that whan I was in
prosperytye/ allthoughe it seme but small in valewe/ yet I wold
not gladly haue departid w^t it for the valewe of a M^l li/ Therfore
I beseche you take it in gree and where it aboughte yor necke for
my sake/ And as often as ye shall happen to loke vppon it/ haue
me in remembraunce vnto the kynges ma^tie as opportunytie
shall serue you/ vnto whos highnes and Clemencye I desyer you
to haue me most lowely commendyd/ ffor whos Charitable
disposicion towardes me I can do no thyng but oonly mynyster
my prayer vnto god for the preseruacion of his Royall estate
long to reygn in honour helthe & quyot lyfe/ I ame hys obedyent,
subiect, vassayle, & poore chapleyn And so do entend (god
willyng) to be/ duryng my lyfe/ Accomptyng that of my selfe
I ame of no estymacion nor of no substaunce but oonly by hyme
& of hyme/ whome I love better than my self/ and hathe Iustly
& truly serued to the best of my grosse wytt/ And w^t that he toke
m^r Norres by the hand and bad hyme farewell/ And beyng not

2 bareheded *canc. before* barehedyd 5 & *canc. before* as he; byfore *interl.*;
had *canc. before* had   6 haue/ Than] *MS.* haue Than   13 bag
canc. before baccke   16 on *canc. before* there   20 haue *interl.*
21 in *interl.*   25 haue me most] *MS.* haue most   32 my *canc.*
after than   34 f. re *canc. after* not

104   Life of Cardinal Wolsey

goon but a small distaunce/ he retourned & called m^r Norres agayn/ And whan he was retorned (he sayd vnto hyme) I ame sory q^d he/ that I haue no condygn token to send to the kyng/ but if ye wold at this my request present the kyng w^t this poore
5 foole/ I trust hys hyghnes wold accept [f. 53] hyme well/ suerly for a noble mans pleasure he is worthe a M^l ^{li}/ so Mr Norres toke the ffoole w^t hyme/ w^t whome my lord was fayn to send vj of tall yomen w^t hyme to conduct & convey the foole to the Court/ ffor the poore foole toke on & fired so in suche a rage
10 whan he sawe that he must nedes departe frome my lord/ yet notw^tstandyng they conveyed hyme w^t m^r Norres to the Court where the kyng receyved hyme most gladly///
After the departure/ of Mr Norres w^t hys token to the kyng my lord Roode strayt to Assher an howsse appurteynyng vnto
15 the bysshopriche of wynchester/ Cituat w^t in the Countie of Surrey not ferre frome hampton Court/ where my lord and his ffamely contynued the space of iij^{re} or iiij^{or} wekes w^tout beddes/ shetes table clothes/ Cuppes/ and disshes to eate our meate/ or to lye in/ howbeit there was good provision of all kynd of
20 victualles and of drynk bothe bere & wyn wherof ther was sufficient & plentie// My lord was of necessite compelled to borowe of the bysshope of Carlylle and of sir Thomas Arundell bothe disshes to eate hys meate in And plate to drynke in and also lynnyn clothes/ to occupie/ And thus contynued he in thys
25 straynge estate vntill the feast of alhaloutyd was past/ **Yt chaunced** me vppon alhalou day in the mornyng to come there in to the great chamber to geve myn attendaunce where I found master Cromwell leanyng in the great wyndowe w^t a prymer in his hand sayeng of our lady mattens (w^{che} had byn
30 synce a very straynge syght) he prayed not more earnestly/ than the teares distilled frome his eyes/ whome I bad god morowe/ And w^t that I perceyved the teares vppon his chekes/ to whome I seyd/ wye m^r Cromwell what meanyth all this yor sorowe// ys

5 for *canc. before* suerly   6 noble] *MS.* noble noble; M^l ^{li}/ so] *MS.* M^l ^{li} so   8 w^t/ *canc. before* to the   9 & *canc. before* on   10 sh *canc. after* whan   15 bysshopriche of wynchester/] *MS.* bysshopriche/ of wynchester   18 Coppes *canc. before* Cuppes   21 compelled] *MS.* complled   24 lynen *canc. before* lynnyn; g *canc. after* lynnyn; he in *interl.*   25 hall all *canc. before* the   28 found *interl.*   31 I *interl.*   33 Cromwell] w *written over* ll

Life of Cardinal Wolsey 105

my lord in any daynger for whome ye lament thus/ or is it for
any losse that ye haue susteyned by any mysadventure/ Nay,
nay/ q^d he/ it is my onhappie Adventure/ w^{che} ame lyke to losse
all that I haue travelled for all the dayes of my lyfe for doyng of
my mayster trwe & [f. 53^v] dyligent seruyce/ why sir/ q^d I/ 5
I trust ye be to wyse to commyt any thyng by my lordes com-
maundeme^t other wyse than ye owght to do of right wherof ye
haue any cause to dought/ of losse of yor goodes/ well, well, q^d
he/ I cannot tell but all thynges (I se byfore myn eyes) is as it is
taken/ And thys I vnderstand right well/ that I ame in disdayn 10
w^t most men/ for my m^r sake and suerly w^{t}out Iust cause/ howbeit an yll name oons gotten wyll not lightly be put a way/ I
neuer had any promocyon by my lord to thencrease of my
lyvyng/ And thus myche wyll I say to you/ that I do entend (god
wyllyng) this after none whan my lord hathe dyned to ride to 15
london and so to the Court/ where I wyll other make or marre or
I come agayn/ I wyll put my self in the prese to se what any man
is Able to lay to my charge of ontrouthe or mysdemeanor/
Mary sir/ q^d I/ In so doyng/ in my conceyt ye shall do very well
& wysely (besechyng god to be yor gwyde & send you good luke) 20
evyn as I wold my self and w^t that I was called in to the Closett
to se & prepare all thyng redy for my lord/ who entendyd that
day to sey masse there hymeself And so I dyd/ And than my lord
came thether w^t his Chapleyn/ oon doctor Marshall sayeng first
his mattens & herd ij masses on his knees/ And than after he was 25
confessed he hyme self seyd masse/ And whan he had ffynesshed
masse & all his dyvyn seruyce/ retorned in to his chamber/ where
he dynned among dyuers of his doctors where as m^r Cromwell
dynned also/ And sittyng at dynner it chaunced that my lord
commendyd the true & faythfull seruyce of his gentilmen & 30
yomen wher vppon m^r Cromwell toke an occasion to say to my
lord that in concyence he owght to consider ther treuthe & loyall
seruyce/ that they dide hyme in this his present necessitie w^{che}
neuer forsakyth hyme in all his troble/ yt shall be well don

4 all *canc. before* all that   5 *a single indecipherable letter canc.*
after &   8 any *canc. after* dought/ of; well *canc. before first* well; *first* well,
interl.   18 able *canc. before* Able   19 Mary] r *written over* y; in
interl.   20) *canc. before* & send   26 self *interl.*   34 in *canc.*
before his

therfore sayd he/ for yor grace to caulle theme byfore you/ all thes yor most worthy gentilmen & right honest yomen/ And lett them vnderstand that ye right well consider ther pacience, treuthe & faythfulness/ and than geve them yor commendacion
5 w^t good wordes & thankes w^{che} shalbe to them great [f. 54] corage to sustayn yor myshape in pacient mysery And to spend ther lyfe And substaunce in yor seruyce/ Alas Thomas/ q^d my lord/ vnto hyme ye knowe I haue no thyng to geve theme/ And wordes w^tout deades be not often well taken ffor if I had as I
10 haue had of late/ I wold depart w^t them so ffrankly As they shold be well content but no thyng hathe no savour And I ame a shamed and also sory that I ame not able to requyte ther faythfull seruyce/ And allthoughe I haue cause to reioyse consyderyng the ffidelite that I perceyve in the nomber of my
15 seruauntes who wyll not departe frome me in my myserable estate but be as dyligent, obedyent And seruysable abought me as they ware in my great tryhumphant glorye yet do I lament agayn the want of substaunce/ to distribut among them/ why sir q^d m^r Cromwell/ haue ye not here a nomber of chapleyns to
20 whome ye haue departed very liberally w^t sperytuall promocions/ In so myche as Somme may dispend by yor graces preferment A M^l markes by the yere And Some .V.^{Cth} markes And some more and some lesse/ ye haue no oon chapleyn w^t in all yor howsse or belongyng vnto you but he may dispend at the
25 least well by yor procureme^t or preferment/ iij^C markes/ yerely who had all the profettes and avuntages at yor handes And thes yor seruauntes non at all And yet hathe yor poor seruauntes taken myche more payn for you in oon day than all yor Idell chapleyns hathe don in a yere/ therfore if they woll not freely and frankeley
30 consider yor liberalitie/ And depart w^t you of the same goodes gotten in yor seruyce/ nowe in yor great Indygence & necessitie/ it is pitie that they lyve/ And all the world woll haue them in Indignacion & hatred for ther abhomynable Ingratytude to ther m^r & lord/ I thynke no lesse/ Thomas/ q^d my lord/ wherfore

1 caulle *canc. before* caulle; all *interl*.   8 knowe *canc. before* knowe
13–14 consyderyng *interl*.   14 to consyder *canc. before* the ffidelite
22 C *canc. after* Some   26 the *interl*.; and avuntages *interl*.; and *canc. before* at.   27 non at all *interl*.   32 lyfe *canc. before* lyve   33 abhomynable] *MS.* abhomynablie

cause all my seruauntes to be callyd & to assemble w^tout in my great chamber After dynner and se them stand in order/ And I wyll declare vnto them my mynd accordyng to yoo^r advise/ After that the bordes end was taken vppe Mr Cromewell came to me & sayd/ hard ye not what my lord sayd evyn [f. 54^v] nowe/ yes sir/ q^d I/ that I dyd/ well than/ q^d he/ assemble all my lordes seruauntes vppe in to the great chamber/ And so I did and whan they ware all there assembled I assigned all the gentilmen to stand on the right side of the chamber/ And the yomen on the lyft side/ And at the last my lord came thether apparelled in a whyht rochett vppon a violett gown of clothe lyke a bysshope who went strayt in to the great wyndowe/ **Standyng there**/ a while and his chapleyns aboughte hyme beholdyng the nomber of his seruauntes devydyd in ij partes cowld not speke vnto them for tendernes of his hart the floode of teares that distilled frome his eyes declared no lesse/ the w^{che} perceyved by his seruauntes caused the fountayns of water to Gushe owt of ther faythefull hartes down ther chekes in suche aboundaunce/ as it wold cause a Cruell hart to lament/ at the last after he had torned his face to the wall & wyped his eyes w^t his hand kercheffe he spake to them after this sort in effect/// **Most**/ faythfull gentilmen/ and trewe hartyd yomen/ I do not oonly lament yor personal presence aboughte me/ but I do lament my necligent Ingratitude towardes you all/ on my behalf/ In whome hathe byn a great default that in my prosperytie hathe not don for you/ as I myght haue don other in word or deade w^{che} was than in my power to do/ But than I knewe not my Ioyelles & specyall treasures that I had of you (my faythfull seruauntes) in my howsse but nowe approved experience/ hathe taught me/ and w^t the eyes of my discression (w^{che} byfore ware hyd) do perceyve full well the same/ there was neuer thyng that repen-tythe me more that euer I dyd than dothe the remembraunce

3 accordyng *canc. before* accordyng   5 nowe *canc. after* evyn   8 whan *interl.*   10 ru *canc. before* yomen *and* on *before* on   14 demvydyd *canc. before* devydyd   15 cowld *canc. before* cowld   15–16 of *canc. before* of teares   18 *first* ther *and* faythefull *interl.*; faythe *canc. before* faythefull   19 lament/at] *MS.* lament at   21 in *canc. before* after; after *interl.*   22 lament *canc. before* oonly   24 who *canc. after* behalf/   25 not *interl.*   29 ap *of* approved *interl.*   30 byfore *canc. before* byfore   31 same/ there] *MS.* same there

of my oblyvyous necligence & ongentilnes that I haue
not promoted or preferred you to condygn Romes & prefermentes accordyng to yor demerites/ howebeit it is not onknowen
vnto you all that I was not so well furnysshed of temperall
5 avaunceme^{tes} as I was of sperytuall prefermentes/ And if I shold
haue promoted you to any of the kynges offices & Romes/ than
shold I haue encurred the Indignacion of the kynges seruauntes/
who wold not [f. 55] myche lett to report in euery place behynd
my bake that there cowld no office or rome of the kynges gyft
10 eskape the Cardynall & his seruauntes/ And thus shold I incurre
the obloquye & slaunder byfore all the hole world/ But nowe it
is come to this passe that it hathe pleased the kyng to take all
that euer I haue in to his possession/ So that I haue no thyng
laft me but my bare clothes vppon my bake the w^{che} be but
15 symple in comparyson to thos that ye haue seen me haue or this/
howebet if they may do you any good or pleasure/ I wold not
stykke to devyde them among you/ yea/ and the skyne of my
bake if it myght countervaylle any thyng in valewe among you/
but good gentilmen & yomen my trusty & faythefull seruauntes/
20 of whome no prynce hathe the lyke/ in my oppynyon/ I most
hartely requyer you to take w^t me some pacience a littill whyle/
ffor I dought not but that the kyng consideryng the offence
suggested ayenst me by my mortall ennemyes to be of small
effect woll shortly I dought not restore me agayn to my lyvynges
25 so that I shall be more able to devyd some part therof yerely
among you/ wherof ye shalbe well assured/ ffor the surplusage
of my revenues what so euer shall remayn at the determynacion
of my accomptes/ shalbe (god wyllyng) distributed among you/
ffor I woll neuer hereafter esteme the goodes & riches of this
30 oncertyn world but as a vayn thyng/ more than shalbe sufficient
for the mayntenaunce of myn estate & dignytie that god hathe
or shall call me vnto in this world duryng my lyfe/ And if the
kyng do not thus shortly restore me/ than woll I se you bestowed
accordyng to yor owen requestes/ and wright for you owther to
35 the kyng or to any other noble person w^t in this Realme to
reteyn you in to seruyce/ for I dought not but that the kyng or

2 pro *canc. before* Romes   7 shold *interl.*   8 place *canc. before*
place   18 in valewe *interl.*   23 me *interl.*   25 therof
interl.   31 god *interl.*

Life of Cardinal Wolsey

any noble man or worthy gentilman of this Realme woll credytt
my letter in yor commendacion/ Therfore in the meane tyme/
myn advyse is that ye repayer home to yor wyfes (suche as hathe
any) And suche among you as hathe none to take thys tyme to
visett yor parentes and frendes in the Contrie/ Ther is none of
you all but oons in a yere wold requyer licence/ [f. 55^v] to visit
yor wyfes & other of yor frendes/ take this tyme (I pray you) in
respect therof/ And at yor retourne I wyll not refuse you if I
shold begge w^t you/ I consider that the seruyce of my howsse
hathe byn suche and of suche a sort that ye be not meate or apte
to serue no man vnder the degree of a kyng/ Therfore I wold
whishe you to serue no man but the kyng/ who I ame suer wyll
not reiect you/ Therfore I desier you to take yor pleasures for a
monyth and than ye may come agayn vnto me/ And I trust by
that tyme the kyng ma^{tie} wyll extend hys clemency vppon me/
Sir q^d m^r Cromwell/ there is dyuers of thes your yomen that
wold be glad to se ther ffrendes but they lake mony/ therfore
here is dyuers of yor Chaplens/ who hathe receyued at yor
handes great benefices & highe dignytes/ lett them therfore nowe
shewe them selfes vnto you as they are bound by all humanytie
to do/ I thynke ther honestie & charite ys not so slender and
voyed of grace that they wold not se you lake where they may
helpe to refresshe you/ And for my part Allthoughe I haue not
receyued of yor graces gyft any oon penny towardes thencrese of
my yerely lyvyng yet wyll I departe w^t you this towardes the
dispetche of yor seruauntes (And delyuerd hyme v^{li} in gold)
And nowe lett vs se what yor chapleyns wyll do/ I thynke they
wyll departe w^t you myche more than I haue don/ who be more
able to geve you a pound than I oon penny/ Goo to maysters q^d
he to the Chapleyns/ In so myche as some gave hyme/ x^{li}/ Some
x^{en} marc/ Some C^s/ And so some more and Some lesse as at that
tyme ther powers did extend/ wherby my lord Receyved among
theme as myche mony of ther liberalitie as he gave to eche of his
yomen a quarters wages & bord wages for a monyth/ And they

1 worthy *interl.*   2 you *canc. before* my   3 I *canc. before*
myn   4 hathe] *MS.* hahe   7 tyme *interl.*   13 you/
Therfore] *MS.* you Therfore   16 yomen] *MS.* yoman   20 are
interl.   28 *two indecipherable letters canc. before* I   32 g *canc.*
before Receyved

departed down in to the hall/ where some determyned to goo to ther frendes/ And some sayd that they wold not departe frome my lord vntill they myght se hyme in better estate/ My lord retorned in to his chamber lamentyng the departure frome his
5 seruauntes makyng his mone vnto m^r Cromwell who comforted hyme the best he cowld/ And desired my lord to geve hyme leave to goo to london where he wold other make or marre or he came agayn (w^{che} was allwayes his comen sayeng) than after long Commynycacion w^t my lord in secret he departed [f. 56] and
10 toke his horsse and Rode to london at whos departyng I was bye/ whome he bade farewell/ And sayd/ ye shall here shortly of me And if I spede well I wyll not fayle to be here agayn w^t in thes ij dayes/ And so I toke my leave of hyme/ And he rode forthe on his Iourney/ Sir Rafe Sadler (nowe knyght) was than his Clarke/
15 and rode w^t hyme//

After that my lord had Supped that nyght (beyng allhalou day at nyght) And all men goon to bed/ yt chaunced so abought mydnyght/ that oon of the Porters came vnto my chamber doore And there knokked/ And wakyng of me perceyved who it was/
20 Axed hyme what he wold haue/ that tyme of the nyght/ sir q^d the porter/ there is a great number of horsse men at the gate that wold come In/ sayeng to me that it is sir Iohn Russhell/ And so it apperys to me by his voyce/ what is yor pleasure that I shall doo/ Mary q^d I/ goo down agayn And make a great fier
25 in yor lodge ayenst I come to drye them/ for it rayned all that nyght the sorest that it dyd all that yere byfore/ than I Roose and put on my nyght gown/ And came to the gattes And asked who was there/ w^t that m^r Russell spake whome I knewe by his voyce/ And than I caused the porters to opyn the gattes and lett
30 them all In/ who ware wette to the skyn desyryng m^r Russell to goo in to the loge to the fier/ And he shewed me that he wase come frome the kyng/ vnto my lord in messwage w^t whome he requyred me to speke/ Sir/ q^d I/ I trust yor newes be good/ yea I promyse you on my fidelitie/ q^d he/ And so I pray you showe
35 hyme/ I haue brought hyme suche newes that wyll please hyme

3 my lord *interl.*   8 comen] *MS.* coen   10 his leave *canc. before* his   12 ye shall here of me *canc. before* I wyll   21 is *interl.*   23 it *canc. before* yor   25 drye *interl.*; dry *canc. before* them   26 r *canc. after* the; roose *canc. before* Roose   31 me *interl.*   35 hyme *canc. before* hyme/ I *and* you *before* suche

Life of Cardinal Wolsey 111

right well/ Than will I goo q^d I/ and wake hyme/ And cause
hyme to rise/ I went Incontynent to my lordes chamber doore/
and waked my lord who asked me what I wold haue/ Sir sayd I/
to shewe you that sir Iohn Russell is come frome the kyng who
is desirous to speke w^t you/ And than he called vppe oon of his
gromes to lett me In/ And beyng w^t in/ I told hyme what a
Iourney Mr Russell had that nyght/ I pray god/ q^d he/ all be for
the best/ [f. 56^v] yes sir q^d I/ he shewed me/ And so bad me tell
you that he had brought you suche newes as ye woll greatly
reioyse there at/ well than/ q^d he/ god be praysed and wellcome
be his grace/ goo ye and fetche hyme vnto me/ And be that tyme
I woll be redy to talke w^t hyme/ than I retorned frome hyme to
the logge/ And brought m^r Russhell frome thence to my lord/
who had cast on his nyght gown And whan m^r Russell was come
in to his presence/ he most humbly Reuerencyd hyme vppon his
knee/ whome my lord bowed down and toke hyme vppe and
bad hyme welcome/ Sir q^d he the kyng commendyth hyme vnto
you/ And delyuerd hyme a great Ryng of gold w^t a Turkkas for
a tokyn/ And willyd you to be of good chere/ who lovythe you
as well as euer he dide/ and is not a littill disquyoted for yor
troble/ whos mynd is full of yor remembraunce/ In so myche as
his grace byfore he satt to Supper called me vnto hyme/ And
commaundyd me to take this Iourney secretly to visit you to yor
comfort the best of my power/ And sir if it please yor grace I
haue hade this nyght the sorest Iourney for so littill a way that
euer I had to my remembraunce/ My lord thanked hyme for his
paynnes and good newes/ And demaundyd of hyme if he had
Supped/ And he seyd nay/ well than q^d my lord to me/ Cause
the Cookes to provyd some mete for hyme/ And cause a
chamber w^t a good ffier to be mad redy for hyme that he may
take hys rest a while vppon a bed/ all w^{che} commaundeme^t I
fulfylled/ And in the mean tyme my lord & m^r Russell ware in
very secrett commynycacion/ And in fynne/ Mr Russell went

5 you *interl.*   7 he *canc. before* M^r 8 yees *canc. after* best/
12 hyme to *interl.*; my lord *interl. and canc. after* hyme   14 gere *canc.
before* nyght; nyght] *MS.* / nyght   16 vppe *interl.*   20 a littill *interl.*
21 troble] *MS.* trobled   22 he *canc. before* called   25 that *canc.
before* that   29 s *canc. before* mete   31 commaundeme^t] *MS.*
commaunde^t

to his chamber takyng his leave of my lord for all nyght/ And
sayd he wold not tary but a while for he wold (god wyllyng) be
at the Court at Grenew^che agayn byfore day/ ffor he wold not
for any thyng that it ware knowen his beyng w^t my lord that
night/ And so beyng in his chamber havyng a small repast/
Rested hyme a while vppon a bedd whillest his seruauntes
Supped & dried them selfes by the ffier/ [f. 57] And than
incontynent he roode a waye w^t spede to the Court/ And shortly
after hys beyng there/ my lord was restored agayn vnto plenty of
howsshold stuff, vessell and plate/ And of all thynges necessary
some part so that he was indifferently ffurnysshed muche better
than he was of latte/ And yet not so aboundauntly as the
kynges pleasure was/ the default wherof was in the officers &
in suche as had the ouer sight of the delyuere therof/ And
yet my lord reioysed in that littill in comparison to that he had
byfore///

Nowe lett vs retourne agayn to m^r Cromwell to se howe he
hathe sped sence his departure last frome my lord/ **The case**
stode so that ther shold begyn shortly after Allhaloutyd the
parlyament/ And beyng w^t in london devised w^t hyme self/ to be
oon of the Burgious of the parliament/ And chaunced to mete w^t
oon sir Thomas Russhe knyght (a specyall frend of his) whos
Sonne was appoynted to be oon of the Burgious of that parlia-
ment/ of whome he opteyned his rome/ And by that means put
his foote in to the parliament howsse/ Than w^t in ij or iij^re dayes
after his entre in to the parliame^t/ he came vnto my lord to
Assher/ w^t a myche pleasaunter Countenaunce/ than he had at
his departure/ And meatyng w^t me byfore he came to my lord
sayd vnto me/ that he had oons adventured to put in his foote
where he trusted shortly to be better regardyd or all ware don/
And whan he was come to my lord they talked to gether in
secrett maner And that don he roode owt of hand agayn that
nyght to london/ because he wold not be absent frome the
parliament the next mornyng/ There cowld no thyng be spoken

---

5 night/ And] *MS.* night And   6 *two indecipherable letters canc. after*
hyme a   8 shortly *interl.*   11 he *interl.*   13 by *canc. after*
wherof was   18 sped *canc. before* sped; last *interl.*   21 *second* of]
MS. of of   22 his)] *MS.* his/   25 howsse *canc. before* howsse
30 better *interl.*   30–31 don/ And] *MS.* don And

ageynst my lord in the parliament howsse but he wold answer
it incontynent or elles take day vntill the next day/ ayenst w^{che}
tyme he wold resorte to my lord to knowe what Answere he shold
make in his behalf/ In so myche that there was no matter alleged
ayenst my lord but that he was euer redy furnysshed w^t an 5
sufficient Answere/ So that at lengthe for his honest behauour in
his m^{rs} case he grewe in to suche estymacion in euery mans
oppynyon that he was estymed to be the [f. 57^v] most faythe-
fullest seruaunt to his m^r of all other/ wherin he was of all men
greatly commendyd/ Than was there brought a byll of Articles 10
in to the parliament howsse to haue my lord condempned of
treason/ Ayenst w^{che} byll m^r Cromwell enveyed so discretly, w^t
suche wytty perswacions & depe reasons that the same byll
cowld take there no effect/ than ware hys ennemyes compelled
to endyght hyme in a Premunire/ And all was don oonly to the 15
entent to entitill the kyng to all his goodes & possessions the
w^{che} he had gathered together and purchased for his Colleges
in Oxford & Ipsew^{che}/ And for the mayntenaunce of the same
(w^{che} was than abyldyng in most Somptious wyse) wherin whan
he was demaundyd by the Iugges (w^{che} ware sent hyme purposly 20
to examyn hyme what answere he wold make to the same) he
seyd/ The kynges highnes knowyth right well wether I haue
offendyd hys ma^{tie} & his lawes or no/ in vsyng of my prerogatife
legantyn for the w^{che} ye haue me endighted/ Notw^tstandyng I
haue the kynges lycence in my Coffers vnder his hand & broode 25
seale/ for excersisyng and vsyng the auctorytie therof in the
largest wyse w^tin his highenes domynyons/ the w^{che} remaynyth
nowe in the handes of my Ennemyes/ therfor bycause I woll not
stand in question or triall w^t the kyng in his owen case/ I ame
content here of myn owen ffranke wyll & mynd in yor presence 30
to confesse the offence in the indyghtment/ And put me holly
in the mercy & grace/ of the kyng/ hauyng no doughtes in his
godly disposicion & charitable concience/ whome I knowe hathe
an highe discression to concyder the trouthe and my humble
submyssion & obedyence/ And allthoughe I myght Iustly stand 35

1 answer] *MS.* answered   6 for *interl.*   8 most *canc. after* the
9 he *canc. before* he   10 in *canc. before* a   20 for that *canc. after*
hyme   32 hauyng *interl.*; put *canc. before* no   35 thoughe *of*
allthoughe *interl.*

Life of Cardinal Wolsey

in the tryall w^t hyme ther in/ yet I ame content to submyt my self to his clementsye/ And thus myche ye may say to hyme in my behalf/ that I ame Intierly his obedyencer/ and do entend (god wyllyng) to obey & fulfyll all his pryncely pleasure in euery
5 thyng that he will commaund me to do/ whos wyll & pleasure I neuer yet disobeyed or repugned/ but was allwayes contentyd & glade to accomplysshe his desier & commaundement (byfore god) whome I owght most rathest to haue obeyed/ the w^che necligence nowe greatly repentithe me/ Notw^tstandyng [f. 58]
10 I most hartely requyer you/ to haue me most humbly to hys Royall ma^tie/ commendyd for whome I do & wyll pray for the preseruacion of his Royall person long to rayn in honour, prosperyte & quyotnes and to haue the victory ouer his mortall & kankard ennemyes/ And they toke ther leave of hyme &
15 departyd/ **Shortly after** the kyng sent the Duke of Norffolk vnto hyme in message/ (but what it was I ame not certeyn) But my lord beyng Aduertised that the Duke was commyng evyn at hand/ he caused all his gentilmen to wayt vppon hyme down thoroughe the hall in to the base Court to receyve the Duke at
20 the entre of the gattes and commaundyd all his yomen to stand still in the hall in order/ And he and his gentilmen went to the gattes/ where he encountred w^t my lord of Norffolk whome he receyved/ bare hedyd/ who embraced eche other/ And so led hyme by the Arme thoroughe the hall in to his chamber/ And as
25 the Duke passed thoroughe the hall/ at the vpper end therof he torned agayn his visage down the hall Regardyng the number of the tall yomen/ that stode in order/ there/ & sayd/ Sirs/ q^d he/ yor diligent & faythefull seruaunce vnto my lord here (yor m^r) in this tyme of his Calamyte hathe purchased for yor self/ of all noble
30 men/ myche honestie/ In so myche as the kyng commaundyd me to say to you in his graces name/ that for yor trewe & lovyng seruyce that ye haue don to yor m^r/ his highnes woll se you all furnysshed at all tymes w^t seruyce accordyng to yor demerittes/ w^t that my lord Cardynall put of hys cappe/ And sayd to my

---

5 will *interl.*   7 to *canc. before* & glade; his *canc. before* his   8 to haue obeyed] *MS.* to obeyed   11 I *canc. before* do   12 his *interl.*   16 certeyn)]) *written over* /   18 awayt *canc. before* wayt; wayt *interl.*   22 w^t *interl.*; lord *canc. before* lord   26 *two indecipherable letters canc. before* torned   34 that *interl.*

lord of Norffolk/ Sir/ q^d he/ thes men be all approved men wherfore it ware pitie they shold want other seruyce or lyvynges/ And beyng sorrey that I ame not able to do for them as my hart dothe whisshe/ Do therfore requyer you my good lord to be good lord vnto theme/ and extend yor good word for theme when ye shall se opportunytie/ at any tyme hereafter/ And that ye wyll preferre ther dyligent & faythfull seruyce to the kyng/ Dought ye not therof/ q^d my lord of Norffolk/ but I wyll do for them the best of my power/ and when I shall se cause I wylbe an earnest sewter for them to the kyng/ And Some of you I wyll [f. 58^v] Retayn myself in seruyce for yor honestes sake/ And as ye haue begon/ so contynewe and remayn here still w^t my lord vntill ye here more of the kynges pleasure/ goddes blessyng & myn be w^t you// And so went vppe in to the great chamber to dynner/ whome my lord Cardynall thanked & sayed vnto hyme yet my lord of all other nobyll men I haue most cause to thanke you/ for yor noble hart & gentill nature w^che ye haue shewed me behynd my bakke/ as my seruaunt Thomas Cromwell hathe made report vnto me/ but evyn as ye are a noble man in deade so haue ye shewed yor self no lesse to All men in Calamytie/ And in especyall to me/ And evyn as ye haue abated my glory & highe estate and brought it full lowe/ so haue ye extendyd yor honorable fauour most charitably vnto me beyng prostrate byfore ye/ forsothe sir ye do Right well deserue to bere in yor armez the noble & gentill lion/ whos naturall Inclinacion is that whan he hathe vanqiesshed Any best And seyth hyme yelded lyeng prostrate byfore hyme at his foote/ than wyll he shewe most clemency vnto his vanquysht & do hyme no more harme/ ne suffer any other devouryng beste to dammage hyme/ whos nature and qualitie ye do ensewe/ therfore thes verses may be Ascribed to yor lordshyppe/ w^che be thes/

Parcere prostratis/ Scit nobilis Ira leonis/
Tu quoque fac Simile/ quisquis regnabis in orbem/

1 Norffolk *canc. before* Norffolk *over* &; 7 fa *canc. before* faythfull 22 for *canc. before* and; and *interl.*; it *interl.* do *interl.* 25 the] *MS.* the the 2 th *canc. before* it; or] *written* 18 behynd] h *written over* g 24 do *canc. before* do; 30 and *interl.* 31 askribed *canc. before* Ascribed

W^t that the water was brought them to wasshe byfore dynner/ to the w^{che} my lord called my lord of Norffolk to washe w^t hyme/ but he refused of Curtesy/ And desired to haue hyme excused/ And sayed that it became hyme not to presume to
5 wasshe w^t hyme any more now than yt dyd byfore in his glory/ yes forsothe q^d my lord Cardynall ffor my Auctory & dignyte legantyn is goon wherin consisted all my highe honour/ A Strawe q^d my lord of Norffolk for yor legacye/ I neuer estemed yor honour/ the more or higher for that/ but I regarded yor
10 honour for that ye ware Archebysshope of yorke and a Cardynall/ whos [f. 59] estate of honor surmountythe any duke nowe beyng w^t in this realme/ And so wyll I honor you/ And acknowloge the same And beare you reuerence accordyngly therfore I beseche you content yor self for I woll not presume/ to wasshe
15 w^t you/ And therfore I pray you hold me excused/ than was my lord Cardynall constrayned to washe alone/ And my lord of Norffolk all alon also/ whan he had don/ And whan he had don my lord Cardynall wold fayn haue had my lord of Norffolk to sytt down in the chayer in the Inner side of the table/ but suerly
20 he refused the same also w^t myche humblenes/ than was there sett an other chayer for my lord of Norffolk ouer ayenst my lord Cardynall/ on the owt side/ of the table/ the w^{che} was by my lord of Norffolk based some thyng benethe my lord/ And duryng the dynner all ther commynycacion was of the dyligent seruyce
25 of the gentilmen w^{che} remayned w^t my lord there/ attendyng vppon hyme there at dynner/ And howe myche the kyng and all other noble men dothe esteme theme/ w^t worthy commendacions for so doyng And at thys tyme howe littill they be estemed in the Court that are come to the kynges seruyce/ and forsaken
30 ther m^r in his necessitie/ wherof some he blamed by name/ and w^t this Commynycacion the dynner beyng endyd/ they roose frome the table and went together in to my lordes bedd Chamber/ where they contynued in Consultacion a certyn season/ And beyng there/ yt chaunced m^r Shelley the Iuge to

---

3 hyme *canc. before* to   5 glory *canc. before* glory   7 sto *canc. before* consisted   11 surmountythe] *MS.* surmoumtythe
13 beare *canc. before* beare   16–17 of Norffolk all *interl.*   18 haue *canc. before* fayn   21 an other *canc. before* chayer   22 b *canc. before* was

come thether sent frome the kyng/ wherof Relacion was made to my lord/ w^{che} caused the Duke & hyme to breke vppe ther commynycacion/ And the Duke desired to goo in to some chamber to repose hyme for a season/ And as he was commyng owt of my lordes chamber he mete w^t Mr Shelley to whome m^r Shelley made Relacion of the cause of hys commyng/ And desierd/ the duke to tary & assist hyme in doyng of hys messwage/ whome he denyed and sayd/ I haue no thyng to do w^t yor messwage wherin I woll not meddell And so departed in to a Chamber where he toke his rest for an hower or ij [f. 59^v] And in the mean tyme my lord issued owt of hys chamber/ And came to m^r Shelley to knowe his message/ who declared vnto hyme (after dewe salutacion) That the kynges pleasure was to haue his howesse at westminster (than Called yorke place) belongyng to his bysshopriche of yorke/ entendyng to make of that howsse a palice Royall/ And to possesse the same accordyng to the lawes of thys hys graces realme/ his highnes hathe therfore sent for all the Iugges and for all his learned Councell to knowe ther oppynyons in the assuraunce therof/ In whos determynacions it was fully resolued that yor grace shold recognyse byfore a Iugge the right therof to be in the kyng & his Successors/ And so his hyghnes shalbe assured therof/ Wherfore it hathe pleased his ma^{tie} to appoynt me by his commaundeme^t to come hether to take of you this recognysaunce/ who hathe in you suche Affiaunce/ that ye will not refuse so to do accordyngly/ Therfore I shall desier yor grace to knowe yor good will therin/ Mr Shelley/ q^d my lord/ I knowe that the kyng of his owen nature is of a Royall stomake/ and yet not wyllyng more than Iustice shall leede hyme vnto by the lawe/ And therfore I councell you & all other fathers of the lawe & learned men of his Councell to put no more in to his hed than the lawe may stand w^t good concience/ ffor whan ye tell hyme (this is the lawe) it ware well done ye shold tell hyme also/ that allthoughe thys be the lawe/ yet this is concyence/ ffor lawe w^t out concyence is not good to

4 he *interl.* 5 che *canc. after* m^r 6 hys *canc. before* the
13 was *interl.* 17 realme/ his] *MS.* realme his; therfore *canc. before and after* therfore; therfore *interl.* 19 pleasures *canc. before* oppynyons; it *interl.* 20 I *canc. before* Iugge 21 as *canc. before* so
22 Wher for his *canc. before* Wherfore 25 r *canc. before* not
30 s *canc. after* the 32 well *interl.*] *MS.* wold *interl.*

be gevyn vnto a kyng in councell to vse for a lawfull right/ but allwayes to haue a respect to Concyence/ byfore the rigor of the comen lawe/ ffor (laus est facere q^d decet/ non q^d licett)/ the kyng owght of his Royall dignytie and prerogatife to mytigat
5 the Rigor of the lawe where concyence hathe the most force/ tharfore in his Royall place of equall Iustice/ he hathe constitute a Chauncelour/ an officer to excecut Iustice w^t clemencye/ where concyence is oppressed by the Rigor of the lawe/ And therfore the Court of Chauncery hathe byn heretofore [f. 60] comenly called
10 the Court of concyence/ by cause it hade Iurysdiccion to commaund the highe mynysters of the Comen lawe to spare execucion & Iugeme^t where concience had most effecte/ therfore I say to you in this case allthoughe you and other of yor profession perceyve by yor learnyng that the kyng may by an
15 order of yor lawes lawfully do that thyng w^{che} ye demaund of me/ howe say you m^r Shelley may I do it w^t Iustice & concyence/ to geve that thyng away frome me & my Successors w^{che} is non of myn/ if this be lawe w^t concience/ shewe me yor oppynyon/ I pray you/ fforsothe my lord/ q^d he/ there is some concyence in
20 this case/ but hauyng regard to the kynges highe power/ And to be employed to a better vse & purpose/ it may the better be suffred w^t concyence/ who is sufficient to make recompence/ to the chirche of yorke w^t doble the valewe/ That I knowe well/ q^d my lord/ but here is no suche condicion/ nother promysed ne
25 agreed/ but oonly a bare & symple departure w^t an others right for euer/ And if euery bysshope may do the lyke/ than myght euery prelate/ geve away the patremony of ther chirches w^{che} is non of thers And so in processe of tyme leve no thyng for ther Successors/ to mantayn ther Dignytes/ w^{che} all thynges con-
30 sydered shold be but small to the kynges honour/ Sir I do not entend to stand in termes w^t you in this matter/ but lett me se yor commyssion/ to whome m^r Shelley shewed hyme the same/ And that seen and perceyved by hyme sayed agayn/ thus/ Mr Shelley/ q^d he/ ye shall make report to the kynges highnes/ that
35 I ame his obedyent subiect & faythfull chapleyn & bedman whos

5 where concyence *interl.*   11 Comen] *MS.* Coen   14 the *canc. before* an   22 is *canc. after* who   30 s *canc. before* but; honour/ Sir] *MS.* honour Sir   32 hyme *interl.*   33 th this *canc. before* thus   35 sub. . *canc. before* subiect

Royall commaundemet & request I wyll in no wyse disobey but most gladly fulfill & accomplysshe his pryncely will & pleasure in all thynges and in especyall in this matter in as myche as ye the ffathers of the lawes say that I may lawfully do it/ therfore I charge yor conciences & dischargethe myn/ howbeit I pray you shewe his matie frome me/ that I most humbly desier his highenes to call to his most gracious remembraunce/ that there is bothe hevyn & hell/ [f. 60ᵛ] And there wt the Clarke was called who wrott my lord recognysaunce/ And after some secret talke/ mr Shelley departed/ Than Roose my lord of Norffolk frome his repose/ And after Somme comynycacion wt my lord/ he departed/

Thus/ contynued my lord at Assher who receyved dayly messwages/ frome the Court/ wherof some ware not so good as some ware badd/ but yet myche more evyll than good/ ffor his ennemyes perceyvyng the great affeccon that the kyng bare allwayes toward hyme/ devysed a mean to disquyot & disturbe his pacience thynkyng therbye to geve hyme an occasion to frett & chafe that deathe shold rather ensewe than encreace of helthe or lyfe the wche they most desired/ They feared hyme more after his fall than they did before in his prosperytie/ doughtyng myche hys readopcion in to auctorytie by reason that the kynges fauour remayned still towardes hyme in suche sorte/ wherby they myght rather be in daynger of ther estates than in any assuraunce/ ffor ther cruelltie mynesterd by ther malicious Invencions surmysed & brought to passe ayenst hyme// Therfore they toke this order among theme in ther matters/ that dayly they wold send hyme some thyng or do some thyng ayenst hyme wherin they thought that they myght geve hyme a cause of hevenes or lamentacion/ As some day they wold cause the kyng to send for iiijor or v of hys gentilmen/ frome hyme to serue the kyng/ And some other day they wold lay matters newly Invented ayenst hyme/ An other day they wold take frome hyme some of

4 wt out *canc. before* therfore   11 comynycacion *interl.*   15 ware badde *with the* re *written over* s *canc. before* ware   16 enneyes *canc. before* ennemyes   19 sh *canc. before* deathe   20 two *indecipherable letters canc. before* or   22 myche *canc. after* doughtyng; he *canc. before* hys *and* au *before* auctorytie; hys *interl.*   25 to hyme *with* to *interl. canc. before* by   27 toke this] *MS.* toke/ this   30 fynd *canc. before* cause

hys promocions or of ther promocions whome he preferred byfore/ than wold they fetche frome hyme some of his yomen/ in so myche as the kyng toke in to seruyce xvj^{en} of theme at oons/ and at oon tyme/ put them in to his gard/ this order of lyfe he
5 led contynually/ that there was no oon day, but or euer he went to bed he had an occasion greatly to chafe or frette the hart owt of his bellye/ but that he was a wyse man and bare all ther malice in pacyence/ At Cristmas he fill sore syke that he was lykly to dye/ Wherof the kyng beyng aduertysed was very sory
10 therfore/ And sent doctor buttes his graces phecision vnto hyme to se in what estate he was/ Doctor Buttes [f. 61] came vnto hyme and fyndyng hyme very syke lyeng in his bedd and perceyvyng the daynger he was in/ repayred agayn vnto the kyng/ of whome the kyng demaundyd sayeng/ howe dothe
15 yonder man haue you seen hyme/ yea sir q^d he/ howe do ye lyke hyme/ q^d the kyng/ fforsothe/ sir q^d he/ yf you wold haue hyme deade/ I warraunt yor grace/ he wyll be deade w^t in this iiij^{or} dayes (if he receyve no comfort frome you shortly and m^{rs} Anne/ Mary (q^d the kyng) (God forbod) that he shold dye)/ I pray you
20 good Mr Buttes goo agayn vnto hyme And do yor cure appon hyme/ ffor I wold not loose hyme for xx M^l li/ Than must yor grace/ q^d m^r Buttes/ send hyme first some comfortable message/ as shortly as is possible/ Evyn so wyll I/ q^d the kyng/ by you/ And therfore make sped to hyme agayn/ And ye shall delyuer
25 hyme frome me thys Rynge/ for a tokyn of our good wyll and fauor towardes hyme (in the w^{che} ryng was engraved the kynges visage w^t in a Rubye as lyvely counterfeyt as was possible to be devysed) thys Ryng he knowyth very well for he gave me the same/ And tell hyme that I ame not offendyd w^t hyme in my
30 hart no thyng At All/ And that he shall perceyve (and god send hyme) lyfe very shortly/ Therfore byd hyme be of good cheare and pluke vppe his hart & take no dispayer/ And I charge you come not frome hyme vntill ye haue brought hyme owt of all

---

1 promocions *canc. after* hys; to *canc. before* whome   3 in *interl.*   4 and *canc. before* put; his *canc. before* lyfe; they *canc. before* he   4–5 he led *interl.*   5 led w^t hyme *canc. before* contynually   6 or] *written over* &   12 bedd *canc. before* bedd   16 wold *interl.*   19 mary *canc. before* Mary; god f *canc. before* (God   23 wyll I/ q^d] *MS.* wyll/ I q^d/; by *interl.*   31 hyme *canc. before first* hyme; lyfe *interl.*   32 f *canc. before* vppe

Life of Cardinal Wolsey 121

daynger of deathe/ And than he spake to m^rs Anne sayeng/
Good swett hart I pray you at this my instaunce (as ye love vs)
to send the Cardynall a token w^t comfortable wordes/ And in so
doyng ye shall do vs a lovyng pleasure/ She beyng not mynded
to disobey the kynges earnest request (what so euer she 5
entendyd in hyr hart towardes the Cardynall) toke incontynent
hir tablett of gold hangyng at hir girdell And delyuerd it to m^r
Buttes w^t very gentill & comfortable wordes/ in commendacion
to the Cardynall/ And thus m^r Buttes departed and made spedy
retorne to Assher to my lord Cardynall/ After whome the kyng 10
sent Doctor Clement/ Doctor Wotten/ & doctor Cromer the
scott/ to consult and assist Mr Buttes for my lordes helthe/ After
that m^r Buttes had byn w^t my lord and delyuerd the kynges
& m^rs Annes tokens vnto hyme/ w^t the most comfortablest
wordes he [f. 61^v] cowld devyse on ther behalf/ wherat he 15
reioysed not a littill/ aduauncyng hyme a littill in his bedd And
receyved thes tokens most Ioyfully thankyng m^r Buttes for his
comfortable newes & paynnes/ Mr Buttes shewed hyme further
more that the kynges pleasure was that he shold mynester vnto
hyme for hys helthe/ And for the most assured and brefe wayes 20
to be had for the same/ hathe sent Doctor wotten/ Doctor
Clement/ And Doctor Cromer/ to Ioyn w^t hyme in counsell &
mynystracion/ Therfore my lord/ q^d he/ it ware well don that
they shold be called in to visett yor person & estate/ wherin
I wold be glad to here ther oppynyons/ trustyng in allmyghty 25
god that thoroughe his grace and assistaunce we shall ease you
of yor paynnes and rid you clean frome yor dissease and
Infirmytie/ wherw^t my lord was well pleased & contented to
here ther Iugeme^tes/ ffor in deade he trust more to the Scottysshe
doctor than he did to any of thother/ by cause he was the very 30
occasion that he inhabytid here in Englond/ and byfore he gave
hyme partly his exebicion/ in Paris/ than whan they ware come
in to hys chamber and had talked w^t hyme/ he toke vppon hyme
to debate his dessease learnedly among theme/ So that they

---

1 spake *canc. before* than   2-3 vs) to] *MS.* vs/ to   5 the k *canc.*
before earnest   16 hyme a littill *interl.*   20 and brefe *interl.*
23 mynystracion/ Therfore] *MS.* mynystracion Therfore   24 in *of*
wherin *interl.*   26 we shall *canc. after* grace   28 *superscript* ^t *canc.*
between w *and* h *of* wherw^t

myght vnderstand that he was seen in that art// After they had taken order for mynystracion it was not long or they brought hyme owt of all daynger & feare of dethe/ And w^{t}in iiij^{or} dayes they sett hyme on his feete/ And gott hyme a good stomake to his
5 meate/ thys don/ And he in a good estate of amendeme^t/ they toke there leave/ to departe/ to whome my lord offered his reward/ the w^{che} they refused seyeng that the kyng gave them in specyall commaundeme^t to take no thyng of hyme for ther paynnes and mynystracion/ ffor at ther retourne/ his highnes
10 seyd that he wold reward theme of his owen costes/ And thus w^t great thankes they departid frome my lord/ whome they lefte in good estate of recouere//

After thys tyme my lord dayly amendyd/ and so contynued still at Assher vntill Candyllmas/ ayenst w^{che} ffeast the kyng caused
15 to be sent hyme iij^{re} or iiij^{or} Cartloodes of stuffe/ And most parte therof was lokked in great standerdes (excepte beddes & kytchyn stuffe) wherin was bothe plate [f. 62] and Riche hangynges/ And chappell stuffe/ Than my lord beyng thus ffurnysshed was therw^t well contented/ Allthoughe/ they whome the kyng
20 assigned did not delyuer hyme so good ne so riche stuffe as the kynges pleasure was/ yet was he Ioyous therof And rendred most humble thankes to the kyng/ And to theme that appoynted the seyd stuffe for hyme/ Sayeng to vs his seruauntes At the openyng of the same stuffe in the standerdes/ the w^{che} we
25 thought and sayd it myght haue byn better if it had pleased them that appoynted it/ Nay sirs q^d my lord/ to vs/ he that hathe no thyng is glad of somwhat thoughe it be neuer so littill/ And allthoughe it be not in comparison halfe so myche & good as we had byfore/ yet we reioyse more of this littill than we dyd byfore
30 of the great aboundaunce that we than hade/ And thanked the kyng very myche for the same/ trustyng after thys to haue myche moore/ therfore lett vs all reioyse & be glade that god & the kyng hathe so graciously remembred to restore vs to some

---

4 good *canc. before* gott; gott *interl.*   7 y *canc. after* first the; thy *canc. before* them   15 vnto my lord *canc. after* sent; hyme *interl.*   24 byfore *canc. after* stuffe; hyme/ that ware *canc. before* in; that where q^d he/ *canc. after* standerdes/; the w^{che} *interl.*   25 and sayd *interl.*   26 sirs *interl.*   28 so *canc. before* halfe   29 herof *canc. before* we reioyse   30 than *interl.*   32 myche *and be interl.*; of *canc. before* that

thynges to mayntayn our estate lyke a noble person/ Than
commaunded he m^r Cromwell beyng w^t hyme to make sewt to
the kynges ma^{tie} that he myght remove thence to some other
place/ ffor he was wery of that howsse of Assher/ for w^t contynuall vse therof the howsse waxed onsavery/ supposyng that if
he myght remove frome thence he shold myche soner recouer
his helthe/ And also the Councell had putt in to the kynges hed
that the newe gallery at Assher (w^{che} my lord hade late byfore his
fall newly sett vppe/) shold be very necessary for the kyng to
take down & sett it vppe agayn at westminster/ w^{che} was don
accordyngly/ And standes at this present day there/ the takyng
a way therof byfore my lordes face was to hyme a Corrysife/
w^{che} was Invented by hys ennemyes oonly to torment hyme/ the
w^{che} in dede discoraged hyme very sore to tary any lenger there/
Nowe m^r Cromwell thought it but vayn & myche folly [f. 62^v]
to move any of the kynges Councell to assist & preferre hys sewte
to the kyng (among whome rested the nomber of hys mortall
ennemyes) for they wold owther hynder his removyng or elles
remove hyme ferder frome the kyng than to haue holpen hyme
to any place nyghe the kynges comen trade/ Wherfore he
refused any sewte to theme & made oonly sewte to the kynges
owen person/ whos sewte the kyng gracyously hard And thought
it very convenyent to be graunted And thoroughe the specyall
mocyon of m^r Cromwell the kyng was well contentyd that he
shold remove to Rychemond w^{che} place my lord had a littill
byfore repayred to his great cost & charge/ ffor the kyng had
made an exchaunge therof w^t hyme for hampton Court/ all this
his removyng was don w^t out the knowlege of the kynges
Councell/ for if they myght haue had any Intelligence therof
byfore/ than wold they haue perswaded the kyng to the contrary/
but whan they ware aduertised of the kynges graunt & pleasure/
they dissimuled ther countenaunces in the kynges presence/ ffor

---

4 wase *canc. after* howsse   5 waxed onsavery/] *MS.* waxed/
onsavery   6 recouer *canc. before* remove   11 and *canc. after*
accordyngly/   12 therof *interl.*   13 Inventyde *with* d *written
over* f *canc. before* Invented; Invented *interl.*   14 very sore *interl.*
16 his *canc. before* & *and* pro *before* preferre   19 ferder *interl.*; ferre
canc. before frome; e *canc. after* than   20 comen *interl.*   21 oon
canc. before oonly; oonly *interl.*   24 well *interl.*   29 Co *canc.
before* Councell

they ware greatly affrayed of hyme/ lest his nyghe beyng to the kyng myght at lengthe some oon tyme resort to hyme and so call hyme home agayn/ consideryng the great affeccion & love that the kyng dayly shewe towardes hyme/ Wherfore they doughted hys risyng agayn if they found not a mean to remove hyme shortly frome the kyng/ In so myche that they thought it convenyent for ther purpose to enforme the kyng vppon certeyn consideracions w^{che} they Invented/ that it ware very necessary that my lord shold goo down in to the Northe/ vnto his benefice of yorke/ where he shold be a good staye for the Contree/ to the w^{che} (the kyng supposyng that they had ment no lesse than good faythe) grauntyd and condyssendyd to ther suggestion w^{che} was fferced w^t so wonderfull Imagyned consideracions/ that the kyng (vnderstandyng no thyng of ther Intent) was lightly perswaded to the same/ **Whervppon** the Duke of Norffolk commaundyd m^r Crommwell (who had dayly accesse vnto hyme) to say to my lord that it is the kynges pleasure that he shold w^t spede goo to his benefice where lyethe his cure/ and looke to that accordyng to his dewtie/ Mr Cromwell at his next repayer to my lord declared vnto hyme what my lord of Norffolk sayd/ who lay [f. 63] than at Richemonde/ howe it was determyned that he shold goo to his benefice/ Well than Thomas/ q^d my lord/ seyng ther is non other remedy I do entend to go to my benyfice of wynchester/ And I pray you Thomas so shewe my lord of Norffolk/ contentyd sir/ q^d m^r Cromwell/ And Accordyng to hys commaundeme^t dyd so/ to the w^{che} my lord of Norffolk answerd/ and seyd what wyll he do there/ Nay/ q^d he/ lett hyme goo in to his provynce of yorke/ wherof he hathe receyved his honor/ and there lyethe the sperytuall borden & charge of his concyence/ as he owght to do/ and so shewe hyme/ The lordes who ware not all his ffrendes/ hauyng intelligence/ of his entent/ thought to w^tdrawe his appetite ffrome wynchester/ wold in no wyse per‑ mytt hyme to plant hyme self so nyghe the kyng/ Movyd therfore the kyng to geve my lord but a pencion owt of wynchester

1 re *canc. after* nyghe   2 to *canc. before* some   4 hyme/ Wherfore] *MS.* hyme Wherfore   6 thought *interl.*   11 lesse] *MS.* lesse)   11–12 than good faythe *interl.*   12 fo *canc. before* was   21 to go to *canc. before* that   24 so *interl.*   25 sir *interl.*   27 and seyd *interl.*; in *interl.*   29 of his *canc. before* &   32 no *canc. before* in

Life of Cardinal Wolsey 125

and to distribut all the rest among the nobilitie & other of
his worthy seruauntes And in lyke wyse to do the same w^t the
revenues of Seynt Albons and of the revenues of his Colleges in
Oxford & Ipswhiche/ the w^{che} the kyng toke in to his owen
handes/ Wherof m^r Cromwell had the receypte & gouernaunce 5
a fore be my lordes assigneme^t/ In consideracion therof it was
thought most convenyent that he shold haue so styll/ Not-
w^{t}standyng owt of the reveneus of wynchester & seynt Albons
the kyng gave to some oon noble man iij^C markes & to some C^{li}
And to some more & to some lesse accordyng to the kynges 10
royall pleasure/ Nowe m^r Cromwell executed his office the
w^{che} he had ouer the londes of the colleges so Iustly and exactly
that he was had in great estimacion/ for his wytty behauor
therin/ And also for the treu, faythfull & dyligent seruyce
extendyd towardes my lord his m^r/ That it came at lengthe so to 15
passe that thos to whome the kynges ma^{tie} hade gevyn any
Annuites or ffees for terme of lyfe by patent/ owte of the
fornamed Revenewes/ cowld not be good but duryng my lordes
lyfe/ for as myche as the kyng had no lenger estate or title
therin/ w^{che} came to hyme by reason of my lordes attendure in 20
the premunire/ And to make ther estates good & sufficient
accordyng to ther patentes/ it was thought necessary to haue my
lordes confirmacion vnto ther grauntes/ And this to be brought
aboughtt there was non other [f. 63^v] mean but to make sewte to
m^r Cromwell to atteyn ther confirmacion/ at my lordes handes/ 25
whome they thought myght best/ opteyn the same/ Then began
bothe noble man & other who had any patentes of the kyng owte
other of Wynchester or Seynt Albons/ to make earnest sewte to
m^r Cromwell for to Solicite ther causes to my lord to gett of
hyme his confirmacions/ And for his paynnes therin susteyned/ 30
they promysed euery man not oonly worthely to reward hyme
but also to shewe hyme suche pleasures as shold at all tymes lye
in ther seuerall powers/ Wherof they assured hyme/ Wherin
m^r Cromwell perceyvyng an occasion and a tyme gevyn hyme/

2 And *canc. before* And   16 my lord *canc. after* whome; the kynges *interl.*; anuites gevyn *with* gevyn *interl. canc. before* gevyn   17 by patent *interl.*   19 they kyng *canc. before* the   22 necessary *interl.*
23 grauntes] *MS.* graauntes   31 not *canc. before* they   34 an *canc. after* and; a *interl.*

to worke for hyme selfe And to bryng the thyng to passe w^che he long wysshed for/ Entendyd to worke so in thes matters to serue ther desiers/ that he myght the soner bryng his owen enterprice to purpose/ Than at his next resort to my lord he moved hyme privyely in this matter to haue his councell and hys advyse/ And so by ther wytty hedes it was devysed that they shold worke to gether by oon lyne to bryng by ther pollecyes m^r Cromwell in place & estate where he myght do hymeself good and my lord myche profett///

Nowe began matters/ to worke to brynge Mr Cromwell in to estymacion in suche sort as was afterward myche to his encrease of dygnyte And thus euery man hauyng an occasion to sewe for my lordes confirmacion made nowe earnest travell to m^r Cromwell for thes purposes/ who refused non to make promyse that he wold do hys best in that case/ And havyng a great occasion of accesse to the kyng for the disposicion of dyuers londes wherof he had the order & gouernaunce/ by means wherof and by his witty demeanor/ he grewe contynually in to the kynges favor/ as ye shall here after in this history/ But first lett vs resorte to the great busynes abought the assuraunce of all thes patentes w^che the kyng hathe gevyn to dyuers noble men & other of his seruauntes wherin m^r Cromwell made a countenaunce of great sewte to my lord for the same that in processe of tyme he serued all ther tornes so that they had ther purposes/ And he ther good wylles/ thus roose hys name & frendly acceptaunce w^t all men/ the fame of his honestie & wisdome sounded so in the kynges eares that [f. 64] by reason of his accesse to the kyng he perceyved to be in hyme no lesse wysdome than ffame had made of hyme report/ for as myche as he had the gouernaunce & receyptes of thos londes w^che I shewed you byfore/ And the conference that he had w^t the kyng therin enforced the kyng to reput hyme a very wyse man and a meate Instrume^t to serue his grace/ As it after came to passe/

Sir nowe the lordes thought long to remove hyme ferther

3 b *canc. before* myght   4 re s *canc. before* resort   5 privyely *interl.*; for *canc. after* matter; to haue his councell and *interl.*   8 he *interl.*   9 good *canc. before* good *and after* myche; good *interl.*; *two indecipherable letters canc. before* my; profett] *MS.* & profett   23 c *canc. before* great   24 processe of] *MS.* processe/ of   28 to *interl. after* perceyved

Life of Cardinal Wolsey 127

frome the kyng and owte of hys comen trade/ Wherfore (among
other of the lordes) my lord of Norffolk seyd to m^r Cromwell/
Sir/ q^d he/ me thynkythe/ that the Cardynall yor m^r/ makythe
no hast northeward/ shewe hyme that if he goo not a way
shortly/ I woll rather then he shold tary still/ teare hyme w^t my 5
teathe/ Therfore I wold advyse hyme to prepare hyme a waye/
as shortly as he can/ or elles he shalbe sent forward/ Thes
wordes m^r Cromwell reported to my lord at his next repayer to
hyme/ who than had a Iust occasion to resort to hyme for the
depeche of the noble mens & others patentes/ And here I wyll 10
leave of this matter & shewe you of my lordes beyng at
Richemond

My lord havyng licence of the kyng to repayer & remove to
Richemond wherfore my lord made hast to prepare hyme
thetherward And so he came and lodged w^tin the great parke 15
there/ w^che was a very pritty howsse & a nett/ lakyng no necessarie Romes that to so small a howsse was conuenyent &
necessary where was to the same a proper garden garnysshed w^t
dyuers plesaunt walkes & alies/ my lord contynued in thys loge
frome the tyme that he came thether shortly after Candylmas 20
vntyll it was lent w^t a privye nomber of seruauntes by cause of
the smalnes of the howsse/ And the rest of hys famely went to
bord wages/ I wyll tell you a certyn tale/ by the way of Com-
mynycasion **Sir as my lord** was accustumed towardes nyght
to walke in the garden there to sey his seruyce/ it was my 25
chaunce than to wayt vppon hyme there/ and standyng still in an
alie/ [f. 64^v] wyllest he in an other walked w^t his chapleyn
sayeng of his seruice/ And as I stode I aspied certyn Images of
beastes counterfeit in tymber standyng in a corner vnder the
loge wall/ to the w^che I repayred to behold/ Among whome I 30
sawe there a Dwn Cowe/ wheron I mused most by cause it semed
me to be the most lyvelyest entaylled among all the rest/ My
lord beyng (as I sayd) walkyng on the other side/ of the Garden/
perseyved me/ came sodenly apon me at my bake onwares

1 comen] *MS.* coen   3 m^re *canc. before* m^r   9 an *canc.*
before a   20 shortly *interl.*   21 small nom *canc. before*
privye   23 his *canc. before* bord; tell you *interl.*   26 hyme
interl.   29 temp *canc. before* tymber   31 mused *canc. before*
mused

sayd what haue ye espied here that ye so attentyfely looke vppon/ fforsothe if it please yor grace/ q^d I/ here I do behold thes entaylled Images the w^{che} I suppose ware ordened for to be sett vppe w^t in some place/ abowght the kynges place howbeit sir among them all I haue most considered the Dwn Cowe/ the w^{che} as it semyth me/ the worke man hathe most apertly shewed hys Connyng/ yea marye sir/ q^d my lord/ vppon thys dwn Cowe dependyth a certyn prophesy/ the w^{che} I woll shewe you for paraduenture ye neuer hard of it byfore/ Ther is a sayeng/ q^d he/ that whan this Cowe ridyth the bull/ than prest beware thy skull/ w^{che} prophecye nother my lord that declared it ne I that hard it/ vnderstod theffect of thys prophecye/ allthoughe that evyn than it was a workyng to be brought to passe/ ffor this Cowe the kyng gave as oon of his beastes appurteynyng of antiquytie vnto his Ereldome of Richemond w^{che} was his auncyent enheritaunce/ this prophecy was after expoundyd in this wyse/ This doon Cowe (because it was the kynges beast) betokened the kyng/ And the bull bytokened m^{rs} Anne Bulloyn (w^{che} was after Quene & the kynges wyfe)/ bycause hyr ffather Sir Thomas Bulloyn gave the same best in his cognysaunce/ So that whan the kyng had maried hyr (the w^{che} was than onknowen to my lord/ or to any other at that tyme/) Than was thys prophecy thought of all men to be ffulfilled// ffor what a nomber of prestes bothe religious & seculer lost ther heddes for offendyng of suche lawes as was than made to bryng this prophecye to effect yt is not onknowen to all the world// [f. 65]

Therfor it was Iuged of all men that this prophecy was than ffulfyll whan the kyng & she ware Ioyned in mariage/ Nowe howe darke & obscure ridelles and prophecyes be/ you may behold in thys same/ ffor byfore it was brought to passe/ there was not the wysest prophicier cowd perfectly discus it/ as it is nowe come to effect & purpose/ Trust therfore (be myn advyse) to no kynd of darke Riddelles & prophecyes/ where ye may (as many hathe byn) be disseyved and brought to distruccion/ And many tymes

---

1 vnto me *canc. before* sayd 5 this *interl. and canc. before* Dwn
6 apertly *interl.*; apertly *canc. before* shewed 9 byfore/ Ther] *MS.* byfore Ther 12 not *canc. before* theffect 13 it *interl.* 14 gave *canc. before* the 21 w^{che} *interl.* 29 and *interl.* 31 as it byfore/ *canc. before* as 34 be *canc. before* be; be *interl.*

the Imagynacions & travelous busynes to avoyd suche darke & straynge prophecyes hathe byn the very occasion to bryng the same the soner to effect & perfeccion/ therfore lett men beware to devyn or assure them selfes to expound any suche prophecyes/ ffor who so doyth/ shal first dissayve them selfes/ And secondly bryng many in to errour/ thexperience hathe byn lately experyenced (the more pitie) But if men woll nedes thynke them selfes so wyse to be assured of suche blynd prophecyes/ And wyll worke ther wylles therin/ owther in avoydyng or in ffulfillyng the same/ god send hyme well to sped/ for he may as well and myche more soner take dammage/ than to avoyd the daynger therof/ lett prophecyes alone a goddes name/ Applie yor vocacion And commytt thexposicion of suche darke riddelles And obscure prophecyes to god that disposyth theme as his devyn plesure shall see cause/ to allter & chaynge all yor enterprices & Imagynacions to nothyng & disceyve all yor expectacions and cause you to repent yor great folly/ the w^{che} whan ye feale the smert wyll yor self confesse the same/ to be bothe great foly & myche more madnes/ to trust in any suche ffantazes/ lett god therfore dispose theme/ who gwerdenythe and punysshethe/ accordyng to mens desertes & not to all mens Iugementes//// [f. 65^v]

You have hard here byfore what wordes the Duke of Norffolk had to m^r Cromwell towchyng my lordes goyng in to the northe to his benyfice of yorke/ at suche tyme as m^r Cromwell declared the same to my lord/ to whome my lord answered in thys wyse/ Marie Thomas/ q^d he/ than it is tyme to be goyng if my lord of Norffolk take it so/ Therfore I pray you goo to the kyng and move his highnes in my behalf and sey that I wold w^t all my hart goo to my benefice in yorke but for want of mony/ desyryng his grace to assist me w^t some mony towardes my Iourney ffor ye may sey that the last monye that I receyved of his ma^{tie} hathe byn to littyll to pay my debtes/ compelled by his Councell so to do/ therfore to constrayne me to the payment therof/ & his highenes hauyng all my goodes hathe byn to

1 the *canc. before* suche 4 sef *canc. before* selfes 5 be *canc. after* shal; be dissayved *canc. after* first 7 wolbe *canc. before* woll 11 and *interl.*; da *canc. before* take 14 to god *interl.* 16 all *interl.* 19 to *canc. before* in 20 to me *canc. before* accordyng 27 you *interl.* 32 to pay *canc. before* to pay 33 compell *canc. before* constrayne

myche extremyte/ wherin I trust hys grace wyll haue a charitable respecte/ ye may sey also to my lord of Norffolk and other of the councell that I wold departe if I had mony/ Sir q⁰ mʳ Cromwell I wyll do my best and after other Commynycacion he departed
5 agayn & went to london// My lord than in the begynnyng of lent removed owt of the loge in to the Charterhowsse of Richemond/ where he lay in a lodgyng (wᶜʰᵉ Doctor Collett (sometyme dean of powlles) hade made for hyme self) vntill he removed northeward wᶜʰᵉ was in the passion weke/ after/ And he
10 had to the same howsse a secrett gallery wᶜʰᵉ went owt of his Chamber in to the Charterhowsse chirche/ whether he resortyd euery day to ther seruyce/ And at after nones he wold sytt in contemplacion wᵗ oon or other of the most auncyent ffathers of that howsse in his sell/ who among theme & by ther councell
15 perswadyd frome the vaynglory of thys world/ And gave hyme dyuers shirtes of heare the wᶜʰᵉ he often ware after ward (wherof I ame certyn) And thus he perceuered for the tyme of his abode there in godly contemplacion/ Nowe whan mʳ Cromwell came to the Court he chaunced to move my lord of Norffolk that my
20 lord wold gladly depart northeward but for lake of mony wherin he desyred his assistaunce to the kyng/ Then went they bothe Ioyntly to the kyng/ to whome My lord of Norffolk declared how my lord wold gladly depart northeward if he wanted not mony to bryng hyme thether/ The kyng thervppon referred the
25 assignemeᵗ therof to the Councell/ where vppon they ware in dyuers oppynyons/ some sayed he shold haue none for he had sufficient but late delyuerd hyme/ Some wold he shold [f. 66] haue sufficient & anowghe/ And some contrarywyse wold he shold haue but a small Somme/ And some thought it myche
30 ayenst the Councelles honor/ and myche more ayenst the kynges highe dignyte/ to se hyme want the mayntenaunce of his estate wᶜʰᵉ the kyng had gevyn hyme in this Realme and also hathe byn in suche estymacon wᵗ the kyng and in great auctorytie/ vnder hyme in this realme/ yt shold be rathe a great

6 lent removed owt] *MS.* lent owt   13 or other *interl.*; fah *canc. before* ffathers   17 contynued there *canc. before* perceuered   19 move] *MS.* moved   21 kyng/ Then] *MS.* kyng Then   22 to *interl. before* whome   32 gevyn *canc. before* gevyn; gevyn *interl.*   34 auctory.. *canc. before* auctorytie

Life of Cardinal Wolsey 131

slaunder (in forrayn Realmes) to the kyng & his hole councell to se hyme want that latly had so myche/ and nowe so lyttill/ therfore rather than he shold lake (q^d oon among theme) that rather than he shold lake/ allthoughe he neuer did me good or any pleasure yet wold I lay my plate to Gagge for hyme for a 5 M^l li Rather than he shold depart so symply as some wold haue hyme for to do/ lett vs do to hyme as we wold be don vnto consideryng his small offence and his in estymable Substaunce that he oonly hathe departyd w^t all for the same oonly for satisfieng of the kynges pleasure Rather then he wold stand in 10 defence w^t the kyng in defendyng of hys case/ As he myght Iustly haue don as all ye knowe/ lett not malice cloke thys matter wherby that pitie & mercy may take no place/ ye haue all yor pleasures fulfillyd w^{che} ye haue long desired/ And nowe suffer concyence to mynester vnto hyme some liberalitie/ the day may 15 come that some of vs may be in the same case/ ye haue suche alteracions in persons as well assured as ye suppose yor selfes to be and to stand vppon as suer a ground/ And what hangythe ouer our heddes we knowe not/ I can say no more nowe do as ye lyst/ Than after all this they began agayn to consult in this 20 matter/ And after long debatyng and reasonyng aboughte the same/ yt was concludyd that he shold haue by the way of prest a M^l marces/ owt of wynchester bysshopriche byfore hand of his pencion w^{che} the kyng had grauntyd hyme owt of the same/ for the kyng had resumed the hole revenues of the bysshopriche/ 25 of wynchester in to his owen handes/ yet the kyng owt of the same had grauntyd dyuers great pencyons vnto dyuers noble men & vnto other [f. 66^v] of his Councell So that I do suppose/ all thynges Accompted hys part was the lest So that whan thys determynacion was fully concludyd they declared the same to 30 the kyng/ who strayt wayes commaunded that M^l marces to be delyuerd owt of hand to m^r Cromewell and so it was/ The kyng callyng m^r Cromwell to hyme secretly/ bad hyme to resort to hyme agayn whan he had receyved the seyd Somme of mony/ And accordyng to the same commaundeme^t/ he repayred agayn 35 to the kyng/ to whome the kyng sayd shewe my lord yor m^r

8 the *canc. after* consideryng; his *interl. before* small   16 case/ ye] *MS.* case ye   19 h *canc. before* our   25 by *canc. before* revenues
31 wayes commaunded that] *MS.* wayes that; *superscript* li *canc. before* marces

allthoughe our Councell hathe not assigned any sufficient Somme of mony to beare hys charges/ yet ye shall shewe hyme in my behalf that I woll send hyme a M^{l} ^{li} of my benyvolence/ And tell hyme that he shall not lake/ And byd hyme to be of good
5 chere/ Mr Cromewell vppon his knee most humbly thanked the kyng (on my lordes behalf) for his great benyvolence & noble hart towardes my lord/ whos comfortable wordes/ q^d he/ of yor grace/ shall reioyse hyme more than iij^{re} tymes the valewe of yor noble reward/ And therw^t departed frome the kyng and
10 came to my lord directly to richemond/ To whome he delyuerd the mony and shewed hyme all the argume^t in the councell w^{che} ye haue hard byfore w^t the progresse of the same/ & of what mony it was & wherof it was levyed w^{che} the Councell sent hyme And of the mony w^{che} the kyng sent hyme And of his
15 comfortable wordes/ wherof my lord reioysed not a littill & greatly comforted/ And after the receypt of this mony my lord consultyd w^t m^r Cromwell abought his departure & of his Iourney w^t the order therof//

Than my lord prepared all thynges w^t spede for his Iourney
20 in to the northe/ Sent to london for lyuere clothes for his seruauntes that shold ride w^t hyme thether/ Some he refused suche as he thought ware not mete to serue/ And some agayn of ther owen mynd desired hyme of his fauour to tary still here in the Sowthe/ beyng very lothe to enbandon ther natife contrie/
25 ther parentes/ wyfes & childerne/ wherw^t he most gladly licenced w^t his good wyll & fauour And rendered vnto theme his hartie thankes for ther paynfull seruyce & long tariaunce w^t hyme in his troblesome dekay & ouerthrowe/ So that nowe/
[f. 67] all thynges beyng ffurnysshed towardes this Iourney
30 w^{che} he toke in the begynnyng/ of the passion weke/ byfore Ester/ And so rode to a place than the Abbottes of westminster called hendon/ And the next day he removed to a place called the Rye where my lady Parre lay/ the next day he roode to Royston and lodged in the monastory there/ And the next he removed to

8 than] *MS.* than than 9 yor *interl*. 13 levyed/ *canc. before* &
14 the *canc. before* his; his *interl*. 17 the *canc. before* m^r 20 northe/ Sent] *MS.* northe Sent 21 in to the *canc. before* thether 24 lothe *canc. before* lothe 30 w^{che} *interl*.; the same *canc. before* in

huntyngdon/ And there lodged in the Abbey/ And frome thence he removed to Peterboroughe And there lodged also w^{t}in the Abbey beyng than Palmesonday where he made hys abode vntyll the thursday in Ester weke/ w^{t}all his trayn/ wherof the most part went to bord wages in the town havyng xijth Cartes to carry his stuffe of his owen w^{che} came frome his collage in Oxford where he had lx^{ore} Cartes to Cary suche necessaryes as belonged to his byldynges there// Vppon Palmesonday he went in procession/ w^t the monkes beryng his Palme/ settyng forthe godes seruyce right honorably w^t such syngyng men as he than had remaynyng w^t hyme/ And vppon maundy Thursday he made his maundy in our ladys Chappell/ hauyng lix^{ti} poomen whos feet he than wasshed wyped & kyssed/ eche of thes poore men had xij^d in mony iij elles of Canvas to make theme shirtes/ a payer of newe shoes/ A Cast of Brede/ iij^{re} red herynges/ and iij^{re} whight herynges and the ode person had ij^s/ Vppon Esterday in the mornyng he rode to the resurreccion/ And that day he went in procession in his vesture Cardynall w^t his hatt & hode vppon his hed/ And he hymeself sang there the highe masse very devoutly/ And graunted cleane remyssion to all the herers and there contynued there all the holledayes//

My lord contynuyng/ at Peterboroughe after this maner entendyng to remove frome thence sent me to sir willam ffitzwillam a knyght w^{che} dwelt w^t in iij^{re} or iiij^{or} mylles of Peterboroughe to provyde hyme there a lodgyng vntill monday next folowyng on his Iourney northeward/ And beyng w^t hyme/ to whome I declared my lordes request/ and he beyng therof very glad/ reioysed not a littill that it wold please my lord to vysit his howsse in his waye/ sayeng [f. 67^v] that he shold be (the kyng ma^{tie} excepted) most hartilest welcome to hyme of any man a lyve/ And that he shold not nede to discharge the cariage of any of hys stuffe for his owen vse duryng the tyme of his beyng there but haue all thynges furnysshed redy ayenst hys commyng/ to occupie (his owen bedd excepted) Thus vppon my

1 Royston *canc. before* huntyngdon   2 Peterbury *with first* r *interl.*
canc. after to   4 Ester the thursday *with* the thursday *interl. canc.*
after vntyll   6 his collage in *interl.*   9 bey *canc. before* beryng
13 wyped *interl.*   18 had *canc. before* hatt   21 allowdays *canc.*
before holledayes   23 rev *canc. before* remove; thence *interl.*   29 be
interl.   30 ma^{tie} *interl.*

134   *Life of Cardinal Wolsey*

report made to my lord at my retorne/ he reioysed of my
messwage/ comaundyng me therw^t to geve warnyng to all his
officers & seruauntes to prepare them selfes to remove frome
Peterboroughe vppon Thursday next/ than euery man made all
5 thynges in suche redynes as was convenyent payeng in the town
for all thynges as they had taken of any person for ther owen
vse/ ffor w^{che} cause my lord caused a proclamacion to be made
in the town/ that if any person or persons in the town or contrie
there ware offendyd or greved ayenst any of my lordes
10 seruauntes/ that they shold resort to my lordes officers of
whome they shold haue redresse/ and truly answered/ as the
case Iustly requered/ So that all thynges beyng ffurnysshed my
lord toke his Iourney frome Peterboroughe vppon the Thursday
in Ester weke/ to M^r ffitzwillam where he was Ioyously receyved
15 and had right worthy & honorable entertaynme^t at the oonly
charges & expences of the seyd M^r ffitzwillam/ all his tyme
beyng there/ The occasion that moved m^r ffitzw^m thus to reioyse
of my lordes beyng in his howsse/ was that he some tyme beyng
a merchaunt of london and shereve there fill in debate w^t the
20 Citie of london vppon a Grudge bytwen the Aldermen of the
benche and hyme vppon a newe corporacion that he wold
erected there of a newe mystery called merchaunt tayllours contrarye to the oppynyon of dyuers of the benche of aldermen/ of
the Citie of london/ w^{che} caused hyme to geve & surrender his
25 Clooke/ and departed frome london & inhabyted w^t in the
Countrie/ And ayenst the malice of all the seyd aldermen and
other rewlers in the Comen wele/ of the Citie/ my lord defendyd
hyme/ and reteyned hyme in to seruyce/ whome he made first
his Treasorer of his howsse/ & than after his highe Chamberlayn/
30 And in conclusion (for his wysdome/ gravytie/ port/ and
eloquens/ beyng a gentilman of a comly stature)/ made hyme
oon of the kynges Councell/ and so contynued all his lyfe after
ward/ Therfor in [f. 68] consideracion of all thes gratitudes
receyved at my lordes handes as well in his trobyll as in his

2 me *interl.*   3 hyme *canc. before* them; them *interl.*   5 suche
canc. before suche   7 procla *canc. before* proclamacion   8–9 in the
town or contrie there *interl.*   9 ayenst] *MS.* aynst   14 was
interl.   15 right *interl.*   17 of hi *canc. before* beyng   22 of a
newe mystery *interl.*   27 Comen] *MS.* Coen   34 mynestred
by *canc. before* receyved; receyved at *interl.*

Life of Cardinal Wolsey

preferment/ was most gladest (lyke a faythfull frend of good remembraunce) to requyt hyme w^t semblable gratuytie and right Ioyous/ that he had any occasion to mynyster some pleasure suche as lay than in his power to do/ Thus my lord contynued there vntill the monday next/ where lakked no good 5 chere of costly vyandes bothe of wyn and other goodly entertaynemet/ So that vppon the seyd monday my lord departed frome thence vnto Stampford where he lay all that nyght/ and the next day he removed frome thence vnto Grantham and was lodged in a gentilmans howsse called/ m^r hall/ and the next day 10 he rode to Newarke/ & lodged in the Castell all that nyght/ The next day he roode to Southewell a place of my lordes w^t in iij^{re} or iiij^{or} myles of Newarke/ where he entendyd to contynewe all that Somer/ as he dyd after// here I must declare to you a notable tale of commynycacion/ (w^{che} was don at m^r ffitzw^m 15 byfore his departyng frome thence) bytwen hyme & me/ the w^{che} was this/ **Sir my lord** beyng in the Garden at m^r ffitzw^m walkyng and sayeng of his evynsong w^t hys Chapleyn/ I beyng there gevyng attendaunce vppon hyme/ his Evynsong fynesshed commaundyd his Chapleyn that bare vppe the trayn of his 20 gown wyllest he walked/ to delyuer me the same and he to goo aside whan he had don/ And after hys chapleyn was goon a good distaunce owt of any heryng/ he sayd vnto me/ in this wyse/ ye have q^d he/ byn late at london/ fforsothe my lord/ q^d I/ not late/ sence that I was there to bye yor lyueres for yor seruauntes/ And 25 what newes q^d he/ was there than hard ye no commynycacion ther of me/ I pray you tell me/ Than perceyvyng that I had a good occasion to talke my mynd playnly vnto hyme/ sayd/ Sir if it please yor grace/ it was my chaunce to be at a Dynner in a certyn place w^t in the Citie/ where I among dyuers other honest 30 & worshipfull gentillmen/ happed to sitt [f. 68^v] w^{che} ware for the most part of my old famylier acquayntaunce/ wherfore they ware the more bolder to enter in commynycacion w^t

1 lyke a] *MS.* lyke/ a   2 to requyt *canc. before* to; ti *canc. before first* t *of* gratuytie   6 bothe *canc. before* of costly   6–7 entertaynem^{et}/ So] *MS.* entertaynem^{et} So   7 he *canc. before* my; my lord *interl.* 10 lodged in *interl.*   21 tall *canc. before* walked; to delyuere *canc. before* to delyuer *and* his *before* the; the same *interl.*; trayn *canc. before* and   24 very *canc. after* not   25 not *canc. before* sence; f *canc. before* for   30 in *interl.* 31 happed to Suppe *canc. before* happed

me/ vnderstandyng that I was still yor graces seruaunt/ Axid me a questyon w^{che} I cowld not well assoyll theme/ what was that/ q^d my lord/ fforsothe sir/ q^d I/ ffirst they axid me howe ye dyd And howe ye accepted yor aduersitie & troble & the losse of yor
5 goodes/ to the w^{che} I answered that ye ware in helthe (thankes be to god) And toke all thyng in good part/ And sir it semed me that they ware all yor Indifferent frendes lamentyng yor dekay & losse of yor Rome & goodes/ doughtyng myche that the sequell therof cowld not be good in the Comen welthe/ ffor
10 often chayngeng of suche officers w^{che} be ffate fed in to the handes of suche as be lean and hongerd for riches woll suer travell by all means to gett aboundaunce & so the poore Comens be pillyd & extorted for gready lucre of Riches & treasure/ they sayd that ye ware full fed and entendyd nowe myche to the
15 auauncme^t of the kynges honor & the comen welthe/ Also they marvelled myche that ye beyng of so excellent a wytt and highe discression wold so symply confesse yor self gyltie in the premunyre/ wherin/ ye myght full well haue stand in the triall of yor case/ ffor they vnderstod by the report of some of the kynges
20 Councell learned that in yor case (well considered)/ ye had great wrong/ to the w^{che} I cowld make (as me thought) no sufficient Answere but sayd that I dought not but that yor so doyng was vppon some greatter consideracion than my wytt cowld vnderstand/ ys this/ q^d he/ the oppynyon of wyse men/ yea forsothe
25 my lord/ q^d I/ and allmost of all other men// Well then/ q^d he/ I se that ther wysdomes perceyve not the ground of the matter that moved me so to do ffor I considered that my ennemyes had brought the matter so to passe ayenst me/ and conveyed it so that they made it the kynges case/ and caused the kyng to take
30 the matter in to his owen handes & quarell/ And after that he had vppon occasion therof seased all my goodes & possession in

2 well *interl.*   3 ye dyd *canc. after* howe   9 can *canc. before* cowld; cowld *interl.*; Comen] *MS.* Coen   10 chayngeng *interl.*; chaynge of *canc. before* of   11 and hongerd *interl.*; an *interl. and canc. after* and; of *canc. before* for   14 to *canc. before* myche   15 comen] *MS.* coen   18 styfe *canc. before* in *and* the *before* the; the *interl.*   20 that *canc. before* ye   21 cowld *canc. before* cowld   22 so *interl.*   23 consideracion] *MS.* considericion; I *canc. before* my   25 of *canc. before* allmost   26 th . . than *interl. and canc. before* I; I se that *interl.*; that *canc. before* of   27 enneis *canc. before* ennemyes   28 that *canc. before* and; and *interl.*; they *interl. and canc. before* conveyed

Life of Cardinal Wolsey

to his demayns/ And than the quarell to be his/ he wold rather than yeld or take a foyell in the lawe/ and therby restore [f. 69] to me all my goodes agan/ wold soner (by the procuremeᵗ of my ennemyes and evyll wyllers) Imagyn my vtter vndoyng & distruccion/ Wherof the most ease therin had byn for me perpetuall Imprisonmeᵗ/ And rather then I wold Ieopard so ferre/ or put my lyfe in any suche hasard/ yet had I most levest to yeld & confesse the matter commyttyng the hole some therof as I did vnto the kynges Clemency & mercy and lyve at large lyke a poore vykare/ than to lye in prison wᵗ all the goodes & honour that I hade/ And therfore it was most best way for me (all thynges consideryd) to do as I haue don/ than to stand in triall wᵗ the kyng ffor he wold haue byn lothe to haue byn noted a wrong doer/ And in my submyssion the kyng (I dought not) had a great remorse of concyence/ wherin he wold rather pitie me than malygne me/ And also there was a contynuall serpentyn ennemye abought the kyng that wolld I ame well assured if I had byn found styfe necked/ called contynually vppon the kyng in his eare (I mean the nyght Crowe)//// wᵗ suche a vehemencye/ that I shold (wᵗ the helpe of hir assistaunce) have opteyned soner the kynges indignacion/ than his lawfull fauour and his ffauor oons lost (wᶜʰᵉ I trust at this present I haue) wold neuer haue byn by me recouered/ therfore I thought it better for me to kepe still his lovyng favour/ wᵗ losse of my goodes & dignytyes than to wynne my goodes & substaunce wᵗ the losse of hys love & pryncely fauour/ wᶜʰᵉ is but oonly deathe// Quia indignacio principis mors est/ And thys was the specyall ground and cause that I yelded my self gyltie in the premunire/ wᶜʰᵉ I perceyve all men knewe not/ wherin sence/ I vnderstand the kyng hathe conceyved a certyn pryke of concyence/ who toke secretly to hyme self the matter more grevous in his secrett stomake than all men knewe/ for he knewe wether I did offend hyme ther in so

1 beyng *canc. after* And 5 therin *and* for me *interl.*; had *canc. before* had 7 moste leves *canc. before* most; most levest *interl.* 8 matter *canc. after* hole; some therof *interl.* 10 than *canc. before* lyke; to *interl.* 11 hade *canc. before* hade 12 to *interl. before* stand 16 was *interl.*; serpenteyn *canc. before* serpentyn; serpentyn *interl.* 20 assistaunce) have opteyned] *MS.* assistaunce opteyned 25–26 pri *written over* & *and canc. before* pryncely; pryncely] *MS.* prynly 26–27 princy *canc. before* principis 29 & *canc. after* kyng 30 secretly *interl.*

grevously (as it was made) or no/ To whos concyence I do commytt my cause/ trowthe/ & equytie// And thus we left the substaunce of all this commynycacion/ allthoughe we had myche more talke/ yet is this sufficient to cause you to vnderstand as
5 well the cause of his confession in his offence/ as also the cause of the losse of all his goodes & treasure/// [f. 69ᵛ]

Nowe lett vs/ retorne were we left/ My lord beyng in the Castell of Newarke/ entendyng to ride to Southwell wᶜʰᵉ was iiijᵒʳ myles frome thence/ toke nowe his Iourney thetherward
10 ayenst Supper/ where he was fayn for lake of reparacion of the bysshopes place/ wᶜʰᵉ appurteyned to the see of yorke/ to be lodgyd in a prebendaries howsse ayenst the seyd place/ And there kepte howsse vntill wytsontyd next ayenst wᶜʰᵉ tyme he removed in to the place newely amendyd & repayred/ And there
15 contynued the most part of the Somer/ Sewerly not wᵗout great resort of the most worshipfullest gentilmen of the Contrie/ And dyuers other/ of whome they ware most gladly entertayned & had of hyme the best chere he could devyse for theme whos gentill & famylier behauour wᵗ theme caused hyme to be greatly
20 beloved & estemed/ thoroughe the hole contrie there aboughtes/ he kept an noble howsse and plentie bothe of meate & drynke/ for all commers bothe for riche & Poore/ And myche almes gevyn at his gate/ he vsed myche charite & pite/ among his poore tenauntes & other/ allthoughe the fame therof was no pleasaunt
25 sownd in the eares of his ennemyes and of suche as bare hyme no good wyll/ howebeit the Comen people woll report as they fynd cause/ ffor he was myche more famylier among all persons than he was accustumed/ And most gladdest whan he had an occasion to do them good/ he made many agrementes and concordes
30 betwen gentillman & gentillman/ And bytwen some gentillmen & ther wyfes that had byn long a Sonder and in great troble/ and dyuers other agrementes bytwen other persons/ makyng great assembles for the same purpose and feastyng of them not sparyng for any costes where he myght make a peace/ and
35 amytie/ wᶜʰᵉ purchased hyme myche love & frendshipe in the

5 all *canc. after* well   10 of *interl. after* lake   11 wa *canc. before* to be   21 noble *canc. before* noble; of *canc. before* bothe
26 wyll/ howebeit] *MS.* wyll howebeit; Comen] *MS.* Coen   33 t *canc. before* not

Contrie// yt chaunced that vppon Corpus xpi Eve after supper he commaundyd me to prepare all thyng for hyme in a redynes/ ayenst the next day/ for he entendyd to syng highe masse in the mynster/ that day And I not forgettyng his commaundeme^t/ gave lyke warnyng to all his officers of hys howsse & other of my 5 ffellowes/ to forse that all thynges appurteynyng to ther romes ware fully furnysshed to my lordes honor/ [f. 70] This don I went to my bed/ where I was skantly a slepe & warme but that oon of the porters came to my chamber doore/ callyng vppon me/ and sayd there was ij gentillmen/ at the gat that wold gladly speke 10 w^t my lord frome the kyng/ w^t that I arose vppe and went incontynent vnto the gate w^t the porter/ demaundyng what they ware that so ffayn wold come In/ they seyd vnto me that ther was m^r Breerton/ oon of the gentilmen of the kynges privye chamber/ And m^r Wrothesley w^{che} ware come frome the kyng empost/ to 15 speke w^t my lord/ than hauyng vnderstandyng what they ware caused the Porter to lett them In/ And after ther entre they desired me to speke w^t my lord w^tout delay for they myght not tary/ at whos request I repayred to my lordes chamber & waked hyme that was a slepe/ but whan he hard me speke/ he de- 20 maundyd of me what I wold haue/ Sir q^d I/ ther be bynethe in the porters loge m^r Breerton gentilman of the kynges pryvye Chamber/ and m^r writhesley come frome the kyng to speke w^t you/ they wyll not tary therfore they besech yor grace to speke w^t you owt of hand/ well than q^d my lord byd them come vppe 25 in to my dynyng chamber/ and I wyll prepare my self to come to theme/ than I resorted to them agayn/ And shewed them that my lord desired them to come vppe vnto hyme & he woll talke w^t theme w^t a right good wyll/ they thanked me & went w^t me vnto my lord and assone as they perceyved hyme beyng in his 30 nyght apparell dyd to hyme humble reuerence/ whome my lord toke by the handes demaundyng of theme howe the kyng his souerayn lord did/ sir seyd they/ right well in helthe & mery/

1 yet it *canc. before* yt   6 ap *canc. before* appurteynyng   8 had *canc. before* was; was *interl.*; in *canc. before* but   10 wold *canc. after* gat   11 vppe *canc. before* vppe   13 ffayn wold come] *MS.* ffayn come   16 lord/ than] *MS.* lord than; vnderst *canc. after* hauyng   19 at *interl.*   21 q^d I] I *written over* h   24 you/ they] *MS.* you they   25 yo *canc. before* w^t; hand/ well] *MS.* hand well   28 them *interl.*; he *interl.*   32 ther *canc. before* his

(thankes be vnto our lord)// Sir q^d they/ we must desier you to
talke w^t you a part/ w^t a right good wyll/ q^d my lord/ who drewe
them a side in to a great wyndowe/ and there talked w^t theme
secretly/ and after long talke they toke owt of a male/ a certyn
5 Coffer couered w^t grean veluett/ and bound w^t barres of siluer
& gylt/ w^t a looke of the same/ hauyng a key w^che was gylt w^t the
w^che they opened the same chest/ owt of the w^che they toke a
certyn Instrume^t or writyng conteynyng more then oon skyn of
parchement/ [f. 70^v] havyng many great Seales hangyng at yt/
10 where vnto they put more waxe for my lordes Seale/ the w^che
my lord Sealed w^t his owen seale & subscrybed his name to the
same/ And that don they wold nedes departe/ And for as myche
as it was after mydnyght/ my lord desired them to tarye & take a
bed/ they thanked hyme/ And seyd they myght in no wyse tary
15 for they wold w^t all spede to the Erle of Shrewesburys directly
w^tout lett by cause they wold be there or euer he stered in the
mornyng/ And my lord perceyvyng ther hasty spede/ caused
them to eate suche cold meate as ther was in store w^tin the
howsse and to drynke a coppe or ij of wyne/ And that don he
20 gaue eche of theme iiij^or old Souerayns of gold desiryng them
to take it in gree sayeng that if he had byn of greatter abyllitie/
ther reward shold haue byn better/ And so takyng ther leave/
they departyd/ and after they ware departed/ as I hard sey they
ware not contentid w^t ther reward/ In deade they ware not none
25 of his indifferent ffrendes w^che caused them to accept it so
disdaynously howebeit if they knewe what littill stoore of mony
he had at that present they wold I ame suere (beyng but his
Indyfferent frendes) they wold haue gevyn hyme harty thankes/
But no thyng is more lost or cast a way/ than is suche thynges
30 w^che is gevyn to suche Ingrate persons/ My lord went agayn to
bed And yet all his watche & disturbaunce that he had that
nyght notw^tstandyng/ he song hyghemasse the next day as he
appoynted byfore/ There was none in all his howsse that knewe
of the commyng or goyng of thes ij gentilmen and yet there lay
35 w^t in the seyd howsse many worshipfull strayngers//

After thys sort/ and maner my lord contynued at Southewell

2 talke *canc. before* talke   4 make *canc. before* male   15 my
lord *canc. before* the   18 them *interl.*   31 that he had that
interl.   32 nyght *interl.*   33 of *canc. before* in; in *interl.*

Life of Cardinal Wolsey 141

vntill the latter end of Grease tyme/ at w^{che} tyme he entendyd to
remove to Scrobye/ w^{che} was an other howsse/ of the bysshopriche of yorke/ and ayenst the day of his removyng he caused all
his officers to prepare as well for provysion to be made for hyme
there as also for cariage of his stuffe and other matters con- 5
cernyng his estate/ his removyng and entent was not so secrett/
but that it was [f. 71] knowen/ abrode in Contrie/ w^{che} was
lamentable to all his neyghbors/ abought Southwell/ and as it
was lamentable vnto them/ so was yt as myche Ioy to his neygh-
bors abought Scrobye/ Ayenst the day of his removyng dyuers 10
knyghtes & other gentilmen of worshype in the Contrie/ came
to hyme to Sowthewell entendyng to accompany & attend vppon
hyme in that Iourney the next day And to conducte hyme
thoroughe the fforest vnto Scrobye/ but he beyng of ther
purpose aduertised howe they did entend to haue lodged a 15
great stagg or tweyn for hyme by the waye/ purposly to shewe
hyme all pleasure & disporte they cowld devyse and havyng
(as I seyd) therof Intelligence was very lothe to receyve any
suche honor & disport at ther handes not knowyng howe the
kyng wold take it and beyng well assured that his ennemyes 20
wold reioyse myche to vnderstand that he wold take vppon
hyme any suche presumpcyon/ wherby they myght fynd an
occasion to enforme the kyng howe sonpmtyous & pleasaunt he
was notw^tstandyng his aduersite and ouerthrowe/ And so to
bryng the kyng in to a wrong oppynyon of small hope/ in hyme 25
of reconsilme^t/ but rather that he sowght a mean to opteyn the
fauour of the Contrie/ to w^tstand the kynges procedynges w^t
dyuers suche Imagynacions wherin he myght soner catche
displeasure than fauour & honour/ And also he was lothe to
make the worshipfull gentilmen privye to this his Imaginacion 30
lest parauenture that they shold conceyve some toye or fantzy
in ther hedes by means therof and so to eschewe ther accustumed
accesse and absent theme selfes frome hyme/ w^{che} shold be as
myche to hys greve/ as the other was to his comfort/ therfore he

3 rem *canc. before* removyng   7 knowen *canc. after* it was   9 yt *canc. before* yt   11 & *canc. before* knyghtes   16 or tweyn *interl.*
17 hyme *canc. before* and   21 *a single indecipherable letter canc. before* take   24 by *canc. after* to   26 wold wold *with first* w *written over* b *canc. after* he   30 priyy *canc. before* privye   34 ther *canc. before* his

devysed this meane way/ (as hereafter folowyth) w^{che} shold rather be taken for a laughyng disport than other wyse/ ffirst he called me vnto hyme secretly at nyght goyng to his rest/ And commaundyd me in any wyse most secretly that nyght to cause
5 .vj.th or .vij.^{en} horsses besides his mewle for his owen person to be made redy by the breke of the day for hyme/ and for suche persons as he appoynted to ride w^t hyme to an Abbey called welbeke/ where he entendyd to logge by the way to Scrobye/ wyllynge me to be also in a redynes/ [f. 71^v] to ride w^t hyme/
10 And to call hyme so early that he myght be on horssebake after he had hard masse by the brekyng of day/ Sir/ what wyll you more/ All thynges beyng accomplisshed accordyng to his commaundeme^t And the same fynysshed & don/ he w^t a small nomber byfore appoynted mounted vppon his mewle settyng
15 forthe by the brekyng of the day towardes welbeke w^{che} is abought xvj^{en} mylles frome thence/ whether my lord & we came byfore vjth of the cloke in the mornyng and he went strayt to his bed levyng all the gentilmen strayngers in ther beddes at Sowthewell no thyng privye of my lordes secrett departure/ who
20 expectyd his vppe risyng vntill it was viijth of the Clocke/ but after it was knowen to theme/ and to all the rest there remaynyng behynd hyme/ than euery man went to horsbake/ gallopeng after supposyng to ouertake hyme/ but he was at his rest in welbeke or euer they roose owt of ther beddes in Sowthewell/ And so
25 ther cheafe huntyng and Coursyng of the great Stagge was disapoynted & dassht/ but at ther thether resort to my lord syttyng at dynner the matter was gested & laughed owte/ merylye/ and all the matter well taken/ My lord the next day removed frome thence/ to whome resortyd dyuers gentillmen of
30 my lord therle of Shrewsburys seruauntes to desier my lord in ther m^{rs} name to hunt in a parke/ of therles called worsoppe parke/ the w^{che} was w^t in a myle of welbeke/ and the very best & next waye for my lord to travell thorowghe on his Iourney where myche plenty of game was layed in a redynes to shewe

1 w^{che} *canc. before* (as   2 be *interl.*; f *canc. before* a   3 bed *canc. before* rest   9 to be in a *canc. before* to ride   13 small *canc. before* small   17 he *interl.*   18 l *canc. before* levyng   32 w^{che} was w^t] *MS.* w^{che} w^t; *two indecipherable letters canc. before* very

hyme pleasure/ howbeit he thanked my lord ther m^r for his
gentilnes and theme for ther paynnes/ sayeng that he was no
meate man for any suche pastyme/ beyng a man other wyse
disposed/ suche pastyme & pleasure ware meate for suche noble
men as delight therin/ Neuerthelesse/ he cowld do no lesse than
to accompte my lord of Shrewsbury to be myche his frend in
whome he found suche gentilnes & noblenes in his honorable
offer/ to whome he rendered his most lowly thankes/ but in no
wyse they cowld entreat hyme to hunt allthoughe the worshipfull
gentilmen beyng in his company provoked him all that they
cowld do therto/ yet he wold not consent desyryng theme to be
contented/ sayeng that he came not in to the Contrye [f. 72] to
frequent or folowe any suche pleasures or pastymes/ but oonly
to attend to a greatter Care that he had in hand wch was his
dewtie, study & pleasure And w^t suche reasons & perswasions he
pacified them for that tyme/ howbeit yet as he rode thoroughe
the parke bothe my lord of Shrewsburys seruauntes And also
the forescyd gentilmen moved hyme/ oons agayn byfore whome
the dere lay very fayer for all pleasaunt/ huntyng and Coursyng/
but it wold not be/ but made as myche sped to ride thorowghe
the parke/ as he cowld/ And at the issue owte of the parke/ he
callyd therles gentilmen & the kepers vnto hyme/ desiryng
theme to haue hyme commendyd to my lord ther m^r/ thankyng
hyme for hys most honorable offer & good wyll/ trustyng
shortly to visit hyme at his owen howsse/ And gave the kepers
xl^s for ther payns & diligence/ who conducted hyme thoroughe
the parke And so rode to an other abbey called Rofford Abbey/
And after he rode to blythe Abbey/ where he lay all nyght/ And
the next day to Scrobye where he contynued vntill after
Michelmas mynystryng many deades of charitie/ Most Comenly
euery Sonday (if the whether did serue) he wold travell vnto
some paryshe chirche/ there abought and there wold say hys
devyn seruyce And other here or say masse hyme self/ causyng
some oon of hys Chaplyns to preche vnto the people/ And that
don he wold dynne/ in some honest howsse/ of that town/ where

1 & *canc. before* for   3 of *canc. before* other   4 yt is *canc. before*
suche pastyme   11 h *canc. before* theme   16 as] *MS.* as as; rose *canc.*
before rode   17 al *canc. after* seruauntes   23 the *canc. before*
hyme   24 hys *canc. before* hys   29 Skroerby *canc. before* Scrobye

144   *Life of Cardinal Wolsey*

shold be distributed to the poore a great almes/ as well of mete & drynke/ as of monye/ to supplye the want of sufficient mete/ if the nombor of the poore did so exced of necessitie/ And thus w^t other good deades practasyng & excercisyng duryng his
5 abode at Scrobye as makyng of love dayes and aggreme^{tes} bytwen partie & partie/ beyng than at varyaunce/ he/ dayly frequentyng hyme self abought suche busynes/ & deades of honest charitie// [f. 72^v]

Than abought/ the feast of Seynt Michell next ensuyng my
10 lord toke his Iourney towardes Cawood Castell/ the w^{che} is w^{t}in vij^{en} myles of yorke/ And passyng thether he lay ij nyghtes and a day at Seynt Oswaldes Abbeye where he hymeself confirmed Childerne in the Chyrche frome viijth of Clocke in the mornyng vntyll xj^{en} of the clocke at none/ And makyng a short
15 dynner resortyd agayn to the chirche at oon of the cloke/ And there began agayn to confirme moo childern vntill iiij^{or} of the cloke/ where he was at the last constrayned for werynes to sitt down in a chayer/ the nomber of the childerne was suche/ that don he sayd his Evynsong and than went to Sopper/ And rested
20 hyme there all that nyght/ And the next mornyng he applied hyme self to departe towardes Cawood and or euer he departed he confirmed all most an Cth childerne more And than rode on his Iourney/ And by the way ther ware assembled at a stone Crosse standyng vppon a greane w^t in a quart^r of a myle of
25 fferyebrigg abought the number of CCth childerne to confirme/ where he allighted and never removed hys foote vntill he had confirmed theme all/ And than toke his mewle/ agayn and roode to Cawood where he lay long after w^t myche honour and love of the Contrie/ bothe of the worshipefull and of the symple/
30 excercysyng hyme self in good deades of charitie/ And kepte there an honorable & plentifull howsse/ for all commers/ And also bylt & repayred the Castell w^{che} was than greatly dekayed hauyng a great multitude of artifycers and laborers/ above the nomber of CCCth persons dayly in wages/ And lyeng there he
35 had Intelligence/ by the gentilmen of the Contrie/ that vsid to

---

4 excersi *canc. before* excercisyng   9 abought *canc. before* the
12 hymeself *interl.*   19 dyn *canc. before* Sopper   22 childerne more] *MS*. childerne/ more   23 stone *interl.*   27 meu *canc. before* mewle   34 wages/ And] *MS*. wages And; he *canc. before* lyeng

repayer vnto hyme/ that there was sprong a great varyaunce &
deadly hate/ bytwen sir Richard Tempest & m^r Bryan hastynges
than but a squyer w^{che} was after made knyght/ bytwen whome
was lyke to ensue great murder onlesse some good mean myght
be found to redresse the Inconvenyence that was most lyklyest
to ensue/ my lord beyng therof aduertised laymentyng the case
made suche means by his wysdome & letters w^t other perswasions that thes ij gentilmen ware content to resort to my
lord to Cawood/ and there to abyde his order/ hyghe & lowe/
than was there a day [f. 73] Appoynted of there assembly byfore
my lord/ At w^{che} day they Came/ not w^{t}out great nomber on
eche partie/ wherfore ayenst w^{che} day my lord had requyred
many worshipfull gentilmen to be there present to assist hyme
w^t ther wysdomes to appease thes ij worthy gentilmen/ beyng
at deadly foode/ and to se the kynges peace kepte/ commaundyng no more of ther nomber to enter in to the Castell w^t
thes ij gentilmen than vj persons of eche of ther menyall
seruauntes and all the rest to remayn w^{t}out in the town or where
they listed to repayer/ And my lord hyme self issuyng owte of
the gattes callyng the nomber of bothe parties byfore hyme
strayntly chargeng them most earnestly to obserue & kepe the
kynges peace/ in the kynges name/ vppon ther parelles w^{t}out
owther braggyng or quarellyng eyther w^t other and caused
theme to haue bothe beare and wynne sent theme in to the
town/ And than retourned agayn in to the Castell beyng abought
ix^{en} of the cloke/ And bycause he wold haue thes gentilmen to
dyne w^t hyme at his owen table/ thought it good/ in avoydyng of
further Inconvenyence/ to appeace ther rancore byfore/ where
vppon he called theme in to his Chappell/ And there w^t the
assystence/ of the other gentilmen he fill in to commynycacion
w^t the matter/ declaryng vnto theme the dayngers & myschefes
that thoroughe ther wylfulnes & foly ware most lyklyest to
enswe/ w^t dyuers other good exhortacions/ Notw^{t}standyng the
parties layeng And allegyng many thynges for there defence/

2 Tempest *canc. before* Tempest   4 e *canc. before* ensue *and* a *before*
great   5 Inconvenye *canc. before* Inconvenyence; was *interl*   14 to
pas *canc. before* to; gentilmen *canc. before* gentilmen   20 byfore *canc.*
before byfore   25 ix *canc. after* abought   30 of the . wors the
other *canc. before* of   34 layeng *canc. before* layeng

Sometyme Addeng eche to other stout & dispyghtfull wordes of diffyaunce the w^che my lord & the other gentilmen had myche a do to qualifie/ ther malices was so greate/ howbeit at lengethe/ w^t long contynuaunce// wyse argume^tes & depe perswasions made by my lord they ware aggreed & fynally accordyd abought iiij^or of the cloke at after none/ And so made theme ffrendes/ And as it semed they bothe reioysed & ware right well contentyd therw^t/ to the great comfort of all the other worshipfull gentilmen/ causyng theme to shake handes and to go arme in Arme to dynner/ And so went to dynner/ thoughe it was very late/ to dynne/ yet notw^tstandyng [f. 73^v] they dyned together w^t thother gentilmen at my lordes table where they dranke lovyngly eche to other w^t countenaunce of great Amytie/ After dynner my lord caused them to discharge ther rowtes & assemble that remayned in the town and to retayn w^t theme no mo seruauntes than they ware accustumed most comenly to ride w^t/ And that don/ thes gentillmen ffulfillyng his commaundeme^t taried at Cawood and lay there all nyght whome my lord entertayned in suche sort that they accepted his noble hart in great worthynes trustyng to haue of hyme a specyall Ioyell in ther contrie/ hauyng hyme in great estymacion & fauour/ as it appered after ward by ther behauor & dymeanor towardes hyme//

Yt ys not/ to be/ doughted but that the worshipefull persons As doctors and prebendaries of the cloos of yorke/ wold & did resort vnto hyme accordyng to ther dewties as vnto ther father & patron of ther sperytuall dignyties/ beyng at his first commyng in to the contrie/ ther chirche of yorke beyng w^tin vij^en myles/ wherfore ye shall vnderstand that Doctor hikden Deane of the chirche of yorke w^t the treasorer and dyuers other hed officers of the same repayred to my lord welcommyng hyme most Ioyously in to the contrie sayeng that it was to theme no small comfort to se hyme among theme as ther cheafe hed w^che hathe byn so long absent frome theme/ beyng all that while lyke

3 & *canc. after* qualifie; geat *canc. before* greate   4 & *canc. before* / wyse and depe *before* &   5 at *canc. before* they; g *canc. after* accordyd
7 as *interl.*; contentyd *interl.*   7–8 con contendyd *canc. before* therw^t
10 wase *canc. before* was   16 to ride *canc. before* most   17 fully *canc. before* ffulfillyng   19 s *canc. after* noble   20 of *canc. before* a; of hyme *interl. and canc. before* in   34 absence *canc. before* while

ffatherlesse childerne & comfortles trustyng shortly to se hyme among them/ in his owen chirche/ yt is/ q^d he/ the especyall cause of all my travell in to this Contrie not oonly to be among you for a tyme but also to spend my lyfe w^t you as a very father and a mutuall brother/ Sir than/ q^d they/ ye must vnderstand that the ordenarie Ruelles of our chirche hathe byn of an auncyent Custume/ wherof allthoughe ye be hed & chefe gouernor yet be ye not so well acquaynted w^t theme as we be/ therfore we shall vnder the supportacion of yor grace/ declare some part therof to you/ as well of our auncyent Customes As of the lawse & vsage/ of the same/ Therfore ye shall vnderstand that where ye do entend to repayer vnto vs/ the old lawe & custume of our chirche hathe byn that the archebisshope beyng our chefe hed & pasture as your grace nowe be/ myght ne owght not to come above the quyer doore nor haue any stalle in the quyer/ vntill [f. 74] he by dewe order ware there stalled/ ffor if ye shold happen to dye byfore yor stallacion ye shold not be buried above in the quyer but in the body of the same chirche benethe/ therfore we shall (vna voce) requyer yor grace/ in the name of all other our brotherne/ that you wold vouchesalve to do herin as yor noble predecessors & honorable fathers hathe don/ And that ye wyll not infrynge or violate any of our laudable ordynaunces & constitucions of our chirche/ to the obseruaunce & preseruacion wherof we be obliged by vertue of an othe at our first admyttaunce to se them obserued & fulfilled to the vttermost of our powers/ w^t dyuers other matters remaynyng of Record in our treasory howsse/ among other thynges// Thos recordes/ q^d my lord/ wold I gladly se/ And thos seen & digested/ I shall than shewe you further of my mynd/ And thus of thys matter they ceassed commynycacion and passed forthe in other matters/ So that my lord assigned theme a day to bryng in ther recordes/ at w^{che} day they brought w^t them ther reiester boke of record/ wherin was writtyn ther constitucions and auncyent Rewles wherevnto all the fathers & mynesters of the chirche of yorke ware most cheafely bound bothe to se it don & performed

1 & *interl.*   5 brother/ Sir] *MS.* brother Sir   7 be *interl.*
10 & *canc. before* As   11 vsed *canc. before* vsage   12 y *canc. before* vs   14 is *canc. before* be   22 infrynge *canc. before* infrynge
27 Ac *canc. before* our   28 my lord/ wold] *MS.* my/ lord wold

and also to performe & obserue the same them selfes/ And whan
my lord had seen/ rede/ & considered theffect of ther recerdes
And debated w^t theme substancyally therin/ he determyned to
be stalled there in the mynstere the next monday after Alhalou-
5 day/ Ayenst w^{che} day there was made necessarye preparacion/
for the furniture therof/ but not in so sumptious a wyse as his
predecessors did byfore hyme/ ne yet in suche a sort as the
comen fame was blowen a brode of hyme/ to his great slaunder/
and to the reporters myche more dishonestie to forge suche
10 lyes & blasfemous reportes wherin ther is no thyng more
ontrewe/ The trowthe wherof I perfectly knowe/ for I was made
pryvye to the same/ And sent to yorke to forse all thyng to prepare accordyng for the same/ w^{che} shold haue byn myche more
meane & basse than all other of his predicessors hertofore hathe
15 don/ yt came so to passe that vppon hallhalouday oon of the hed
officers of the chyrche w^{che} shold (by vertue of his office) haue
most doynges in this stallacion came to dynne w^t my lord at
Cawood and sittyng at dynner they fill in commynycacion
[f. 74^v] for the order of his stallacion/ who sayd to my lord that
20 he owght to goo vppon clothe frome seynt Iames chapell
(standyng w^{t}out the gattes of the Citie of yorke) vnto the
mynster the w^{che} shold be distributed among the poore/ My
lord heryng this made answere to the same in this wyse/
Allthoughe/ q^d he/ that our predycessors went vppon clothe
25 right Somptiously/ we do entend (god willyng) to goo a foote
frome thence w^{t}out any suche glory/ in the vamppes of my
hosyn/ for I take god to be my very Iuge that I presume not to
goo thether for any tryhumphe or vaynglory/ but oonly to fulfyll
the obseruaunces & Rewles of the chirche to the w^{che} (as ye say)
30 I ame bound/ And therfore I shall desier you all to hold you
contentyd w^t my symplycyte/ And also I commaund all my
seruauntes to goo as humbly w^{t}out any other sumptyous apparell
than they be costumably vsed & that is comly & decent to were/
ffor I do assure you I do entend to come to yorke vppon Sonday

2 b *canc. after* my 6 furniture] *MS.* furtiature 8 comen]
MS. coen 10 bl *canc. before* & 11 ontrewe/ The] *MS.*
ontrewe The 12–13 d *canc. after* prepare 15 byn *canc. before*
don 17 stallacion came to] *MS.* stallacion to 21 the Citie of
interl. 26 of *canc. before* of; of *interl.* 27 be *canc. before* be
33 & that is *interl.*; to where/ *canc. before* comly

at nyght and lodge there in the Deans howsse and vppon
monday to be stalled & there to make a dynner for you of the
cloose and for other worshipfull gentylmen/ that shall chaunce
to come to me at that tyme/ And the next day to dynne w^t the
Mayor and so retorne home agayn to Cawood that nyght/ And
thus to fynysshe/ the same wherby I may at all tymes resort to
yorke mynster w^{t}out other scripulosite or offence to any of you/
This day cowld not be onknowen to all the Contrie but that some
must nedes haue knowlege therof/ wherby that notice was gevyn
vnto the gentillmen of the Contrie/ And they beyng therof as
well aduertised as Abbottes/ Priors & other of the day of this
solemnyzacyon/ sent in suche provision of dayntie victualles that
it is allmost Incredyble/ wherfore I omyt to declare vnto you
the certyntie therof/ As of great & fatt beafes/ muttons/ wyld-
fowle/ and venyson bothe red & falowe and dyuers other dayntie
meates suche as the tyme of the yere dyd serue/ sufficyent to
furnysshe a great & somptious feast/ all w^{che} thynges ware
onknowen to my lord/ for as myche as he beyng preventyd and
disapoynted of his reasonable purposed entent/ by cause he was
arrestyd as ye shall here hereafter/ So that [f. 75] the most part
of this provision was sent to yorke/ that same day that he was
arrested and the next day folowyng/ ffor his arrest was kept as
cloose & secrett frome the contrie as it cowld be/ by cause they
doughted the people w^{che} had hyme in great love & estymacion/
for his accustumed charitie/ & liberalitie vsed daylye among
theme w^t famylier gesture & countenaunce/ w^{che} be the very
means to allewer the love & hartes of the people in the northe
parties/ **Or euer I wad** any ferther in this matter I do entend
to declare vnto you what chaunced hyme byfore this his last
troble at Cawood as a sygne or token gevyn by god what shold
folowe of his end or of troble w^{che} did shortly ensue/ the sequell
wherof was of no man (than present) owther premedytate or
Imagyned/ therfor for as myche as it is a notable thyng to be
considered I wyll (god wyllyng) declare it as truly as it chaunced

8 Contre *canc. before* Contrie   13 the *canc. after* you   14 bukes
canc. after fatt   16 ye *canc. after* of   20 here hereafter/]
MS. here/ hereafter   24 hyme] *MS.* hymee   31 or *interl.*;
shold *canc. before* did; did *interl.*; At the w^{che} doyng/ *canc. before* the
33 Imagyned/ therfor] *MS.* Imagyned therfor; notable *canc. before* notable
34 to *canc. before* it as

accordyng to my symple remembraunce/ at the w^{che} I my self
was present//

My lordes accustumed Ennemyes in the Court abought the
kyng had nowe my lord in more dowght than they had byfore
5 hys fall/ consideryng the contynuall fauour that the kyng bare
hyme/ thought that at lengthe the kyng myght caulle hyme home
agayn/ And if he so did/ they supposed that he wold rather
Imagyn ayenst theme/ than to remytt or forgett ther Crueltie
w^{che} they most oniustly Imagened ayenst hyme// warfore they
10 compased in ther hedes that they wold owther by some means
dispatche hyme by some synester Accusacion of treason/ or to
bryng hyme in to the kynges highe indignacion by some other
wayes/ this was ther dayly Imagynacion & studye/ hauyng as
many spyalles and as many eyes to attend vppon his doynges (as
15 the poettes fayn Argos to haue)/ So that he cowld nother worke/
or do any thyng but that his ennemyes had knowlege therof
shortly after/ Nowe at the last they espied a tyme wherin they
caught an occasion/ to bryng ther purpose to passe thynkyng
therbye to haue of hyme a great avauntage/ ffor the matter beyng
20 oons disclosed vnto the kyng in suche a vehemencye as they
purposed/ they thought the kyng wold be moved ayenst hyme w^t
great displeasure/ And that [f. 75^v] by them executyd & don/
the kyng vppon ther Informacion/ thought it good that he shold
come vppe to stand to his triall/ w^{che} they lyked no thyng at
25 all/ Notw^tstandyng he was sent for after thys sort/ ffirst they
devysed that he shold come vppe apon arest in ward the w^{che}
they knewe right well wold so sore greve hyme that he myght be
the weker to come in to the kynges presence to make answere/
wherfore they sent sir walter welshe knyght (oon of the
30 gentilmen of the kynges privye chamber)/ down in to the
Contrie vnto the Erle of Northehumberland (who was brought
vppe in my lordes howsse) w^t a Commyssion/ And they twayn
beyng in commyssion/ Ioyntly to arrest my lord of haulte treason/
thys conclusion fully resolued/ they caused m^r walsshe to
35 prepare hyme selfe to thys Iourney w^t this commyssion and

11 to *canc. before* dispatche; some *interl.* 12 kynges *interl.* 14 as
canc. before and 20 they *interl.* 25 all/ Notw^tstandyng] *MS.*
all Notw^tstandyng 28 come *canc. before* come 33 hal *canc.*
before haulte

Life of Cardinal Wolsey 151

Certyn Instruccions annexed to the same/ who made hyme redy to ride and toke his horsse at the Court gate Abought oon of the clocke at none vppon halhalou day/ towardes the Northe/ **Nowe ame** I come to the place where I wyll declare the thyng that I promysed you byfore of a certyn token of my lordes troble w^{che} 5 was thys/ **My lord** syttyng at dynner vppon Alhalou day in Cawood castell hauyng at his bordes end dyuers of his most worthiest chapleyns syttyng at dynner to kepe hyme company for lake of Strayngers/ ye shall vnderstand that my lordes great crosse of Syluer accustumably stode in the corner at the tables 10 end leanyng ayenst the tappett or hangyng of the chamber/ And whan the tables end was taken vppe/ & a convenyent tyme for theme to arryse/ And in arryssyng frome the tabyll/ oon doctor Augusteyn/ the phisicion beyng a venycian borne/ hauyng a boystors gown of blake veluett vppon hyme/ As he wold haue 15 come owt at the tables end his gown ouerthrewe the crosse that stode there in the corner/ And the Crosse raylyng down along the tappett it chaunced to fall vppon doctor Bonners hed w^{che} stod among other by the tappett makyng of Curtesy to my lord and w^t oon of the poyntz of the [f. 76] crosse Raced hys hed a 20 littill that the blode ran down/ the company standyng there ware greatly astoned w^t the chaunce (my lord syttyng in his chayer) lokyng vppon them perceyved the chaunce/ demaundyd of me beyng next hyme what the matter ment of ther soden abasshemet/ I shewed hyme howe the Crosse fyll vppon doctor 25 Bonners hed/ hathe it/ q^d he/ drawen any bloode/ yea forsothe my lord/ q^d I/ as it semythe me/ w^t that he cast down hys hed lokyng very soberly vppon me a good while w^{t}out any word spekyng/ at the last/ q^d he/ shakyng of hys hed/ **Malum Omen**/ And therw^t sayd grace/ and rose frome the table/ And went in to 30 his bed chamber there lamentyng makyng his prayers/ Nowe marke the sygnyficacion howe my lord expoundyd this matter vnto me after ward at Pountfrett Abbey/ ffirst ye shall vnderstand that by the Crosse w^{che} belonged to the dygnytie of yorke/ he

8 sytt *canc. before* syttyng; syttyng *interl.*   11 at *canc. before* ayenst
12 a *and* tyme for *interl.*; for tyme of *with* for tyme *interl. canc. before* tyme
16 w^t *canc. before* his   17 there *interl.*   20 brake *canc. before*
Raced; Raced *interl.*   21 down/ the] *MS.* down the   23 vppon
them *interl.*   25 doctor] *MS.* doctors   27 I thynke so *interl.*
and canc. before as

vnderstode to be hymeself/ And by Augusteyn he vnderstode that ouerthrewe the Crosse to be he that shold accuse hyme/ by means wherof he shold be ouerthrowen/ the fallyng vppon m^r Bonners hed (who was m^r of my lordes faculties & sperytuall
5 Iurisdiccions) w^{che} was dampnefied by the ouerthroweng of the crosse by the phisicion/ And by the drawyng of blode betokned deathe/ w^{che} shortly after came to pas/ Abought the same very tyme of the day of thys myschaunce m^r walshe toke hys horsse at the Court gate/ as nyghe as it cowld be Iuged/ And thus my
10 lord toke it for a very sygne or token of that w^{che} after enswed if the circumstaunce be equally considered & noted/ Allthoughe no man was there present at that tyme that had any knowlege of m^r walshes commyng down/ or what shold followe/ wherfore as it was supposed that god shewed hyme more secrett knowlege
15 of his lattere dayes & end of his troble than all men supposed/ w^{che} appered right well by dyuers talkes (that he had w^t me at dyuers tymes) of his last end/ And nowe that I haue declared vnto you theffect of this prodegye and sygn/ I wold retorne agayn to my matter//// [f. 76^v]
20 **The tyme drawyng** nyghe of his stallacion sittyng at dynner vppon the ffriday next byfore monday on the w^{che} he entendyd to be stalled at yorke/ the Erle of Northumberland and m^r walshe w^t a great company of gentilmen/ as well of therles seruauntes as of the Contrie w^{che} he had gathered together to accompany
25 hyme in the kynges name (not knowyng to what purpose or to what entent) came in to the hall at Cawood (the officers sittyng at dynner/ and my lord not fully dyned) but beyng at his freuctes/ nothyng knowyng of therles beyng in his hall/ The first thyng that therle dyd after he came in to the Castell com-
30 maunded the Porter to delyuer hyme the kayes of the gattes who wold in no wyse delyuer hyme the kayes/ allthoughe he ware very roughly commaundyd in the kynges name to delyuer theme/ to oon of therles seruauntes/ Seyeng vnto therle/ Sir ye do entend to delyuer them to oon of yor seruauntes to kepe theme & the

---

1 hy *canc. after* vnderstode; to be *interl.*   8 of the day *interl.*
11 ther was *canc. after* Allthoughe   12 was *interl.*   20 and *canc. before* at   22 and m^r] *MS.* and/ m^r 26 who *canc. before* came
27 dynner/] / *written over*)   30 gattes of *canc. after* hyme the; gattes *canc. before* gattes; gattes *interl.*

gattes and to plant an other in my rome/ I knowe no cause whye
ye shold so do/ and this I assure you that yor lordshipe hathe
no oon seruaunte but that I ame as able to kepe theme as he/ to
what purpose so euer it be/ And also the keyes ware delyuerd
me by my lord my M^r w^t a charge bothe by othe & by other 5
preceptes & commaundeme^{tes} therfore I beseche yor lordshipe
to pardon me/ thowghe I refuse yor commaundeme^t ffor what
so euer ye shall commaunde me to do that belongyth to my
office/ I shall do it w^t a right good wyll as Iustly as any other of
yor seruauntes/ w^t that q^d the gentilmen there present vnto 10
therle (heryng hyme speke so stoutly lyke a man & w^t so good
reason) Sir/ q^d they/ he is a good ffellowe & spekythe lyke a
faythfull seruaunt vnto his m^r/ and lyke an honest man/ therfore
geve hyme yor charge and lett hyme kepe still the gattes/ who we
dought not wyll be obedyent to yor lordshipes commaundeme^t/ 15
Well than/ q^d therle/ hold hyme a boke and commaund hyme to
lay his hand vppon the boke/ where at the porter made some
dought/ but beyng perswadyd by the gentilmen there present/
was contentid/ and layed his hand vppon the boke/ to whome/
q^d therle/ thou shall swere to kepe well & truly thes gattes to the 20
kynges our soueraĵn lordes vse and to do all suche thynges as
we shall commaund the in the kynges name beyng his hyghnes
commyssioners and as it shall seme to vs at all tymes good as
long as we shalbe here in the Castell/ And that [f. 77] ye shall
not lett in nor owte at thes gattes but suche as ye shalbe com- 25
maundyd/ by vs frome tyme to tyme/ And vppon this othe he
receyved the kayes at therles and m^r walshes handes/ of all thes
doynges knewe my lord no thyng/ for they stopped the stayers
that went vppe in to my lordes chamber where he sate/ so that
no man cowld passe vppe agayn that was come down/ At the last 30
oon of my lordes seruauntes chaunced to loke down in to the
hall at a loope that was vppon the stayers and retorned to my
lord that shewed hyme that my lord of Northumbeland was in
the hall/ where at my lord marvelled and wold not beleve hyme
at the fyrst but commaundyd a gentilman/ beyng his gentilman 35

2 you *canc. before* you; you that *interl.*   10 seruauntes/ w^t] *MS.*
seruauntes w^t 12 / q^d they/ *interl.*   15 o *canc. before* obedyent
15–16 commaundeme^t/ Well] *MS.* commaundeme^t Well   31 of *interl.*;
loke *canc. before* loke   33 & *canc. before* that shewed   34 not *interl.*

vssher to goe down & bryng hyme perfight word/ Who goyng
down the stayers lokyng down at the loope/ where he sawe therle/
who than retorned to my lord & shewed hyme that it was very
he/ than/ q^d my lord/ I ame sory that we haue dyned for I feare
5 that our officers be not stored of any plenty of good ffysshe/ to
make hyme suche honorable chere/ as to hys estate ys con-
venyent/ Notw^tstandyng he shall haue suche as we haue/ w^t a
right good wyll and lovyng hart/ lett the table be standyng still
and we woll goo down and meate hyme/ and bryng hyme vppe
10 and than he shall se howe ferreforthe we be at our dynner/ w^t
that he put the table frome hyme/ and rose vppe/ goyng down
he encountred therle vppon the myddes of the stayers/ commyng
vppe/ w^t all hys men abought hyme/ And as sone as my lord
espied therle he put of hys cappe/ and sayd to hyme/ my lord ye
15 be most hartely welcome (And therw^t they enbraced eche other)
Althoughe my lord/ q^d he/ that I haue often desired and wysshed
in my hart to se you in my howsse/ yet if ye had lovyd me as I
do you/ ye wold haue sent me word byfore of yor commyng to
thentent that I myght haue receyved you accordyng to yor
20 honor & myn/ Notw^tstandyng ye shall haue suche cheare as I
ame able to make you w^t a right good wyll/ trustyng that ye wyll
accepte the same of me as of yor very old & lovyng frend/ hopyng
hereafter to se you oftener whan I shalbe more able and better
provydyd to receyve you/ w^t better fare/ [f. 77^v] And than my
25 lord toke my lord of Northeumberland by the hand & led hyme
vppe in to the Chamber/ whome folowed all therles seruauntes
where the table stode in thestate that my lord left it whan he
rose/ sayeng vnto therle/ Sir nowe ye may perceyve howe
ferforthe we ware at our dynner/ my lord led therle to the fier
30 sayng my lord ye shall goo in to my bed chamber where is a
good fier made for you/ and there ye may shyfte yor apparell
vntill yor chamber be made redy therfore lett yor male be
brought vppe and or euer I goo I pray you geve me leave to take
thes gentilmen yor seruauntes by the handes/ And whan he had

2 at the loope *canc. after* lokyng down; my lord *canc. before* therle   8 table *canc. before* table   11 vppe/ goyng] *MS.* vppe goyng   17 he *canc. after* if; ye *interl.*   24 the *canc. before* my   28 rose/ sayeng] *MS.* rose sayeng   34 g *canc. before* thes

Life of Cardinal Wolsey 155

taken theme all by the handes/ he retourned to therle & sayed
Ah my lord I perceyve well that ye haue obserued my old
preceptes & Instruccions w^che I gave you whan ye ware abydyng
w^t me in yor youthe/ w^che was to cheryshe yor fathers old
seruauntes wherof I se here present w^t you a great nomber/   5
sewerly my lord ye do therin very well and nobly and lyke a wyse
gentilman/ ffor thes be they that will not oonly serue & love you/
but they wyll also lyve & die w^t you/ and be treu & faythfull
seruauntes to you/ And glade to se you prosper in honor/ the
w^che I beseche god send you w^t long lyve///   10
Thys sayd/ he toke therle by the hand & led hyme in to hys
bedd chamber and they beyng there all alone (save oonly I that
kepte the doore/ accordyng to my dewtie beyng gentilman
vssher) thes ij lordes standyng at a wyndowe/ by the chymney
in my lordes bedd chamber/ therle tremlyng sayed w^t a very faynt   15
& softe voyce/ vnto my lord/ layeng his hand vppon his arme/
My lord/ q^d he/ I arrest you of hyghe treason/ w^t w^che wordes my
lord was marvelously astonyed standyng bothe still a long space
w^tout any ferther wordes/ but at the last/ q^d my lord/ what
movyth you or by what auctorytie do you this/ fforsothe my   20
lord/ I haue a commyssion to warraunt me/ & my doynges/
where is yor commyssion/ q^d my lord/ lett me se yt/ Nay sir that
you may not/ q^d therle/ well than/ q^d my lord/ I wyll not obey
yor arrest/ ffor ther hathe byn bytwen some of yor predicessors
& myn great contencyon & debate growen vppon an auncient   25
grudge/ w^che may succed in you w^t lyke inconvenyence as it
hathe done here tofore/ therfor onlesse I se yor Auctoryte and
commyssion I wyll not obey you/ Evyn as/ [f. 78] they ware
debatyng this matter bytwen them in the chamber/ So busyly
was m^r walshe arrestyng of Doctor Augustyn/ the phisicion/ at   30
the doore w^tin the portall whome I hard saye vnto hyme/ goo in
thou traytor or I shall make the/ And w^t that I opyned the
portall doore And the same beyng opyn/ m^r walshe thrust
doctor augustyn in byfore hyme w^t vyolence/ thes matters on

1 retourned] *MS*. retou*rr*ned   8 die w^t you/] *MS*. die/ w^t you
9 prosper] *MS*. propser   10 you *canc. after* beseche; to *canc. before* send *and* he *before* lyve   13 doore/] / *written over*)   14 vssher)]) *written over* /   20 by *interl*.   21 q^d therle *canc. after* lord/
27 tofore/ therfor] *MS*. tofore therfor

bothe the sides/ astonyied me very sore/ musyng what all this
shold mean/ vntill at the last m^r walshe beyng entered the
chamber/ began to plukke of hys hode/ the w^che he had mad
hyme w^t a Cote of the same clothe/ of Cotten/ to thentent that
5 he wold not be knowen/ And after he had pluke it of/ he kneled
down to my lord/ to whome my lord spake first sayeng thus
(commaundyng hyme to stand vppe)/ Sir here my lord of
Northumberland hathe arrested me of treason but by what
auctorytie or commyssion he shewyth me not but saythe he
10 hathe oon/ if ye be privye therto or be Ioyned w^t hyme therin/
I pray you shewe me/ In dead my lord/ q^d m^r walshe/ if it please
yor grace/ it is trewe that he hathe oon/ well than seyd my lorde
I pray you lett me se it/ sir I beseche yor grace hold vs excused/
q^d m^r walshe/ ther is annexed vnto our commyssion a Sedell w^t
15 certyn Instruccions w^che you may in no wyse be prive vnto/ why
q^d my lord/ be yor Instruccions suche that I may not se theme/
parauenture if I myght be privye to them I cowld the better
helpe you to performe theme/ yt is not onknowen vnto you bothe
I ame assured but I haue byn privye & of councell in as waytie
20 matters as this is/ ffor I dought not for my part but I shall
prove & cleare my self to be a trewe man/ ayenst thexpectacion/
of all my Cruell ennemyes/ I haue an vnderstandyng where
vppon all this matter growyth/ well there is no more to do I
trowe gentilman ye be oon of the kynges privye chamber yor
25 name I suppose is (walshe) I ame content to yeld vnto you/ but
not to my lord of Northumberland/ w^tout I se his commyssion/
And also you are a sufficyent commyssion/ yor self in that
behalfe in as myche as ye be oon of the kynges privy chamber/
ffor the worst person there/ is a sufficient warraunt to arrest the
30 greattest peere of this realme/ by the kynges oonly com-
maundeme^t w^tout any commyssion/ Therfore I ame redy to be
ordered & disposed att yor wyll/ put ther fore the kynges

1 all *interl.* 7 hyme *interl.* 10 Io *canc. before* w^t
12 lord *canc. before* lorde 15 wyse *interl.* 19 ass *canc. before*
ame 21 cleare] r *written over either* l *or* h 22 ennemyes/ I] *MS.*
ennemyes I 25 name *interl.* 27 in *canc. before* yor 28 as
interl. before ye 31 co *canc. before* commyssion; redy to be *interl.*
32 ed *of* ordered *and* & *interl.*; to *canc. before* ordered; & *canc. before* &; wyll/
put] *MS.* wyll put; the kynges *interl.*

Life of Cardinal Wolsey 157

commyssion and yor auctory in execucion/ a goddes name/
[f. 78^v] And spare not and I wyll obey the kynges wyll &
pleasure/ ffor I feare more the crueltie of my onmercyfull
ennemyes/ than I do my treuthe & allegyaunce/ wherin I take
god to witnes I neuer offendyd the kynges ma^{tie} in word or dede
And therin I dare stand face to face w^t any man a lyve hauyng
Indifferency w^tout parcyalitie/ Than came my lord of Northumberland vnto me standyng at the portall doore/ And commaundyd me to avoyd the chamber (And beyng lothe to depart
frome my m^r) stode still and wold not remove/ to whome he
spake agayn & seyd there is no remedy ye must nedys departe/
w^t that I loked vppon my lord (as who sayth shall I goo) vppon
whome my lord loked very hevely/ And shoke at me hys hed/
perceyvyng by hys countenaunce/ it boted me not to abyd/ And
so I departed the chamber/ And went in to the next chamber/
where abode many gentilmen of my fellowes and other/ to
learne of me somme newes of the matter w^t in/ To whome I
made report/ what I sawe & hard/ w^{che} was to them great hevynes
to here/ Than therle called dyuers gentilmen in to the chamber
w^{che} ware for the most part of his owen seruauntes/ And after
therle & m^r walshe had taken the keyes of all my lordes cofferrs
frome hyme/ they gave the charge & custody of my lordes person
vnto thes gentilmen/ they departed and went aboughte the
howsse to sett all thynges in order that nyght ayenst the next
mornyng entendyng than to depart frome thence/ w^t my lord
beyng Saturday the w^{che} they deferred vntill Sonday bycause all
thynges cowld not be brought to passe as they wold haue it/ They
went busely a bought to conveye doctor Augustyn a way to
london ward w^t as myche spede/ as they cowld sendyng w^t
hyme dyuers honest persons to conduct hyme who was tied
vnder the horsse belly And this don whan it was nyght/ thes
commyssioners assigned ij Grommes of my lordes to attend
vppon hyme in his chamber that nyght/ where they lay/ And the
most part of the rest of therles gentilmen seruauntes whatched

1 yor *canc. before* commyssion, in *before* and, *and* & *before* in; and yor *and* in *interl.*   15 de *canc. before* I   17 howe *canc. after* newes; of *interl. before* the   20 after *interl.*   27 all th *canc. before* cowld   28 to *canc. before* a way   34 of *canc. before* part; gentilmen *interl.*; wath *canc. before* whatched

in the next chamber and abought the howsse contynually vntill
the morowe/ And the porter kept the gattes so that no man
cowld goo in ne owt vntill the next mornyng at w^{che} tyme my
lord rose vppe supposyng that he shold haue departed that day//
5 howbeit he was kept closse secretly in his [f. 79] chamber
expectyng contynually his departure frome thence/ Than therle
sent for me in to his owen chamber/ And beyng there/ he commaundyd me to goo in to my lord and there to geve attendaunce
vppon hyme/ And charged me vppon an othe that I shold
10 obserue certyn Articles/ And goyng away frome hyme towardes
my lord/ I met w^t m^r walshe/ in the Court/ who called me vnto
hyme & led me in to hys chamber/ And there shewed me that
the kynges highnes bare towardes me his pryncely fauour for
my dyligent & true seruyce that I dayly mynestred towardes my
15 lord & m^r/ wherfore/ q^d he/ the kynges pleasure is/ that ye shalbe
abought yor m^r as most cheffest person in whome his highnes
puttyth great confidence/ And assured trust/ whos pleasure is
therfore that ye shalbe sworne vnto hys ma^{tie} to obserue certyn
articles in writyng the w^{che} I wold deliuere you/ Sir/ q^d I/ my lord
20 of Northumberland hathe all redy sworne me to dyuers
articles/ yea/ q^d he/ but my lord cowld not delyuer you the
articles in writyng as I ame commaundyd specyally to do
therfore I delyuer you this byll w^t thes articles/ to the w^{che} ye
shalbe sworne to fulfill/ Sir than/ q^d I/ I pray you to geve me
25 leave to pervse theme or euer I be sworne to se if I be able to
performe theme// w^t a right good wyll/ q^d he/ And whan I had
pervsed theme and vnderstod that they ware but reasonable &
tollerable/ I answered that I was contented to obey the kynges
pleasure and to be sworne to the performaunce of them/ And so
30 he gave me an newe othe/ And than I resorted to my lord where
he was in his chamber syttyng in a chayer the table beyng
couered redy for hyme to goo to dynner/ but as sone as he
perceyved me commyng in/ he fill in to suche an woofull
lamentacion w^t suche rewfull termes & waterye eyes/ that it wold
35 haue caused the flyntiest hart to haue relented & burst for
sorowe/ And as I and other cowld comforted hyme but it wold

3 goo *interl.*; owte *canc. before* owt; ro *canc. before* at   9 hyme] *MS.* hyyme   18 hi *canc. before* ma^{tie}   36 sorye *canc. before* sorowe

not be/ ffor nowe/ q^d he/ that I se this gentilman/ (meanyng by
me) howe faythefull/ howe diligent/ And howe paynfull, synce
the begynneng of my troble/ he hathe serued me/ Abandonyng
his owen contrie/ his wyfe & [f. 79^v] childerne/ his howsse &
famelye/ his rest & quyotnes/ only to serue me/ And remembryng 5
w^t my self that I haue no thyng to reward hyme for his honest
merytes grevythe me not a littill/ And also the sight of hyme
puttythe me in remembraunce of the nomber of my faythfull
seruauntes/ that I haue here remaynyng w^t me in this howsse
whome I did entend to haue preferred & auaunced to the best 10
of my power frome tyme to tyme as occasion shold serue/ but
nowe alas I ame preventyd/ & haue no thyng laft me to reward
theme/ ffor all is depryved me/ and I ame laft here ther desolat
& myserable m^r bare & wretched/ w^tout helpe or socoure but of
god alone// howbeit/ q^d he/ to me (callyng me by my name)/ 15
I ame a trewe man and therfore ye shall neuer receyve shame of
me for yor seruyce/ I perceyvyng his heuynes & lamentable
wordes sayd thus vnto hyme/ my lord I mystrust no thyng yor
trewthe/ And for the same I dare & wyll be sworne/ byfore the
kynges person and hys honorable Councell/ wherfore (knelyng 20
vppon my knee byfore hyme)/ sayd/ my lord comfort yor self and
be of good chere/ the malice of yor oncharitable ennemyes nor
ther ontrouthe shall neuer prevayle ayenst yor truethe and
faythfulnes/ ffor I dought not but commyng oons to yor
answere/ my hope is suche that ye shall so acquyt & cleare yor 25
self of all ther surmysed & fayned accusacions that it shall be to
the kynges contentacion and myche to yor auauncement &
restitucion of yor former dygnyte & estate/ yea/ q^d he/ if I may
come to myn answere I feare no man a lyve/ ffor he lyvyth not
vppon the yerthe that shall loke vppon this face (poyntyng to 30
his owen face)/ shall be able to accuse me of any ontrouthe/ And
that knowyth myn ennemyes full well/ w^che woll be an occasion
that I shall not haue Indifferent Iustice/ but woll rather seke
some other synyster wayes to distroy me/ Sir/ q^d I/ ye nede not
therin to dowght the kyng beyng so myche yor good lord as he 35
hathe allwayes shewed hyme self to be/ in all yor trobles/ w^t that
came vppe my lordes meate/ and so we left our commynycacion/

13 th *canc. before* is   14 socoure] *MS.* soco*ur*re   21 k *canc. before* my *knee*

I gave hyme water & satt hyme down to dynner (w^t whome sate dyuers of therles gentilmen)/ notw^tstandyng my lord did eate very littill meate/ but wold many tymes burst owte sodenly in teares w^t the most sorowfullest [f. 80] wordes that hathe byn
5 hard of any wofull creature/ And at the last he fetched a great sighe frome the bottome of his hart sayeng thes wordes of scripture/ *O constancia martirum laudabilis/ O charitas inextinguibilis/ O paciencia/ Invincibilis// Que licet inter pressuras persequencium visa sit despicabilis// Invenietur in laudem et*
10 *gloriam et honorem in tempore tribulacionis/* And thus passed he forthe his dynner in great lamentacion & hevynes/ who was more fed & moysted w^t sorowe & teares than w^t owther pleasaunt metes or dylicate drynkes// I suppose there was not a drie eye among all the gentilmen/ syttyng at the table w^t hyme/
15 And whan the table was taken vppe/ it was shewed my lord that he could not remove that nyght (who expected none other all that daye)// q^d he/ evyn whan it shall seme my lord of Northumberland good/ the next day my lord prepared hyme self (beyng Sonday) to ride/ whan he shold be commaundyd/ And
20 after dynner/ be that tyme that therle hade appoynted all thyng in good order w^t in the castell/ yt drewe fast to nyght/ there was assigned to attend vppon hyme fyve of vs his owen seruauntes and no mo/ that was to sey/ I/ oon chapleyn/ his barbor & ij Gromes of his chamber/ And whan he shold goo down the
25 stayers owt of the great chamber my lord demaundyd for the rest of his seruauntes/ therle answered that they ware not farre (the w^che he had enclosed w^t in the Chappell by cause they shold not disquyot his departure) sir I pray you/ q^d my lord/ lett me se theme or euer I depart or elles I woll neuer goo owt of this
30 howsse/ alake my lord/ q^d therle/ they shold troble you therfore I beseche you to content yor self/ well/ q^d my lord/ than wyll I not depart owt of this howsse but I wyll se theme & take my leave of theme in this chamber/ And his seruauntes beyng inclosed in the chappell hauyng vnderstandyng of my lordes

2 ge *with* g *written over* s *canc. before* gentilmen   5 at *interl.*   6 s *canc. before* sayeng   8 ter *of* inter *interl.*   9 despicabilis] *MS.* desplicabilis; e *canc. after* Invenietur   13 pleasaunt] *MS.* pleasauntes; metes *interl.*   21 d *canc. before* nyght   22 fyve *and* vs *interl.*   23 v seruauntes *canc. before* and   33 byfore I goo owt of *canc. before* in; in *interl.*

departyng awaye and that they shold not se hyme byfore his departure/ began to grudge and to make suche a rewfull noyce/ that the commyssioners dowted some tumult or enconvenyence to aryse by reason therof/ thought it good to lett them passe owt to my lord/ and that don they came to hyme in to the great chamber where he was [f. 80ᵛ] and there they kneled down/ byfore hyme among whome was not oon drie eye/ but pytifully lamentyd ther maysters fall and troble/ to whome my lord gave comfortable wordes and worthy praysis for ther dyligent faythfullnes & honest treuthe/ towardes hyme/ assureng them that what chaunces so euer shold happen vnto hyme that he is a true man and a Iust to his souerayn lord and thus wᵗ a lamentable maner shakyng eche of them by the handes was fayn to departe the nyght drewe so fast vppon theme/ My lordes mewle & our horsys ware redy brought in to the Inner Court where we mounted/ and commyng to the gate/ wᶜʰᵉ was shett the porter opened the same/ to lett vs passe/ where was redy attendyng a great nomber of gentilmen wᵗ ther seruauntes (suche as therle assigned) to conduct & auttend vppon hys person/ that nyght to Pumfrett and so forthe as ye shall here/ here after/ But to tell you of the nomber of people of the Contrie that ware assembled at the gates wᶜʰᵉ lamentyd his departyng/ was wonderous/ wᶜʰᵉ was abought the nomber of iij Mˡ persons/ who at the opynyng of the gattes after they had a sight of his person/ cried all wᵗ a lowd voyce/ god save yoʳ grace/ god save yoʳ grace/ the fowlle evyll take all theme that hathe thus taken you frome vs we pray god that a very vengeaunce may light vppon theme/ thus they ran crieng after hyme thoroughe the town of Cawood they lovyd hyme so well/ for suerly they had a greate losse of hyme bothe the poore & the Riche/ ffor the poore had of hyme great releafe/ and the riche lakked his councell in any busynes that they had to do/ wᶜʰᵉ caused hyme to haue suche love among theme/ in the Contrie/ Than rode he wᵗ his conductors towardes Pumfrett/ and by the way as he rode he axed me if I had any famylier acquayntaunce among thes gentilmen that rode wᵗ

2 departure] *MS.* depture   3 enconvenyence] *final* e *frayed away at edge of page*   4 to arisse *canc. before* to aryse; reso *canc. before* reason   5 to *interl. before* the   6 was] s *frayed away at edge of page*   12 sh *canc. before* wᵗ   29 theme *canc. before second* hyme   32 the *canc. before* suche

hyme/ yea sir sayd I what is yor pleasure/ mary/ q^d he/ I haue left a thyng behynd me w^{che} I wold fayn haue/ Sir sayd I if I knewe what it ware I wold send for it owt of hand/ Then sayed he lett the messanger goo to my lord of Northumberland/ and desier
5 hyme to send me the [f. 81] Red bokerham bagg lyeng in my Almery in my chamber sealed w^t my seale/ w^t that I departed frome hyme/ and went strayt vnto sir Roger lasselles knyght who was than Steward to therle of Northeumberland beyng among the rowt of horssemen as oon of the cheaffest rewlers/
10 whome I desired to send some of hys seruauntes bake vnto therle his m^r for that purpose the w^{che} grauntted most gently my request and sent incontynent oon of his seruauntes vnto my lord to Cawood for the sayd bagg/ who did so honestly his mesuage that he brought the same to my lord Immedyatly after
15 he was in his chamber w^t in the Abbey of Pumfrett where he lay all nyght/ In w^{che} bagg was no other thyng enclosed but iij^{re} shyrtes of heare w^{che} he delyuerd to the chapleyn his gostly father very secretly/ ffurthermore as we roode toward Poumfrett my lord demaundyd of me/ whether they wold lede hyme that
20 nyght/ fforsothe sir/ q^d I/ but to Poumfrett/ Alas/ q^d he/ shall I goo to the Castell and lye there & dye lyke a beast/ Sir I can tell you no more what they do entend but sir I wyll enquyer here among thes gentilmen of a specyall frend of myn whoo is cheafe of all ther councell/ w^t that I repayred vnto the sayd
25 sir Roger lasselles knyght desiryng hyme most earnestly that he wold vouche salve to shewe me whether my lord shold goo to be logged that nyght who answered me agayn that my lord shold be lodged w^t in the abbey of Poumfrett and in non other place/ and so I reported to my lord who was glade therof/ so that w^t in
30 nyght we came to Poumfrett Abbey & there logged And therle remayned still all that nyght in Cawood castell/ to se the dispeche of the houshold/ And to establysshe all the stuffe/ in some sewertie w^tin the same/ The next day they removed w^t my lord

2 I wold] *MS.* I I wold   4 and desier hyme/ *canc. after* Northumberland/   5 buke/ *canc. before* bagg   7 knyght *interl. and canc. before* knyght; knyght *interl.*   9 rewlers *canc. before* rewlers 16 nyght/ In] *MS.* nyght In   19 whether *interl.*   20 nyght/ fforsothe] *MS.* nyght fforsothe   21 of *canc. before* and   22 do *interl.*   23 d *canc. after* myn   24 councell/ w^t] *MS.* councell w^t   25 h *canc. after* most

Life of Cardinal Wolsey 163

towardes Dancaster desyryng that he myght come thether by
nyght by cause the people folowed hyme wepyng & lamentyng/
and so they dyd neuer the lesse allthoughe he came in by torche
lyght/ crieng (god save yor grace) god save yor grace my good
lord Cardynall/ runnyng byfore hyme w^t Candelles in ther 5
handes/ Who caused me therfore to ride hard by his mule to
shadowe hyme frome the people/ and yet they perceyved hyme
cursyng his ennemyes/ And/ [f. 81^v] thus they brought hyme to
the blake ffreers w^t in the w^che they logged hyme that nyght/
And the next day we removed to Sheffeld parke where therle of 10
Shrewsbury lay w^t in the loge/ and all the way thetherward the
people cried & lamented as they dyd in all places as we rode
byfore/ And whan we came to the parke of Sheffeld nyghe to the
logge my lord of Shrewesbury w^t my lady his wyfe a trayn of
gentillwomen And all my lordes gentilmen & yomen/ standyng 15
w^tout the gattes of the logge to attend my lordes commyng to
receyve hyme w^t myche honor whome therle enbraced sayeng
thes wordes/ My lord/ q^d he/ yor grace is most hartely welcome
vnto me And glade to se you in my poore logge the w^che I haue
often desired/ And myche more gladder if you had come after an 20
other sort/ Ah my gentill lord of Shrowesbury/ q^d my lord/
I hartely thanke you/ And allthoughe I haue no cause to reioyce/
yet as a sorowefull hart may Ioye/ I reioyce my chaunce w^che is
so good to come in to the handes & custody of so noble a person/
whos approved honour & wysdome hathe byn allwayes right 25
well knowen to all nobell estates/ And sir howe so euer my
ongentill accusers hathe vsed ther accusacions ayenst me/ yet
I assure you and so by fore yor lordshipe and all the world I do
protest that my demeanor & procedynges hathe byn Iust and
loyall towardes my souerayn & liege lord/ of whos behauor & 30
doynges yor lordshipe hathe had good experyence/ And evyn
accordyng to my trowthe & faythfulnes/ so I beseche god helpe
me in this my calamytie/ I dought no thyng of yor trouthe/ q^d
therle/ therfore my lord I beseche you be of good chere/ and
feare not/ for I haue receyved letters frome the kyng of his owen 35
hand/ in yor fauour And entertaynyng the w^che you shall se/ Sir

6 handes/ Who] *MS.* handes Who   9 that] hat *written over* o
23 a *interl.*   24 th *canc. after* good   30 lyge *canc. before* liege;
of *interl.*

I ame no thyng sory but that I haue not wherw^t worthely to receyve you & to entertayn you accordyng to yor honour & my good wyll/ but suche as I haue ye are most hartely welcome therto desiryng you to accept my good wyll accordyngly/ ffor
5 I woll not receyve you as a prisoner but as my good lord and the kynges trewe faythfull subiecte/ And here is my wyfe/ come to salute you/ whome my lord kyst barehedyd/ and all hir gentilwomen/ [f. 82] and toke my lordes seruauntes by the handes as well gentilmen & yomen/ as other/ than thes ij lordes went
10 arme in arme in to the logge conductyng my lord in to a fayer Chamber at thend of a goodly gallery w^t in a newe tower where my lord was lodged/ there was also in the myddes of the same Gallery a trauers of Sarcenet drawen so that thoon part was preserued for my lord & thother part for therle////

15 **Than departed all the** great nomber of gentillmen and other that conducted my lord to therles of Shrewsburyes/ And my lord beyng there contynued there xviij^{en} dayes after/ vppon whome therle appoynted dyuers gentilmen of his seruauntes to serue my lord for as myche as he had a small nomber of
20 seruauntes there to serue/ and also to se that he laked no thyng that he wold desier/ beyng serued in his owen chamber at dynner and Supper as honorably and w^t as many dayntye disshes as he had most comenly in his owen howsse beyng at libertie/ And oons euery day therle wold resorte vnto hyme And sitt w^t
25 hyme commonyng vppon a benche in a great wyndowe in the Gallery And thoughe therle wold right hartely comfort hyme yet wold he lament so pitiously that it wold make therle very sory & hevye for his greve/ Sir sayd he/ I haue & daylye do receyve letters frome the kyng commaundyng me to entertayn
30 you as oon that he lovythe and hyghely fauoryth wherby I perceyve ye do lament w^{t}out any great cause myche more than ye nede/ to do/ And thoughe ye be accused (as I thynke in god fayth) oniustly/ yet the kyng can do no lesse but put you to yor triall/ the w^{che} is more for the satisfieng of some persons/ than he

2 ente *canc. before* entertayn; entertayn you] you *written over* w^t 4 you *interl.*; & *canc. before* accordyngly   10 and *canc. before* conductyng   20 to ser *canc. before* there   26 com *canc. before* comfort   28 do *canc. before* daylye   32 d *canc. before* nede; ye be *interl.*; thyng *canc. before* thynke; thynke *interl.*   34 the *interl. after* for

Life of Cardinal Wolsey

hathe for any mystrust in yor doyenges/ Alas/ q^d my lord/ to therle/ ys it not a pitious case that any man shold so wrongfully accuse me vnto the kynges person And not to come to myn Answere/ byfore his ma^{tie}/ ffor I ame well assured (my lord) that there is no man alyve or deade that lokythe in this face of myn/ 5 is able to accuse me of any disloyaltie towardes the kyng/ Oh howe myche than dothe it grevythe me/ that the kyng shold haue/ [f. 82^v] any suspycyous oppynyon in me to thynke that I wold be false or conspire any evyll to his Royall person/ who may well consider that I haue no assured frend in all the world 10 in whome I put my trust but oonly in his grace/ ffor if I shold goo abought to be traye my souerayn lord and prynce/ in whome is all my trust and confidence byfore all other persons/ all men myght iustly thynke & report/ that I lakked not oonly grace but also bothe wytte & discression/, Nay, Nay, my lord I wold rather 15 adventure to shed my hart bloode/ in his defence/ as I ame bound to do by myn allegeaunce/ and Also for the savegard of my self/ than to Imagen his distruccion/ ffor he is my stafe that supportethe me/ And the wall that defendyth me/ ayenst my malygnaunt ennemyes/ and all other who knowythe best my 20 trewthe byfore all men and hathe had therof best & longest experyence/ therfore to conclude/ it is not to be thought that euer I wold goo abought or entend maliciously or trayterously to travell or whyshe/ any preiudice/ or dammage to his Royall person/ or Imperyall dignytie/ but as I sayd/ defend it w^t the 25 shedyng of my hart blode/ and procure all men so to do/ And it ware but oonly for the defence of myn owen person/ and symple estate (the w^{che} my ennemyes thynke I do so myche esteme) hauyng non other refuge/ to flee to for defence or socoure in all aduersitie/ but vnder the shadowe of his ma^{ties} wyng/ Alas my 30 lord/ I was in a good estate nowe & in case of a quyot lyvyng right well content therw^t/ but the ennemy that neuer slepithe but studyeth & contynually Imagynyth/ bothe slepyng & wakyng my vtter distruccion/ perceyvythe the contentacion of

2 it *interl*. 6 disho *canc. after* any; disloyaltie *interl*.; dylloyalltie/ *canc. before* towardes 7 than dothe *interl*. 12 p *canc. before* and 16 to *interl. and canc. before* adventure 20 knowythe best *interl*.; knowyst best *canc. before* my 22 experyence/ therfore] *MS.* experyence therfore 23 wold *interl*. 24 to *interl. before* travell 28 & *canc. before* I 34 to *canc. before* my

my mynd/ doughted that ther malicious & cruell dealyng wold
at lengthe growe to ther shame & rebuke/ goythe abought
therfore to prevent the same w^t shedyng of my blode/ but frome
god (that knowythe the secrettes of ther hartes And of all
5 others) it cannot be hyd/ ne yet onrewardyd whan he shall se
opportunytie/ ffor my good lord if ye wyll shewe yor self so
myche my good frend as to requyer the kynges ma^{tie} by yor
letters/ that my accusers may come byfore my face in his
presence/ And there that I may make answere/ I dought not
10 but ye shall se me acquyte my self of all ther [f. 83] malicious
accusacions/ And vtterly confound them/ ffor they shall neuer
be able to prove by any dewe probacions that euer I offendyd
the kyng in wyll thought & deade/ therfore sir I desier you and
most hartely requyer yor good lordshipe to be a meane for me
15 that I may answere vnto my accusers byfore the kynges ma^{tie}//
The case is his/ and if ther accusacions shold be true/ than shold
it touche no man but hyme most earnestly/ wherfore it ware
most convenyent that he shold here it hyme self in propir person/
but I feare me/ that they do entend rather to depeche me then
20 I shold com byfore hyme/ in his presence/ for they be well
assured And very certeyn that my trouthe shold vanquesshe
ther ontrouthe/ And surmysed accusacions w^{che} is the specyall
cause that movythe me so earnestly to desier to make my
Answere/ byfore the kynges ma^{tie}/ the losse of goodes// the
25 slaunder of my name/ ne yet all my troble grevyth me no thyng
so myche as the losse of the kynges fauour/ and that he shold
haue in me suche an oppynyon w^{t}out deserte/ of ontrouthe/ that
hathe w^t suche travell & payn serued his heyghenes so Iustly/
so paynfully and w^t so faythfull an hart to his profett & honor/ at
30 all tymes/ And also agayn the trouthe of my doynges ayenst ther
oniust accusacyons/ proved most Iust and loyall shold be myche
to my honestie/ and do me more good than to attayn great
treasure/ As I dought not but it wyll if they myght be Indifferently hard/ Nowe my good lord way ye my reasonable request/

1 that *interl.* 3 therfore to *canc. before* therfore 4 of *interl. before*
ther 12 dewe *interl.* 16 be *canc. before* shold be 17 hyme]
y *written over* e 18 ly *canc. after* convenyent 19 I en *canc.*
before they 31 do *canc. before* be *and* most *after* be 33 bu *canc.*
before not

And lett charitie/ and trouthe move yor noble hart w^t pitie to
helpe me in all this my trowthe/ wherin ye shall take no maner
of slaunder or rebuke (by the grace of god)// Well than/ q^d my
lord of Shrewsbury/ I woll wright to the kynges ma^{tie}/ in yor
behalf declaryng to hyme by my letters howe grevously ye
lament his displeasure & Indignacion/ And what request ye
make for the triall of yor trewthe towardes his heyghnes/ Thus
after thes commynycacions & dyuers others (as bytwen theme
dayly was accustumed) they departed a sonder/ where my lord
contynued the space after of a fouerthnyght haueng goodly &
honorable entertaynme^t whome therle wold often requyer hyme
to kyll a doo or ij ther in the parke/ [f. 83^v] who allwayes
refused all maner of earthely pleasures & disportes owther in
huntyng or in other games/ but applied his prayers contynually
very devoutly/ So that it came to passe at certyne season sittyng at
dynner in his owen chamber hauyng at his bordes end that same
day (as he dyuers tymes had to accompanye hyme)/ a messe of
therles gentillmen & chappleyns/ And etyng of Rosted wardens at
thend of his dynner/ by fore whome I stode at the table dressyng
of thos wardons for hyme beholdyng of hyme perceyved hys
Colour often to chaynge and alter dyuers tymes wherby I Iuged
hyme nott to be in helthe/ w^{che} caused me to leane ouer the table/
sayeng onto hyme/ softly/ Sir me semys yor grace/ is not well at
ease/ he answered agayn and seyd/ forsothe no more I ame/ for
I ame/ q^d he/ sodenly taken/ abought my stomake/ w^t a thyng
that lyethe ouerthwart my brest as cold as a whetston/ the w^{che}
is but wynd/ therfore I pray you take vppe the clothe/ and make
ye a short dynner/ and resort shortly agayn vnto me/ And after
that the table was taken vppe/ I went & sat the wayters to dynner
w^tout in the Gallery/ And resorted agayn to my lord where I
found hyme still syttyng where I left hyme very evyll at ease/
Norw^tstandyng he was in commynycacions w^t the gentilmen
sittyng at the bordes end/ And asson as I was entred the Chamber
he desired me/ to goo down to the pottecarie/ And to enquyer

1 noble *interl.*   8 theme *interl.*   20 hyme] *MS.* hymee   22 o *canc.*
before ouer   29 that *interl.*; that that *with second* that *interl. canc.*
before table; *a superfluous* the *is interl. after the cancellation and before* table
30 I *canc. before* And; And *interl.*   32 commynycacions] s *written over* e
33 sittyng *interl.*   34 to *canc. after* down; to *interl. before* the

of hyme/ whether he had any thyng that wold breke wynd vpward/ and accordyng to hys commaundeme^t I went my way towardes the pottecarye/ and by the way I remembord oon article of myn othe byfore made vnto m^r walshe/ w^{che} caused me first to goo to therle/ and shewed hyme bothe what estate he was in/ & also what he desired at the potticaries hand for his releafe/ w^t that therle caused the pottecarie to be called Incontynent byfore hyme/ of whome he demaundyd whether he had any thyng to breke wynd that troblyth oon in his brest/ And he answered that he had suche gere/ than q^d therle/ fetche me some hether/ the w^{che} the pottecarie brought in a whight paper a certyn wyht confeccion/ vnto therle/ who commaundyd me to geve the assay therof to the pottecarie/ and so I did byfore hyme/ And than I departyd therw^t bryngyng it to my lord byfore whome I toke also the assay therof And delyuerd the same [f. 84] to my lord who receyved the same holy all together at oons/ and Imedyally after he had receyved the same/ sewerly he avoydyd excedyng myche wynd vppward/ loo q^d he/ nowe ye may se that it was but wynd/ but by the means of this recepte/ I ame (I thanke god) well eased/ And so he rose frome the table and went to hys prayers as he accustumedly did after dynner/ And beyng at hys prayers there came vppon hyme suche a laske/ that it caused hyme to goo to his stoole/ And beyng there therle sent for me/ And at my Commyng he sayd/ ffor as myche as I haue allwayes perceyved in you to be a man in whome my lord yor m^r hathe great affiaunce/ and for my experyence/ knowyng you to be an honest man/ (w^t many moo wordes of commendacions than nedes here to be reherced)/ sayed it is so that my lord yor lamentable m^r hathe often desyred me to wright to the kynges ma^{tie} that he myght come vnto his presence to make answere to his accusacions/ And evyn so haue I don/ ffor thys day haue I receyved letters frome hys grace/ by sir willam kyngstone

---

3 and by the way *interl*.   4 by *canc. after* made   6 what] t *written over* h   9 that t *canc. after* wynd   10 he *canc. before* answered   12 wyht *interl*.   15 to *canc. after* same   16 lord *canc. before* lord   18 h *canc. before* loo *and* e *after* se   19 ame *interl*.   24 *a single indecipherable letter canc. before* allwayes   25 of *canc. after* man   26 affiaunce] *MS.* affiaaunce   27 here to *canc. before* than   28 be *interl*.   31 so *interl*.   32 kyngstone] *MS.* kygnstone

knyght wherby I do perceyve that the kyng hathe in hyme a
very good oppynyon/ and vppon my often request he hathe sent
for hyme by the seyd sir w^m kyngston to come vppe to answere
accordyng to hys owen desier/ who is in his chamber/ wher for
nowe is the tyme come that my lord hathe often desired to trie
hyme self & his truthe (as I trust) myche to hys hono^r/ And I
put no doughtes in so doyng that it shall be for hyme the best
Iourney that euer he made/ in all his lyfe/ Therfore nowe I wold
haue you to play the part of a wyse man/ to breke fyrst this
matter vnto hyme so wittely & in suche a sort that he myght take
it quyotly in good parte/ for he is euer so full of Sorrowe/ & dolor
in my company that I feare me he wyll take it in evyll part/ And
than he dothe not well for I assure you (and so shewe hyme) that
the kyng is hys good lord And hathe gevyn me the most worthy
thankes for his entertaynme^t desiryng & commaundyng me so to
contynewe/ not doughtyng but that he wyll right nobly acquyte
hyme self towardes hys heyghnes/ Therfore goo yor wayes to
hyme/ and so perswad w^t hyme that I may fynd hyme in good
quyot at my commyng for I wyll not tary long after you/ Sir/ q^d
I/ I shall if it please yor [f. 84^v] lordshipe endevour me to
accomplyshe your commaundeme^t to the best of my power
but sir I dought oon thyng/ that whan I shall name (sir w^m
kyngeston) he wyll mystrust that all is not well because he is
Constable of the tower/ And Capteyn of the Gard hauyng
xxiiij^tl of the gard to attend vppon hyme/ Mary it is treuthe q^d
therle/ what therof thoughe he be constable of the tower/ yet he
is the most meatest man for his wysdome/ and discression to be
sent abought any suche messwage/ And for the gard it is for
none other purpose but oonly to defend hyme/ Ayenst all them
that wold entend hyme any evyll owther in word or deade/ And
allso they be all or for the most part suche of hys old seruauntes
(as the kyng toke of late in to hys seruyce) to thentent that they
shold attend vppon hyme most Iustly and dothe knowe best
howe to serue hyme/ well sir/ I wyll do what I can/ And so
departed toward my lord/ And at my repayer/ I found hyme
syttyng at the vpper end of the Gallery vppon a trussyng chest

3 y *canc. after* the   4 for *interl.*   8 nowe *interl.*   12 it *interl.*
20 s I shall *canc. before* endevour *and* th *after* me   24–25 hauyng
xxiiij^tl of the gard *interl.*   33 attend *interl.*   36 t *canc. before* trussyng

of hys owen/ w^t hys beedes & staffe in his handes/ And espieng
me commyng frome therle/ he demaundyd of me/ what newes
nowe/ q^d he/ fforsothe/ sir q^d I/ the best newes that euer came to
you if yor grace can take it well/ I pray god it be what is it/ q^d
5 he/ ffor sothe/ q^d I/ my lord of Shrewesbury perceyvyng by yor
often commynycacion/ that ye ware allwayes desyrous to come
byfore the kynges ma^{tie}/ And nowe as yor most assured frend
hathe travelled so w^t his letters vnto the kyng/ that the kyng
hathe sent for you by m^r kyngeston/ And xxiiij^{ti} of the gard to
10 conduct you to his highnes/ M^r kyngesston/ q^d he/ rehersyng his
name oons or twyse/ And w^t that clapped his hand vppon his
thyghe/ And gave a great sighe/ Sir/ q^d I/ yf yor grace cowld or
wold take all thynges in good parte/ it shold be myche better for
you/ content yor self therfore for goddes sake/ And thynke that
15 god and yor frendes hathe wrought for you accordyng to yor
owen desier/ Dyd ye not allwayes whisshe/ that ye myght cleare
yor self by fore the kynges person/ Nowe that godd & yor
frendes hathe brought yor desier to passe/ ye will not take it
thankfully/ yf ye consider yor treuthe and loyaltie vnto our
20 souerayn lord ayenst the w^{che} yor ennemyes cannot prevayle (the
kyng beyng yor good lord as he is) you knowe well that the kyng
can do no lesse than he dothe/ you beyng to his highnes accused
of some heynous cryme/ but cause you to be brought to yor
triall/ And there to receyve accordyng to yor demerittes the
25 w^{che} his highenes trustithe and sayth no lesse but that you shall
prove yor self a Iust man to his ma^{tie}/ [f. 85] wherin ye haue
more cause to reioyse than thus to lament or mystrust his
fauorable Iustice/ ffor I assure you yor ennemyes be more in
dought & feare of you/ than you of them/ that they whisshe that
30 thyng (that I trust) they shall neuer be able to bryng to passe w^t
all ther wyttes the kyng (as I seyd before) beyng yor Indifferent
& syngular good lord & frend/ And to prove that he so is/ se ye
not howe he hathe sent gentill m^r kyngeston/ for you w^t suche
men as ware yor old treu seruauntes and yet be/ as fferre as it
35 becommythe them to be/ oonly to attend vppon you for the want

3 sir q^d I] *MS.* sir I   5 I *canc. before* I   18 hathe b brought
canc. before hathe   22 to *interl.*; seruaunt *canc. before* accused
25 heyghes *canc. before* highenes   26 trust *canc. before* Iust   30 be
ha *canc. before* be   33 kyngstos *canc. after* m^r

of yor owen seruauntes/ willyng also mr kyngeston/ to reuerence
you wt as myche honour as was dewe to you in yor hyghe estate/
And to convey you by suche easy Iourneyes as ye shall commaund hyme to do/ and that ye shall haue all yor desiers &
commaundemetes/ by the way/ in euery place to yor graces 5
contentacion and honor/ wherfore sir I humbly beseche yor grace/
to emprynt all thes Iust perswasions wt many other Imynent
occasions/ in yor discression/ and be of good cheare/ I most
humbly wt my faythfull hart requyer yor grace/ wherwt ye shall
pryncypally comfort yor self/ & next geve all yor frendes & to me 10
& other of yor seruauntes good hope of yor good spede/ well well/
than qd he/ I perceyve more than ye can Imagyn or do knowe/
experyence/ of old hathe taught me/ And therwt he rose vppe
and went in to his chamber/ to his cloose stoole/ the ffluxe
trobled hyme so sore/ and when he had don he came owt agayn 15
and Immedyatly my lord of Shrewsbury came in to the Gallery
vnto hyme wt whome my lord mett/ And then they bothe
sittyng down vppon a benche in a great wyndowe/ therle axed
hyme howe he did/ And he most lamentably (as he was
accustumed) answered thankyng hyme for his gentill enter- 20
taynmet/ Sir/ qd therle/ if ye remember ye haue often whisshed
in my company to make answere byfore the kyng/ And I as
desirous to helpe yor request/ as you to whishe/ beryng toward
you my good wyll/ hathe writtyn especyally to the kyng in yor
behalf makyng hyme also privye of yor lamentable sorowe/ that 25
ye inwardly receyve for his hyghe displeasure/ who acceptyth all
thynges & yor doynges therin as frendes/ [f. 85v] be accustumed
to do in suche cases/ wherfore I wold advyse you to pluke vppe
yor hart and be not agast of yor ennemyes/ who I assure you
haue you in more dowght than ye wold thynke/ perceyvyng that 30
the kyng is fully mynded to haue the heryng of yor case byfore
his owen person/ nowe sir if ye can be of good chere/ I dought
not but this Iourney wche ye shall take towardes his highnes
shalbe myche to yor auauncemet and An ouerthrowe of yor
ennemyes/ the kyng hathe sent for you by that worshypfull 35

1 to honour you wt *canc. before* to   7 other *interl.*   9 *a single indecipherable letter canc. before* grace; grace *interl.*   11 well/ *interl.*
14 sto *canc. before* cloose   24 wyll/ hathe] *MS.* wyll hathe   31 grace *canc. before* case   32 person/ nowe] *MS.* person nowe

knyght m^r kyngeston/ And w^t hyme xxiiij^ti of yor old seruauntes/ w^che be nowe of the Gard to defend you ayenst yor onknowen ennemyes to thentent that ye may savely come vnto his ma^tie/ Sir/ q^d my lord/ as I supposse m^r kyngeston is Constable of the tower/ yea, what of that,/ q^d therle/ I assure you he is oonly appoynted by the kyng for oon of yor ffrendes & for a discrett gentilman/ as most worthy to take vppon hyme the save conduct of yor person/ for w^tout faylle the kyng fauorethe you myche more/ And beryth towardes you a specyall secrett fauor ferre other wyse than ye do take it/ well sir/ q^d my lord/ as god wyll so beit/ I ame subiect to fortune And to ffortune I commytt my self beyng a trewe man redy to accepte suche ordynance as god hathe prouydyd for me/ And ther an end/ sir I pray you where is m^r kyngeston/ Mary/ q^d therle/ if ye wyll I woll send for hyme/ who wold most gladly se you/ I pray you than/ q^d he/ send for hyme/ at whos message/ he came Incontynent/ and assone as my lord espied hyme commyng in to the gallery he made hast to encounter hyme/ M^r kyngeston came towardes hyme w^t myche reuerence/ at his approche he kneled down and saluted hyme on the kynges behalf/ whome my lord (bareheded) offred to take vppe/ but he still kneled/ Than/ q^d my lord/ m^r kyngeston/ I pray you stand vppe/ And leve yor knelyng vnto a very wretche/ replett w^t mysery not worthy to be estemed but for a vile abiecte/ vttirly cast a way w^tout desert/ And therfore good m^r kyngeston/ stand vppe or I woll my self knele down by you/ w^t that m^r kyngeston stod vppe sayeng w^t humble reuerence/ Sir the kynges ma^tie hathe hyme commendyd vnto you/ I thanke his hyghnes/ q^d my lord/ I trust he be in helthe & mery/ the w^che I beseche god long contynewe/ yea w^tout dought/ q^d m^r kyngeston/ And sir he hathe [f. 86] commaundyd me/ first to sey vnto you that you shold assure yor self that he berythe you as myche good wyll & fauour as euer he dyd/ And wyllyth you to be of good chere/ And where report hathe byn made vnto hyme/ that ye shold commytt ayenst his Royall ma^tie certyn haynous

5 tower *canc. before* tower   9 specyall *interl.*   11 *a single indecipherable letter canc. before* subiect   14 *three indecipherable letters canc. before* kyngeston   16 hyme/ at] *MS.* hyme at   17 he espied/ *canc. before* my   17–18 to enco *canc. before* to; to encounter] *MS.* encounter; hyme/ M^r] *MS.* hyme M^r   22 wredche *canc. before* wretche   24 abeiect *canc. before* abiecte   27 you/ I] *MS.* you I

Life of Cardinal Wolsey 173

Crymes/ w^{che} he thynkythe to be vntrewe/ yet for the mynystracion of Iustice in suche casis requysit/ And to avoyd all suspecte/ parcyallytie/ can do no lesse/ at the least/ than to send for you to yor triall/ mystrustyng no thyng yor trowthe & wysdome but that ye shalbe able to acquyt yor self ayenst all 5 complayntes & accusacions exibyted ayenst you/ And to take yor Iourney towardes hyme at yor owen pleasure/ commaundyng me to be attendaunt vppon you w^t mynestracion of dewe reuerence/ And to se yor person preserued frome all dammage And Inconvenyences that myght ensewe/ and to elect all suche 10 yor old seruauntes (nowe his) to serue you by the way/ who hathe most experyence of yor diett/ Therfore sir I beseche yor grace to be of good chere/ And whan it shall be yor good pleasure to take yor Iourney I shall geve myn attendaunce/ M^r kyngeston/ q^d my lord/ I thanke you for yor good newes/ And sir herof assure yor 15 self/ that if I ware as able and as lustie/ as I haue byn but of late/ I wold not fayle to ride w^t you in post/ but sir I ame disseased w^t a fluxe that makyth me very weke/ But m^r kyngeston/ all thes confortable wordes w^{che} ye haue spoken be but for a purpose to bryng me in a fooles paradice/ I knowe what is provydid for me/ 20 Notw^tstandyng I thanke you for yor good will & paynnes taken abought me/ And I shall w^t all spede/ make me redy to ride w^t you to morowe/ And thus they fill in to other commynycacion bothe therle and m^r kyngeston/ w^t my lord who commaundyd me to forse and provyde that all thynges myght be made redy to 25 departe/ the morowe after/ I caused all thynges to be thrust vppe & made in a redynes as fast as they could convenyently/ whan nyght came that we shold goo to bed my lord waxed very syke/ thoroughe hys newe desease/ the w^{che} caused hyme contynually frome tyme to tyme/ to goo to the stolle all that nyght/ In so 30 myche frome the tyme that his desease toke hyme/ vnto the next day he had above l^{ti} stoolles So that he was that day very weke/ the matter that he avoyded was [f. 86^v] wonderous blake/ the w^{che} phisicions call Colour Adustum/ And whan he perceyved

5 all *canc. before* yor *and* accusacions *before* self   8 dewe] d *written over* r   14 attendaunce *canc. before* attendaunce   16 b *canc. before* byn   20 bryng] r *written over* e   25 made redy] *MS.* made/ redy   26 be *canc. before* departe   27 they] *MS.* thy   30 stoole *canc. before* stolle   31 the *interl. before* tyme   34 whan *interl.*; perceyved *canc. before* perceyved

it he sayd vnto me/ if I haue not/ q^d he/ some helpe shortly yt will cost me my lyfe/ w^t that I caused oon doctor Nicholas a Phisicion beyng w^t therle to loke vppon the grosse matter that he avoyded vppon sight wherof he determyned/ howe he shold
5 not lyfe past iiij^{or} or .v. dayes/ yet notw^{t}standyng he wold haue ridden w^t m^r kyngeston that same day if therle of Shrewsbury had not byn/ Therfore in consideracion of hys Infirmyte they caused hyme to tary all that day/ And the next day he toke his Iourney w^t m^r kyngeston/ And the Gard/ And as son as they
10 espied ther old m^r in suche a lamentable estate/ lamented hyme w^t wepyng eyes whome my lord toke by the handes And dyuers tymes by the way as he rode he wold talke w^t theme some tyme w^t oon and some tyme w^t an other/ At nyght he was lodged at an howsse of therle of Shrewsburys called hardwyke hall/ very
15 evyll at ease/ the next day he rode to Nothyngham/ And ther lodged that nyght more sykker/ and the next day we rode to leycester abbey and by the way he waxed so sykke/ that he was dyuers tyme lykly to haue fallen frome his mewle/ And beyng nyght or we came to the abbey afore seyd/ where at his commyng
20 in at the gattes the Abbott of the place w^t all his Covent mett hyme w^t the light of many torches whome they right honorably receyued w^t great reuerence/ To whome my lord sayd/ ffather abbott I ame come hether to leave my bones among you/ whome they brought on his mewle to the stayers foote of his chamber/
25 and there lighted And m^r kyngeston than toke hyme by the Arme/ and led hyme vppe the stayers (who told me afterward that he neuer Caried so hevy a burden in all his lyfe) And asson as he was in his chamber he went incontynent to his bedd very sykke/ this was vppon Satorday at nyght/ and there he contynued
30 sykker & sykker/ vppon Monday in the mornyng as I stode by his beddes side/ abought viijth of the Clocke/ the wyndowes beyng cloose shett/ hauyng waxe lightes burnyng vppon the Cupbord/ I behyld hyme As me semed drawyng fast to hys end/ he perceyued my shadowe vppon the wall [f. 87] by his beddes

7 in consideracion] *MS.* inconsideracion   10 a *interl.*; w^t *canc. before* hyme   12 by *canc. before* by   13 other/ At] *MS.* other At   14 where he lay all nyght *canc. before* very   16 the *canc. before* the   22 ffather *canc. after* sayd/   27 gathered lyfted lyfted so heuy a burden *with* lyfted lyfted *interl. canc. before* Caried   29 Satorday] *MS.* Storday   32 be *canc. before* beyng

Life of Cardinal Wolsey

side/ Asked who was there/ Sir I ame here/ q^d I/ howe do you/ q^d he/ to me/ very well sir if I myght se yor grace well/ what is it of the clocke/ q^d he/ to me/ for sothe sir/ q^d I it is past viij^th of the clocke/ in the mornyng/ viij^th of the clocke/ q^d he/ that cannot be rehersyng dyuers tyme/ viij^th of the Clocke/ viij^th of 5 the Clocke/ Nay/ nay/ q^d he/ at the last/ it cannot be viij^th of the cloke/ ffor by viij^th of the Clocke ye shall loose yor m^r/ for my tyme drawyth nere that I must depart owt of this world w^t that m^r doctor Palmes a worshipfull gentilman beyng his chapleyn/ & gostly father standyng bye bad me secretly demaund of hyme 10 if he wold be shreven/ And to be in a redynes towardes god what so euer shold chaunce/ at whos desier I asked hyme that question/ what haue you to do/ q^d he/ to aske me any suche question/ And began to be very angry w^t me/ for my presumpcion vntill at the last/ Mr Doctor toke my part And talked w^t hyme in latten And 15 so pacyfied hyme/ And after Dynner M^r kyngeston sent for me in to hys chamber/ And at my beyng there/ Sayd to me/ So it is that the kyng hathe sent me letters by this gentilman (Mr Vyncent) oon of yor old companyons who hathe byn late in troble in the tower of london for mony that my lord shold haue 20 at his last departyng frome hyme/ w^che nowe cannot be found/ wherfore the kyng at this gentilmans request for the declaracion of his trewthe/ hathe sent hyme hether w^t his graces letters dyrected vnto me/ commaundyng me by vertue therof to examyn my lord in that behalf/ And to haue yor councell herin 25 howe yt may be don that he may take it well & in good part/ this is the cheafe cause of my sendyng for you/ wherfore I pray you what is yor best Councell to vse in thys matter for the true acquytall of this gentilman/ Sir q^d I/ as touchyng that matter/ my symple Advice shalbe this/ that ye yor owen person shall 30 resort vnto hyme/ and visit hyme/ And in commynycacion breake the matter vnto hyme/ And if he woll not tell the treuthe/ ther be that can satysfie the kynges pleasure therin/ And in any wyse speke no thyng of my ffellowe vyncent/ And I wold not advyse you to tract the tyme w^t hyme for he is very syke/ I 35

1 Axed *canc. before* Asked 7 *a single indecipherable letter canc. before* by
10 to *canc. before* demaund 12–13 question/ what] *MS.* question
what 13 to do *interl.* 26 he *canc. before* yt; this *interl.* 28 in
interl. 30 s. *canc. before* Advice

feare me he wyll not lyve past to morowe in the mornyng [f. 87ᵛ] Then went mʳ kyngeston vnto hyme And asked first howe he did And so forthe procedyd in Commynycacion/ wherin mʳ kyngeston demaundyd of hyme the seyd mony/ sayeng that
5 my lord of Northumberland hathe found a boke at Cawood that reportithe howe ye had but late xv ᶜˡⁱ in redy mony And oon penny therof wyll not be found/ who hathe made the kyng privy by his letters therof/ wherfore the kyng hathe writtyn vnto me/ to demaund it of you if ye do knowe where it is become/ ffor it
10 ware pitie/ that it shold be embeselled frome you bothe/ therfore I shall requyer you in the kynges name to tell me the treuthe herin to thentent that I may make Iust report vnto his maᵗⁱᵉ/ what answere ye make ther in/ wᵗ that my lord pawsed a whyle And sayd/ Ah good lord howe myche dothe it greave me/
15 that the kyng shold thynke/ in me suche disceyt wherin I shold disceyve hyme of any oon penny that I haue/ Rather than I wold (mʳ kyngeston) embesell or deceyve hyme of a myght I wold it ware molt & put in my mouthe/ wᶜʰᵉ wordes he spake twyse or thrice very vehemently/ I haue no thyng ne neuer had (god
20 beyng my Iuge) that I estemed or had in it any suche delight or pleasure but that I toke it for the kynges goodes hauyng but the bare vse of the same duryng my lyfe/ And after my deathe/ to leave it to the kyng wherin he hathe but prevented myn entent and purpose/ And for this mony that ye demaund of me/ I
25 assure you it is none of myn for I borowed it of dyuers of my ffrendes to bury me & to bestowe among my seruauntes wᶜʰᵉ hathe taken great paynnes abought me/ lyke trewe and faythfull men/ Notwᵗstandyng if it be his pleasure to take thys mony frome me/ I must hold me therwᵗ content/ yet I wold most
30 humbly beseche his maᵗⁱᵉ to se them satysfied of whome I borowed the same/ for the discharge of my concience/ who be they/ qᵈ mʳ kyngeston/ That shall I shewe you/ I borowed CCˡⁱ therof of sir Iohn Alyn/ of london/ And CCˡⁱ of sir Richard Gressham/ And CCˡⁱ of the mʳ of Savoye/ And CCˡⁱ of Doctor
35 hykden dean of my College in Oxford/ And CCˡⁱ of the

5 Cawood *canc. before* Cawood   7 found/ who] *MS.* found who   10 pityee *canc. before* pitie   17 of *interl.*   18 it *canc. before* molt *and* mouthe *before* mouthe; mouthe/ wᶜʰᵉ] *MS.* mouthe wᶜʰᵉ   26 bestowe *canc. before* bestowe   28 thys] y *written over* e

Life of Cardinal Wolsey 177

Treasorer of the Chirche of yorke/ And CC^{li} of the Dean of yorke/ And CC^{li} of parson Elis my chapleyn [f. 88] And an C^{li} of my Steward (whos name I haue fforgotten) trustyng that the kyng wyll restore theme agayn ther mony for it is none of myn/ Sir/ q^d m^r kyngeston/ there is no dought in the kyng (ye nede not to mystrust that) but whan the kyng shalbe aduertised therof (to whome I shall make report of yor request) that his grace woll do as shall become hyme/ but sir I pray you where is this mony/ M^r kyngeston/ q^d he/ I will not conceyll it frome the kyng/ I woll declare it to you or I dye/ by the grace of god/ take a littill pacience w^t me I pray you// well sir than I woll troble you no more at this tyme trustyng that ye wyll shewe me to morowe/ yea that I wyll m^r kyngeston/ for the mony is save a noughe/ And in an honest mans kepyng/ who wyll not kepe oon Penny frome the kyng/ and than m^r kyngeston went to his Soper/ howbeit my lord wexid very syke most lyklyest to dye that nyght/ And often Swowned/ And as me thought drewe toward fast hys end vntill it was iiij^{or} of the Clocke in the mornyng/ At w^{che} tyme I Asked hyme howe he dyd/ well/ q^d he/ if I had any meate I pray you geve me some/ Sir ther is none redy/ I wys ye be the more to blame/ ffor you shold haue allwayes some meate for me in a redynes to eate whan my stomake seruyth me/ Therfore I pray you gett me some/ for I entend thys day (god willyng) to make me strong to thentent I may occupie my self in Confession and make me redy to god/ Then sir q^d I/ I wyll call vppe the Cookes to provyd some meate for you/ And woll also if it be yor pleasure call for m^r Palmes that ye may Comen w^t hyme vntill yor meate be redy/ w^t a good wyll/ q^d he/ And ther w^t I went first and called vppe the Cooke/ commaundyng hyme to prepare some meate for my lord And than I went to m^r Palmes and told hyme what case my lord was in/ wyllyng hyme to rise and to resort to hyme w^t spede/ And than I went to m^r kyngeston and gave hyme warnyng that as I thought he wold not lyve/ Aduertysyng hyme that if he had any thyng to say to hyme that

5 m^r kyngeston/] *MS.* m^r/ kyngeston; nede *interl.*   7 but *canc. before* that   8-9 mony/ M^r] *MS.* mony M^r 13 kyngeston/] / *written over*)   15 kyng/ and] *MS.* kyng and   20 ye *canc. before* I   22 d *canc. before* redynes   27 k *canc. before* Palmes   30 than *canc. before* than   33 he *interl.*; lyfe *canc. before* lyve

he shold make haste for he was in great daynger/ In good fayth/ q^d m^r kyngeston/ ye be to blame for ye make hyme beleve that he is sykkyr and in more daynger [f. 88^v] then he is/ Well sir q^d I/ ye shall not say an other day but that I gave you warnyng as I am bound to do/ in discharge of my dewtie/ Therfore I pray you what so euer shall chaunce lett no necligence/ be ascribed to me herin/ for I assure you his lyfe is very short/ do therfore nowe as ye thynke best// Yet neuerthelesse he arose & made hyme redy and came to hyme after he had eaten of a Colas made of a chykken a sponefull or too/ At the last q^d he/ wherof was this Colas made/ forsothe sir/ q^d I/ of a Chikkyn/ wye/ q^d he/ it is fastyng day and saynt Androwes Eve/ what thoughe sir q^d Doctor Palmes/ ye be excused by reason of yor syknes/ yea/ q^d he/ what thoughe I wyll eate no more/ than was he in confession the space of an hower// And whan he had endyd his confession m^r kyngeston bade hyme god morowe (for it was abought vjj^{en} of the clocke in the mornyng) And Asked hyme howe he did/ Sir/ q^d he/ I tary but the wyll & pleasure of god/ to render vnto hyme my symple sowlle in to hys dyvyn handes/ Not yet so sir/ q^d m^r kyngeston/ w^t the grace of god ye shall lyve & do very well if ye wyll be of good cheare/ M^r kyngeston my desease is suche that I cannot lyve/ I haue had some experyence in my desease/ And thus it is/ I haue a ffluxe w^t a contynuall ffevour/ the nature wherof is this/ that if there be no alteracion w^t me of the same w^t in viijth dayes than must owther ensue excorriacion of the Intraylles/ or ffrancye/ or elles present deathe/ And the best therof is deathe/ And as I suppose this is the viijth day And if ye se in me no alteracion/ than is there no remedye (allthoughe I may lyve a day or twayn)/ but deathe w^{che} is the best remedy of the three// Nay sir in good fayth q^d m^r kyngeston/ ye be in suche dolor & pensyvenes doughtyng that thyng that in deade ye nede not to feare/ w^{che} makyth you myche wors than ye shold be/// well, well, M^r kyngeston/ q^d he/ I se the matter ayenst me howe it is framed/ But if I had serued god as dylygently as I haue don the kyng he wold not

3 bele *canc. before* beleve; in *interl.*   4 gave *canc. before* gave
14 syknes/ yea] *MS.* syknes yea   16 bad *canc. before* bade   19 sowlle] le *written over* &   20 kyngeston *canc. before* kyngeston   26 ex *canc. after* owther   30–31 q^d m^r kyngeston/ *interl.*; ye *canc. before* in

haue gevyn me ouer in my gray heares/ howbeit thys is the Iust
reward that I must Receyve for my worldly dyligence & paynnes
that I haue had to do hyme seruyce/ oonly to satysfie his vayn
pleasures/ not regardyng my godly dewtye [f. 89] wherfore I pray
you w^t all my hart to haue me most humbly commendyd vnto 5
his Royall ma^{tie} besechyng hyme in my behalf to call to hys most
gracious remembraunce All matters procedyng bytwen hyme
& me/ frome the begynnyng of the world vnto thys day/ and the
progresse of the same/ And most cheafely in the waytie matter/
yet dependyng/ (meanyng the matter newly begon bytwen hyme 10
& good quen katheryn) than shall his concyence declare
whether I haue offendyd hyme or no/ he is suer a prynce of a
Royall Corage/ And hathe a pryncely hart/ And rather than he
wyll owther mysse or want any parte of hys wyll or apetite/ he
wyll put the losse of oon half of hys realme in daynger/ ffor I 15
assure you/ I haue often kneled byfore hyme in his privye
chamber on my knes the space of an hower or too/ to perswade
hyme frome hys wyll & apetide/ but I cowld neuer bryng to
passe to diswade hyme therfroo/ Therfore m^r kyngeston/ if it
chaunce hereafter you to be oon of hys privye councell (as for 20
yor wysdom & other qualites ye be mete so to be) I warne you
to be well advysed & assured what matter ye put in his hed/ ffor
ye shall neuer pull it owt agayn/ And sey furthermore that I
requyer his grace (in goddes name) that he haue a vigilent eye/
to depresse this newe peruers sekte of the lutarnaunce that it do 25
not encrease w^{t}in his domynyons thoroughe hys necligence/ in
suche a sort as that he shalbe fayn at lengthe to put harnoys
vppon hys bake to subdewe them As the kyng of Beame did/
who had good game to se his rewde Commyns (than enfected
w^t wycklyfes heresies) to spoyell and murder the sperytuall men 30
& Religious persons of hys Realme/ the w^{che} fled to the kyng &
his nobles for socours ayenst ther frantyke rage/ of whome they
could gett no helpe of defence/ or refuge/ but laughed theme to

2 receyve *canc. before* Receyve; worldly (*MS.* wordly) *interl.*   3 do *interl.*
4 dewte to *canc. before* godly   5 me *interl.*   11 the *canc. before*
good   13 *a single indecipherable letter canc. between the* o *and* r *of*
Corage   16 privy *canc. before* privye   19 diswade *canc. before*
diswade   22 ye pu *canc. before* in   25 to *interl.*; lutarnaunce]
first n *written over* y   29 rewde *interl.*   32 ther *canc. before*
ther; ther *interl.*

scorne hauyng good game at ther spoyle & consumpcion not regardyng ther dewties nor ther owen defence/ And whan thes erronyous heretykes had subdued all the clargy and sperytuall persons takyng the spoyell of ther riches/ bothe of [f. 89ᵛ]
5 chirches/ monastorys/ And all other sperytuall thynges havyng no more to spoyle caught suche a Corage of ther former libertie/ that/ than they disdayned ther prynce and souerayn lord/ wᵗ all other noble personages And the hed gouerners of the Contrie/ And began to fall in hand wᵗ the temporall lordes to slee &
10 spoyle theme wᵗout pitie or mercye most cruelly/ In so myche that the kyng and other hys nobles ware constrayned to put harnoyes vppon ther bakkes to resist the ongodly powers of thes traterous heretykes And to defend ther lyves & liberties/ who pitched a feld Royall ayenst theme/ in ʷᶜʰᵉ fyld thes traytors so
15 stowtly encounterd/ that the parte of theme ware so cruell & vehement/ that in fyne they ware victors/ and slewe the kyng/ the lordes & all the gentilmen of the Realme/ leavyng not oon person that bare the name or port of a gentilman a lyve/ or of any person that had any Rewle or auctorytie in the Comen wele/
20 by means of ʷᶜʰᵉ slaughter they haue lyved euer synce in great mysery & pouertie/ wᵗ out an hed or gouernor but lyved all in Comen lyke wyld bestes/ abhorred of all Cristyan nacions/ lett this be to hyme an evydent example to avoyd the lyke daynger I pray you good mʳ kyngeston/ Ther is no trust in rowttes
25 or onlawfull Assembles of the comen pepolle ffor whan the ryotouse multytud be assembled there is among theme no mercy or consideracion of ther bounden dewtie/ As in the history of kyng Rycherd the second/ oon of hys noble progenytors ʷᶜʰᵉ in that same tyme of wykclyffes sedicious oppynyons/ dyd not the
30 Comens/ I pray you/ rise ayenst the kyng & nobles of the Realme of Englond/ wherof some they apprehendyd whome they wᵗout mercye or Iustice put to deathe/ And did they not fall to spoylyng & Robbery to thentent they myght bryng all thyng in comen/ And at the last wᵗout discression or reuerence/ spared

9 lordes *canc. before* temporall   14 stoutly *canc. before* Royall; Royall *interl.*; wᶜʰᵉ fyld] *MS.* wᶜʰᵉ/ fyld; so *interl*   19 Comen] *MS.* Coen   21 out *interl.*   22 bestes *canc. before* wyld   25 r *canc. after* whan the   26 multytud *interl.*; hedes *canc. before* be   27 consideracion] *MS.* consideraciion   28 Rycherd] R *written over* I   29 r *canc. after* the

Life of Cardinal Wolsey   181

not in ther rage to take the kynges most Royall person owt of the
tower of london/ and Caried hyme abought the Citie most
presumptiously/ causyng hyme (for the preseruacion of hys lyfe)
to be aggreable to ther lewd proclamacions/// Dyd not also that
trayterouse herityke/ sir Iohn OldCastell pytche a feld ayenst 5
kyng herry the .v.^{th} ayenst whome the kyng was constrayned to
encontre in his Royall [f. 90] person/ to whome god gave the
victory/// Alas m^r kyngeston/ if thes be not playn presedentes
and sufficyent perswasions to admonysshe a prynce to be
circumspect ayenst the semblable myschefe/ and if he be necly- 10
gent/ than wyll god stryke and take frome hyme his power/ and
dymynysshe his regally/ takyng frome hyme his prudent
councellours and valyaunt capteyns/ and leave vs in our owen
handes w^t out hys helpe & ayed/ And than wyll ensewe myschefe vppon myschefe/ Inconvenyence vppon Inconvenyence/ 15
barynes & skarcyte of all thynges/ for lake of good order in the
comen welthe to the vtter distruccion & desolacion of this noble
Realme/ ffrome w^{che} myschefes god for hys tender mercy defend
vs/ Mayster kyngeston farewell I canno more but whyshe all
thyng to haue good successe/ my tyme drawyth on fast I may 20
not tary w^t you/ And forgett not (I pray you) what I haue seyd
& charged you w^tall ffor whan I ame deade/ ye shall parauenture
remember my wordes myche better// And evyn w^t thes wordes
he began to drawe his speche at lengthe/ And his tong to fayle/
his eyes beyng sett in his hed whos sight faylled hyme/ than we 25
began to put hyme in remembraunce of Cristes passion and sent
for the Abbot of the place to annele hyme/ who came w^t all
spede/ and mynestred vnto hyme all the seruyce to the same
belongyng/ And caused also the gard to stand by bothe to here
hyme talke byfore his deathe & also to be wytnes of the same/ 30
And incontynent the Clocke strake viij^{th}/ at w^{che} tyme he gave
vppe the gost & thus departed he this present lyfe/ And callyng
to our remembraunce his wordes the day byfore howe he sayd

1 to *canc. before* in; most *interl.*   2 presumptio *canc. before* most
4 the *canc. before* that; that *interl.*   6 constrayned] *MS.* conⁿstrayned
7 hyme *canc. before* in   12 as *canc. before* takyng   14–15 myschefe
vpon/ *canc. before* myschefe vppon   24 leg *canc. before* lengthe
25 be *canc. before* eyes   30 his dethe *canc. before* the; the same
interl.   31 stake *canc. before* strake; strake *interl.*   32 he *interl.*
33 byfore *canc. before* byfore

that at viijth of the Cloke we shold lose our mayster/ oon of vs lokyng vppon an other/ supposyng that he proficied of hys departure/ **Here is thend** and ffall of pryde and Arrogauncye of suche men exalted by ffortune to honour & highe dygnytes/
5 ffor I assure you in hys tyme of auctoryte & glory/ he was the haultest man in all his procedynges that than lyved/ hauyng more respect to the worldly honor of hys person/ than he had to his sperytuall profession/ wherin shold be all meknes, hymylitie, & charitie/ the processe wherof I leave to theme that be learned
10 & seen in the dyvyn lawes/// [f. 90^v]

After that he was departyd/ m^r kyngeston sent an empost to the kyng to Aduertise hyme of the deathe of the late Cardynall of yorke/ by oon of the Gard that bothe sawe & hard hyme talke & die/ And than M^r kyngeston callyng me/ vnto hyme & to
15 thabbott went to consultacion for the order of hys buriall/ After dyuers commynycacions it was thought good that he shuld be buried the next day followyng for m^r kyngeston wold not tarie the retourne/ of thempost/ And it was ferther thought good that the mayor of leycester and hys bretherne shold be sent for to se
20 hyme personally deade/ in Avoydyng of ffalce Rumors that myght hape to sey that he was not deade/ but still lyvyng/ than was the mayor and hys bretherne sent for And in the mean tyme/ the body was taken owt of the bed where he lay deade/ who had vppon hyme next his body a shirt of heare besydes his
25 other shirt w^{che} was of very fynne lynnyn holond clothe/ this shirt of heare was onknowen to all hys seruauntes beyng contynually attendyng vppon hyme in his bedd chamber except to his chapleyn w^{che} was his gostly father/ wherin he was buried and layed in a Coffen of bordes/ hauyng vppon his dead Corps
30 all suche vestures & ornamentes as he was professed in whan he was consecrated bysshope & Archebysshope/ As myter crosseer ryng & palle w^t all other thynges appurtenaunt to his profession/ And lyeng thus all day in his Coffen opyn and bare faced that all men myght se hyme lye there deade/ w^tout ffaynyng/ than whan

2 procefied *canc. before* proficied; proficied *interl.*   3 yet *canc. after* departure/   4 suche *interl.*   7 worldly] *MS*. wordly; honor *interl.*   8 shold *interl.*   13 hyme *interl.*   16 bury *canc. before* be   18 it was *interl.*   21 lyvyng/ than] *MS*. lyvyng than   24 here *canc. before* heare   27 bedd *interl.*   33 that the *canc. before* that

the mayor, hys bretherne & all other had sen hyme lyeng thus vntill iiij^{or} or .v. of the cloke/ at nyght he was caried so down in to the chyrche/ w^t great solempnyte/ by the Abbott & Couent w^t many torches lyght syngyng suche seruyce as is dewe for suche ffuneralles/ And beyng in the churche the Corps was sett in our 5 lady chappell w^t many dyuers tapers of waxe burnyng abought the hearsse/ And dyuers poore men syttyng abought the same holdyng of Torches lyght in ther handes who watched abought the dead body all nyght wyllest the Chanons sang dirige/ and other devout Orisons/ And abought iiij^{or} of the cloke in the 10 mornyng they sang masse and that don and the body entired M^r kyngeston w^t vs beyng his seruauntes ware present at hys seyd ffuneralles and offered at hys masse/ And be that tyme that all thynges was fynysshed and all Ceremonyes that to suche a person was decent & conuenyent it was abought vj of the cloke/ 15 in the mornyng/ Then prepared we to [f. 91] horsebake/ beyng seynt Androwes day thappostell And so toke our Iourney towardes the Court beyng at hampton Court where the kyng than lay And after we came thether w^{che} was vppon seynt Nicholas Eve we gave attendaunce vppon the Counsell for our 20 depeche/ vppon the morowe I was sent for by the kyng to come to hys grace/ And beyng in m^r kyngestons chamber in the Court had knowlege therof And repayryng to the kyng I found hyme shotyng at the Rownds in the parke on the baksyde of the garden/ And perceyvyng hyme occupied in shotyng/ thought it 25 not my dewtie/ to troble hyme/ but leaned to a tree entendyng to stand there and to attend hys gracious pleasure/ beyng in a great study/ At the last the kyng came sodynly behynd me where I stode/ And clappt his hand vppon my sholder/ And whan I perceyved hyme I fyll vppon my knee/ to whome he 30 sayd/ callyng mee by my name/ I woll/ q^d he/ make an end of my game/ And than woll I talke w^t you/ And so departed to his marke whereat the game was endyd/ than the kyng delyuerd hys bowe to the yoman of hys bowes And went his way in ward to the place/ whome I folowed/ howbeit he called for sir Iohn 35

7 hersse *canc. before* hearsse   9 chana.s *canc. before* Chanons   11 m^r *canc. after* don   12 and *canc. before* w^t 19 was *interl.*   21 mor *canc. before* morowe   25 shotyng *canc. before* shotyng   33 endyd/ than] *MS.* endyd than

Gagge w^t whome he talked vntill he came at the garden posterne gate/ And there entred the gate beyng shett after hyme w^{che} caused me to goo my wayes/ And beyng goon but a lyttyll distance/ the gate was opened agayn/ And there sir harry Norres
5 called me agayn commaundyng me to come in to the kyng who stode behynd the doore in a nyght gown of Russett velvett furred w^t Sabelles/ byfore whome I kneled down beyng w^t hyme there all alon the space of an hower & more dewryng w^{che} tyme he examyned me of dyuers waytty matters concernyng my
10 lord/ whysshyng that leuer than xx M^l ^{li} he had lyved/ than he asked me for the xv^{Cli} (w^{che} m^r kyngeston moved to my lord byfore his deathe) Sir sayd I I thynke that I can tell yor grace partely where it is/ yea can q^d the kyng than I pray you tell me and you shall do vs myche pleasure/ nor it shall not be on-
15 rewardyd/ Sir sayd I if it please yor highnes/ After the departure of Davyd Vyncent frome my lord at Scrobye who had than the custody therof/ leavyng the same w^t my lord in dyuers bagges sealed w^t my lordes seale/ delyuerd the same mony in the same bagges sealed vnto a certyn prest (whome I named to the kyng)
20 savely to kepe to his vse/ ys thys trewe/ q^d the kyng/ yea sir q^d I w^{t}out all dought/ [f. 91^v] the prest shall not be able to denye it in my presence/ ffor I was at the delyuere therof/ well than/ q^d the kyng/ lett me alone kepe thys gere secrett bytwen yor self and me/ And lett no man be privye therof/ ffor if I heare any
25 more of it/ than I knowe by whome it is come to knowlege/ iij^{re} may/ q^d he/ kepe councell if ij be away/ And if I thought that my cappe knewe my councell/ I wold cast it in to the fier and burne it/ And for yor trewthe & honestie/ ye shall be oon of our seruauntes/ and in that same rome w^t vs that ye ware w^t yor old
30 m^r/ therfore goo to sir Iohn Gage/ our vice chamberlayn/ to whome I haue spoken alredy to geve you yor othe & to admytt you our seruaunt in the same Rome/ And than goo to my lord of Norffolk and he shall pay you/ all yor hole yeres wages w^{che} is x^{li}/ is it not so q^d the kyng/ yes forsothe/ sir q^d I/ And I ame

3 caused] c *written over* t   4 gate *interl.*   7 Sabelles *canc. before* Sabelles *and* s *before* byfore; I *canc. after* whome   8 w^t *canc. before* the   9 of *canc. before* of   10 *superscript* ^{li} *canc. after* xx   14 vs *canc. before* vs; vs *interl.*   15 if *canc. before* sayd   20 Ys *canc. after* vse/   26 thought *interl.*; knewe *canc. before* that   32 you *interl.* 34 so *interl.*

behynd therof for iij^{re} quart^{rs} of a yere/ that is trewe/ q^d the kyng/ for so we be enformed therfore ye shall haue yor hole yeres wages w^t oure reward delyuerd you by the Duke of Norfolk/ the kyng also promysed me ferthermore to be my syngular good & gracious lord whan so euer occasion shold serue/ And thus I departed frome hyme And as I went I mett w^t m^r kyngeston commyng frome the councell who commaundyd me in ther names/ to goo strayt vnto theme for whome they haue sent for by hyme/ And in any wyse/ q^d he/ for goddes sake/ take good hede what ye say/ ffor ye shall be examyned/ of suche certyn wordes as my lord yor late m^r hade at hys departure/ And if you tell theme the treuthe/ q^d he/ what he sayd you shold vndo yor self for in any wyse they wold not here of hyt/ therfore be circumspect what answere ye make/ to ther demaund/ why sir/ q^d I/ howe have ye don/ therin yor self/ Mary q^d he I haue vtterly denyed that euer I hard any suche wordes/ and he that opened the matter first/ is fled for feare w^{che} was the yoman of the gard that rode empost to the kyng frome leycester/ therfore goo yor wayes/ god send you good spede/ And whan ye haue don come to me in to the Chamber of presence where I shall tary yor commyng to se howe you spede/ And to knowe howe ye haue don w^t the kyng/ Thus I departed and went dyrectly to the councell chamber doore/ and as sone as I was come I was called in among them/ And beyng there/ My lord of Norffolk spake to me first and bad me welcome to the Court/ And sayd my [f. 92] lordes thys gentilman hathe bothe Iustly And paynfully serued the Cardynall hys m^r lyke an honest & diligent seruaunt/ therfore I dought not but of suche questyons as ye shall demaund of hyme/ he wyll make Iust report/ I dare vndertake the same for hyme/ howe say ye/ it is reported that yor m^r spake certyn wordes evyn byfore his departure owt of thys lyfe/ the truthe wherof I dought not ye knowe/ And as ye knowe I pray you report & feare not for no man/ ye shall not nede to swere

1 / yere *canc. after* a 8–9 for *interl. before* by 11 I *canc. before* you 11–12 you tell *interl.* 12 told *canc. before* theme; I *canc. before* you; you *interl.*; my *canc. before* yor; yor *interl.* 13 wold not *interl.* 15 haue ye *canc. before* have 18 leycester/ therfore] *MS.* leycester therfore 19 whan *interl.* 26 my lordes] *MS.* my/ lordes; ar *canc. before* And 30 hyme/ howe] *MS.* hyme howe; reported *canc. before* spake 33 to *interl.*

hyme/ therfore goo to howe saye you/ is it trewe that is reported/ ffor sothe sir I was so diligent attendyng more to the preseruacion of his lyfe/ than I was to note & marke euery word that he spake/ And sir in deade he spake many Idell wordes as men in suche
5 extremes/ the w^{che} I cannot nowe remember/ yf it please yor lordshypes to call byfore you m^r kyngeston he wyll not fayle to shewe you the truthe/ Mary so haue we don alredy/ q^d they/ who hathe byn here presently byfore vs/ And hathe denyed vtterly that euer he hard any suche wordes spoken by yor m^r/ at
10 the tyme of hys deathe or at any tyme byfore/ fforsothe my lordes/ q^d I// than I can say no more for if he hard them not I cowld not heare theme/ for he hard as myche as I/ and I as myche as he/ therfore my lordes it ware myche foly for me to declare any thyng of ontrouthe w^{che} I ame not able to Iustefie/
15 loo/ q^d my lord of Norffolk I told you as myche byfore/ therfore goo yor wayes/ q^d he/ to me/ you are dismyst/ And come agayn to my chamber anon for I must nedes talke w^t you/ I most humbly thanked theme & so departed/ And went in to the Chamber of presence/ to mete w^t m^r kyngeston/ whome I found standyng in
20 Comynycacion w^t an auncyent gentillman vssher of the kynges privy chamber called m^r Ratclyfe/ And at my Commyng M^r kyngeston demaundyd of me if I had byn w^t the Councell and what answere I made theme/ I sayd agayn that I had satisfied them sufficyently w^t my answere/ And told hyme the maner of
25 it And than he asked me howe I sped w^t the kyng/ I told hyme partely of our commynycacion/ And of hys graces benyvolence/ and pryncely lyberalitie/ and howe he commaundyd me to goo to my lord of Norffolk/ As we ware spekyng of [f. 92^v] hyme/ he came frome the Councell in to the chamber of presence/ asson
30 as he aspied me he came in to the wyndowe where I stode/ w^t m^r kyngeston and m^r Ratclyfe to whome I declared the kynges pleasure/ thes ij gentilmen desired hyme to be my good lord/ Nay q^d he/ I woll be better vnto hyme than ye wene for if I could haue spoken w^t hyme byfore he came to the kyng I wold haue

1 hyme/ therfore] *MS.* hyme therfore   3 mak. *canc. before* marke
7 we *interl.*   8 vse *canc. after* byfore   12 theme *canc. after* heare   16 you are] *MS.* yor are   17 y *canc. before* w^t; you/ I] *MS.* you I   21 Ratclyfe *canc. before* Ratclyfe   24 w^t *canc. after* them   27 he *interl.*   29 to *interl.*; counsell the *canc. before* chamber   32 to *canc. before* my

had hyme to my seruyce/ (the kyng excepted) he shold haue don no man seruyce in all Englond but oonly me/ And loke what I may do for you/ I woll do it w^t a right good wyll/ Sir than/ q^d I/ woll it please yor grace to move the kynges ma^{tie} in my behalf to geve me oon of the Cartes & horsys that brought vppe my 5 stuffe w^t my lordes w^{che} is nowe in the tower to carie it in to my Contrie/ yea marie wyll I/ q^d he/ and retorned agayn to the kyng for whome I taried still w^t m^r kyngeston/ And m^r Ratclyfe/ who sayd that he wold go in and helpe my lord in my sewte/ w^t the kyng/ And incontynent my lord came forthe and shewed me 10 howe the kyng was my good & gracious lord// And hathe gevyn me vj of the best horsse that I can chose amongest all my lordes Cart horsse w^t a Cart to Carye my stuffe/ And .v. markes for my Costes homwardes/ And hathe commaundyd me/ q^d he/ to delyuer you X^{li} for yor wages beyng behynd on payed And xx^{li} 15 for a reward/ who commaundyd to call for m^r Secretorye to make a warraunt for all thes thynges/ than was it told hyme/ that m^r Secretory was gon to hanworthe for that nyght/ than commaundyd he oon of the messengers of the chamber to ride vnto hyme in all hast for thes warrauntes and wylled me to mete w^t 20 hyme the next day at london And there to receyve bothe my mony my stuffe & horsse/ that the kynge gave me/ And so I dyd/ of whome I receyved all thynges accordyng/ And than I retorned in to my Contrie And thus endyd the lyfe of my late lord & m^r/ the Riche & tryhumphant legat and Cardynall of 25 Englond/ on whos sowle Iesu haue mercy Amen/

ffinis Q^d. G. C.

[f. 93] **Who lyste** to Rede And consider w^t an Indyfferent eye this history may behold the wonderouse mutabilitie/ of vayn honours/ the bryttell Assuraunce of haboundaunce/ the 30 oncertyntie of dignytes the fflateryng of fayned frendes/ And the tykkyll trust to worldly prynces/ wherof thys lord Cardynall

3 wyll/ Sir] *MS.* wyll Sir   7 the *canc. before* the   9 my *canc. after* helpe   11 . . lord *canc. before* &   13 Ad *canc. before* And; And *interl.*   14 my *interl. and canc. before* my; my *interl.*; ye my *with* my *interl. canc. after* my   17 Secretory *canc. before* warraunt; then *canc. before* hyme   20 ha *canc. before* all; all *canc. before* wylled   22 & *canc. after* mony; my *interl.*   24 late *interl.*   25 legat *interl.*; & legate *canc. before* of

hathe felt bothe of the swette & the sower in eche degrees/ As fletyng frome honors/ losyng of Riches/ deposed frome Dignytes/ fforsaken of ffrendes// And the inconstantnes of prynces fauour/ Of all w^{che} thynges he hathe had in this world the full felycyte as
5 long as that ffortune smyled vppon hyme/ but whan she began to frown howe sone was he depryved of all thes dremyng Ioyes And vayn pleasures/ the w^{che} in XX^{ti} yeres w^t great travell, study, and paynnes opteyned/ ware in oon yere and lesse (w^t hevynes, care, & sorowe) lost and consumed/ O madnes/ O
10 folyshe desier/ O fond hope/ O gredy desier of vayn honors, dignyties, and Ryches/ O what inconstant trust And assuraunce is in Rollyng ffortune/ wherfore the prophett sayd full well/ Tezaurisat et ignorat cui congregabit ea/ who is certyn to whome he shall leave his treasure & riches that he hathe gathered
15 together in this world it may chaunce hyme to leave it vnto suche as he hathe purposed/ But The wyse man saythe/ that an other person who parauenture he hated in his lyfe shall spend it owt & consume it/

13 to whome *interl.*   14 that *canc. before* he shall   15 it may chaunce hyme to leave it *interl.*   16 by his *canc. after* purposed; testament or other wyse *canc. before* | But; But *interl.*   17 t *canc. before* his

BIBLIOGRAPHY TO THE NOTES

The following bibliography includes all the titles which are frequently referred to in the notes. Full references to works cited only once are given as they occur.

Alumni Cantabrigienses, ed. John Venn and J. A. Venn, Part I, 'Earliest Times to 1751', 4 vols., Cambridge, 1924–7.
Athenae Cantabrigienses, ed. C. H. Cooper and Thompson Cooper, 2 vols., 1, 1500–85, Cambridge, 1858.
Bacon, Francis, *History of the Reign of King Henry VII*, ed. J. Rawson Lumby, Cambridge, 1892.
Busch, Wilhelm, *England Under the Tudors*, tr. from the German by Alice M. Todd, London, 1895.
Cameron, T. W., 'The Early Life of Thomas Wolsey', *English Historical Review*, iii (1888), 458–77.
The Chronicle of Calais, ed. J. G. Nichols, Camden Society, xxxv, 1846.
Chronicle of King Henry VIII, tr. from the Spanish by M. A. Sharp Hume, London, 1889.
Collier, J. Payne, *The History of English Dramatic Poetry*, 3 vols., London, 1831.
Doran, John, *The History of Court Fools*, London, 1858.
Fiddes, Richard, *The Life of Cardinal Wolsey*, London, 1724. The title 'Collections' refers to the second part of Fiddes's work in which he printed numerous materials relating to Wolsey.
Forrest, William, *The History of Grisild the Second*, ed. W. D. Macray, Roxburghe Club, London, 1875. See also Appendix A.
Friedmann, Paul, *Anne Boleyn*, 2 vols., London, 1884.
Fuller, Thomas, *The Church History of Britain*, 6 vols., ed. J. S. Brewer, Oxford, 1845.
Grove, Joseph, *The History of the Life and Times of Cardinal Wolsey*, 2nd ed., 4 vols., London, 1748.
Hall, Edward, *The Vnion of the Two Noble and Illustre Famelies of Lancastre & Yorke*, London, 1542, 1548, 1550. Reprinted, London, 1809. Cited as 'Hall's *Chronicle*'.
Harpsfield, Nicholas, *The life and death of Sr Thomas Moore*, ed. E. V. Hitchcock and R. W. Chambers, London, E.E.T.S., o.s. 186, 1932.
Herford, C. E., *Studies in the Literary Relations of England and Germany in the Sixteenth Century*, Cambridge, 1886.
Holmes, John (ed.), *The Life of Cardinal Wolsey*, London, 1852.
Hughes, Philip, *The Reformation in England*, 3 vols., London, 1950–4.

Hunter, Joseph, *Who Wrote Cavendish's Life of Wolsey?* London, 1814. Reprinted in Singer (1825 ed.), II, xiii–lxxii.

Jacqueton, G., 'La Politique extérieure de Louise de Savoie,' *Bibliothèque de L'École des Hautes Études*, LXXXVIII (1892).

Lavisse, Ernst, *Histoire de France*, V, Parts 1 and 2, Paris, 1903–4.

Le Neve, John, *Fasti Ecclesiae Anglicanae*, revised and continued by T. Duffus Hardy, 3 vols., London, 1854.

Leonard, Frederic, *Recueil des Traitez*, 6 vols., Paris, 1693.

Letters and Papers Foreign and Domestic of the Reign of Henry VIII, ed. J. S. Brewer, J. Gairdner, and R. Brodie. Revised ed. by Brodie, 1920. Preface to Vol. IV of the original ed. by Brewer. Referred to as 'LP'.

Mackie, J. D., *The Earlier Tudors 1485–1558* (Oxford History of England), Oxford, 1952.

Mattingly, Garrett, *Catherine of Aragon*, Boston, 1941.

Merriman, R. B., *The Life and Letters of Thomas Cromwell*, 2 vols., Oxford, 1902.

Muller, J. A., *Stephen Gardiner and the Tudor Reaction*, New York, 1926.

Nichols, John, *The History and Antiquities of the County of Leicester*, 4 vols. in 8, 1795–1815.

[Northumberland Household Book]—*The Regulations and Establishment of the Household of Henry Algernon Percy, the Fifth Earl of Northumberland*, ed. Thomas Percy, London, 1827.

Pocock, Nicholas, *Records of the Reformation*, 2 vols., Oxford, 1870.

Pollard, A. F., *Wolsey*, London, 1929.

The Privy Purse Expences of King Henry the Eighth, ed. N. H. Nicolas, London, 1827.

Registrum Thome Wolsey [Wolsey's Winchester Register], ed. F. T. Madge and H. Chitty, The Canterbury and York Society, XXXII, Oxford, 1926.

Roper, William, *The Lyfe of Sir Thomas Moore, knighte*, ed. E. V. Hitchcock, E.E.T.S., o.s. 197, London, 1935, reprinted 1958.

Roy, William and Barlowe, Jerome, *Rede me and be nott wrothe*, Strasburg, 1528. Reprinted by Arber, London, 1871.

Seebohm, Frederic, *The Oxford Reformers*, Everyman edition, London, 1914.

Sergeant, Philip W., *The Life of Anne Boleyn*, 2nd ed., New York, 1924.

Singer, S. W., *The Life of Cardinal Wolsey*, 1st ed., Chiswick, 2 vols. [with the poems], 1825; 2nd ed., 1 vol., London, 1827.

Skelton, John, *Works*, ed. A. Dyce, 3 vols., Boston, 1866.

[Spanish Calendar]—*Calendar of Letters, Despatches, and State Papers preserved in the Archives at Simancas, etc.*, ed. G. A. Bergenroth, London, 1862, et seq.

[State Papers]—*State Papers of the reign of Henry VIII*, 11 vols., London, 1830–52.
Stowe, John, *The Survey of London*, Everyman edition, London, 1912.
Van Ortroy, F., 'Vie du Bienheureux Martyr Jean Fisher', *Analecta Bollandiana*, x (1891), 121–365 and xii (1893), 97–287.
[Venetian Calendar]—*Calendar of State Papers ... in the Archives and Collections of Venice*, ed. Rawdon Brown, London, 1864 et seq.
Wordsworth, Christopher [ed.], *Ecclesiastical Biography*, 4th ed., 4 vols., London, 1853. The *Life of Wolsey* occupies pp. 459–672 in vol. 1.

HISTORICAL AND EXPLANATORY NOTES

3/16–17 **not geveng**: not give.

4/13 **than to quenche**: than have quenched.

4/18 **or of affeccion**: or out of affection (for Wolsey). Cavendish emphasizes the lack of prejudice that is to characterize his narrative.

4/29 **an honest ... Ipsewiche**: Wolsey's early years are summarized by Pollard (pp. 11–13), who suggests 'the latter part of 1472 or early in 1473' as the most probable date for his birth. Cavendish's own account of Wolsey's Maundy (below, 133/11 ff) in 1530, when he washed the feet of 'fifty-nine poor men', is best interpreted, as Pollard shows, so as to give the above dates. The will of Wolsey's father (Singer, pp. 502–3) was proved on 15 October 1496. As Skelton and other detractors of the cardinal liked to point out, he was in fact a butcher 'and apparently of some truculence' (Mackie, p. 287, n. 1). On the other hand, Cavendish's 'honest poore man' is supported by the fact that he was also a churchwarden.

5/1–2 **bacheler ... age**: If Wolsey proceeded B.A. in 1487–8, it becomes difficult to account for the next few years of his life. He was ordained on 10 March 1498 and, at some time prior to that date, had been elected fellow and had received his M.A. In 1499 he was Senior Bursar at Magdalen and also Master of Magdalen College School. The university and college records, as Pollard (p. 12, n. 2) points out, do not give us any insight into his activities during the early nineties.

5/4 **learnyng, was made**: A typical instance of Cavendish's habit of omitting subject pronouns when the context is clear enough to avoid confusion. Here, supply 'he' (Wolsey) before 'was'.

5/6 **the lord Marques Dorsett**: Thomas Grey, first Marquis (1451–1501). By his second wife Cicely, whom he had married before 23 April 1475, he had seven sons and eight daughters. His two eldest sons died young and the third, Thomas (1477–1530) succeeded to the title at his father's death (below, 6/22) on 20 September 1501. If the second Marquis was one of Wolsey's pupils 'At scole', this would presumably mean that Wolsey was instructing there as early as 1490.

5/9–10 **Ayenst ... season**: This was apparently Christmas, 1499. Wolsey was instituted at Limington, near Ilchester in Somerset (the diocese of Bath and Wells) on 10 October 1500 (Fiddes, p. 5).

5/18 **Ordynarie:** 'One who has, of his own right and not by special deputation, immediate jurisdiction in ecclesiastical cases, as the archbishop in a province, or the bishop or bishop's deputy in a diocese' (*O.E.D.*).

5/22–3 **sir Amys Pawlett:** Sir Amias Paulet or Poulet (d. 1538). Tradition has it that Wolsey was disciplined 'for disorderly conduct at a fair where he had drunk to excess' (Singer, p. 68), but the story seems to go back no further than to Sir John Harington. Paulet became Treasurer of the Middle Temple in 1521. We do not know precisely when Wolsey restricted him to the Temple, but he was free again in 1524. Cavendish's '.v. or vj yeres' would place the beginning of his confinement in 1518–19.

5/25–6 **to sett ... feete:** i.e. to put him in the stocks. The *O.E.D.* does not record the phrase 'to set by the feet'.

6/32 **sir Iohn Nanfant:** As Singer (p. 70, n. 6) noted, Cavendish seems to have confused Sir Richard Nanfan with his father, Sir John. Sir Richard (d. 1507), who must be intended here, was the son of Sir John Nanfan, who had been Sheriff of Cornwall in 1451 and 1457. He received his 'great rome' (Deputy of Calais) sometime after 1488. Wolsey's chaplaincy with him probably dates from about 1503, for it was not long thereafter that Sir Richard returned to England, retiring to Birtsmorton, Worcestershire. A natural son, John, presumably named after Sir Richard's father, inherited his estates. Nanfan seems to have recommended Wolsey to Henry VII at his death in 1507 (Pollard, p. 13). Cavendish does not mention Wolsey's service as chaplain to Archbishop Deane, a position which he held from 1501 until the bishop's death on 15 February 1502/3.

7/14 **Doctor ffoxe:** Richard Foxe (1448?–1528). His patronage of Wolsey is amply attested (Pollard, pp. 14–16). As Bishop of Winchester, he would have been visitor of Magdalen College after 1501; this, plus his own affiliation with the college as a student earlier, may help to account for his interest in the young Wolsey. There is good evidence, however, that Foxe later opposed both Wolsey's war policy and the arbitrariness of his home rule (Pollard, pp. 102, 108–9, 190). Foxe's parting advice to Wolsey (LP, II, 1814) was 'and, good my lord, when the term is done, keep the Council with the king wherever he be,' a statement that implicitly confirms Cavendish's account (below, p. 12) of Wolsey's efforts to separate king and Council.

7/16 **sir Thomas lovell:** Sir Thomas Lovell (d. 1524) was a student at Lincoln's Inn about 1473 and fought at Bosworth Field under Richmond in 1485. On 12 October 1485 Henry VII made him Chancellor of the Exchequer for life and thereafter he was frequently employed by the king. The two offices that Cavendish assigns to him here, Master of the Wards and Constable of the Tower, he did not receive until 1509 under Henry VIII, when he was confirmed as Chancellor of the Exchequer. Like Foxe, he seems to have been forced into retirement by Wolsey's rise and, after 1516, took little part in public affairs. Cf. W. C. Richardson, *Tudor Chamber Administration* (Baton Rouge, 1952), pp. 111-15.

7/20 Supply 'they' (the Counsellors) before 'thought' and 'him' (Wolsey) before 'a'.

7/23 **an ambassette . . . Maxymylian:** Cavendish's story of Wolsey's mission cannot be confirmed by the contemporary documents that have survived. Historians are now inclined to discredit many of its details, particularly his account of the time (about eighty hours) in which the journey was accomplished. T. W. Cameron thought that the mission might have occurred in 1507 but could offer no better authority for his view than a statement made by Bacon in his *Life of Henry VII*. Busch (pp. 381-2) believes that Cavendish's narrative refers to a mission made to the Bishop of Gurk on or about 23 August 1508. Wolsey was again in the Netherlands in October of that year and the correspondence relating to the second mission (partially preserved in LP, I, 426-452) alludes to an earlier mission made by him. Busch notes, however, that Wolsey could not have left the king 'at Richmond' (below, 8/9-10), for Henry was absent from there between the end of July and the end of August. Moreover, 'Maximilian . . . was staying at Dordrecht . . . and Wolsey could not have made the journey from Calais there in less than a day.'

7/33 **his grace presence:** Genitives without *s* are frequent in Cavendish even when the possessive word does not end with an *s*-sound; cf. 'monythe wages' 38/32-3, 'for my m^r sake' 105/11, 'my lord recognysaunce' 119/9.

9/1-4 **And hauyng . . . redy:** The construction is clumsy and somewhat redundant. Modern usage requires a comma after 'he' (l. 3).

10/9 Supply 'he' (Wolsey) before 'prepared'.

10/17 **the Deanry of lyncolne:** Wolsey was collated to this office on 2 February 1509. Henry VII undoubtedly intended the benefice as a reward for his chaplain's services but the date argues against Cavendish's statement that the appointment resulted directly from the mission to Maximilian. By 4 June 1509 Wolsey had also received the Deanery of Hereford (Pollard, p. 13, n. 5).

10/21–2 **and after . . . almener:** Supply 'was' before 'after'. Wolsey did not become royal almoner until 8 November 1509 (Brodie's Preface to new ed. of LP, p. xiv) under Henry VIII. Pollard attributes his failure to achieve promotion in the first months of the new reign to the influence of Margaret of Beaufort, who apparently distrusted him.

10/34 **kyng or Cayser:** A Middle-English alliterative phrase, still common in the sixteenth century. See Langland (B. xix. 134), 'To be kaisere or kynge of the kyngedome of Iuda,' and note Spenser's suggestive use of the phrase in his description of Mammon's Cave (*F.Q.*, II, vii, 5. 8), 'The antique shapes of kings and kesars straunge and rare'.

10/35 ff. The death of Henry VII. Henry VIII succeeded to the throne on 22 April 1509 and was crowned with Catherine, whom he had married on 11 June, on 25 June.

11/2 **the second Salomon:** Apparently a commonplace description of Henry VII. The phrase is used by William Forrest (pp. 30, 37–9) and later by Bacon (p. 211), who may possibly have taken it from Cavendish. The *O.E.D.*'s first example is from the 1554 edition of Hawes's *Pastime of Pleasure*.

11/7–8 **I Omyt . . . Cronycles:** Hall, for example, devotes some seven pages (506–12) to the description of the funeral and coronation ceremonies.

11/25–6 **sir Richard Emsons . . . howsse:** Sir Richard Empson (d. 1510). Empson had been given land in the parish of St. Bride in Fleet Street on 5 August 1507. His house there was granted to Wolsey on 18 October 1509 (Fiddes, p. 19). See *D.N.B.*

12/5 **other auncyent councellours:** Besides Foxe and Lovell, who have already been mentioned, these were Warham, Archbishop of Canterbury; Ruthal, Secretary to the King and Bishop of Durham; Thomas Howard, Earl of Surrey; Shrewsbury, the Lord Steward; Herbert, Lord Chamberlain; Lord Darcy, Sir Edward Poynings, and Sir Harry Marney. See Pollard's (pp. 10–11) analysis of the Council during Wolsey's early years and G. R. Elton, *Tudor Revolution in Government* (Cambridge, 1953), pp. 62–3.

13/23–5 The sentence involves an anacoluthon after 'qualites' (l. 25) which has been occasioned by the participle 'clymmyng'

(l. 23) and the repetition of the subject 'Thys Almosyner (l. 23) . . . he' (l. 25).

13/29 **the warres:** Henry VIII had joined the holy league with the Pope, following Ferdinand's lead, on 13 November 1511. The disastrous Fuenterrabia expedition of June 1512 was recouped by the campaign of 1513 (here described by Cavendish) that followed upon Henry's treaty of 5 April 1513 with Julius, Ferdinand, and Maximilian.

14/16 **passed . . . Calice:** Henry arrived in Calais with a retinue of 11,000 men on 30 June 1513. He left Calais for Thérouanne on 21 July (*Chronicle of Calais*, pp. 13–14). The city fell on 23 August.

14/24 **Maximylian:** Henry met Maximilian before Thérouanne on 12 August (Mackie, p. 279) 'and there the emperowre had wages of the kynge' (*Chronicle of Calais*, p. 14). Fiddes (p. 60) reports that the emperor received £25 per day for his services.

14/28 **that . . . to take:** The shift from the noun clause to the infinitive is confusing. Either 'for an emperor to take wages' or 'that an emperor should take wages'.

14/33 **Tourney:** Tournai, besieged early in September, capitulated on 21 September.

15/2–3 **gave . . . see:** Wolsey received Tournai in 1513 from Henry, but was never able to take possession of the see. A French bishop-elect, Louis Guillard, had already been appointed and for four years Wolsey carried on a controversy with him through his agent Sampson. See Polydore Vergil's account of the quarrel (*Anglica Historia*, Camden Society, 1950, p. 233) and, for Sampson, the note to 79/22 below.

15/8 **he retourned . . . Englond:** Henry returned to Calais on 19 October and sailed for England on the 21st.

15/10 **asskyrmouche:** The 'skirmish' to which Cavendish refers was the famous 'Battle of the Spurs'. Hall (p. 550) tells us that 'The Frenchmen call this battaile the iourney of Spurres because they ranne away so fast on horsbacke'. The 'Duke of longvyle' was Louis d'Orleans (d. 1516), who, while a prisoner in England, helped to negotiate the marriage treaty between Henry's sister Mary and Louis XII of France. The 'Countie Clermount' was Antoine, second Count of Clermount (d. 1530), the king's Chamberlain.

15/12 **the See of lyncolne:** Wolsey was nominated to the see of Lincoln on 1 January 1514 (Hall, p. 567), although his predecessor, Dr. William Smith, did not die until 2 January. The papal bulls are dated 6 February and his consecration took place on 26 March.

Dr. William Smith (1460?-1514) had been translated to Lincoln from Coventry and Lichfield on 31 January 1496. He dropped out of public affairs after Margaret of Beaufort's death in 1509, and thereafter devoted his time and wealth to benefactions. Cavendish's account of Wolsey's appropriation of his goods is confirmed by the bill of articles against the cardinal of 1 December 1529 (LP, IV, 6075), where he is also charged with the same practice after his accession to the bishoprics of York, Durham, and Winchester.

15/20 **Doctor Baynbryge:** Christopher Bainbridge (1464?-1514), Archbishop of York, English ambassador at Rome (1509-14), and close friend of Julius II, died in Rome about 13 July 1514, allegedly poisoned by his chaplain, Rinaldo de Modena. The circumstances surrounding his death and the subsequent investigation of them are ably elucidated by Pollard (pp. 21-4). Wolsey's agent, Silvester de Giglis, Bishop of Worcester, was implicated in the affair but was acquitted. As soon as the news of Bainbridge's death reached England (5 August), Wolsey was given the temporalities of York; he paid the fees for his promotion principally out of Bainbridge's estate. The papal bulls are dated 15 September 1514.

15/28 **Caunterburye:** Wolsey's controversies with William Warham (1450?-1532), Archbishop of Canterbury, were to flare up a number of times during the cardinal's career. Warham already had a long record of faithful service to the crown. He served on several diplomatic missions between 1488 and 1503, was Bishop of London in 1501, and was given the archbishopric (succeeding Deane, Wolsey's old patron) on 29 November 1503. It was Warham who consecrated Wolsey a cardinal in November 1515 (below, p. 16) and delivered up the seal to him on 22 December of that year. The *D.N.B.*, echoing Fiddes and Grove, endeavours to show that little personal enmity existed between Wolsey and Warham, but modern opinion (cf. Pollard, p. 108, n. 2) has tended to confirm Cavendish's account of the 'grudge' between them. In his later life, Warham was forced to give in to the policies of Wolsey and Henry VIII. He was chief counsel for Catherine at the divorce trial, but was of little use to her, giving as his reason '*Ira principis mors est*', a maxim which Wolsey could also find occasion to quote after his fall (below, 137/26-7).

16/4-5 **Caused his Crosse ... hym:** After Wolsey received the cardinalate, he had two crosses borne before him (below, 17/28 ff.), one as archbishop and the other as cardinal, or, as Cavendish has it, 'for his legacye'. At the Westminster ceremony in which Wolsey received the red hat, no cross was borne before Warham; 'and none was ever borne again before him in Wolsey's presence. . . . Warham had not even one in his own province, when it was illumined by Wolsey's superior lustre' (Pollard, p. 57).

16/13 **legatus de latere:** Wolsey did not obtain his 'legacy' until 17 May 1518 and then 'simply as a colleague to watch and control Campeggio' (Pollard, p. 170), who was coming to England to encourage interest in a crusade. In 1519 Leo X prolonged the commission for two years and, under Adrian VI, two further extensions were granted. Wolsey finally managed to secure his commission for life from Clement VII. Pollard (Ch. V) has an admirable discussion of the whole question of the legateship and the problems it created. The crux of the difficulties lay in the fact that, as legate de latere, Wolsey was a special papal envoy and hence responsible only to the Pope, while, as Chancellor and subject of Henry, he owed his allegiance to the British crown. Before him, legates de latere had been given only temporary appointments (as Campeggio's was in 1518); his unprecedented power stemmed from the union of spiritual and temporal jurisdictions in his own person.

17/1 Supply 'he' (Wolsey) before 'thought'.

17/9 **Chauncelour of Englond:** Wolsey received the Chancellorship on 24 December 1515, two days after Warham's resignation (above 15/28 and n.). Warham had been Lord Chancellor since 21 January 1504.

17/17 **to convocatt Caunterbury:** In 1523 Wolsey called Warham's convocation at St. Paul's before him in Westminster. This action is said to have inspired Skelton's famous lines: 'Gentle Paule laie downe thy swearde;/For Peter of Westminster hath shaven thy beard.' Even after his fall and shortly before his planned installation at York, he called a convocation of his province without waiting for a regular mandate from the king (Pollard, pp. 292–3).

17/19–20 **takyng . . . Dyoces:** The cardinal's far-reaching powers of appointment are fully discussed by Pollard (pp. 204–8). The technical term 'prevencyon' (l. 24, below) refers to 'the privilege in Canon Law possessed or claimed by an ecclesiastical superior of taking precedence of or forestalling an inferior in the execution of an official act regularly pertaining to the latter' (*O.E.D.*). The seventh of the articles against Wolsey in 1530 specifically mentions his abuse of this power (LP, IV, 6075).

17/33 **the bysshopryche of Duresme:** Wolsey had acquired Bath and Wells *in commendam* by a bull of 30 July 1518 and had received its temporalities on 28 August of that year. He resigned this see for Durham in February 1523 (Le Neve, III, 293). When Foxe died on 5 October 1528 Wolsey received Winchester, which he held *in commendam* by a bull of 8 February 1529 (Le Neve, III, 16).

17/33 **the Abbey of seynt Albons:** Wolsey received St. Albans from Henry on 17 December 1521 (Pollard, p. 321); it was, at this time, the richest abbey in England and had, in 1535, revenues amounting to £2102 per year. Upon Wolsey's fall in 1529 it was given to Robert Catton, Prior of Norwich, who died two years later. Pollard comments (pp. 173–4) that 'it was almost unprecedented for an English archbishop to hold an English bishopric *in commendam*, and it was a still more flagrant abuse for a secular priest like Wolsey to hold such an improper *commendam* as St. Albans. . . .' Wolsey's various *in commendam* holdings were in direct violation of a decree of the Lateran Council of 1512–17.

17/33–4 **in Commendam:** This term was used to describe the tenure of a benefice 'commended' or given in charge to a qualified clerk or layman, to hold until a proper incumbent was provided for it, or according to a later practice, bestowed upon a layman or secular ecclesiastic, with enjoyment of the revenues for life.

18/3 **in ferme . . . hereford:** Cavendish seems confused in listing the bishoprics which Wolsey 'farmed out' for their non-resident incumbents. Bath was held by Hadrian de Castello or Corneto from 1504 until 1518, when he was deprived and the bishopric given to Wolsey himself (above, 17/33 and n.). Castello had formerly held Hereford (1502–4), but from 1504 onwards that see was occupied by Englishmen. Worcester was held by three 'strangers' during Wolsey's period of power: Silvester de Giglis (for whom see above, 15/20 and n.), 1498–1521; Giulio de Medici, later Pope Clement VII, 1521–22; and Jerome de Ghinucci, 1522–35. Cavendish does not mention Campeggio's possession of Salisbury, 1524–34, and Ateca's (Catherine's Spanish confessor) occupancy of Llandaff, 1517–36. It is just possible that Cavendish's confusion arose from his belief that Campeggio was Bishop of Bath. This error may have originated in his recollection that Campeggio stayed at Bath Place while he was in London in 1528 and 1529. See 77/9–10 and n.

18/26 **the order of his howsse:** The number of servants here listed by Cavendish totals about 406 to 409 people, depending on how the 'nine or ten' lords, each with two servants (20/8–9), are added into the account. This total does not include the miscellaneous 'retainers and suitors' (21/11–12). Cavendish's round number of 500 is thus approximately correct, but the actual count of 406–9 squares even better with the total of 429 which is given in the assessment of Wolsey's household for the subsidy of 1526 (LP, IV, 2972 and 6185). Pollard (p. 327), estimating that the number of those who would not have been assessed for the subsidy must have been as great as the number of those who were, gives the total number of servants as 'little if at all short of a thousand'.

18/32 **Cofferer:** An officer of the Royal Household, next under the controller, who had the supervision of the other officers.

18/35 **surveyour of the Dressor:** An officer of a household who superintended the preparation and serving of food. The 'dresser' was a sideboard or table on which food was dressed.

19/12 **gentilman for the monthe:** The phrase is not recorded by the *O.E.D.* It apparently means an officer appointed by the month who was replaced at the end of that time by another gentleman. But I have found no other evidence for such a rotating office in Wolsey's household.

20/4 **Pillers berers:** Those who bore Wolsey's 'pillars' which he had introduced as symbols of his office. Cf. *O.E.D.* (s.v. *Pillar* 5).

20/6 **xij . . . wayters:** It was probably in this group of servants that Cavendish himself served his master. In the list of Wolsey's suite that disembarked at Calais in 1527 he is listed among the 'Awdiences' (*Chronicle of Calais*, p. 40). The word 'audience' in this sense does not occur in the *O.E.D.*; it seems to mean 'gentleman-in-waiting' as distinct from 'gentleman-usher' proper. See the introduction, pp. xix–xx.

20/9–10 **the Erle of Derby:** Edward Stanley (1508–72), the second but eldest surviving son of Thomas Stanley, second earl, who died on 23 May 1521. The third earl was one of Wolsey's wards during his minority.

20/23 **Clarke of the Crowne:** An officer of Chancery who issued writs for the summoning of peers in the House of Lords, and writs of election for members of the House of Commons.

20/23 **ridyng Clarke:** 'One of the six Clarks of the Chancery, who takes his turn for his year to have the controlling of all Grants which passe the great Seal' (Phillipps, *Riding Clark*, 1658, cited in *O.E.D.*, s.v. *Riding*, ppl. a.).

20/23–4 **Clarke of the hamper:** Clerk of the Hanaper, that department of the Chancery into which fees were paid for the sealing and enrolment of charters and other documents.

20/24 **Chaffer of waxe:** A chafe-wax was 'an officer attending on the Lord Chancellor, whose duty it was to prepare the wax for sealing documents' (*O.E.D.*).

20/24–5 **Clarke of the Chekke:** Normally an officer in the royal household who kept the check-roll, keeping a check on the other servants in the fulfilment of their duties.

20/33 **Clarke of the Grean clothe:** An officer of the Board of Green Cloth (named from the green-covered table at which its business was originally transacted), a department of the Royal Household, consisting of the Lord Steward and his subordinates, which has control of various matters of expenditure, and legal and judicial authority within the sovereign's court-royal (after *O.E.D.*).

21/22–3 **he was . . . Charles the 5:** Charles V became emperor on 28 June 1519; his grandfather Maximilian had died (below, l. 25) on 12 January of that year. Cavendish's statement that the cardinal was sent to the emperor on two occasions seems to be erroneous, for, between 1519 and his fall in 1529, Wolsey's only special mission to Charles occurred in the summer of 1521. It is this journey which Cavendish describes in some detail in the following pages. In 1520, Wolsey was with Henry at the Field of the Cloth of Gold and, on their return from Guisnes and Ardres, both monarch and minister met Charles at Gravelines, outside Calais, on 10 July. On 26 May 1520 Wolsey had been deputed by Henry to meet Charles at Dover. Perhaps Cavendish conceived of one of these meetings as having entailed a journey to Bruges on the cardinal's part. It may be noted, however, that in his actual description (pp. 21–2) he speaks of Wolsey's mission as if it had occurred only once. Thus we find him referring to 'his Ambassett', not 'his Ambassetts', at 22/28.

21/23–4 **that nowe . . . lord:** Good evidence that this portion of the *Life* was written before the news of Charles's abdication (January 1556) reached England. Philip and Mary were married on 25 July 1554 and thus Cavendish, who tells us that he began his book on 4 November, must have written this passage sometime after 4 November 1554. See the introduction, pp. xxvi–xxvii.

21/28 **so worthy an Ambassett:** The *Chronicle of Calais* says that Wolsey arrived on the continent on 2 August 1521. On 12 August he left for Bruges and there, on 25 August, concluded a treaty between Henry and Charles. He returned to Calais on 29 August and remained there until 27 November (*Chronicle of Calais*, pp. 30–1 and Mackie, p. 311).

Historical Notes 203

22/6–7 **dischargyng . . . charges:** i.e. paying all his bills for him and his train.

22/13 **ne allthoughe:** i.e. not even if.

22/18 **And there serued lyueres:** Hall's account (p. 625) of the entertainment given to Wolsey's retinue is equally indicative of the emperor's hospitality: 'The Englishe lordes, knightes, esquiers, yomen of the kynges gard & other beyng to the nomber of .iiii. C. lx. horse, were well lodged euery man after his degree and euery lodgyng furnished with fewell, bread, bere, wyne, Beues, Muttons, Veles, Lambes, Venison, and all maner deintie viand aswell in fishe as fleshe, with no lacke of spices and bankettyng dishes.'

24/19 **the Crane in the vyntrie:** The Vintry was 'a large house built of stone and timber, with vaults for the stowage of wines' (Stowe p. 214); it gave its name to the ward in which it stood. The Crane is explained by Stowe as 'the Three Cranes' lane, so called not only of a sign of three cranes at a tavern door, but rather of three strong cranes of timber placed on the vintry wharf by the Thames side, to crane up wines with. . . .'

26/8 **the lord Sandes:** William Sandys (d. 1540), Baron Sandys of 'The Vine', near Basingstoke, Hampshire, was a great favourite of Henry VIII. In 1509, upon the young king's accession, he was made a Knight of the Body and his debts were remitted. Treasurer of Calais in 1517, he was created Baron Sandys on 27 April 1523. He did not become Lord Chamberlain until 15 April 1526, when he received the office by reversion at the death of the Earl of Worcester. Thus the masque which Cavendish here describes must have occurred at some time after that date.

26/9 **sir herry Gywldford:** Like Sandys, Sir Henry Guildford (1489–1532) was one of the young courtiers with whom Henry surrounded himself soon after his accession. He was knighted on 30 March 1512 and, after the expedition of 1513, became Master of the Revels. He was noted for his ability in devising entertainments and was frequently so employed by Henry. After Wolsey's fall, Guildford was one of the members of the committee on the articles of impeachment and he later received a pension from Wolsey's Winchester revenues.

27/9–10 **to whome . . . cast at:** i.e. they set various pieces of coin before each of the company, casting dice with the guests for them. The antecedent of 'whome' is apparently 'most worthyest' (l. 8).

27/33 **sir Edward Neveyll:** Sir Edward Neville (d. 1538), another of Henry's favourites in the early years of his reign. He was knighted at Tournai, 25 September 1513. In 1516, he became a gentleman of the privy chamber and Master of the Buckhounds and, from then until 1538, when he was implicated in the Poles' conspiracy and executed with Montagu and Exeter, he held many offices in the royal household. He is reputed to have been a fine soldier and a handsome courtier, a description that is borne out by Cavendish's short characterization of him.

28/3 **dasht owt w**t: Either 'ran from the room' or 'broke forth with'. In view of the fact that the King apparently does not leave the room until l. 8 below, the latter seems more likely. The *O.E.D.* (s.v. *Dash* 2.b.) cites this passage from Holinshed's *Chronicle* where the 'with' is omitted and defines the phrase as meaning 'drove impetuously forth or out'. Cavendish's intransitive usage is not recorded.

29/3 **Venus . . . goddesse:** Wolsey's complaint in Cavendish's poems has the lines: 'Thus Venus the goddesse that called is of love/ Spared not with spight to bryng me from above' (II, 14).

29/4–5 **She brought . . . gentillwoman:** Cavendish's mention of Anne Boleyn introduces us to the highly controversial question of the Divorce. Modern historians, like their predecessors, have disagreed considerably on both the facts of the matter and the interpretation that is to be placed upon them. The most recent account (Mackie, pp. 322 ff.), while emphasizing the role that Wolsey played in supporting the king's attempt to divorce Catherine, is inclined to credit the king himself with the germinal idea. Hughes (I, 157–9) places the sole responsibility for all the proceedings squarely on Henry's shoulders. Anne's own refusal to acquiesce in Henry's wishes until it became certain that she would be queen undoubtedly 'fired' (the metaphor is Cavendish's) the king's passion to the utmost. Despite the contention of Pollard (p. 19, n. 2), followed by Mackie (p. 323) that the idea of the divorce first arose in 1514, an examination of the relevant items in the *Venetian Calendar* (see also Mattingly, pp. 127 and 320–1) would tend to show that the question did not arise before the winter of 1526–7.

29/9 **sir Thomas Bolayn:** Most historians now agree with Cavendish's account of the manner in which Sir Thomas Boleyn (1477–1539) achieved the royal favour which he enjoyed between 1522 and the downfall of his daughter and son. His dislike of Wolsey probably went back to 1515 when the cardinal succeeded in convincing Henry that his promise to Boleyn of the treasureship of the royal household should be denied or at least postponed (Pollard, p. 222, n. 1). Boleyn became Comptroller of the Household in 1520 but he did not receive the treasurership until April 1522, a date which, interestingly enough, corresponds to the presumed date of the Percy-Anne episode (see below, 29/34 and n.). Friedmann (I, 43) gives the following list of Boleyn's appointments between 1522 and 1525: '... on the 24th of April, 1522, the patent of treasurer of the household; five days later the stewardship of Tunbridge, the receivership of Bransted, and the keepership of the manor of Penshurst; in 1523 the keepership of Thunderby and Westwood Park, and in 1524 the stewardship of Swaffham. Having by all these lucrative employments obtained sufficient means to sustain the dignity, Sir Thomas was in 1525 created Lord Rochford.' In addition, he became a Knight of the Garter in 1523. On 8 December 1529, one week after the articles against Wolsey were presented in Parliament, Boleyn became Earl of Wiltshire and Ormond, and, on 24 January 1530 Lord Privy Seal.

29/19 **his Sonne:** George Boleyn, Viscount Rochford. Arrested on 2 May 1536, after the famous May Day tournament, he was executed, on a charge of 'incest and treason', on 17 May, two days before Anne met the same fate.

29/24-5 **I will ... you:** The 'do' in l. 24 is redundant; 'declare you,' i.e. 'declare unto you'.

29/25-6 **beyng very yong ... ffraunce:** If, as most authorities now incline to believe, Anne was born in 1507, she would have been only seven years old when she first went to France in 1514 with Henry VIII's sister, Mary. It is, of course, by no means certain that she was in France so early and some historians have believed that it was Anne's sister, Mary, who is referred to as 'M. Boleyne' in the list of Mary's suite (Friedmann, II, 316-22). The 'ffrenche Quene' was Claude, Francis I's consort (d. 1524). Cavendish confuses his chronology when he asserts that Anne did not return to England until 'the ffrenche Quene dyed' (ll. 27-8, below). The Percy episode occurred in 1522 and Anne must have been back in England by January of that year when Francis I wrote that 'Mr. Boullan's daughter had returned to her country' (LP, III, 1994). She took part in an entertainment at Wolsey's house on 4 March 1522 (Revels Accounts, LP, III, pp. 1558-9).

29/34 **my lord Percye:** Henry Algernon Percy, sixth Earl of Northumberland (1502?-37), was brought up, according to the custom of the period, in Wolsey's household. Knighted in 1519, he had been destined by his father to be the husband of Mary Talbot, daughter of the Earl of Shrewsbury, from as far back as 1516. His affair with Anne, says the *D.N.B.* (s.v. Anne Boleyn), can be shown to have taken place as early as 1522 'by the most conclusive evidence'. In October of that year Percy was sent to the North, serving there as Deputy Warden of the Marches. For a full discussion, see Brewer's Preface to LP, IV, pp. ccxliii–ccxliv. He married Mary Talbot in late 1523 or early 1524, but their union was a most unhappy one. She soon returned to her father and later, in 1532, accused Percy of a precontract with Anne. When this matter came up again in 1536 at the time of Anne's indictment, Percy vehemently denied the existence of any precontract (see his letter in Singer, pp. 464–5).

30/10–11 **revealed . . . Cardynall:** If Henry did conceive an affection for Anne as early as 1522, he certainly kept his project well concealed for some years thereafter. It would seem that at the moment he was more interested in Anne's sister, Mary; moreover, it is probable that the projected marriage between Anne and the son of the Earl of Ormond (mentioned as early as September 1520) was the real cause of Henry's interference at this time. At 31/7–9 Wolsey tells Percy that Henry 'entendyd to haue preferred hir/vnto an other person/wt whome the kyng hathe travelled allredye/'.

30/16–17 **byfore vs his seruauntes:** For the first time in his narrative Cavendish speaks of himself as an eye-witness to the events which he describes. We are thus enabled to date his entry into Wolsey's service as occurring at least as early as 1522. See the introduction, p. xix.

31/20–1 **right noble parentage:** Sir William Boleyn (d. 1515), Anne's paternal grandfather, had married Margaret Butler, daughter of Sir Thomas Ormond, who was later seventh Earl of Ormond. Anne's father had married the lady Elizabeth Howard, daughter of Thomas Howard, afterwards second Duke of Norfolk. For Howard, see below (94/23 and n.).

32/5 **Yes qd he:** The 'yes' is spoken by Percy, to whom 'he' refers. Wolsey then continues with 'I warraunt the . . .'

33/29 **I haue . . . Boyes:** Northumberland had two other sons besides Henry: Sir Thomas Percy (d. 1537) and Sir Ingelram Percy (d. 1540). The old earl did not carry out the threat that Cavendish here depicts him as making; his eldest son succeeded to the title at his father's death on 19 May 1527.

34/10 **the same:** i.e. the precontract ('assuraunce') between Anne and Percy.

34/11–12 **oon . . . doughters:** For Mary Talbot, see above (29/34 and n.) and, for the Earl of Shrewsbury, below (140/15 and n.).

34/13–14 **Anne Bolloyn . . . offendyd:** Cavendish is probably right in associating the origin of Anne's opposition to the cardinal with the Percy episode. Her father and Wolsey had never been friends and, in 1529, the cardinal sharply rebuked Boleyn (below, 87/14 ff.). For an earlier dispute between them, see above (29/9 and n.). In 1527 Anne would have been further incensed by the knowledge that Wolsey was scheming to marry Henry to Renée, the sister of Claude, Francis I's queen (Pollard, p. 222 and below, 62/7 ff.). Certainly, as Cavendish notes, Wolsey can be exonerated from any blame in the Percy affair; in this case he was merely carrying out the will of his master.

34/19–20 **commaundyd... Court:** Cavendish speaks as if Anne's stay with her father (at Hever, the family manor, in Kent) was not long. This is in accord with the tradition that she was again in France before 1525. She returned to the Court sometime between 1525 and 1527 but the circumstances of her recall are obscure.

35/4–5 **allthoughe . . . hir:** Either 'although she knew that he had a great affection unto her' or 'despite the fact that the king had a great affection unto her'. The 'that' seems to make the first more likely. Cavendish apparently meant to set up an antithesis between 'affection' (1. 5) and 'great love' (1. 6).

35/21–2 **a perfect Grysheld:** See Appendix A.

35/27 **Comenwell:** *MS.* Coen well. Other editors have read 'scene well' but 'scene' in this sense (*O.E.D.* 10) is not recorded before 1679. Cavendish frequently omits the abbreviation mark for *m* in 'co*m*en' (e.g. 78/34) and 'well' is a normal variant of 'wele' or 'weal'.

35/29 **caught an occasion. . . . :** The opposition to Wolsey in the Council was led by Norfolk and the Boleyns, supported (at least later) by Suffolk (Pollard, pp. 222–3). Wolsey's efforts to reduce the nobility to a level with 'other meane subiectes' had already caused a great deal of dissent. As early as 1516, according to Hall (p. 585), the cardinal had 'punyshed also lordes, knyghtes, and men of all sortes for ryottes, beryng and mayntenaunce in their countreyes, that the poore me*n* lyued quyetly, so that no man durst beare for feare of imprisonment: but he him selfe and his serua*un*tes, which were well punished therfore.'

36/32–3 **that . . . Imagyned:** Cavendish presumably alludes to speculations about the divorce. It is this topic which he takes up when he 'comes to the place' on p. 74, where the 'dyuers Imagynacions' are again mentioned.

Historical Notes

37/1 Than began: For the Battle of Pavia and the events which led up to it, see Appendix B.

37/17–18 that an Ambassett . . . Emprour: For the details of these negotiations, which took place in the summer of 1523, see Lavisse (V, ii, 29–30) who gives a full account of the treaties that were signed by Henry VIII, Charles V, and the Duke.

37/23–4 oon . . . men: Apparently the Marquis of Pescara, Ferdinando Francesco d'Avaloz, Charles V's general with whom Bourbon joined forces in an effort to raise the siege of Pavia.

37/25–6 sir Iohn Russell: The English plan to enlist the aid of Bourbon against the French had begun as far back as June 1523, when Sir John Russell (1486?–1555) was sent to the Duke for the first time (LP, II, 3217). Russell came to an agreement with Bourbon in early September and was back in England by the 26th. He set off again with £12,000 in October 1523 and remained with or near Bourbon until after Pavia. He got more money in 1524, but sent it back to England. It is not certain that payments to Bourbon were completely cut off, but there can be little doubt that Wolsey was already beginning to shift to the French side (Mackie, pp. 314–15). Cavendish carries the cardinal's 'policy' a step further when he mentions (below, 41/28) a 'leage' between Henry and Francis which was captured by Bourbon at Pavia. No pact had been signed, although Wolsey was certainly thinking along such lines.

Russell had a long and active career under Henry, Edward, and Mary. It was he who, on 1 November 1529, brought Wolsey a ring from the king (below, 110/22). On 19 January 1550 he was created Earl of Bedford for his service in suppressing the rebels at St. Mary's Clyst.

38/16 Iohn Iokyn: The fullest account of the mission of Jean Joachim de Passano is given by Jacqueton (pp. 53 ff.). This secret agent, a man of mystery to Hall as well as to Cavendish, was a Genoese, the secretary of Fregosa, governor of Genoa, who was resident at the French court as early as 1520. Joachim was at the Field of the Cloth of Gold in that year and seems to have become maître d'hôtel to Louise of Savoy shortly thereafter. He arrived in London on 22 June 1524, having disguised himself as an Italian merchant while on the Continent waiting for a safe-conduct. Cavendish probably retails the common gossip of the day when he makes him to be 'a man byfore of no estymacyon'. Hall (p. 691), contrary to Cavendish's statement that Joachim stayed at Richmond (below, l. 23), says that the envoy 'was kept close in the house of doctor

Larke, a Prebendary of sainct Steuens, and euery daie priuely spake with the Cardinall'. This Thomas Lark was the brother of Wolsey's mistress. De Praet, the imperial ambassador, protested vigorously against Joachim's presence and was temporarily imprisoned by Wolsey for his interference (Pollard, p. 138, n.). Joachim was joined by Jean Brinon, another ambassador, on 22 January 1525; the two colleagues succeeded so well in their mission that on 6 March, three days before the news of Pavia reached London, they could write to Louise that Wolsey 'said he was beginning to be considered a Frenchman [cf. Cavendish's comment, above, ll. 11–12], and was willing, for their sakes, to be as good a Frenchman as he had been a Spaniard, for he had only helped the Spaniards from necessity' (LP, IV, 1160).

39/23–4 (**as I dought . . . vs:** The parentheses seem to be incorrectly placed; Cavendish apparently means the Duke to say 'and I have no fear that he will deceive us.'

41/21 **Suspectyng . . . entre:** i.e. not in the least suspecting the duke's entry.

42/2–3 **he went . . . Rome:** Contrary to Cavendish's account, Bourbon did not advance immediately upon Rome; his disgruntled troops finally broke into the city on 6 May 1527. Clement VII was imprisoned in Castle Angelo and Wolsey had an added reason for his trip to France. Bourbon died in the first assault. The Pope was not released by the emperor until December 1527, when he was allowed to go to Orvieto. It is perhaps worth noting that Rome was sacked by Italian and Spanish troops in September 1526 as well as in 1527; Cavendish may have confused the two different attacks, the second of which was far more severe than the first. Even so, a good year and one half intervened between Pavia and the first assault on the holy city.

42/22–3 **And therfore . . . successe:** The second clause partially repeats and partially explains the first. One might paraphrase 'and thus it is that they come to such an end and that their affairs have such an outcome [success].' Cavendish's 'suche' is, of course, ironic.

42/31–2 **if the kyng . . . ffraunce:** This was Wolsey's own reaction when he first heard the news of Francis's capture (Mackie, pp. 313–14).

43/16 **the ffrenche kynges delyuere:** Wolsey had managed to make peace with France on 30 August 1525, when the so-called 'Treaty of the Moor' was signed at his palace of that name between

Rickmansworth and Northwood (LP, IV, 1600). Contrary to Cavendish's statement that Wolsey dictated terms to the emperor (below, l. 19), this treaty had little effect on the Treaty of Madrid which Charles V forced on Francis in the following January (Pollard, p. 148). Francis was released on 17 March 1526 after his two eldest sons, Francis, the Dauphin (1517-36), and the Duke d'Orleans (1518-59), were delivered to Charles as hostages.

44/13 **ther Cheafe** mrs: Most modern historians agree with Cavendish's statement that, during Wolsey's journey to France, Anne ingratiated herself with Henry as she had not been able to do before. See, for example, Mattingly's account (pp. 257-8). How much the cardinal knew of this while he was in France is perhaps open to question, but it is interesting to note that Sir William Fitzwilliam saw fit to tell him in a letter of 31 July (LP, IV, 3318) from Beaulieu that the king was supping daily with Norfolk, Suffolk, Exeter, and Rochford. Wolsey certainly learned of what had been going on when he returned in September (below, 64/10-11 and n.). By 26 October Mendoza, the imperial ambassador, could report that Norfolk and the Boleyns had become 'heads of a league against Wolsey and [that] Wolsey himself [was] "now trying all he can to prevent the divorce" for fear of Anne becoming queen' (Pollard, p. 222, quoting *Spanish Calendar*, 1527-29, p. 432).

44/18-19 **this Iourney:** Cavendish's vividly detailed description of the cardinal's mission can be strikingly substantiated from many passages in the *Letters and Papers* and from Hall's account (pp. 728-32). Wolsey's commission, under which he was appointed 'King's lieutenant and plenipotentiary in France,' is set out in LP, IV, 3186 (18 June 1527). He was impowered to secure the ratification of the treaties of Westminster made the previous April, in which war on the emperor had been agreed upon (Pollard, pp. 152-4). Moreover, he intended to get himself made vicar-general during the Pope's imprisonment and, if possible, to call a special conclave at Avignon. Finally, he was to break the news of the king's plans for a divorce to Francis I. Despite Cavendish's suspension of judgement (below ll. 19-20), there can be little doubt that Wolsey saw his mission as a grand moment in his career.

44/21-2 **after ... therof:** i.e. after it had been decided that he should undertake the embassy.

44/25-6 **thys noble ambassett:** LP, IV, 3216 gives a partial list of the members of Wolsey's suite and mentions that it contained '900 horse'. Unfortunately, the MS. (Cotton Caligula D. x. f. 103) is mutilated; otherwise we should probably find that it, like the *Chronicle of Calais* (pp. 38–40), mentions a 'mastar Caundishe' in Wolsey's train. The Chronicle confirms the 900 horses of the *Letters and Papers*; Hall (p. 728) says Wolsey left London with 'twelue hundreth horse'.

44/29–30 **Than ... forward:** Wolsey left London on 3 July 1527. His itinerary to Dover is summed up in LP, IV, 3231 (cf. *State Papers*, I, 196).

45/16 **sir Richard wyltchers howsse:** Wolsey actually stayed at Sir *John* Wiltshere's house on this occasion (LP, IV, 3231). Sir John was at this time Controller of Calais (see LP, IV, p. 2227 and no. 2507). Wordsworth notes (p. 519) that his house was Stone Place, 17 miles from London, 2 miles beyond Dartford, and near Greenhithe.

45/18 **The next day:** 4 July.

45/21 **the iij^de day:** 5 July. See Wolsey's letter to Henry from there (LP, IV, 3231).

45/23 **The iiij^th day:** 6 July. See LP, IV, 3243, 3244, and 3247. Wolsey left Canterbury on 10 July and sailed from Dover on the 11th.

45/28 **the feast of Seynt Thomas:** 7 July, the feast of St. Thomas of Canterbury. Cavendish's description of the festival closely follows that of Hall (p. 728): 'and at Cauntorburie he rested, & there to the people declared the destruction of Rome, & howe the Pope was in captiuitie with many Cardinalles: wherfore he caused a Letany to be song by the monkes of Christes Church, after this maner. S, Maria, ora pro Clemente papa. S^e Petri ora pro Clemente papa. & so furthe al ye letany: then he exhorted the people to fast & pray for his deliueraunce.'

46/7 **launceknyghtes:** 'Originally the German word (*landsknecht*) denoted the mercenary foot-soldiers belonging to the imperial territory, in contra-distinction to the Swiss; but it was very early applied in a wider sense' (*O.E.D.*). Cavendish uses the term here to refer to the German (Lutheran) mercenaries in the pay of the Duke of Bourbon who committed so many outrages at Rome in 1527.

46/7 **The next day:** Cavendish left Wolsey on 8 July and reached Calais that evening. He remained there until the morning of the 11th, when the cardinal arrived. In LP, IV, 3254 Wolsey writes that he embarked between three and four in the morning on 11 July and reached Calais by nine.

Historical Notes

46/15 recevyed in procession, etc.: For the cardinal's activities while in Calais and the preparations for his advance into France, see LP, IV, 3262, 3269, 3279, and 3288. On 13 July, Wolsey issued a 'Proclamation for establishing of trade and merchandizing and traffique with the towne and marches of Callice, with divers immunities and freedoms concerning the same' (LP, IV, 3262; text in the *Chronicle of Calais*, pp. 102–9). This is apparently the 'marte' that Cavendish (below, 64/3) speaks of Wolsey as founding upon his return to Calais in September. Hall (p. 729) assigns the event to July and implies that the mart failed because Calais 'was a towne of warre', which made it impossible for the merchants to have complete freedom of movement, and because 'the hauen is not able to receiue greate Hulkes and Carikes that come to a marte'. The establishment of the mart was evidently intended as an affront to the emperor, with whose Flemish merchants the English had long been accustomed to trade.

46/23–4 clean remyssion: Wolsey, as Papal Legate, had the power to grant Plenary Indulgences, which remitted all of the temporal punishment due to sin. He repeats this special blessing later at Peterborough after his fall (below, 133/20) and in France (below, 49/26) he gives 'certyn dayes of pardon', i.e. a Partial Indulgence, or partial remission of temporal punishment, to the citizens of Boulogne.

46/29 Monsur de Bees: Du Biez's visit to Wolsey apparently did not occur until the 17th (LP, IV, 3269 and 3279). Oudart, Seigneur du Biez (d. 1553) was Chamberlain to the king, Captain of Boulogne (June 1523), and later Marshall of France (1542).

46/35 he called byfore hyme: Wolsey's speech to his retainers must have occurred on 21 July, for he left Calais on the 22nd and arrived at Boulogne that evening.

47/25 wyllyng and commaund you: So MS. There should perhaps be a full stop before 'wyllyng'. Supply 'I' (Wolsey) as the subject of 'wyllyng' and 'commaund'. The shift from the participle to the finite verb, though frequent in Cavendish, is more confusing than usual in this instance.

48/2–3 oon of the gentilmen: This 'Rice' is mentioned in the *Chronicle of Calais* (p. 40) as one of Wolsey's 'Awdiences' in the 1527 embassy. He may have been the John ap Price or ap Rhys mentioned in the *D.N.B.* (XLVI, p. 329), who was a servant of the king in 1519, and later officiated as a servitor at the coronation of Anne Boleyn. It is not impossible, however, that he is to be identified with Sir

John ap Price (d. 1573?) who was a visitor of the monasteries and seems to have been in Cromwell's service at least as early as 1532 (*D.N.B., ibid.*).

48/29-30 **the brode seale:** On his 1521 mission to Bruges Wolsey had not hesitated to take the Broad Seal with him, thus holding up royal business in England (Pollard, p. 92; LP, III, 1650, 1675, 1680, and 1762). By September 1527 Henry needed the Seal again and commanded Taylor to seal and deliver some letters patent immediately. But the Master of the Rolls first wrote to Wolsey to ask his permission before acting on the king's order.

48/32 **it began ... vehemently:** Cf. Wolsey's letter to Henry (LP, IV, 3289, 22 July) where the cardinal tells of his meeting at Sandingfield with the Lieutenant of Picardy (below, 49/6-7); mentions three pageants that were presented for him (Hall, p. 729, describes them); notes that the day was very wet and stormy; and describes his visit to 'Our Lady Churche' (below, 49/23).

48/34-49/1 **the Cardynall of lorrayn:** For this gentleman and his three brothers see below (52/23 and n.).

49/6 **le Countie Brian:** Philippe de Chabot, Admiral de Brion (1480-1543), who had been appointed Admiral by Francis after Bonivet's death at Pavia.

49/8 **Stradiates and Arbanoys:** A sort of light-armed cavalry. Cf. Jean Nicot's description of these troops (*Thresor De La Langue Francoyse*, Paris, 1606, Sig. C): '... celuy qui habite en cette contrée de Macedoine, ou d'Epire comme aucuns veulent. Et à present on appelle en particulier Albanois ces hommes de cheual armez à la legere, autrement dite Stradiote, ou Stradiots (par la consone moyenne) qui portent les chappeaux à haute testiere, desquels on se sert pour cheuaux legers, qui viennent dudit pais d'Albanie, dont les Papes se seruent encore de ce temps és garnisons de plusieurs villes du Saint Siege.'

49/11 **ffor my lord ... Emprour:** Wolsey feared that he might be attacked from Charles V's domains in Burgundy and the Low Countries.

49/28 **The next mornyng:** 23 July. On the 24th Wolsey writes to Henry of his arrival at Montreuil (LP, IV, 3294) and tells him that the Prior of the White Friars (probably Cavendish's 'oon learned', below, l. 31) made him an oration.

50/4-5 **le Cardynall pacyfike:** Cf. Hall (p. 730), 'and euer he was called *Cardinalis pacificus* the Cardinall pacifique, and so was writen at the gate of his lodging [at Amiens]'.

Historical Notes

50/7 The next day: 24 July (LP, IV, 3295). The mayor's secretary made him an oration on this occasion.

50/16 kyng lowice: Henry's sister, Mary (1496–1533), had married Louis XII of France (1462–1515) at Abbeville on 9 October 1514. Louis died on 1 January 1515, and Mary, who had agreed to the marriage only on the condition that she would be allowed to choose for herself the next time, married Suffolk in the following spring.

50/17–18 the Duke of Suffolk: Like Wolsey, Charles Brandon, Duke of Suffolk (d. 1545), had risen to power from the lower ranks of society. His father had been Henry VII's standard bearer at Bosworth Field and was killed there by Richard III himself. Charles is not heard of until Henry VIII's reign, but he soon became a great favourite of the young king. He was Marshall of the 1513 expedition and on 1 February 1514 became Duke of Suffolk. His precipitate marriage to Henry's sister in 1515 brought him into temporary disfavour, but he escaped with a heavy fine. Suffolk plays an important part in the drama of Wolsey's fall; see below (90/24 ff. and n. and 98/1 ff.).

50/18–19 And beyng w^{t}in ... Gallery: The sentence, as it stands, is elliptical. We might paraphrase 'once one was within he could see that the house was constructed in the manner of a gallery'. The gallery-like shape of the house might imply that it was uncomfortable; consequently Cavendish notes, in the next line that 'notwithstanding it was very necessary' (comfortable).

50/20 viijth or x^{en} dayes: Wolsey remained at Abbeville from 24 July until 3 August (LP, IV, 3337).

50/25 Pynkney castell: The cardinal reached Picquigny on 3 August and lodged there at a 'castle of Mons. Vidams' (LP, *ibid.*).

50/31 Edward the iiijth: Cavendish could have read of this meeting at Picquigny (29 August 1475) in Hall (pp. 318 ff.), who gives a very full account. The phrase 'Cronycles of Englond' might suggest that Cavendish is speaking of the so-called 'Saint Albans Chronicle,' published by Wynkyn de Worde in 1515 and 1528 as *The Cronycles of Englonde*. But this chronicle stops at the year 1460 with the coronation of Edward IV. Since no other chronicle of the period bore this title, we should probably take Cavendish's phrase as a generic reference to the various history writers who had described the event.

50/34–5 that the ffrenche kyng ... Amyens: Francis I arrived in Amiens on 3 August (Hall, pp. 729–30).

Historical Notes

51/9–10 **Madame Regent:** This was the famous Louise of Savoy (1476–1531), with whom Wolsey had many dealings during his career. For a full account of the relationship between them, see Jacqueton.

51/11 **the Quene of Naver:** Marguerite d'Orleans, sister of Francis I and Duchess of Alençon, had become Queen of Navarre by her marriage to Henri d'Albret, King of Navarre, on 3 January 1526.

51/23 **Souches:** These were Switzers or 'Swissers', hired Swiss mercenaries. Cavendish's form goes back ultimately to the French 'Suisse', Wolsey, in the *State Papers* (I, 207), writes 'Swiches'. Neither form is recorded by the *O.E.D.*

51/31 and 33 Supply 'was' before 'conveyed' in both lines.

51/34 **The next mornyng:** 4 August.

52/6–7 **the kyng... hyme:** The cardinal gave his own description of this encounter in a letter to Henry of 9 August (LP, IV, 3337).

52/23–5 **The Cardinal of Lorraine, the Duke of Lorraine, Monsieur de Guise, and Monsieur Vaudemont:** All four of these noblemen were, as Cavendish notes, brothers, and sons of René de Lorraine (d. 1508). Antoine, Duke of Lorraine (d. 1544), the oldest surviving son, succeeded to the title at the age of nineteen. Claude, the second son (d. 1550), had just been created Comte de Guise by Francis I (January 1527) for service done in the king's wars. Jean, the third son (d. 1550), was Cardinal and Archbishop of Reims and Lyon. Louis, the fourth son (d. 1528), was Comte de Vaudemont.

52/25–6 **apparelled ... Purpull veluett:** John Croke, one of Wolsey's chancery clerks, disagrees about the colour of the king's outer garments. On 21 August (LP, IV, 3369) he wrote to Cromwell that 'the French king ... did were that day that he met first with my Lord's gra[ce a gown] of black velvet, which was here and there cut and laid [in with] white sarcenet, and tied together with small aglets of go[ld.]'

52/32 **that he ... horsse:** The 'he' probably refers to Wolsey, whose mule had already given him trouble at Boulogne. On that occasion Wolsey wrote to Henry that he could not describe the pageants presented before him because his mule shied so much during them (LP, IV, 3289).

53/16–17 **The next day:** 5 August. Wolsey's visit took place at three in the afternoon. Francis's 'disease' was a chaffed leg that had already caused him to delay his meeting with Wolsey. The cardinal found it so swelled that the king could not stand (LP, IV, 3317 and 3337).

216   *Historical Notes*

53/27 **ij wekes& more:** Wolsey himself remained at Amiens until after 30 August (LP, IV, 3391). He arrived at Compiègne on 1 September (LP, IV, Appendix, no. 117, p. 3122). Francis left Amiens on Monday, 19 August (LP, IV, 3365), so that Cavendish's 'two weeks and more' proves to be fairly exact.

53/28–9 **the Assumpcion:** 15 August. But Cavendish seems to have confused the activities of that day with the solemn swearing of the peace on 18 August. For the Treaty of Amiens (dated 18 August) see LP, IV, 3356. On the feast of the Assumption Wolsey said mass at Amiens and gave the sacrament to the lady regent (LP, IV, 3369); afterwards he dined with the king. Croke describes the ceremonies of the 18th as follows: 'The French king and Regent in one traves, which was passing [lofty and on the] south side of the high altar, and on the north side a little mount of three steps for Wolsey, [on which] was set a cloth of estate and two chairs without any trav[es.]' (LP, IV, 3369). Wolsey himself wrote that he had been to the cathedral with Francis on the 14th for evensong and he noted that there 'were two traverses, one for me, and one for the French king' (LP, IV, 3350). The passage that begins with the words 'And in the feast of the Assumpcion' (53/28–9) and ends with 'as my lord dyned w^t hyme' (54/20) is omitted in most of the secondary manuscripts, perhaps for religious reasons.

53/30 **de noster dame:** Cf. the variant form 'de notre dame' at 51/7.

54/21–2 **that the kyng . . . Amyens:** Cavendish is in error in reporting that Wolsey and Francis left together. See above (53/27 and n.).

54/25 **beyng vppon a ffriday:** This must have been Friday, 30 August, for Wolsey was in Compiègne on 1 September. Cavendish, of course, notes the day of the week in order to explain the bit of bad luck that overtook him on his way; like his master, the gentleman-usher may have been somewhat given to 'superstition'—and this despite (or perhaps partly because of) his violent disclaimer later (below, 128/28ff.). The 'littill village' was Moreuil, about twelve miles from Amiens and nine from Montdidier.

55/10 **monsur Creekey:** Jean, sire de Crecqui, who was governor of Montreuil in 1526. He married Jossine de Soissons in 1497 and seems to have died in 1543.

55/29 **my lorde of Suffolk:** For Suffolk, see above (50/17–18 and n.).

56/24–6 **an Englysshe man . . . offence:** The Tudor Englishman was quite different in this respect from his more sober descendants of the present day. Cf. Wordsworth's note (pp. 533–4) on this passage, where he cites a letter of Erasmus on this, for the sixteenth century, peculiarly English custom. Note also Whytford's *Pype of Perfection* (1532, fol. 213ᵛ), 'it bycommeth nat therfore yᵉ persones religious to vse any touchyng/ nor to folowe the maner of seculer persones/ yᵗ in theyr congresses/ & commune metynges or departyng done vse to kysse/ take handes/ or such other touchinges that good religious persones: shulde vtterly auoyde.' But, later in the *Life* (164/7–8), we find that Wolsey 'kyst barehedyd' my lady Shrewsbury 'and all hir gentilwomen'.

56/25 **Custume**ᵗ: Possibly an error by Cavendish for 'custom' but perhaps a genuine nonce formation. The *O.E.D.*, which does not list 'customent', records the form 'custumhede' from the fourteenth century.

56/34 **ffor she ... Arde**: i.e. with Francis I at the Field of the Cloth of Gold between Guisnes and Ardres in June 1520.

57/6–7 **that nyght ... Montdedyer**: Presumably the night of 30 August. Suffolk had laid siege to Montdidier on 27 October 1523; the town surrendered, after a great bombardment, on the 28th. Cavendish (below, 57/9) reached Compiègne on 31 August.

57/32–3 **the Chauncelor of ffraunce**: Antoine Duprat (1463–1535) had been Chancellor of France since 1515 and held that office until his death. After the death of his wife in 1520, he took orders and was made a cardinal by Wolsey in 1527 (below, 63/31–2).

58/3–4 **the leage**: i.e. the treaties of Westminster, signed 30 April 1527. See above (44/18–19 and n.).

58/6–7 **my lord ... stoutly**: Cavendish is probably wrong in placing this quarrel at Compiègne after the Treaty of Amiens had been signed. The altercation described is almost certainly that which Wolsey related to Henry in a postscript to his letter of 9 August (LP, IV, 3337). The cardinal there speaks of opposition 'between me and the French king's council' that was settled by Madame Regent, who 'came suddenly to my lodging' and 'rated the Chancellor and others soundly' (see below, l. 20, for Louise's visit to Wolsey).

58/25–6 **he hade ... gyrdell**: Cavendish may well be echoing one of Wolsey's own boasts; Roy's *Rede Me* (p. 114) begs for God's judgement 'Agaynst soche a wicked brothell/[Wolsey] Which sayth/ vnder his girthell/He holdeth Kynges and Princes'.

58/27 **the next mornyng:** From this point on in his description of the French mission Cavendish's narrative becomes extremely confused. Events are vividly and accurately described, but the order in which they actually occurred is often violated. The *Letters and Papers* are not complete enough to provide a full solution of the difficulties involved here and the following notes, which are based upon them, must be taken as somewhat tentative.

If the conflict with the French Council (see the note to 58/6-7, above) occurred, as Cavendish implies, at Compiègne, then these letters were probably those of 5 September (LP, IV, 3400), which 'Gunner' could have carried. On the other hand, if the quarrel took place, as has been suggested, about 7-8 August at Amiens, then the letters were presumably those of 9 August (LP, IV, 3337) from Amiens. We know that 'Christopher Gunner' (for whom, see below) was back with Wolsey on 13 September and that Wolsey sent him off again to Henry on that day with the news of his return from France in the near future (LP, IV, 3420 and 3422; see below, 63/26, for Gunner's return in Cavendish). The crux of the problem lies in Cavendish's statement 'the next mornyng after this conflycte', which may be erroneous. Wolsey's letter of 5 September is a long one and it would have been urgent, for in it the cardinal showed that he had heard of the dispatching of Knight to the Pope for the first time. Knight reached Compiègne on 10 September and on the 13th mentions Gunner's arrival. There would thus have been time for the courier to leave Wolsey on the 5th and return eight days later with new instructions for Knight. 'Christopher Gunner' was noted for his speed as a messenger (LP, IV, 2828).

'Gunner's' real name was Christopher Morris, Mores, or Morice (1490?-1544) and he had been one of Henry's gunners (Chief Gunner, 4 February 1527) in the Tower since 1513. He was not knighted until 18 October 1539. Cavendish's reference to him as 'Cristofer Gonner' can be paralleled in Hall's account of the role which he played in the raid on Morlaix, July 1522. Hall describes him, within the space of one paragraph (pp. 642-3), as 'Christopher Morres the master Gunner', 'the Gunner', and 'sir Christopher Gunner'.

59/11 **The next nyght:** Once more Cavendish seems to have confused his sequence of events. This banquet, which was attended by both Francis and his mother, most probably occurred on Monday, 19 August, at Amiens. In LP, IV, 3365, Wolsey writes to Henry that the 'French king, my lady, the king of Navarre, many nobles &

prelates' are to dine with him that night (19 August). He goes on to state that Francis will leave after the dinner to visit certain places in accordance with vows made during his illness (see Cavendish, below, 60/2ff.). The cardinal's words are confirmed by Croke in his letter to Cromwell of 21 August (LP, IV, 3369) where he states that 'after dinner the French king did remove, and, as they sa[y, will] meet with us again at Compiègne'. Cavendish, however, speaks as if the banquet were at Compiègne in the first place and has Francis leaving that town and then returning to it (see below, 60/12, 'Then the kyng Retorned agayn vnto Compigne').

59/14 **madam Reigne:** Renée (1510–1574), daughter of Louis XII and sister of Francis I's queen, Claude, who had died in 1524. Francis was not so much interested in preventing Renée's marriage as in making sure that he did not lose Brittany. In 1515 he had arranged to marry her to Charles of Burgundy and he was not opposed to Wolsey's scheme whereby she might marry Henry VIII (see below, 62/9). She was eventually married to Hercule d'Este, Duke of Ferrara, on 28 June 1528; under the terms of the marriage contract, both she and the Duke renounced all claim to Brittany and received instead Chartres, Gisors, and Montargis.

59/25–6 **the kyng of Naverne:** Henri d'Albret (1503–1555). For his marriage to Francis' sister, Marguerite, see above (51/11 and n.).

59/34–5 **oon madame ffountayn:** Certainty with regard to the identity of this young lady is probably impossible. I can only suggest that she may have been Marie, the daughter of Jacques de Fontaines (d. 1548?) by his second wife, Guyonne de Belloy, whom he married in 1508. Marie was married in 1530 to Thibaut d'Amfreville, Seigneur de Maizières. Her family was from Picardy.

60/6 **Shalme:** The shawm was 'a medieval musical instrument of the oboe class, having a double reed enclosed in a globular mouthpiece' (*O.E.D.*).

60/14 **huntyng ... wyld Swyne:** We have two letters from Sir Anthony Browne to Henry VIII that relate to hunting in France during the 1527 embassy. The first (LP, IV, 3368) was written from Amiens on 21 August and mentions that Browne had been deer hunting with Francis on the 16th. The second (LP, IV, 3437) from Montdidier on 18 September, speaks of Francis's offer to supply Henry with some wild swine. Boar hunting, according to Lavisse (*Histoire*, V, i, 188–9), was much esteemed by Francis I: 'À la chasse, un jour, François Ier lutta seul contre un sanglier. Cet exploit fournit plus tard une matière inépuisable à la chronique, à la poésie, à la peinture. Hercule, le sanglier de Calydon, tout l'attirail mythologique s'y mêla pour l'illustrer.' Cavendish's boar hunt seems to have occurred near Compiègne, probably between 5 and 17 September.

60/26 **Armed ... greyhoundes:** It was apparently the French custom to arm their dogs against the tusks of the *sanglier*. I have not been able to discover any exact description of the armour employed for this purpose, but it may be noted that de Mersan, in his *Manuel du Chasseur* (Paris, 1821, p. 176) defines a 'chien armé' as being so named 'quand il est couvert pour l'attaque du sanglier'.

61/17 m^r **Ratclyfe:** Henry Radcliffe (1506?–1557) was the son of the 'auncyent gentilman' whom Cavendish mentions in his closing scene (below, 186/21). He became Earl of Sussex on 26 November 1542. For the importance of this passage in the dating of the autograph manuscript, see Introduction, pp. xxvi–xxvii.

61/20–1 (**the boore ... chaffed**): The construction would be clearer if the parentheses were to enclose only 'beyng sore chaffed'.

62/5–6 **a certyn boke:** I have not been able to discover any reference to the book which Cavendish describes here. It would seem to have been written in French and published in France. It is not unlikely that the French 'boke' was actually a pamphlet, or perhaps even a broadside against the cardinal. Wolsey may have been able to have the entire edition suppressed and destroyed. We know that he had had agents on the Continent since the first printing of Tyndale's *Testament* in 1526 and that they were very effective. See Arber's Preface to Roy's *Rede Me*.

62/8 **too mariages:** For the proposed marriage between Henry VIII and Renée, see Pollard (p. 222) and Mackie (p. 323). The seventh article of the Treaty of Amiens (LP, IV, 3356) arranges for Mary's marriage to the Duke of Orleans. The subject had been agreed upon in the preceding April at Westminster, when it was arranged that if Francis himself, already engaged to Eleanor, the sister of the emperor, could not marry Henry's daughter, then she was to be given to the Duke.

62/13 **at this present kyng of ffraunce:** For Henry II, see above (43/16 and n.); since he died in 1559, this passage accords with Cavendish's statement that he finished his book on 24 June 1558.

62/19–20 **the people ... there:** Hall (p. 728) tells us 'that for what cause the cardinal went into France no person knew but the king until his return' and reports some of the rumours that were afloat.

62/30 The secondary manuscripts begin again at this point with

Historical Notes 221

'sedicius ontreuthe, etc.' after having omitted everything from 61/19–20, 'a fynne boore spere'. See Appendix E.

63/25–6 **the retourne of Crystopher Gunner:** Probably 13 September; see above (58/27 and n.).

63/35 **my lord Sandes:** For Sandys, see above (26/8 and n.).

64/1 **to Calice:** Wolsey reached Calais and sailed from there on 24 September (LP, IV, 3341 and 3594). For the establishment of the mart, see above (46/15 and n.).

64/10–11 **sir harre wyates howsse:** Hall tells us that Wolsey came to the king at *Richmond* on 30 September (p. 732). Mendoza, the Spanish ambassador, says that Wolsey went 'immediately' to the king at Richmond when he returned and also tells the story of how Anne demanded that she be present at the first interview between Henry and his minister. The king granted her wish, thus letting Wolsey surmise something of what had happened during his mission abroad (*Spanish Calendar*, 1527–9, p. 432). Cavendish seems to have confused the years 1527 and 1528 when he says that Wolsey returned to Henry at Wyatt's house, for it was in 1528 that the king visited the father of the poet (*D.N.B.*). Sir Henry Wyatt (d. 1537) stood high in the royal favour under Henry VII and Henry VIII. His house in Kent was Allington Castle, near Maidstone.

64/20 **an assemble ... starre Chamber:** Wolsey's 'Oracion' on this occasion is reported by Hall (p. 733) in terms very close to those which Cavendish uses; but the chronicler says that Wolsey actually displayed a French seal printed in fine gold as if the league had already been confirmed.

64/32 **the Duchye of Normandye:** The Treaty of Amiens (Leonard, II, 277ff., for the text) does not mention the Duchy of Normandy, but it does stipulate that Francis is to pay Henry a sum of 50,000 écus annually. The freedom which English merchants were to enjoy in France is also noted in the Treaty (Leonard, II, 282; see below, 65/11ff.).

65/32 **Thys greate ambassett:** Francis I issued his commission to his ambassadors on 25 September (LP, IV, 3449); the envoys included Montmorency, the Grand Master; Du Bellay, Bishop of Bayonne; Brinon, President of Rouen; and the Sieur d'Humieres, King's Chamberlain. The mission reached Dover on 13 October (LP, IV, 3494) and arrived in London on 20 October (Hall, p. 733). Cavendish's 'four score persons' is reduced by Hall to sixty.

66/5 **wyne ... mottons:** Hall (pp. 733–4), who also says that the Frenchmen stayed at the bishop's palace, reports that 'the citezens of

London prese*n*ted them with. v. fat oxen, xx. shepe, xii. Swannes, xii. Cranes, xii. Fesantz, iiii. dosyn Partiches, xx. loaues of Suger, Comfettes & other spyce and waxe, and. viii. hoggesheades of wyne with many other thinges which I cannot reherse.'

66/7 **the next Sonday:** Since the 20th of October (the day the embassy arrived) fell on a Sunday, this would have been the 27th. Hall is probably correct when he says (p. 734) 'tewsday' the 22nd, although he gives the wrong month. Cavendish belies his own account when he writes (66/18–19) that the king 'sent incontynent vnto the frenche kyng the lyke order of Englond'. We know (LP, IV, 3508) that the royal commission was dated 22 October, from Greenwich.

66/19 **the Erle of wyltshere:** A double error on Cavendish's part. Thomas Boleyn was not created Earl of Wiltshire until December 1529 and he was not sent on this mission. Its members were Viscount Lisle, John Taylor, Nicholas Carew, Anthony Browne, and Thomas Wriothesley. Francis I acknowledged receipt of the Garter on 10 November (LP, IV, 3565 and 3574). Cavendish repeats his mistake with regard to Boleyn's earldom at 87/1–2; see also his erroneous list of Boleyn's preferments (above, 29/13 ff.).

66/21 **Garter the harold:** Thomas Wriothesley (d. 1534), Garter King of Arms from 1505 until his death and brother of William Wriothesley, the father of the first Earl of Southampton. Thomas Wriothesley, the first Earl, is mentioned later by Cavendish (below, 139/15).

66/26 **a Solompne masse:** 1 November 1527 (Hall, p. 734).

67/4 **the Graund m^r:** Anne de Montmorency, first Duke of Montmorency (1493–1567). He had been taken prisoner at the Battle of Pavia with Francis I and was appointed Grand Master after the king's return from captivity in 1526.

67/25–6 **my lord . . . Supper:** Hall has a lengthy description of the banquet given by the king on 10 November, but does not mention Wolsey's. The cardinal's must have taken place between 1 November and 10 November.

69/13–14 **all the rest . . . yomen:** Apparently 'one chamber was better than another [with regard to its hangings] and all of them were furnished with tall yeomen'.

72/11–12 **who entendyd . . . same:** There is no extant evidence for the cardinal's feast outside of Cavendish's account. As far as can be judged from the materials available, it would seem that the king's banquet in the tiltyard at Greenwich (Hall, p. 735 and Gibson's

Historical Notes

Revels Accounts, LP, IV, 3563) was designed to glorify Wolsey to the highest degree. Hall tells us that the play which was performed depicted the cardinal releasing the Pope from bondage, but it would seem that his source of information was somewhat faulty. According to the Revels Accounts MS. (quoted by Collier, I, 107), the 'enterlude' to which Cavendish (below, 73/5) refers 'was a Latin Moral, in which Luther and his wife were brought upon the stage, and in which ridicule was attempted to be thrown upon them, and the Reformers. It was acted by the children of St. Paul's School under the regulation of their master, John Rightwise, who was most likely the author of the piece presented.' According to Herford (p. 106) this was 'the earliest instance of an original performance in Latin in England— apart, of course, from those of early mysteries'. It would appear that Cavendish is in error when he says that it was in both Latin and French.

73/7–8 **this don ... gentilwomen:** Cavendish speaks of three different companies of maskers (see 'an other maske', below, ll. 17 and 20) where Hall (p. 735) says there were four separate groups.

74/5 **to take ... kyng:** According to Hall, the embassy left on 11 November. Montmorency wrote to Wolsey from Boulogne, telling him of their arrival there, on the 15th (LP, IV, 3580).

74/11–12 **the kynges ... reward:** Robert Amadas the goldsmith presented his bill for a portion of this reward on 19 May 1528. Collier (I, 105) reprints the list of items, which amounted to almost 3,000 ounces of plate.

74/33–4 **the matter ... Cardenall:** Wolsey was certainly aware of the king's desire for a divorce by the spring of 1527, if not before. Cavendish, who does not seem to have known of the cardinal's efforts on the king's behalf both before and during the French embassy, probably picked up the tale of Wolsey's 'perswasion vppon his knees' from his deathbed speech at Leicester Abbey (below, 179/16–17).

75/14–15 **Than assembled ... westminster:** Wolsey called this consistory at his house on 17 May 1527 (LP, IV, 3140). Once more Cavendish confuses the order of events in his narrative.

75/22–4 **in Conclusion ... Iugement:** The passage is difficult to construe. If 'Auncyent fathers of the lawes' (l. 23) refers, as is most likely, to the men 'of long experyence' (above, ll. 13–14) and not to the patristic Church Fathers, then the best paraphrase would seem to run as follows: 'It seemed to me that by the time the session broke up ['by the departure'] the Counsellors were all of one mind [against

224   *Historical Notes*

the king].' But Cavendish may be playing on the several meanings of 'departure', for which see the glossary.

75/32–3 **all the vnyuersites:** Henry's appeal to the Universities of Europe was not made until *after* the divorce trial of 1529.

76/4 **And thervppon agreed:** i.e. and thereupon it was agreed.

76/14–15 **mony ... Clarkes:** Henry's agents often resorted to bribery in their efforts to win over the Universities to the king's side. See Hughes (I, 215–17) for a summary of their activities. Cavendish is right in the main when he says that the commissioners were 'euer in great estymacion'. Dr. John Stokesley, who, together with Richard Croke, was sent to Italy, later became Bishop of London. Croke himself was made sub-dean of Cardinal College, Oxford. Edward Foxe, afterwards Bishop of Hereford, was sent to Paris and Cranmer, who had originated the idea of appealing to the Universities, went to Germany. Only Reginald Pole, who was sent to Paris with Foxe, received no benefits from his role in the affair. He was shortly to become an exile and later returned to England as Cardinal and Archbishop of Canterbury under Mary.

76/26–7 **Sent agayn ... bysshoppes:** There is no evidence to suggest that the long campaign which king and cardinal waged for the appointment of a papal legate who, with Wolsey, would decide on the validity of Henry's marriage to Catherine, was planned and executed on the advice of the bishops. Wolsey held no further convocation after that of May 1527, but instead directed his agents at Rome to press for the appointment of the legate. Clement VII finally granted the commission on 8 June 1528 (LP, IV, 4345).

77/8–9 **ac vice tantum:** i.e. *hac vice tantum* 'for this occasion only'; a special court as opposed to one which met at regular intervals.

77/9–10 **Cardynall Campagious:** Lorenzo Campeggio (1472–1539) had been in England in 1518 as legate de latere and had received the bishopric of Salisbury in 1524, not in 1518, as Cavendish states. Cavendish's reference to him as 'bysshope of Bathe' probably stems from the fact that, while in London, he occupied the house of John Clerk, who was then in possession of that see. Clerk was greatly disturbed when informed that Campeggio should stay at his house. His letter to Gardiner (LP, IV, 4753; see also 4754 and 4768) amply testifies to his irritation.

77/21 **Long ... desier:** Campeggio reached Dover on 28 September. Hall (p. 753) describes his arrival as follows: '& so this Cardinal Campeius by long iorneyes came into England & much preparacion was made to receiue him triumphantly into London, but he was so

Historical Notes 225

sore vexed with the goute that he refused all suche solempnities, & desired hartely that he might without pompe be conueyed to his lodging for his more quiet & rest, & so the ix. day of October he came from saint Mary Ouereys by water to the bishop of Bathes place without Temple barre where he lodged the last tyme he was in England'. Campeggio's own account of his journey is in LP, IV, 4857.

78/1–2 **the kyng . . . Bridewell:** Cavendish passes over without comment the complex series of events that took place between the coming of Campeggio and the actual calling of the court for the trial in May 1529. The account of the trial that follows is compressed in Cavendish's usual manner: Catherine read a formal speech of protestation on 18 June; she appeared in the court again on 21 June and on that day made a speech like that with which Cavendish credits her. She then left the court immediately and Henry's reply followed her departure (Hughes, I, 187–8).

79/6–7 **Quia peccauimus . . .:** Ps. cv, 6 (*A.V.*, cvi, 6), 'Peccavimus cum patribus nostris: iniuste egimus, iniquitatem fecimus.'

79/16 **Doctor Stephens:** Stephen Gardiner (1497?–1555), at this time still Wolsey's secretary but soon (28 July 1529) to be taken into the king's service. He became Bishop of Winchester in November 1531. It was customary to refer to secretaries by their Christian names (see below, l. 25, 'doctor Peter' for Peter Vannes). Gardiner was not at the opening of the trial; he returned from Rome on the evening of 22 June and thereafter took a large part in the proceedings.

79/17 **oon Cooke:** The fullest account of this 'Cooke of Winchester' is contained in the preface to the Canterbury and York Society's edition of Wolsey's *Winchester Register*. He was John Cooke, a notary public of the Winchester diocese, who had been made registrar on 10 December 1524.

79/22 **Doctor Sampson:** Richard Sampson (d. 1554), a former chaplain of Wolsey's and his chancellor at Tournai from 1514 to 1517. He had declined Wolsey's offer to make him head of his household in 1519 and had instead gone into the king's service. One of Henry's chief agents during the divorce proceedings, he was rewarded with the bishopric of Chichester in June 1536.

79/23 **Doctor Bell:** John Bell (d. 1556), Dean of the Arches at the Lateran Council and afterwards chaplain to Henry VIII. He was constantly employed by the king on the divorce between 1527 and 1529. He became Bishop of Worcester on 11 August 1537.

79/25 **doctor Peter:** Peter Vannes (d. 1562), born at Lucca, Italy, had come to England in 1513 as an assistant to Andrea Ammonio, Latin Secretary to the king. After Ammonio's death in 1517, he came under Wolsey's protection and was frequently employed on Italian diplomatic missions. The *Letters and Papers* do not give the date at which he became Latin Secretary to the king, but he held the post on into the reign of Elizabeth. The *D.N.B.* apparently follows Cavendish when it says that Vannes was a proctor at the divorce trial. That this is an error is shown by the official correspondence, which proves him to have been in Rome at this time. See his autograph letter of 10 July 1529 in Pocock (I, 259–61).

79/26 **Doctor Tregonell:** Sir John Tregonwell (d. 1565), an admiralty lawyer after receiving his D.C.L. from Oxford in 1522. Henry VIII soon took him into his service and he proved his usefulness on numerous occasions during the rest of the king's reign.

79/27–8 **Doctor ffissher:** Bishop John Fisher's (1450?–1535) role in the divorce proceedings is too well known to require much comment here. Long an opponent of Wolsey and Queen Catherine's confessor, he was the only bishop to oppose the divorce. Pope Paul III made him a cardinal on 20 May 1535, while he was in prison for denying the royal supremacy; this action probably infuriated Henry VIII into executing him at Tower Hill on 22 June of that year. The anonymous *Life of Fisher* (see Van Ortroy's edition) contains ample testimony to the lamentations which Cavendish notes as arising in Western Europe after his death.

79/28 **Doctor Standysshe:** Henry Standish (d. 1535), one of the king's spiritual counsellors, became Bishop of St. Asaph on 28 May 1518. He spoke against the divorce after Fisher on 29 June 1529, but was distrusted by the Queen. Later he assisted at Anne's coronation and, on 1 June 1535, formally renounced the Pope.

79/34–80/1 **doctor Rydley:** Robert Ridley (d. 1536), the uncle of Nicholas Ridley, the Protestant martyr under Mary. After receiving his D.D. from Cambridge in 1518, he held a number of London benefices and was generally esteemed as 'a man of learning and an opponent of the Reformation' (*D.N.B.*).

80/15 **she sayd in effect:** The words which Cavendish puts into the queen's mouth are remarkably close to those reported by Hall and William Forrest. See Appendices A and C. Hall (pp. 755–6) does not represent Catherine's speech as having occurred at the trial itself but instead assigns it to an interview which she had with the legates before the proceedings commenced. The text of her prepared appeal, which she read three days before her speech, can be found in Pocock (I, 219–22).

80/34 **this xx^ti yeres:** Almost to the day. Catherine and Henry had been married on 11 June 1509; her speech was delivered on 21 June 1529.

81/4 **a true mayed:** Catherine continued to insist on this point throughout the divorce proceedings. Her statement, which was never denied by Henry, was in direct contradiction to many of the depositions that were made during the trial (LP, IV, 5774 for the depositions). Campeggio notes the queen's insistence on her virginity in a letter of 16 June (LP, IV, 5681).

81/15 **fferdynando:** Ferdinand of Aragon (d. 1516).

81/28 **ffor ye . . . Answere:** The legates accepted the queen's protest on Friday, 18 June, but ruled, on the 21st, that it was invalid and that they had legal jurisdiction in the case. On 23 June Henry wrote that the queen, 'Being thrice summoned to appear without effect . . . was pronounced contumax, and cited to appear on Friday next' (LP, IV, 5707). But Catherine never returned to the court.

82/11 **Generall receyvour:** The *O.E.D.* lists the title 'general-receiver' as a variant of 'receiver-general' and defines it as 'a chief receiver, esp. of public revenues'. But Griffith here seems to have functioned as a sort of 'master of ceremonies' as well as treasurer for the Queen.

82/11–12 **m^r Griffithe:** Mattingly (pp. 47–9 and 287) identifies 'Griffithe' with Griffith ap Rhys, the son of Rice ap Thomas (d. 1527); but this Griffith, who had been an attendant upon Prince Arthur, was presumably dead by 1527 when Rice ap Thomas's grandson inherited the family estates (cf. *Cambrian Register*, 3 vols., London, 1796, I, 49–144). The *Letters and Papers* (IV, 2972 and 6121) show that Cavendish's 'Griffithe' was rather a certain Griffin or Griffith Richardes, but I have been unable to obtain any further information about Catherine's receiver-general.

82/22–3 **sayd thus in effect:** Cavendish's words closely resemble those reported by Hall both at the trial and at the Bridewell assembly of 8 November 1528, when Henry had justified himself to 'his nobilitie, Iudges, and counsaylors with divers other persons' (Hall, p. 754). Catherine had issued a formal protest against the proceedings on 7 November (Hughes, I, 180). See Appendix C.

82/29–30 Supply a comma after 'condicyons' and 'they' before 'woll'.

228   *Historical Notes*

82/33–4 **for I . . . herein:** Mackie (p. 322) cites a long list of contemporary statements to illustrate this point. He concludes that 'contemporary opinion must have believed that Wolsey was the author of the divorce'. Cavendish's own belief that the cardinal was innocent of the charge was perhaps based on the king's public support of his minister during this scene.

83/5 **the Bysshope of Biean:** The Bishop of Bayonne at this time was Jean du Bellay (d. 1560), to whom Joachim du Bellay, his second cousin, dedicated *La Défense et Illustration de la Langue Française* in 1549. Du Bellay was French ambassador to Henry VIII, but Cavendish is in error when he refers to him as heading the embassy of 1527. The marriage negotiations of that spring were conducted by Gabriel de Grammont, Bishop of Tarbes. Henry's explanation of his 'scruples' is branded as a lie by Hughes (I, 157). Mackie, on the other hand, considers it 'quite conceivable'. There is no mention of any objection in the minute account of the embassy which was kept by its secretary (LP, IV, pp. 1397–1415).

83/13 **prynce Arthure:** Catherine and Arthur were married on 14 November 1501. Arthur died five months later on 2 April 1502.

84/7 **my lord of lyncolne:** John Longland (1473–1547) became Bishop of Lincoln on 5 May 1521. Both Harpsfield (p. 175, following Roper, p. 31) and the author of the *Life of Fisher* (ed. Van Ortroy, X, 293) implicate Longland in the early plans for the divorce. Henry's own account of the matter, as recorded here by Cavendish, seems to be substantially correct. It is perhaps true that Wolsey tried to force Longland to further the king's wishes, but the bishop himself denied that this was so and later affirmed to his chaplain that he sorely repented having given his consent in the matter (Van Ortroy, X, 291–2, n. 2).

84/13–14 **writyng . . . seales:** Van Ortroy (X, 323, note 1) cites a document from Rymer's *Foedera* (ed. Holmes, t. VI, p. i, p. 119) of 1 July 1529 in which the Bishops of London, Rochester, Carlisle, Ely, St. Asaph, Lincoln, Bath, and Canterbury all recognize that the king has consulted them and certify their consent to the divorce proceedings. This would seem to place the date of the scene here described by Cavendish after 1 July and not before it. Fisher's denial that he had subscribed to such a document is paralleled by a manuscript in the Record Office (LP, IV, 5729) which, according to the Calendar, contains 'a very bitter reply to Fisher, who has corrected some of the King's statements in his own hand in the margin: among others, that he had approved of the reasons for the King's divorce; to which he answers, "Non haec dixi: Certe Cardinalis voluit ut haec dixissem."'

84/18 no hathe/ q^d the kyng: The secondary manuscripts all corrupt this passage to 'No, ha! q^d the king,' thus indicating that their scribes did not understand the original. Singer (I, 157) has the illogical 'No! ha' the!' This type of phrase was apparently not uncommon in the sixteenth century. *John Bon and Mast Person* (1548–1550, p. 3) has 'No dyd' and John Bridges's *Sermon at Paul's Cross* (1571, p. 128) has 'No is'. I owe these references to Professor F. P. Wilson of the University of Oxford. Note also Henry's somewhat similar 'yea can' (below, 184/13). Further examples are cited by W. Franz, *Die Sprache Shakespeares* (4th ed., Halle 1939) § 409.

85/8 The next court day: Apparently 29 June when, according to a letter of Campeggio (LP, IV, 5732), Fisher appeared and stated that the marriage could not be dissolved by any power, human or divine.

85/19 to be very doughtfull: i.e. were very doubtful.

85/24–5 Q^d deus ... separet: Matthew xix, 6; Mark x, 9.

86/9 and 13–14 this honorable persons, this abhomynable presumcyons: Cf. above (80/34) 'this xx^{ti} yeres'. On the form 'this' for 'these' see *O.E.D.* s.v. *These*.

86/25 the bysshope of Carelyle: John Kite (d. 1537), Bishop of Carlisle from 12 July 1521. He seems to have been a good friend of Wolsey and was certainly indebted to him for some of his promotions.

87/5–7 that he ... Bridwell: There is no other evidence for this visit of the cardinals to the queen, but it is certain that they were continually endeavouring to persuade her to comply with the king's wishes. The scene is somewhat similar to that described by Hall (pp. 755–6) as having occurred in the previous November. Cavendish's reference to Thomas Boleyn as 'my lord of wyltchere' (above, ll. 1–2) is anachronistic (see above, 66/19 and n.).

87/19–20 that was ... matter: i.e. of what was likely to ensue with regard to this matter.

89/8 At w^{che} day: Campeggio prorogued the court until 1 October on 23 July. The news had not yet reached England that on 15 July the Pope had revoked the case to Rome (LP, IV, 5777, 5780, and 5791). The legate's postponement was in accordance with the practice of the Roman Curia, which did not sit from the end of July until October, but the point of his action was not missed by the king.

The general tenor of Campeggio's speech certainly reflects his attitude toward the case.

90/24 **the Duke of Suffolk:** Hall (p. 758) reports this scene as follows: 'Charles Duke of Suffolke, seeyng the delay, gaue a great clappe on the Table with his hande and said: by the Masse, now I see that the olde saied sawe is true, that there was neuer Legate nor Cardynall, that did good in Englande and with that saiyng all the Temporall Lordes departed to the King.' Cavendish is the sole authority for Wolsey's reply to the Duke and one may doubt, with Pollard (pp. 109 and 234) that any answer was actually given. Wolsey's reference to an occasion when Suffolk had owed his life to him would seem to allude to the Duke's brief period of disfavour after his marriage to Henry's sister in 1515. Fiddes (p. 95) attempted to show that Wolsey's intercession with the king had saved the Duke's life, but the letters which he cites are not completely convincing.

91/8 **the kynges Commyssioner:** Wolsey's words can be taken as an ironic allusion to Suffolk's conduct in 1515, when he had been sent 'as the kynges Commyssioner in a fforrayn Region' to bring Mary, Henry VIII's sister, back to England after the death of Louis XII. On that occasion Suffolk had not waited for any word from Henry but had instead proceeded impetuously into a marriage of which the king disapproved (see above, 50/17–18 and n.).

91/29 **Thys matter contynued, etc.:** Cavendish's description of the sequence of events between the prorogation of the court and the visit of the two cardinals to the king at Grafton is extremely confused. Most of the happenings which he narrates had occurred before the commencement of the trial: thus the Pope did not 'take delyberacion in respeyght of Iugeme^t', but instead, after revoking the case to Rome, cited Henry to appear there (Hughes, I, 218); Cavendish's reference to 'Bartholmewetyd next' (24 August) is rendered meaningless by the fact that the papal courts would not have opened in any event until October; Gardiner was not sent on any new embassy to the Pope (he had been in Rome from January to June 1529) but instead became the king's secretary and was with him for the rest of the year.

92/15–16 **the grece season:** The 'grease season' for deer was the time when the harts were fat and fit for killing. *O.E.D.* (s.v. Grease 1.b.) says that this was from August until the middle of October.

92/20–1 **that the Cardynall . . . Grafton:** Wolsey had not been invited to the court during the royal progresses which followed upon the termination of the trial. Campeggio had a good deal of difficulty securing permission for him to attend at Grafton on 19 September, when the Italian legate took his farewell of the king.

92/31-2 **yet for as myche ... effect:** Cavendish seems to imply that Henry could not treat Campeggio as he did Wolsey because the Italian cardinal was a foreigner and thus was entitled to special considerations of hospitality. Note the 'hyme oonly' of l. 34 below.

93/3 **no lodgyng ... Court:** Chapuys, the Spanish ambassador, whose account of this meeting between the cardinals and Henry confirms Cavendish's in many details, says that it was the Duke of Suffolk who took care to provide that Wolsey should not be lodged in the palace (*Spanish Calendar*, 1529-30, pp. 253 and 257).

93/4 **Sir herre Norreys:** Henry Norris (d. 1536) had come to the court as a youth and was soon intimate with the king. He took sides against Wolsey at an early date and was looked upon as one of Anne's adherents. His devotion to her was proved in 1536 when he suffered death as a traitor rather than confess that he had had intercourse with her. It is Norris who brings the king's ring to Wolsey after his fall (below, 101/30 ff.); he also figures as one of the mourners in Cavendish's poems (II, 25).

94/9 **I hard ... :** Pollard (pp. 237-8) conjectures that Henry here confronted Wolsey with documentary proof of the cardinal's private dealings with Francis I, Campeggio, and the Pope. Such evidence could perhaps have been provided by Gardiner at his return from Rome on 22 June. Wolsey's apparent pacification of the king at this juncture is scarcely borne out by the events of the next month.

94/16-17 **the kyng ... Anne Boleyn:** Cavendish is the only authority for the ensuing conversation between the king and Anne, but there can be little doubt of the enmity that existed between her and the cardinal at this date.

94/23 **my lord of Norffolk:** Thomas Howard II, Earl of Surrey and third Duke of Norfolk (1473-1554), whose father had opposed Wolsey in the council when the cardinal-to-be first rose to power. He was Anne's uncle and the leader of the opposition to Wolsey at the court. Although his power was great immediately after the cardinal's fall, he never achieved the complete control at which he aimed and narrowly escaped death for treason during the last days of the king's reign when his son, the poet Surrey, was executed.

94/27 **Wynchester:** For Wolsey's acquisition of Winchester, see above (17/33 and n.).

95/8 **a lone:** Cavendish's statement must refer to the loan of 1522, which had not been repaid in 1529, when the Parliament reluctantly turned it into a gift. See Pollard, pp. 132–3.

96/8 **Eston:** Cavendish's detail is confirmed by a letter from Thomas Alford, a former servant of Wolsey's, to Cromwell on 23 September 1529 (LP, IV, 5953). Alford writes that both 'my Lord and the Legate returned to their lodgings at Empson's Place' on the evening of 19 September. It would seem, however, that Campeggio actually stayed at the palace, as Cavendish states (see Pollard's note, p. 238). This Empson was Thomas Empson, the eldest son of Sir Richard (above, 11/25 and n.). His father's estates had been restored to him by an act of 4 Henry VIII and he seems to have been in favour with the king.

96/15 **Doctor Stephyns:** Wolsey, if not Cavendish, must have known that Gardiner had returned from Rome on 22 June, for several letters passed between them during the summer (Pollard, pp. 234–7). It may be true, however, that the cardinal suspected Gardiner of having betrayed him to the king. On 18 September the French ambassador Du Bellay wrote that Wolsey had been betrayed by some of his protégés, a statement that Pollard takes as 'certainly' referring to Gardiner (LP, IV, 5945).

96/32 **The next mornyng:** Alford's letter (LP, IV, 5953) reports that Wolsey was in council with the king on the morning of 20 September and that the king went hunting in the afternoon. Hall's account (p. 759) agrees exactly with Cavendish's except for the references to Anne Boleyn. On 17 October Du Bellay wrote to Montmorency describing the cardinal's state just before his fall. He noted that 'the worst of his evil is that Mademoiselle de Boulen has made her friend promise that he will never give him a hearing, for she thinks he could not help having pity upon him' (LP, IV, 6011).

97/17 **Campagious . . . Rome:** The cardinal left London on 5 October (LP, IV, 5995) but was held up at Dover, as Du Bellay wrote, 'on pretence of want of ships . . . for fear he carries off the treasure of the cardinal of York' (LP, IV, 6003). Campeggio's baggage was searched at Dover (not Calais as Cavendish, below, l. 24, has it), according to Hall (p. 759) 'to se what letters the Cardinal of Yorke had sent to the court of Rome'. The real purpose behind the search seems to have been Henry's desire to get hold of the decretal commission that Campeggio had brought to England but had long since destroyed. The whole story of this bull is fraught with mystery, but it seems to have granted full power in the divorce question to

Campeggio and Wolsey, thus enabling them to proceed to a decision. But Clement VII had stipulated to Campeggio that the decretal was to be shown to the king and Wolsey and then destroyed. For a full account of the matter, see Hughes (I, 176). Campeggio did not sail until 26 October.

97/17–18 **the kynges reward:** The reward which Campeggio received from the king was a considerable one, as is shown by the Treasurer of the Chamber's accounts (LP, V, pp. 303–26) of the expenses necessitated by his departure. His secretary, 'Mr. Florian', received £112 10s. in September 1529 (p. 315); there are three separate payments to Robert Amadas, the goldsmith, 'for plate delivered to Campeggio.' In October the amount was £39 18s. 0½d.; on 9 November Amadas received £200; and on 13 December he was paid an apparently final sum of £169 15s. 6d. (pp. 315–16).

97/30 **terme began:** Michaelmas Term began on 9 October in 1529.

97/34–98/1 **expectyng . . . Norffolk:** Cavendish seems to have compressed two weeks into one at this point in his narrative. The Dukes came for the seal on 17 October, not 11 October; when refused, they returned on the 18th. Dr. Taylor, the Master of the Rolls, delivered the seal to the king on 20 October at Windsor. Wolsey had ample reason to 'expect' the arrival of the Dukes, for on 9 October a bill of indictment for praemunire had been presented in the king's bench.

98/4 **Assher:** Wolsey had begged this palace at Esher from Foxe, Bishop of Winchester, in 1519 and had officially acquired it for himself when he succeeded Foxe in 1528.

98/32 **to take accompte:** The inventory taken here is calendared in the *Letters and Papers* (IV, pp. 2763–70).

100/1 **sir wm Gascoyn:** Sir William Gascoigne, the grandfather of the Elizabethan poet and the founder of the family fortunes. He had been Sheriff of Bedfordshire in 1507, 1514, and 1516 and was knighted by Henry VIII. After Wolsey's fall Gascoigne retired to his estate at Cardington, but he was soon back in service again in the household of John Neville, Lord Latimer. See C. T. Prouty's *George Gascoigne* (New York, 1942), pp. 9–10.

100/20 **And toke his barge:** Hall (p. 760) tells us that Wolsey 'toke his barge, and went to Putney by Water, and there toke his horse and rode to Asher, where he remaigned til Lent after' but he does not give the date of the removal. Chapuys (*Spanish Calendar*, 1529–30, p. 304) writes on 25 October that a ring had been sent to the cardinal; his letter presumably refers to Norris's message (below, 101 ff.).

103/28–9 **I ame ... chapleyn:** The sense is clearer if we omit Cavendish's comma after 'obedyent'. Wolsey had used words very similar to these in a letter to the king which he wrote about 8–9 October (*State Papers*, I, 347). He there signed himself 'your most prostrate poor chaplain, T. Car^lis Ebor., miserimus.'

104/4–5 **this poore foole:** A gloss in one of the secondary manuscripts (Douce 363, fol. 72) reports that the 'fole was called master Williams: owtherwise called Patch. geven to ye kinge from the Cardinall'. A series of anecdotes about Wolsey's fool will be found in John Doran's *The History of Court Fools* (London, 1858), pp. 132–4 and 140–1; he turns up again in Rowley's chronicle play (1605) *When You See Me You Know Me*. Patch is mentioned as in the king's service on 22 January 1530 (Nicolas, *Privy Purse Expences*, p. 19; LP, V, pp. 748, 750, and 752).

104/9 **fired:** Most of the secondary manuscripts read 'for the poor fool took on like a tyrant', thus missing the significance of Cavendish's metaphor.

104/22 **the bysshope of Carlylle, sir Thomas Arundell:** For the bishop see above (86/25 and n.). Sir Thomas Arundell (d. 1552) had, like the Earl of Northumberland, been brought up in Wolsey's household and was one of the cardinal's gentlemen of the privy chamber. Cavendish represents him later in his poems (II, 125).

104/28 **master Cromwell:** The rise of Thomas Cromwell (1485?–1540) in the royal favour after the fall of Wolsey is too well known to require comment here. Good accounts can be found in Merriman's *Life and Letters* and in Hughes (I, 223–7).

105/3 **my onhappie Adventure:** A letter to Cromwell from Stephen Vaughan, his agent at Antwerp, of 30 October 1529 informs him that he is more hated for his master's sake than for any wrong that he has done to anyone (Merriman, I, 65). Cromwell's role in the suppression of monasteries, the revenues of which were to build Wolsey's colleges at Oxford and Ipswich, had a great deal to do with the popular disfavour in which he was held at this time.

105/9–10 **all thynges ... taken:** Cromwell voices his belief that the right or wrong of an action is dependent not upon the action itself but upon the interpretation that people place upon it. He fears 'guilt by association'. For 'taken' cf. the *O.E.D.* quotation (s.v. *Take* v. 42) from Latimer (1553): 'There is a common saying amongst us ... Everything is (say they) as it is taken, which indeed is not so: for every thing is as it is, howsoever it be taken.'

105/12–14 **I neuer ... lyvyng**: Certainly a gross misrepresentation on Cromwell's part. Wolsey had made him collector of revenues for York as early as 1514 and by 1527 almost all of the cardinal's legal business was passing through his hands. Cromwell repeats this statement at 109/23–5.

105/16 **make or marre**: Cavendish later notes this phrase as characteristic of Cromwell (below, 110/8). William Forrest's *Governance of Princes* (see Macray's *Grisild the Second*, pp. 182–3) has a somewhat puzzling passage on what Forrest calls the 'game' of making and marring:

> The world is chaunged from that it hathe beene,
> Not to the bettre but to the warsse farre;
> More for a penye wee haue before seene
> Then nowe for fowre pense, whoe liste to compare:
> This suethe the game called *Makinge or Marre*;
> Unto the riche it makethe a great deale.
> But muche it marrethe to the Commune weale.

Macray (p. 194) notes that such a game was actually prohibited by statute (2 and 3 Philip and Mary, 1555, cap. 9), but can give no description of it. The meaning of Cromwell's 'make or mar' is at any rate obvious.

105/24 **doctor Marshall**: Wolsey wrote from Esher (LP, IV, 6261, no date) that he had sent Dr. Marshall to the king with his seal to give up some York benefices and collate others. This was evidently Cuthbert Marshall (d. 1550), who took his D.D. at Cambridge in 1523 and was prebendary of York from 1526 to 1550. See Cooper, *Athenae*, I, 97 and 538.

106/28 **yor Idell chapleyns**: In Cavendish's poems (II, 18) Wolsey speaks of his

> ... vicious chapleyns walking by my syde,
> Voyde of all vertue, fullfilled with pryde,
> Which hathe caused me, by report of suche fame,
> For ther myslyvyng to have an yll name.

108/32–3 **if the kyng ... me**: Here and at 109/14–15 Cavendish seems to represent Wolsey as expecting to be restored to all his dignities. Henry took the cardinal under his protection on 18 November after he had made his submission to the king. Wolsey did not recover all his revenues, but was allowed to keep York and a pension out of Winchester (see below, 124/34ff.)

109/25 **yet wyll I ... this:** i.e. Yet will I divide this among you.

110/12-13 **thes ij dayes:** Presumably 1-3 November. Cromwell left Wolsey on 1 November. By the 3rd he had obtained his seat in the Parliament that met on that day.

110/14 **Sir Rafe Sadler:** Cromwell refers to Ralph Sadler (1507-87) as 'my servant' in the will which he made on 12 July 1529. Sadler's rise to power began in Cromwell's household; he was made a gentleman of the privy chamber shortly after Henry's minister became Earl of Essex (9 July 1536) and was knighted in 1540.

110/19 Supply 'I' (Cavendish) before 'perceyved'.

110/22 **sir Iohn Russhell:** The *Letters and Papers* (IV, 6024) preserve a letter from Wolsey to Henry thanking the king for the comfort sent him by Sir John Russell. The letter is undated, but is placed under 24 October 1529 by the editors. Pollard (p. 265, n.) suggests that if Cavendish is right Wolsey's acknowledgement should be dated 2 November. For Russell see above (37/25-6 and n.).

112/8-10 **And shortly ... stuff:** If Wolsey arrived at Esher about 25 October, as seems most likely (above, 100/20 and n.), then Cavendish's 'shortly after' apparently contradicts his earlier statement (above, 104/17) that the cardinal's household remained without furnishings for 'three or four weeks'. In actual fact the gift of furniture and supplies from the king seems to have been made on 14 February 1530, two days after Wolsey's pardon had been granted (LP, IV, 6213 and 6214). The schedule appended to the 'Instrument' certifying the king's gift is reprinted by Singer (pp. 507-8). From it we learn that the total value of the king's present was £6,374 3s. 7½d. See below (122/14 and n.).

112/21 **oon of the Burgious:** According to Merriman (I, 67-8), the story that Cavendish tells here must have been a deliberate fabrication on Cromwell's part. A letter from Sadler to Cromwell of 1 November implies that it was through the Duke of Norfolk's influence that Wolsey's secretary entered Parliament. The letter advises Cromwell to see the Duke about what the king wants done in the coming session. Cromwell sat as a member for Taunton; apparently Cavendish's account repeats the story that Cromwell sent back to Wolsey. It would not have done to have told the cardinal that his agent had obtained his seat from Wolsey's worst enemy.

112/22 **sir Thomas Russhe:** Thomas Rush had been associated with Cromwell in the dissolution of the monasteries undertaken by

Wolsey. He sat in Parliament in 1529 as a member for Ipswich (LP, IV, 6043). Cromwell had referred to him as 'my friend' in the will which he made earlier in that year. Rush was not a knight at this time but received the honour later (1 June 1533) at Anne's coronation. His son, to whom Cavendish refers here, was Arthur Rush of Sudborne, Suffolk; he is not listed as a member of this Parliament.

113/10 **a byll of Articles:** These forty-four articles are discussed in detail by Pollard (pp. 258–63). They did not in fact condemn Wolsey, nor did they ask that he should be tried for treason; they merely request that 'he be so provided for, that he never have any power, jurisdiction, or authority hereafter to trouble, vex, and impoverish the commonwealth'.

113/15 **to endyght hyme:** Either Cavendish's original comprehension of events was extremely limited on this point or his later recollections were much more hazy than usual. The bill of indictment for praemunire had been presented in the king's bench on 9 October and on the 22nd Wolsey signed a complete acknowledgement of his guilt. The statute of praemunire under which the cardinal was indicted (16 Richard II, c. 5) is fully discussed by Pollard (pp. 245–51). Its terms provided for the confiscation of the defendant's property.

113/17 **his Colleges:** Wolsey continually deplored the dissolution of his colleges after his fall, but, as Pollard (p. 326) notes, it was the cardinal's own possessiveness which placed them in the king's hands. He had neglected to set them up as corporate entities and had retained absolute control of them for himself. Thus, as his own 'private property', they fell to the crown at his indictment.

113/25 **the kynges lycence:** Wolsey was not indicted for being legate, but for what he had done while he held that office. No one has ever produced the king's licence, but certainly it could not have covered the breaches of common law with which he was charged.

113/29–31 **I ame content . . . indyghtment:** Since Wolsey's submission occurred on 22 October, the visit of the judges, to whom Cavendish represents him as saying these words, must have occurred about the 20th or 21st. A further bill of indictment had been presented on the 20th. The cardinal surrendered to the king not only because he feared what might happen to him if the bishops themselves were to judge him but also because an indictment in the king's bench, unlike an act of attainder, could not issue in the death penalty (Pollard, p. 244).

114/15 **the Duke of Norffolk:** There is no evidence other than

Cavendish's for Norfolk's visit to the cardinal. Its dating presents a problem. We know that the Duke came to Wolsey on the same day that 'master Shelley' arrived to get Wolsey's signature on the transference of York Place to the king (below, 116/34ff.). If the document was the actual deed of recovery against Wolsey (printed by Fiddes, *Collections*, p. 224) then we should probably place Shelley's visit as occurring shortly before its date (7 February 1530). Cavendish (below, 119/9) says that Shelley called a clerk 'who wrott my lord recognysaunce'. It thus appears that the judge's visit referred to an earlier acknowledgement made by Wolsey and not to the actual transfer of February. Henry had taken over York Place as his own by 7 November 1529 (LP, V, p. 316). It seems most likely that Norfolk's visit occurred in November, rather than in February, for by the latter date he was violently expressing his wish that Wolsey should move North to York (below, 127/5–6 and n.).

114/17–18 **was commyng . . . hand:** Elliptical: was coming and was [now] even at hand.

115/24–5 **to bere . . . lion:** After the Battle of Flodden in 1513, the Earl of Surrey (father of Cavendish's Norfolk) was granted an augmentation to his arms which consisted of a red lion, symbolizing Scotland, cut in half and pierced by an arrow. But Wolsey's words probably allude to the fact that Norfolk was entitled to quarter his arms with those of Mowbray (a silver lion on a red field) and Segrave (a silver lion with a crown of gold on a black field). The Duke's retainers thus wore a device which pictured a white lion tearing a red one. The bloody crest that forms the title page of Roy's *Rede Me* (pp. 21–2) is described in the following verses:

> Of the prowde Cardinall this is the shelde
> Borne vp betwene two angels off Sathan.
> The sixe blouddy axes in a bare felde
> Sheweth the cruelte of the red man/
> whiche hathe devoured the beautifull swan.
> Mortall enmy vnto the whyte Lion/
> Carter of Yorche/ the vyle butchers sonne.

The red, of course, refers to Wolsey's robes as a cardinal; the swan is the Duke of Buckingham (executed in 1521); and the 'white lion' represents Norfolk. See Wordsworth's note (pp. 598–9).

115/33–4 **Parcere prostratis, etc.:** I have not been able to locate the exact source of this distich. The first half-line may well echo Virgil's famous 'Parcere subiectis et debellare superbos' in the sixth book of the *Aeneid* and the idea of the lion as the king of beasts who shows mercy to his victims is a classical commonplace. Seneca's *De Clementia* (Loeb edition of the *Moral Essays*, I, 372 and 422) and the following passage from Pliny (*Naturalis Historia*, VIII, 19) may be cited as typical: 'Leoni tantum ex feris clementia in supplices; prostratis parcit: et ubi saevit, in viros potius, quam in foeminas fremit, in infantes non nisi magna fame.' Josse Clichtove, a contemporary of Wolsey (see below, 160/6–7 and n.), speaks of the lion as a type of nobility in his *De vera nobilitate* (Paris 1520): Enimuero leones tantum ex feris clementia vtuntur in supplices, prostratis parcunt, vt eleganti carmine sic notat Ouidius in tertio libro tristium. Quo quisque est maior, magis est placabilis irae. Et faciles motus mens generosa capit. Corpora magnanimo satis est prostrasse leoni: Pugna suum finem, cum iacet hostis, habet.' (Sig. C$_5$; Clichtove is quoting *Tristia*, III, v, 31–4). In *The Thistle and the Rose* (1503) Dunbar says of the lion 'Quois noble yre is proceir [*l.* parcere] prostratis' (l. 119), where the allusion is to the Scottish king's armorial bearings. Finally, it may be noted that Skelton seems to refer to this distich in his 'Elegy on the Earl of Northumberland' (d. 1489; see *Works*, I, 16): 'And, as the lyone, whiche is of bestes kynge, Unto thy subiectes be curteis and benygne.' Northumberland's crest contained a blue lion, just as that of Norfolk quartered a white one.

116/6 **auctory:** Either a slip here (and at 157/1) by Cavendish for his more normal 'auctoryte' or a genuine shortened form of the latter word.

116/7–8 **A Strawe . . . legacye:** 'Norfolk was here expressing at once the respect which conservatives felt for the mediaeval catholic church and the prejudice they entertained against the intruding autocracy involved in the legatine powers which Wolsey had acquired' (Pollard, p. 165).

116/28–9 **at thys tyme . . . seruyce:** Sadler's letter to Cromwell of 1 November 1529 (Merriman, I, 68) reports that 'Other newes at the courte I here none but dyuers of my lorde his seruauntes as Mr. Aluarde Mr. Sayntclere Mr. Forest, Humfrey lisle Mr. Mores & other ben elect and sworne the king his seruauntes.' But Sadler does not mention what the general attitude was with regard to the servants' transfer of allegiances.

116/34 **m^r Shelley:** For the date of Shelley's visit to Wolsey, see above (114/15 and n.). Sir William Shelley (1480?–1549) had been made a serjeant and then a judge by Henry VIII. He was in the Parliament of 1529 and later, although reported to have been hostile to the Reformation, took part in the most important state trials. Among the many appeals which Wolsey wrote after his fall there is one of August 1530 (LP, IV, 6577) to Shelley in which the cardinal beseeches his clemency 'in consideration of their old friendship' with regard to the status of Cardinal College, Oxford.

117/8–9 **I haue ... messwage:** Norfolk was perhaps embarrassed by his own involvement in the York Place transaction. On 11 February 1530 he appeared in Chancery with More and others to acknowledge the deed of recovery against Wolsey (LP, IV, 6210).

118/10 **the Court of concyence:** Chancery formerly consisted of two courts, one of common law and the other of equity. 'The second proceeded upon rules of equity and conscience, moderating the rigour of the common law, and giving relief in cases where there was no remedy in the common-law courts' (*O.E.D.*, s.v. *Chancery*, 2).

118/20–1 **And ... employed:** i.e. 'and [considering] that it is to be employed'.

119/5 **dischargethe:** i.e. 'discharge,' third person for first person, the only instance in the *Life*.

119/16 **the great affeccon:** This was Chapuys' impression when he wrote on 6 February that it would be easy to reinstate the cardinal if it were not for Anne Boleyn, 'for it is thought the King has no ill-will to the Cardinal. His only wish is for the Cardinal's goods' (LP, IV, 6199).

119/18–19 **to geve ... chafe:** A letter from Wolsey to Cromwell (LP, IV, 6226; no date, but placed under February 1530) contains several statements of the cardinal's vexation. Wolsey may be alluding to the petty irritations that Cavendish describes when he says that 'Thys dayly alteration [keeps] me in suche agony that I had lever be ded [than alive]'.

119/24 **in daynger ... estates:** Chapuys, writing of possible French attempts to reinstate the cardinal, says that 'were the affair properly conducted, the result would be greatly to their advantage; but if they fail in the attempt, as seems probable, it will only serve to irritate those now in power and at the head of affairs, whose very lives are at stake' (Pollard, p. 270).

120/8 **At Cristmas ... syke:** Apparently a little after Christmas itself. Early in January Wolsey speaks of 'being entered into the passion of dropsy' (LP, IV, 6224; misdated under 17 February, see Pollard, p. 267, n. 4) and on 19 January Doctor Augustine (for whom see below, 151/13–14 and n.) wrote to Cromwell asking that

Historical Notes 241

Drs. Butts and Cromer be sent. They were to bring leeches and some vomitive electuary and 'No time must be lost'.

120/10 **doctor buttes**: Sir William Butts (d. 1545) who took his M.D. at Cambridge in 1518 and was court physician from 1524 until his death.

120/21 **xx M¹ ˡⁱ**: Cavendish makes Henry use the same phrase after Wolsey's death (below, 184/10).

121/1 **And than ... Anne:** Chapuys reported on 6 February (LP, IV, 6199) that 'a cousin of the Cardinal's physician told me that the lady had sent to visit him during his sickness, and represented herself as favouring him with the King. This is difficult to be believed, considering the hatred she has always borne him.'

121/11 **Doctor Clement:** John Clement (d. 1572), the friend of Thomas More and tutor to his children, who married Margaret Giggs, More's adopted daughter, in 1530. He was later (1544) president of the College of Physicians.

121/11 **Doctor Wotten:** Edward Wotten (1492–1555) was a member of the College of Physicians from 1528 on but does not appear to have attended Henry VIII. He is said to have been the first English physician to take up the systematic study of natural history and his *de Differentiis Animalium* (Paris, 1552) gained him a European reputation.

121/11 **doctor Cromer:** The fullest account of Dr. Walter Cromer (d. 1547) is contained in an article by R. R. James in *The Practitioner*, cxxxiii (1934), 200–7. Cromer became King's Physician in Ordinary to Henry VIII in 1539–40. He had married Alice Whethill, by whom he had four children, in 1528. A list of his medicines for Henry VIII is contained in MS. Sloane 1047, from which it was reprinted by Furnivall for the E.E.T.S. (E.S. 53, 1888). I owe this information to Mr. W. H. Challen.

121/34 **to debate his dessease:** The cardinal would never let himself be outshone, not even in medical matters. See his own diagnosis of the dysentery that killed him (below, 178/22 ff.). In 1519 More had written to the cardinal advising him not to physic himself so much (LP, III, i, p. 154).

122/14 **Candyllmas:** 2 February 1530. Cavendish's description of the 'stuff' which the king sent Wolsey may refer to the gifts of 14 February (LP, IV, 6214; above 112/8–10 and n.). It is possible, of course, that Henry sent two consignments of goods to Esher, one 'shortly after' or 'three or four weeks after' the cardinal arrived there and the other in February; if so, the first present has not been recorded in the *Letters and Papers*.

242   *Historical Notes*

122/16 **beddes, etc.**: The schedule of 14 February specifically mentions 'Plate, Dyvers Apparell of Houshold, as Hangyngs, Beddyng, Napry, and Implements of the Kytchen'.

123/4 **ffor he ... Assher**: It must have been about this time that Wolsey wrote to Gardiner asking his aid in removing from Asher and complaining of the damp and moist air there (LP, IV, 6224, no date). On 1 February Wolsey wrote to Cromwell saying that he could not leave for Richmond as yet (*State Papers*, I, 361). It may be supposed that his removal occurred shortly after this date; this would agree with Cavendish's 'shortly after Candylmas' (below, 127/20).

123/26-7 **ffor the kyng ... hampton Court**: Pollard (p. 325, n. 2) interprets this passage as meaning that the 'exchange' occurred after Wolsey's fall, but Cavendish's description of the cardinal's repairs would make it appear that it took place before his indictment. Wolsey had 'given' Hampton Court to the king in 1524-5, but had continued to occupy it afterwards.

124/1-2 **lest his ... at lengthe**: 'Lest his nigh-being to the king might cause the king'.

124/15 **the Duke of Norffolk**: See the Duke's words to Wolsey at Grafton before his fall (above, 94/27ff.).

124/33-4 **Movyd ... wynchester**: Pollard (p. 273, n. 2) quotes Holmes's text for this passage where the reading is 'a pension of four thousand marks'. That the pension was actually 1,000 marks is shown by the treasurer's accounts (Pollard, *ibid.*, referring to LP, V, p. 318) and by Cavendish himself (below, 131/23). The recipients of these pensions are all mentioned elsewhere in the *Life*. The *Rotuli Parliamentorum* (Rolls of Parliament to supply the deficiencies in the Journals of the House of Lords, clxxxviii) record the passing in 1531 of 'An Act concerning certain Annuities granted out of the Bishopric of Wynchester', which insured the possessors of grants from Wolsey against any loss of their revenues. The cardinal's writs are listed as follows: on 20 February 1530, £100 to Norfolk, who was also made High Steward of the bishopric's rents; £200 to George Boleyn; £40 each to Sir William Fitzwilliam, Henry Guildford, and Sir John Russell; two grants to Henry Norris, one of £100 and the other of £20; on 5 June 1530, 100 marks to Lord Sandys. The pensions amount to about £610 per year. Winchester, in 1535, had lands valued at £3,820 per year. Only George Boleyn received as much as 300 marks (below, 125/9) and Cavendish appears to be incorrect when he says (below, 131/29) that 'hys [Wolsey's] part was the lest'.

127/5-6 **teare ... teathe**: Norfolk's words, as Wordsworth

(p. 610) noted, probably allude to the lion that he displayed on his crest (see above, 115/24–5 and n.). They are strikingly confirmed in one of Chapuys' dispatches (LP, IV, 6199; 6 February 1530), in which the ambassador reports a conversation between Norfolk and Sir John Russell. Norfolk, so runs the letter, asked Russell if he thought that the cardinal would return to power. When Russell replied that this was not unlikely, the Duke 'began to swear very loudly that, rather than suffer this, he would eat him up alive'.

127/20 **Candylmas:** See above (123/4). In 1530 Lent began on 2 March.

127/23 **a certyn tale:** The 'dun cow' prophecy which Cavendish relates here may be alluded to in the last stanza of 'The descripcion of the armes' in Roy's *Rede Me* (p. 20):

> The cloubbe signifieth playne hys tiranny
> Covered over with a Cardinals hatt
> Wherin shalbe fulfilled the prophecie
> Aryse vp Iacke and put on thy salatt/
> For the tyme is come of bagge and walatt
> The temporall cheualry thus throwen downe
> Wherby prest take hede and beware thy croune.

Wordsworth (p. 612) suggested that the lines on the dun cow may explain the fact that, when Anne Boleyn was made Marchioness of Pembroke, her family arms were not quartered on her new crest. Henry, who presumably forbade the 'bull' to be placed on the royal arms, might have been endeavouring to avoid any references to such a 'coupling' which a vulgar prophecy like this one might have aroused in the populace. His other queens were all allowed to include their family arms in their new royal crests. Wolsey's superstitious concern for prophecies and omens is substantiated by several anecdotes that have come down to us. See below (170/10 and n.).

129/31 **the last monye:** Presumably the £3,000 in ready money which was included in Henry's gift of 14 February (Singer, p. 507). For Wolsey's debts after his fall, all of which were taken over by the king, see Pollard (pp. 273–4).

130/7 **Doctor Collett:** John Colet (1467?–1519), the famous Dean of St. Paul's, who had built this house shortly before he died. Colet's dwelling is mentioned in Seebohm's *Oxford Reformers* (Everyman ed., p. 292) and a brief description of it is given in the *Life of Colet* printed by Wordsworth (p. 444).

130/9 **the passion weke:** See below (132/30 and n.).

131/3 **q^d oon among theme:** The council member who speaks here will probably remain unidentified, but it may be suggested that Cavendish is alluding to Sir Thomas More (from whom he could have got the story), the only man in the council who seems to have foreseen the turn that events were to take in the future. Not long before this More had remarked to Roper: 'I haue no cawse to be prowd [of the king's affection], for if my head could winne him a castle in Fraunce . . . it should not faile to goe' (Roper's *Life of More*, p. 21).

131/7 **lett vs do, etc.**: Perhaps echoing Luke, vi, 31, but the phrase is, of course, proverbial.

131/23 **a M^l marces:** See above (124/33–4 and n.). This sum was paid to Wolsey on 18 March (LP, V, p. 318).

132/3 **a M^l li:** Henry entrusted this money to Laurence Stubbs, the cardinal's receiver-general, with specific instructions that it be used only to pay his debts. But even this sum was insufficient to compensate Wolsey's creditors. See Stubbs's letter to Wolsey (LP, IV, 6390) and Pollard (p. 274).

132/16 Supply 'was' before 'greatly'.

132/30 **the passion weke:** Passion Week began on Sunday, 3 April, in 1530. By reckoning back from the date (Palm Sunday, 10 April) of Wolsey's arrival at Peterborough, we find that he left Richmond on Tuesday, 5 April.

132/32 **hendon:** The Abbot of Westminster at this time was John Islip, the last of the great masters of the Abbey. He was succeeded in 1532 by William Boston. The manor of Hendon had been given to Westminster by Richard le Rous in 1312 (Wordsworth, p. 616).

132/32 **the Rye:** Rye House in Hertfordshire, later the scene of the famous 'Rye House Plot' of June 1683. It was owned at this time by Maud Parr (1495–1531), the wife of Sir Thomas Parr (d. 1518) and the mother of Catherine Parr, the sixth and last queen of Henry VIII. See *Wills from Doctors Commons*, Camden Society, LXXXIII, 9–20.

133/2 **to Peterboroughe:** 9 April 1530. The king had been asked for letters of recommendation under the privy seal addressed to the various nobles with whom Wolsey stayed on his route northwards. That to the Abbot of Peterborough is dated 28 March (LP, IV, 6294).

133/4 **the thursday:** 21 April.

133/11 **maundy Thursday:** 14 April. The fifty-nine poor men each represented a year of the cardinal's life. This passage provides the best evidence for the date of Wolsey's birth (see above, 4/29 and n. and Pollard, p. 276, n. 1).

Historical Notes 245

133/17 the resurreccion: 17 April. By 'the resurreccion' Cavendish means the ceremonies connected with Easter. Singer (p. 309) quotes the following passage from the *Processionale secundum usum Sarum* (1555 ed., fol. 72) to illustrate the ritual: 'On Easter Day, before mass, and before the ringing of the bells, let the clerks assemble, and all the tapers in the church be lighted. Then two persons shall draw nigh to the sepulchre, and after it is censed let them take the cross out of the sepulchre, and one of them begin *Christus resurgens*. Then let the procession commence. After this they shall all worship (*adorent*) the cross. Then let all the crucifixes and images in the church be unveiled, etc.'

133/23-4 sir willam ffitzwilliam: Sir William Fitzwilliam (1460?-1534), not to be confused with Sir William Fitzwilliam, Earl of Southampton (d. 1542). Cavendish's Sir William was originally a merchant of London; he was instrumental in obtaining a new charter for the Taylors' Company in 1502 and was frequently in trouble with the City of London as a consequence of his action. See Charles M. Clode, *The Early History of the Guild of Merchant Taylors*, London, 1888, I, 36-7.

The reason why the City became so incensed over the new charter was that it gave the guild the privilege of admitting new members without restriction. Fitzwilliam's quarrel with the City came to a head a few years later when he was appointed Sheriff by the king and the city-elected candidate deposed. The Mayor and aldermen deprived him of his rights as a freeman of the City in consequence, but a Star-Chamber decree of 1511 (in which Wolsey almost certainly had a hand) remitted their decision. Thereafter, Fitzwilliam rose rapidly. Wolsey soon made him Treasurer of his household and a member of the Council. He was knighted in 1522. His house where the cardinal stayed was Milton Manor in Northampton, which Fitzwilliam had purchased in 1506 from Richard Wittelbury.

134/1 he reioysed: Wolsey had good reason to rejoice on this occasion: he had already written to Gardiner complaining about the charges he had to bear at Peterborough (LP, IV, 6299).

134/4 Thursday next: Wolsey left Peterborough on 21 April. He stayed four days with Sir William Fitzwilliam and left for Stamford on Monday, 25 April (below, 135/8).

135/9 the next day: 26 April. The gentleman with whom Wolsey lodged at Grantham was John Hall, Surveyor of Calais, and father of Arthur Hall (fl. 1563-1604) whose *Ten Books of Homers Iliades* (1581) are the first English translation of Homer.

135/10 **The next day:** Wolsey was at Newark on the 27th and rode to Southwell on the 28th. He stayed at the house of Archdeacon Magnus until his own manor at Southwell could be repaired; Magnus had already written to him that he did not have enough room and that, in any event, he would have to reside in his benefice himself (LP, IV, 6341; see below, 138/12 and n.). But the cardinal was not a man to be put off by the complaints of a mere archdeacon.

135/25 **sence . . . lyueres:** i.e. shortly after 18 March (see above, 132/15ff.), when Wolsey was paid the 1,000 marks out of Winchester.

136/9–12 The sentence structure is very compressed: 'for often changing . . . for riches, who will . . . abundance [brings it about that] the poor Commons, etc.'

136/17–18 **confesse . . . premunyre:** For the reasons which prompted Wolsey to this confession see above (113/29–31 and n.). Wolsey's explanation, as recorded by Cavendish in the following passage, is substantially in agreement with the discernible facts.

137/10 **a poore vykare:** A vicar's benefice at this time was worth £20 a year; Wolsey himself had estimated that he would need £4,000 a year to maintain himself after his fall (Pollard, p. 323).

137/19 **the nyght Crowe:** The allusion is, of course, to Anne Boleyn.

137/26–7 **Quia indignacio . . . est:** cf. Proverbs xvi, 14, Indignatio regis, nuntii mortis. Most men of the early Tudor period would have agreed with Wolsey's maxim: a few years later the Duke of Norfolk was to quote it ominously to More (Harpsfield, p. 165, following Roper, pp. 71–2), who replied: 'Is that all, my Lord? Then in good faith is there no mo*re* differens/betweene yo*ur* grace *and* me, but that I shall dye today, *and* yow tomorrowe.' Archbishop Warham had also used it in 1528, when he refused to aid Queen Catherine in her defence (above, 15/28 and n.).

138/12 **a prebendaries howsse:** The house of Archdeacon Magnus, who, despite his complaints (above, 135/10 and n.), had been forced to put Wolsey up for the time. The cardinal moved into his repaired palace at Southwell on 4 June. Whitsunday fell on 5 June in 1530.

139/1 **Corpus xpi** [i.e. Christi] **Eve:** 15 June.

139/12–13 **demaundyng what they ware:** i.e. 'asking who they were'. Cf. *Othello*, I, i, 94, 'What are you? My name is Roderigo.'

139/14 **m^r Breerton:** William Brereton (d. 1536) afterwards executed as one of Anne's lovers. The expense account of his journey with Wriothesley includes the item 'Guide to Southwell, 12d.' (LP, IV, 6489). The document to which Wolsey affixed his signature was the famous petition (dated 13 July 1530) from the clergy and nobility of England to Clement VII, begging him to accede to the king's wishes in the divorce case. As Pollard (p. 287, n. 2) points out, Cavendish was probably unaware of its contents; otherwise, he could scarcely have described the cardinal as so opposed to the divorce.

139/15 m^r **Wrothesley:** Thomas Wriothesley (1505–1550), a servant of Cromwell by February 1524, and Clerk of the Signet by 4 May 1530, the latter office probably accounting for his participation in this journey. He was created Earl of Southampton on 16 February 1547.

140/15 **the Erle of Shrewesburys:** George Talbot, fourth Earl of Shrewsbury (1468–1538), who had already had a long and full career under both Henry VII and Henry VIII. During the divorce he supported the king and gave evidence against the queen at the trial. After Wolsey's arrest, the Earl entertained him at Sheffield Castle for several weeks (below, pp. 163 ff.).

141/1 **vntill . . . Grease tyme:** About 1 September 1530. Cavendish, who is the chief authority for the stages of Wolsey's journey at this point, is not precise on the date. It would seem that the cardinal spent about four or five days on the road and arrived at Scrooby about 6–7 September. He left there 'aboughte the feast of Seynt Michell' (29 September, below 144/9) and reached Cawood on 2–3 October.

144/11 **vij^{en} myles:** Cawood is nine and a half miles from York, not seven.

144/32 **bylt . . . Castle:** On 18 August Cromwell wrote to Wolsey as follows: 'Sir, sum ther be, that doth alledge that Your Grace doth kepe to grete a house and famylye, and that ye are contynually buylding; for the love of God, therefore, I eftesones, as I often tymys have done, most hertelye beseche Your Grace to have respecte to every thing, and consideryng the time, to refraygne your self, for a season, from al maner byldyngges, more then mere necessite requireth' (*State Papers*, I, 366).

145/2 **sir Richard Tempest & m^r Bryan hastynges:** The cause of the quarrel between these two gentlemen must probably remain unknown but it may be noted that Sir Richard Tempest had been knighted at Tournai, 25 September 1513, and had served as Sheriff of York in 1517. He was at the Field of the Cloth of Gold in 1520 and later seems to have been a member of the Duke of Richmond's court in the North (LP, IV, 3551). Bryan Hastings, who appears to have been the younger of the two men, was knighted on 24 May 1533 at Greenwich before the coronation of Anne.

146/10–11 **very late/to dynne:** Dinner during this period usually took place at about ten or eleven o'clock in the morning. The *Northumberland Household Book* (London, 1827, p. 310) says that 'to x of the Clock that my Lorde goos to Dynner'.

146/21–3 **As it appered ... hyme:** See Cavendish's description of their laments at Wolsey's departure from Cawood (below, 161/22 ff.).

146/29 **Doctor hikden:** Doctor Brian Higden (d. 1539) became Dean of York in 1516, succeeding John Young, who had succeeded Wolsey himself on 17 May 1514. He is not to be confused with the Doctor John Higden who was Dean of Cardinal College, Oxford (below, 176/34–5). For Brian Higden, see Le Neve (III, 126).

146/30 **the treasorer:** The Treasurer of York at this time was Lancelot Collynson (d. 1538), who had held the office since 1514 (Le Neve, III, 162).

146/34 **so long ... theme:** A delicate euphemism on the part of the doctors; in fact, Wolsey had never entered his diocese since the day he received the archbishopric.

148/4 **the next monday:** Monday, 7 November.

148/7–8 **the comen fame:** It was not only Wolsey's coming 'enthronisation' that caused rumours to spread about his plans to return to power: he had summoned a convocation to meet at York on 7 November without waiting for the normal royal mandate and apparently intended to go through with it despite the warnings he received (Pollard, pp. 292–3).

148/26–7 **the vamppes of my hosyn:** Wolsey may have been recalling the manner in which his successful rival for the papacy, Adrian VI, had proceeded to his installation as Pope. According to Harpsfield (p. 42 and Chambers' note, p. 324) Adrian had walked barefoot through the city of Rome on his way to St. Peter's in January 1522.

149/4–5 **the Mayor:** The Mayor of York in 1530 was Sir George Lawson (d. 1543), later a nember of Parliament for York. The York Civic Records (*Yorkshire Archaeologial Society*, Record Series, CVI and CVIII, 1942–3) contain numerous notices of his activities.

Historical Notes 249

150/29 **sir walter welshe:** Sir Walter Walsh is frequently mentioned in the *Letters and Papers* and in the *Privy Purse Expences*. He had recently married the widow of Sir William Compton and was undoubtedly in the king's esteem (see LP, IV, 4477). It may or may not be significant that on 31 October 1530 the king made him a present of £10 (*Privy Purse Expences*, p. 85); Walsh started North to arrest Wolsey on 1 November.

150/31 **the Erle of Northehumberland:** Henry Percy, the sixth Earl, who has already figured prominently in the early part of the *Life*. See above (29/34 and n.).

151/13-14 **doctor Augusteyn:** Agostino d'Agostini, a native of Venice and the nephew of Ghinucci, Bishop of Worcester. 'He had entered Wolsey's service about 1527, was given by him the prebend of Wetwang in York cathedral, and was naturalized in 1530. He became in 1532 physician to Wolsey's old colleague Campeggio, was a friend of Sir T. Elyot, kept up a correspondence with Cromwell, and referred to Wolsey as *heros meus felicis memoriae*' (Pollard, p. 296). Cavendish's representation of Agostini as the Judas who betrayed his master does not seem to be supported by the facts of the situation. He was, of course, arrested as a traitor, but this seems to have been due to his role in carrying letters for the cardinal; it is 'practically certain' (Pollard, p. 295) that, once in London, he turned king's evidence and thus implicated the cardinal, but he did not forge the correspondence with the foreign ministers.

151/17 **raylyng:** Apparently *O.E.D. v.* 3: 'flowing, gushing down, usually said of blood'. But Cavendish seems to be using the word in a transferred sense; in his example it is the cross which 'rails down', thus causing blood to flow. Cf. the *O.E.D.*'s quotation from Capgrave: 'Ffro thi eynez lete the water now be thi cheekis reyle.'

151/18 **doctor Bonners:** Edmund Bonner (1500?-69), the famous 'bloody Bonner' of Foxe's martyrology. He had become Wolsey's chaplain in 1529 and had been frequently employed by him as a messenger to Gardiner and Cromwell.

151/29 **Malum Omen:** For Wolsey's superstitions, see the note on the 'dun cow' passage (above, 127/23) and below (170/10 and n.).

151/33 **Pountfrett Abbey:** i.e. at Pontefract Abbey on 6 November after his arrest.

152/21 **the ffriday next:** 4 November 1530.

153/35-154/1 **his gentilman vssher:** Possibly Cavendish himself?

154/17 **to se ... howsse:** As Wordsworth (p. 639) notes, 'this was a very natural expression for Wolsey to use, although it conveys somewhat of a reproof'. The Earl lived at Wressil Castle, only ten miles from Cawood.

155/17 **My lord ... treason:** Hall's account of Wolsey's arrest (p. 773) differs in some details from Cavendish's: 'he [the Earl] ... came to the Manor of Cawod ... and when he was brought to the Cardinal in his chamber, he said to him, my lord I pray you take pacience, for here I arrest you. Arrest me sayd ye Cardinal, yea sayd the erle I haue a commaundement so to do: you haue no such power sayd the Cardinal, for I am both a Cardinal and a Legate de Latere and a pere of the College of Rome & ought not to be arrested by any temporal power, for I am not subiect to that power, wherfore if you arrest me, I will withstand it: well sayd the erle here is the kings Commission (which he shewed him) and therfore I charge you to obey, etc.'

155/25-6 **an aunciente grudge:** Wolsey's reference is apparently to strife that had existed between the earl's ancestors and former Archbishops of York. There was, of course, much bad blood between the earl and his father and the cardinal. The Percy-Anne episode has already been mentioned by Cavendish himself. In 1516, the fifth earl, who was a friend of Buckingham, was imprisoned in the Fleet, 'put there so that Wolsey might have the credit of getting him out' (*D.N.B.*). When the fifth earl died in 1527, the cardinal appropriated, among other effects, his chapel books. See young Percy's letter on the subject (Singer, p. 462).

156/14 **Sedell:** Schedule, 'originally a separate paper or slip of parchment accompanying or appended to a document, and containing explanatory or supplementary matter' (*O.E.D.*).

160/6-7 **thes wordes of scripture:** 'Scripture' in Cavendish's day could refer to any religious writing, not, as now, to the Bible alone. Wolsey's words form part of a liturgical *responsorium* composed by King Robert of France (c. 970–1031). The text is in Migne (*Patrologia Latina*, vol. 141, col. 944) where the only differences from Cavendish's words are 'despicabilis' for 'desplicabilis' (see the emendation) and 'retributionis' for 'tribulacionis'; it continues with the response 'Nobis ergo petimus piis subveniat meritis, honorificati a Patre qui est in coelis. Invenietur in laudem, etc.' According to Migne, the hymn is still sung in France, and is found in 'quelques Processionaux au commun des martyrs' (*ibid.*, col. 902).

It is perhaps worth mentioning that the 'O Constantia' occurs in the *Elucidatorium Ecclesiasticum* (Paris, 1515, I use the Basel edition of 1517) of Jodocus Clichtovaeus (Josse Clichtove, 1472–1543),

Historical Notes 251

where it is the sixth responsorium for the feast of the Blessed Sacrament (Sigs. S_4–S_{4v}). Clichtove, a noted theologian of his day, was director of studies to Louis Guillard, Bishop-elect of Tournai, who disputed that see with Wolsey for over four years (1514–18; see above, 15/2–3 and n.). It is not at all impossible that Clichtove was known personally to the cardinal. His book collects a vast body of ecclesiastical hymns and gives full explanations of their symbology. In his comment on the 'O Constantia' he remarks that 'hoc responsorium elegans admodum & suave, fertur composuisse Robertus rex Franciae, uir non minus literarum & uirtutum splendor, atque regia dignitate spectabilis. In cuius responsorii fronte allusisse dicitur ad nomen reginae uxoris suae, quae Constantia uocabatur, praefigendo id nomen (communiter tamen sumptum) in capite sui operis.' The story is also in Migne (col. 902) and in Helen Waddell's *The Wandering Scholars* (New York, 1927), p. 73.

160/18 **the next day:** Wolsey left Cawood on Sunday, 6 November, reaching Pontefract Abbey that night (below, 162/30).

162/3–4 **lett...Northumberland:** Northumberland had remained behind at Cawood to complete the inventory of Wolsey's possessions. This inventory, signed by the Earl and 'Walter Walch', is calendared in LP, IV, 6748, item 12.

162/7 **sir Roger lasselles:** Sir Roger Lascelles of Sowerby and Brackenbury in Lincolnshire, captain of Norham Castle for the earl. Four letters from him to Northumberland on Scottish affairs are calendared in the *Letters and Papers* (IV, 4674, 4709, 4720 and 4728, all from August and September 1528). James V refers to him as 'Master Leisence' in a letter to Henry VIII of 22 June 1529 (LP, IV, 5706).

162/16–17 **iij^{re} shyrtes of heare:** For William Forrest's comment on Wolsey's hair shirt, see Appendix A.

162/20 **to Poumfrett:** Wolsey's despairing words were no doubt inspired by his knowledge that Pontefract Castle, or 'Pomfret' as it was generally pronounced, had been the scene of state executions in times past. Cf. the words of Lord Rivers in *Richard III* (III, iii, 9–14):

> O Pomfret, Pomfret! O thou bloody prison,
> Fatal and ominous to noble peers!
> Within the guilty closure of thy walls
> Richard the second here was hack'd to death;
> And, for more slander to thy dismal seat,
> We give thee up our guiltless blood to drink.

162/33 **The next day:** Monday, 7 November. Wolsey spent the night at the Blackfriars, Doncaster, and arrived at Sheffield on 8 November.

163/10-11 **therle of Shrewsbury:** For Shrewsbury, see above (140/15 and n.). He had married his second wife, Elizabeth, daughter of Sir Richard Walden of Erith, Kent, about 1512.

164/17 **xviij^{en} dayes after:** This statement is not contradicted by Cavendish's later remark, 'the space after of a fouerthnyght' (167/10), which refers to the number of days Wolsey spent at Sheffield *after* his long lamentation to the earl (below, ll. 27ff.) and not to the whole period of his stay. But Cavendish's eighteen days should be sixteen, for Wolsey arrived on the 8th and left, under Kingston's arrest, on the 24th.

164/34-165/1 **than he ... mystrust:** The word order is inverted: 'than for any mistrust he hath, etc.'

165/1 **Alas/q^d my lord:** The cardinal's lament contains many echoes of the Psalms. Cf., for example, his 'ffor he is my stafe ... ennemyes' (165/18-20) with Ps. xxiii, 4, 'thy rod and thy staff they comfort me'; also Ps. xxxi, 2-3, 'Be thou my strong rock, for a house of defence to save me. For thou art my rock and my fortress; therefore for thy name's sake lead me and guide me.' Note especially how Wolsey's 'hauyng non other refuge ... contynually Imagynyth' (165/29-33) echoes Ps. lvii, 1, 'Yea, in the shadow of thy wings will I make my refuge', and the whole of Ps. lix with its references to the enemies that 'return at evening and wander up and down'. Cf. also Ps. lxi, 2.

167/15 **at certyne season:** By counting back from the day of Wolsey's death (29 November) it can be ascertained that this was Tuesday the 22nd, the date of Kingston's arrival at Sheffield.

168/3-4 **oon article of myn othe:** Evidently Cavendish had sworn that no medicines would be given to the cardinal unless his captors were first informed of the fact.

168/22 **laske:** For the details of Wolsey's disease see below (178/22-3 and n.).

168/32 **sir willam kyngstone:** Sir William Kingston (d. 1540) had been knighted at Flodden in 1513. A favourite of Henry VIII, he was made Constable of the Tower on 28 May 1524.

170/10 **M^r kyngesston/q^d he:** According to an anecdote preserved by Fuller (*Church History*, II, 51) Wolsey had been told that 'he should have his end at Kingston'. For this reason the cardinal is said to have avoided passing through Kingston-on-Thames on his way to the court. Wolsey's reliance on soothsayers and fortune tellers is mentioned in the contemporary *Chronicle of King Henry VIII* (p. 3) and by William Forrest in *Grisild the Second* (p. 52), who also tells of his belief that a woman would cause his fall:

> Hee counseled (men saide) withe Astronomyers
> (Or what other secte I cannot well saye,
> Weare they Sothesayers or weare they lyers),
> Whyther he shoulde fall or florysche alwaye;
> Whois answeare was, he shoulde come to decaye
> By meanys (they fownde) of a certayne woman,
> But what shee sholde bee they coulde not saye than.

For other instances of the cardinal's superstitions, see above (127/23 and n., and 151/29).

171/7 **Imynent:** 'imminent', probably for 'eminent', noteworthy. The *O.E.D.* gives one example (from 1642) of this confusion. But 'imminent' in the sense of 'threatening' is also possible here.

171/12 **I perceyve ... knowe:** Cf. Wolsey's words to Kingston later (173/20): 'I knowe what is provydid for me.' The cardinal believed that he was destined for the Tower and his suspicions are proved to have been correct by an entry in the treasurer's accounts (LP, V, p. 322): 'To Sir Wm. Kingston, captain of the King's Guard, sent to the earl of Shrewsbury with divers of the Guard, for the conveyance of the cardinal of York to the tower, 40 l.'

173/34 **Colour Adustum:** Cavendish's variation of the normal sixteenth-century 'choler adust', a disease whose symptoms were dryness of the body, heat, thirst, black or burnt colour of the blood, and deficiency of serum in it, atrabilious or 'melancholic' complexion, etc. Cavendish's use of the term to refer to the excreted bile is paralleled by the *O.E.D.*'s 1601 example, 'Choler black and adust, what purgeth downward.'

174/2 **doctor Nicholas:** The only reference to this Doctor Nicholas which I have been able to discover occurs in the *Privy Purse Expences* (p. 192), where he is listed as having received a reward from the king. There is a 'Nicholas' mentioned as being in Wolsey's service in a letter from Vannes to the cardinal of 7 June 1529 (LP, IV, 5656), but he is probably not Cavendish's doctor, who is described as 'being w^t therle'.

174/6–7 **if therle ... byn:** i.e. if the Earl of Shrewsbury had not prevented him from doing so.

174/8 **the next day:** 24 November, Wolsey was taken ill on the 22nd, the day of Kingston's arrival, and on the 23rd he was too weak to move (above, 173/32).

174/14 **hardwyke hall:** As the Rev. Joseph Hunter was the first to point out, this was not the famous Hardwick Hall in Derbyshire, later the home of the Countess of Shrewsbury during Elizabeth's reign, but Hardwick-upon-Line in Nottinghamshire, four miles from Newstead Abbey. See Singer's note (pp. 379–80).

174/15 **the next day:** 25 November.

174/16 **and the next day:** Saturday, 26 November.

174/20 **the Abbott:** Richard Pexall or Pexsall, who was Abbot of St. Mary's, Leicester, from 1509 to 1533. Leicester Abbey belonged to the Canons Regular of Saint Augustine, an order in which Wolsey himself was a brother. In 1518 the canons had appealed to the cardinal to maintain their authority over refractory brethren (LP, IV, p. dcxiv, n. 1).

174/30 **vppon Monday:** 28 November.

175/9 **doctor Palmes:** Doctor George Palmes, who, in 1544, became Archdeacon of York. A short account of his preferments is given in Nichols's *History of Leicester* (I, ii, 271, n. 4) and in the *Alumni Cantabrigienses* (I, iii, 302). On 28 January 1531 William Lelegrave wrote to Kingston reporting that Doctor Palmes had told him about a debt of £100 which was owed to Wolsey by the Prior of St. Oswald's in Gloucestershire (LP, V, 66). He is probably the George Palmes referred to at this time in the *Letters and Papers* (V, 572 and 1688) as 'Receiver of the revenues of the Archdeaconry of York'.

175/18–19 **Mr Vyncent:** David Vincent, who had been one of the grooms of Wolsey's privy chamber (LP, IV, 4198, V, p. 325; Pollard, p. 299). Vincent was made Keeper of the Great Wardrobe at Richmond on 29 December 1530, only a month after Wolsey's death (LP, IV, 6803, [29]). In 1532 he received the same office at Greenwich (LP, V, 838, [31]). Cavendish's story of the £1,500 for which Wolsey was accountable to the king rests, as might be expected, solely on his authority. Vincent had left Wolsey at Scrooby in September (below, 184/15–16) and had been arrested later on suspicion of having stolen the money.

176/5 **a boke at Cawood:** The 'book' does not appear in the inventory as calendared in the *Letters and Papers* (IV, 6748, item 12).

176/33 **sir Iohn Alyn:** Sir John Alen or Alyn was a prominent

Historical Notes 255

London alderman, who had been mayor in 1526; he is frequently referred to in the *Letters and Papers*, where we learn that he was one of the commissioners appointed to make inquisition in London of Wolsey's possessions during the summer of 1530 (IV, 6516, item 1) and that the cardinal owed him a sum of £83 12s. 'for arras . . . at his departure northwards' (IV, 6748, item 15).

176/33–4 **sir Richard Gressham:** Sir Richard Gresham (1485?–1549) was not knighted until 18 October 1537, in which year he was Mayor of London. A member of the Mercers' Company, he had had extensive dealings with Wolsey in the past. The cardinal owed him a sum of £226. 12s. 5d. at the time of his arrest at Cawood (LP, IV, 6748, item 15).

176/34 **the m^r of Savoye:** The Master of the Savoy at this time was William Holgill, who was Wolsey's surveyor and who had been active in the dissolution of the monasteries under Cromwell (LP, IV, 633, 2193, 4547, 6329, etc.). The inventory taken at Cawood shows that Wolsey owed him £100, which may or may not be part of the debt mentioned here. The Savoy had been founded as a London palace on 12 February 1246 from a grant of land given by Henry III to Peter of Savoy. It was destroyed by Wat Tyler's mob in 1381. Henry VII rebuilt it as a hospital about 1505 and endowed it in his will.

176/34–5 **Doctor hykden:** Doctor John Higden, who had been elected to the presidency of Magdalen College, Oxford, in 1516; he had resigned in 1525 to become Dean of Cardinal College, a position which he held until 15 January 1531, when all the lands and patronage of the college were finally surrendered to the king (Le Neve, II, 511; III, 561 and, for other preferments held by Higden, II, 190 and III, 223). John Higden may have been a brother of Cavendish's 'Doctor hikden Deane of the chirche of yorke', for whom see above (146/29 and n.).

176/35–177/1 **the Treasorer:** Lancelot Collynson (above, 146/30 and n.).

177/1–2 **the Dean of yorke:** John Higden (above, 146/29 and n.).

177/2 **parson Elis:** Apparently the 'Mr. Elis, the priest', who is referred to in the *Letters and Papers* (IV, 6186) as a member of Wolsey's household at the time of his death. He is perhaps to be identified with the 'Mons. Ellys' who was in the cardinal's suite on the French embassy of 1527 (LP, IV, 3216). We also hear of a 'Sir Nich. Ellys, clk.' who was apparently in Wolsey's service in 1529 and who may have been the 'Elis' mentioned as a bearer of a letter from the cardinal to the Lord Chief Justice about 10 August 1530 (LP, IV, 5331 and 6555).

177/3 **my Steward:** A letter to Wolsey of 10 June 1530 mentions that 'Master Donington' is rumoured to be Wolsey's steward, a man 'who is not beloved in that country' (LP, IV, 6447). This was probably Thomas Donington, one of Wolsey's chaplains, who appears to have been in the king's displeasure in January 1530 (LP, IV, 6164). On 10 August of that year Donington wrote to Cromwell thanking him for his services, which may have entailed some pleading of his cause with the king. The only other reference to Donington which I have been able to discover occurs in a letter of 27 March 1529, where he is said to have failed to perform his duty (LP, IV, 5400). What this duty was or how Donington failed in it is not specified in the letter.

178/12 **saynt Androwes Eve:** Tuesday, 29 November, the day of Wolsey's death.

178/22–3 **I haue ... desease:** For Wolsey's pride in his medical knowledge, see above (121/34 and n.). According to Hall (p. 774), the cardinal died 'for very feblenes of nature caused by purgacions and vomites'. William Forrest (see Appendix A) had heard that his death was brought about from taking 'too, too many' pills. Augustine, who was not with Wolsey at Leicester, wrote to Norfolk about six months later that the cardinal did not die of poison, as had been rumoured, 'sed tremore cordis et atra bili, forsa[n] dolore animi, jampridem contracto' (LP, V, 283, 3 June 1531).

178/28 **the viij**[th] **day:** Wolsey had been taken ill on 22 November (above, 167/15 and n.).

178/34–5 **But if I ... kyng:** A remarkable parallel to Wolsey's dying words is found in Robert Lindsay of Pitscottie's *Historie and Cronicles of Scotland* (ed. A. J. G. Mackay, 3 vols., 1899–1911, Scottish Text Society, I, 393): 'And in the meane tyme the said Schir James Hammilltoun [who is appearing to James V in a vision after the king had had him executed] sould say into the king of Scottland as efter followis: "Thou hes gart slay me wrangouslie and uniustlie, ffor I was innocent of the cryme that was layd to me; thocht I was ane sinner aganis God zeit [i.e. 'yet'] I faillzett not to the. Had I bene allis goode ane servant to my god as I was to the, I had not dieit the deid."' Pitscottie's history was not composed until 1576–9 and it is not impossible that the Scots writer had heard of Wolsey's deathbed words. Cf. also Skelton's *Magnificence* (Works, I, 290): 'In welthe to beware, yf I had had grace,/Never had I bene brought in this case.'

179/13–15 **And rather ... daynger:** As early as 20 August 1528 Du Bellay had written to Montmorency that 'His [Wolsey's] great difficulty is that he knows his master to be the most avaricious man in the world' (LP, IV, 4649).

179/25 **the lutarnaunce:** Wolsey himself had not been unduly severe in his proceedings against heretics. He had burned the reformers' books, but it is a matter of record that 'there is no instance of the extreme penalty being inflicted during Wolsey's legacy by the cardinal himself, his commissaries, or the diocesan synods whose jurisdiction he effectively superseded' (Pollard, p. 214).

179/28 **the kyng of Beame:** For the Bohemian Revolt, see Appendix B.

180/28 **kyng Rycherd:** Wolsey refers to Wat Tyler's rebellion of June 1381. On 14 June Richard II met the rebels at Smithfield and gave them charters of freedom, which were revoked on 2 July. Tyler himself was killed at the Smithfield meeting and John Ball was executed on 14 July.

181/5 **sir Iohn OldCastell:** Sir John Oldcastle (1378?–1417), the original of Shakespeare's Falstaff. He became a Lollard about 1410, was arrested after his failure to recant in 1413, but escaped from the Tower. Recaptured in 1417, he was sentenced as a traitor and heretic and hanged on the same day, 14 December.

181/25–6 **than we began ... passion:** This was the normal deathbed procedure in Cavendish's day. John Mirk's *Instructions for Parish Priests* (E.E.T.S., o.s. 31) lists seven 'specialle interrogacions The whiche a Curat aught to aske euery cristene persone that liethe in the extremytie of dethe'. The seventh and last of these instructs the priest to say: 'Belevest thowe fully that Criste dyed for the, and that thowe may neuer be saved but by the Merite of Cristes passione, and thanne thankest therof god with thyne harte asmoche as thowe mayest? he answerethe, Yee' (pp. 64–5).

182/14–15 **vnto hyme & to thabbot:** Apparently 'calling to the abbot to come unto him also'.

182/15 **the order of hys buriall.** Although Cavendish, naturally enough, does not mention the fact, Wolsey was buried in the so-called 'tyrants' grave' at Leicester Abbey where Richard III had been interred. By 4 December Chapuys had noted that 'gissent tous deux en une mesme eglize, la quelle l'on commence desja appeller la sepulture des tyrans' (Pollard, p. 302).

182/19 **the mayor of leycester:** The Mayor of Leicester in 1530 was William Tebbe, a baker, who had been born about 1480. He died about 1543 and was himself buried at St. Mary's (*Roll of the Mayors . . . of Leicester*, ed. H. Hartopp, Leicester, 1935, p. 58).

183/17 **seynt Androwes day:** 30 November.

183/19–20 **seynt Nicholas Eve:** 5 December. Cavendish saw the king on the next day.

183/35–184/1 **sir Iohn Gagge:** Sir John Gage (1479–1556), who was Henry VIII's Vice-Chamberlain from 1528 until 1540.

184/4 **sir harry Norres:** For Norris, see above (93/4 and n.).

186/21 **m^r Ratclyfe:** Robert Radcliffe or Ratcliffe (1483–1542), the father of Cavendish's 'yong . . . m^r Ratclyfe' (above, 61/17). The elder Radcliffe had been a prominent courtier throughout the reign of Henry VIII and on 8 December 1529 had been made Earl of Sussex.

187/16 **m^r Secretorye:** Stephen Gardiner, for whom see above (79/16 and n.). Gardiner's being at Hanworth is perhaps to be explained by the fact that he had recently (July 1530) received a grant of arable lands and rents in that honour (*D.N.B.*).

187/21 **the next day:** 7 December.

188/13 **Tezaurisat . . . ea:** Psalms xxxviii, 7 (A.V., xxxix, 6).

188/16–17 **an other . . . lyfe:** Perhaps echoing Ecclesiastes vi, 2, 'Vir, cui dedit Deus divitias et substantiam et honorem, et nihil deest animae suae ex omnibus quae desiderat, nec tribuit ei potestatem Deus ut comedat ex eo, sed homo extraneus vorabit illud.' The 'other person' must, of course, be Henry VIII. Cavendish repeats his account of Wolsey's final sentiments in his poems (II, 13), where the cardinal says: 'Some oon, perchance, shall me thereof dyscharge,/ Whom I most hate, and spend it owt at large.'

APPENDIX A

William Forrest's
The History of Grisild the Second (1558)

Cavendish's reference to Queen Catherine as 'a perfect Grysheld' (35/21–2) assumes a larger significance when viewed in the light of the popularity of the Griselda legend in the sixteenth century. It seems to have been the practice of those who sympathized with the Queen's misfortunes to apply to her the name of Boccaccio's heroine.[1] Thus we find William Forrest dedicating his *History of Grisild the Second*[2] to Queen Mary as a token of the grief he felt for her mother's sufferings. It is of interest that Forrest finished his poem on 25 June 1558, one day after Cavendish put his signature to his manuscript of the *Life of Wolsey*. In the course of this poem[3] Forrest describes many of Wolsey's activities in language which often corresponds quite closely to that of the *Life*. It would seem to be by no means impossible that Forrest and Cavendish were friends, and that Cavendish showed Forrest the manuscript on which he was working at some time before June 1558.

Such a possibility is rendered more likely by the fact that Forrest seems to rely very little on the printed accounts of the Queen which were available to him. He does tell us that the Prior of Leicester Abbey informed him that Wolsey wore a hair shirt during his last illness,[4] but his major source of information seems to have come from someone who knew the cardinal well:

> Of whome [Wolsey] ferdre I shall somewhat disclose
> (By honest credyble information)
> Howe hee fell into tribulation.
>   (p. 58; cf. Cavendish's mention of 'some approved
>   & credible person' at 3/18–19)

[1] The legend was, of course, easily accessible to English readers in Chaucer's *Clerk's Tale*.

[2] Ed. by W. D. Macray for the Roxburghe Club (London, 1875). William Forrest, who had, according to Macray, spent some time at Cardinal College, Oxford, was at this time a royal chaplain. See the account of him in the *D.N.B.*

[3] The poem, in which Henry VIII figures as 'Walter' and Catherine as 'Grisild', is in broken-backed stanzas of rhyme royal, the same metre as that of Cavendish's poems.

[4] And to signyfie that hee was penytent,
Certaynlye, the Pryor I herde thus saye. (p. 61)

Whether or not this 'information' came from George Cavendish remains a moot point, but the following stanzas, in which Forrest lists two causes for the fall of the cardinal, are very close to the tenor and phrasing of Cavendish's narrative:

> A certayne younge lorde [Percy] in his Cowrte dyd dwell
> Whoe shewed pretence to this conclusion,
> (Whyther of earnest, other illusion,
> The veary certayntee scace saye I can)
> For to haue macht with the ladye *Anne*.
>
> His lorde (the *Cardynall*) as hee thearof knwe
> He raged withe hym outragyouslye,
> Protestinge he shoulde his entreprise rwe
> If eauer he herde hym vse her companye;
> This was before she was ordayned ladye;
> Whiche from her knowledge was not kept secret,
> Whearfore longe tyme she muche ynwardlye fret.
>   (Cf. the Percy episode in Cavendish, 29/34 ff., especially 30/20–2)
>
> Thother occasion was (as is saide) this:
> When *Walter* on her dyd firste caste his mynde,
> He asked the *Cardynall* what his aduyse is,
> Whoe answearde hym, as after [s]he dyd fynde,
> She was not for hym in anye maner kynde,
> Vnlesse for Concubyne he wolde her take,
> But as his Queene her clearlye to forsake.
>   (pp. 58–9)

Forrest's depiction of Queen Catherine parallels Cavendish's account closely. We learn that

> In perfecte charitee shee alwayes aboade
> And thanked God howe eauer it dyd frame,
>   (p. 57)

and that during the trial, when she made her speech before the king,

> Shee saide, to hym she was true wedded Wife,
> All Christendome ouer can wytnes the same,
> So wolde shee acknowledge duryinge her life,
> Howe eauer otherwise hee pleased her to name;
> As for his owne Royalme, for feare they did frame
> To the fulfillinge of his fixed mynde,
> Witheout respectinge what Conscience dothe bynde.

> Shee added, his Father was thought man of wytt
> And wyttelye he wrought. . . .
> (pp. 82–3)

Most of these details can, it is true, be found in Hall (p. 755) but the following account of Wolsey's death is almost certainly that of an eye-witness, some of it, no doubt, from the Prior of Leicester Abbey, but some, perhaps, from George Cavendish himself:

> Which sodayne nues [Wolsey's arrest] put hym in
> mortal fraye;
> Notwithestandinge, withe muche trobeled harte,
> Backwardys to *Lecestre* he dyd reuert.
>
> In whiche journeyinge by the wayes (doubtles)
> Hee tooke certayne pyllys, his stomake to purge,
> Replenysched with greuous heauynes
> For this sodayne tempestyous surge,
> Rysinge (as he thought) throughe the *Merqueses* grudge;
> So that of necessytee by the waye
> He tooke restynge at *Lecestre* Abbaye;
>
> Wheare, thorowe woorkynge of the said peelys,
> (Whiche, as I herde tell, weare too too manye)
> And thorowe sorowe hymself he theare feealys
> His life to forgoe witheoute all remeadye.
> No longe was the tyme while he dyd theare lye,
> Not passinge eyght dayes at the veary moste,
> Tyll he was foarsed to yealde vpp the goste.
>
> Before he departed, right Christyanlye
> He sent for the Pryor and was confest,
> The Euchariste moste reuerentlye
> Receauynge into his penytent brest,
> Askynge God mercye withe harte moste earnest
> For that (in his tyme) by will, deade and thought,
> Agaynste His goodnes he had euer myswrought.
>
> And to signyfie that hee was penytent,
> Certaynlye, the Pryor I herde thus saye,
> A shurte of heare was his indument
> Next to his bodye, when he thear deadde lay;
> For whome hartelye it behoaueth to praye,
> Sithe hee heere ended so penytentlye,
> To whome (no doubte) God grauntethe His mercye.

> What thoughe he lyued muche remyssyuelye,
> Farre out of the trade of his profession,
> Yeat dyinge (as hee dyd) penytentlye,
> His sowle (no doubtys) hathe heauyns ingression
> By hauynge in harte vycis suppression;
> For, thoughe mannys life bee neauer so infecte,
> God (speciallye) his ende dothe respecte.
> (pp. 60–1)

This is not the place to go into the many different phases of the development of the Griselda legend in sixteenth-century England, but it may perhaps be noted that among the books (in fact, the only vernacular book) which the humanist Vives recommended for the Princess Mary was 'Gresilda vulgata jam fabula'.[1] Cavendish himself later repeats his reference to the Queen in his poems (II, 97), when he makes Henry VIII say she was like

> Unto pacient Greseld, if ever there ware any;
> For lyke hyr paciente there hathe not regned many.

We know also that Ralph Radcliffe had written a play on Griselda in either Latin or English between 1540 and 1542.[2] It is possible that this is the same play as that known as *The Play of Patient Grissell*,[3] generally attributed to John Phillip, which was acted in the early years of Elizabeth's reign. Three further versions of the story may be noted: Dekker's *The Pleasant Comoedye of Patient Grissill* (1603);[4] *The Ancient, True, and Admirable History of Patient Grisel*, a prose tract of 1619; and *The Pleasant and Sweet History of Patient Grissell*, an undated (1630?) tract in prose and verse.[5]

[1] *Privy Purse Expenses of the Princess Mary*, ed. F. Madden (London, 1831), pp. cxxiii–cxxiv.
[2] It is mentioned by Bale, *Index Britanniae Scriptorum*, ed. R. L. Poole and M. Bateson, Oxford, 1902, p. 333. See also C. H. Herford, *Studies in the Literary Relations of England and Germany in the Sixteenth Century*, Cambridge, 1886, pp. 111–12 and C. W. Roberts, *An Edition of John Phillip's 'Commondye of Pacient and Meeke Grissil'*, Univ. of Illinois Abstract of Thesis, Urbana, 1938, pp. 6–11.
[3] Ed. for the Malone Society (1909) by R. B. McKerrow and W. W. Greg. For the problem of authorship, see Roberts, *loc. cit.*
[4] Ed. by Grosart in vol. V of *The Non-Dramatic Works of Thomas Dekker*, Huth Library, London, 1886.
[5] Both the latter pieces were edited for the Percy Society, vol. III, London, 1841, and the former of them also by H. B. Wheatley, London, for the Villon Society, 1885.

APPENDIX B

The Battle of Pavia and the Bohemian Revolt

Cavendish's accounts of the Battle of Pavia (37/1–42/8) and the Bohemian Revolt (179/28–180/22) contain several serious violations of historical fact and embrace errors which go far beyond the simple slips of memory that have been discussed in the Introduction (above, p. xxxviff.). Since both of these events play a considerable part in the development of his biography and since he was not an eye-witness to either of them, I have thought it desirable to append the following discussion of the possible sources from which he may have obtained his information.

I. *The Battle of Pavia*

The revolt of Charles, Duke of Bourbon (1489–1527) from Francis I began in the early 1520s.[1] By 1523 the Duke was negotiating with the agents of Charles V and Henry VIII, with whom he concluded treaties which bound him and his forces to aid them in a coalition against Francis. In August 1524 Bourbon had besieged Marseilles but he was forced to retreat into Italy in September when Francis advanced upon him. The French soon took Milan, fifteen miles north of Pavia, and invested the latter town on 28 October; the Imperial forces, led by Bourbon and Pescara, had meanwhile retired to Lodi, fifteen miles to the east.

In Pavia itself, the gallant Antonio de Leyva commanded the besieged garrison. Despite the difficulty of obtaining supplies, he managed to keep up the morale of his forces, who frequently sallied out against the French army. On the night of 24–25 February 1525 Bourbon and Pescara launched their attack to relieve the town. Their troops

> made a breach at three points in the walls of the park [which surrounded Francis's camp]. The soldiers wore white shirts in order that they might recognize each other; they marched in perfect order, in silence. Then, at daybreak, the imperial army penetrated into the park through the breaches. The French artillery at first ravaged Pescara's troops, who were forced to defile on the flank before it,

[1] The best modern account of the battle (followed in this discussion) is in Ernest Lavisse's *Histoire de France* (Paris, 1900–11), V, i, 217–24 (for the events leading up to Bourbon's revolt) and V, ii, 29–37 (for the battle itself).

but, little by little, the Spanish army became concentrated and entered the royal camp.

It was then that Francis I, abandoning his position, deployed his army before its entrenchments: in the front ranks, the men at arms, commanded by himself and flanked by German mercenaries, in the rear the Duke d'Alençon, further off, facing Pavia, La Palice. The king hurled himself at his enemies, thus masking his artillery, and he did it so quickly that the infantrymen could not follow him. Thus, having overthrown those whom he encountered before him, he found himself cut off, his gendarmes decimated by arquebusiers that Pescara had mixed in with his cavalry. Attacked apart [i.e. cut off from their leader], the foot-soldiers succumbed after an energetic struggle; the Swiss fought badly and broke their ranks in disorder. At that moment, Leyva left Pavia and hurled himself on the camp, while the Duke d'Alençon fled from the field of battle.

(Lavisse, V, ii, 36, my translation)

The king was surrounded and, though he fought bravely, soon captured. 6,000–8,000 French were killed, 'among them the greatest lords of France'. The plain, says Lavisse, 'was covered with blood for several days'.

So runs a modern retelling of the battle; nor does it differ greatly from the accounts of the sixteenth-century historians, none of whom was so confused about Pavia as Cavendish shows himself to be in his narrative. Although Cavendish is correct in his resumé of the events that led up to the investment of the town, he gets the central situation of the siege itself completely reversed. Bourbon was not in Pavia but instead came to its relief with Pescara. Cavendish could have found a correct account of the matter in Hall (pp. 691–3) but he does not seem to have consulted it on this occasion. Other sixteenth-century historians, though they vary in the details of the battle itself, do not make the mistake of putting the Duke in the town. Thus Sleidan,[1] Guicciardini,[2] and, later, de Serres[3] give versions of the battle that accord fairly well with those of modern historians. Stowe and Holinshed, when they adopted Cavendish's narrative, apparently did not notice his

[1] *A Famouse Cronicle of oure time, called Sleidanes Commentaries*, translated out of Latin into Englishe by Ihon Daus. London, 1560, Sig. K5.
[2] *The Historie of Guicciardin, conteining the warres of Italie and other partes*. . . . Reduced into English by Geffray Fenton. London, 1579, Sigs. 4G$_v$ff. A very full account.
[3] *A General Inventorie of the History of France*, by Ihon de Serres, translated by Edward Grimeston, London, 1607, Sigs. Qqq3ff. So also in the folio which Thomas Creede published in 1597, *The Mutable and wauering estate of France from the yeare of our Lord 1460, vntill the year 1595*, Sigs. B$_4$v–B$_5$v.

mistake, for they print his account of the battle without comment. If Cavendish was following a written source in his description of the battle, I have not been able to trace it.

Cavendish is also wrong when he speaks of a 'league' between Francis I and Henry VIII which Bourbon found in Francis's tent and he 'telescopes' history considerably when he makes the Duke set off for Rome 'immediately' after Pavia.[1] On the other hand, some of his details seem to have behind them a certain air of truth. According to Sleidan, there was a famous oration delivered at the battle, but it was made by Pescara outside the town and not by the Duke.[2] Another historian tells of the suffering within Pavia:

> They that were within *Pauia* suffred no smal necessitie of money and municions, the store of wine beginning also to fayle and all other sorts of vittels, except bread: By reason whereof the launce-knightes assembled, and almost in maner of a tumult demaunded their pays, wherevnto, besides their owne insolent dispositions, they were pushed on by incitacion of their capteine, who was feared to haue made some secret contract with the French king.[3]

Thus it would seem that some of Cavendish's details derive in a sketchy way from what must have been items of general news about the battle in the 1520s. Eager to emphasize how great a folly it is 'for any wyse man to take any waytie enterprice for hyme self trustyng all together to his owen wyll not calling for grace to assist hyme in all his procedynges', and perhaps seduced by his fondness for the 'feigned oration',[4] he seems to have allowed himself to deal with history in a much more cavalier manner than was his usual practice in his biography.

[1] For these two errors see the historical notes to 37/25–6 and 42/2–3.
[2] Sleidan, loc. cit.
[3] Guicciardini, op. cit., 4F₃v.
[4] For Cavendish's use of this rhetorical device, which originates in the fictitious speeches of the classical historians, see Wiley's note (op. cit., p. 124). Sidney, in his *Apology* (ed. G. G. Smith, I, 153), speaks deprecatingly of Herodotus and tells how

> both he and all the rest that followed him either stole or vsurped of Poetrie their passionate describing of passions, the particularities of battailes, which no man could affirme, or, if that be denied me, long Orations put in the mouthes of great Kings and Captaines, which it is certaine they neuer pronounced.

But it is only in the speeches of the Duke at Pavia that Cavendish can be shown to have actually 'feigned' his orations. The great speeches at the divorce trial seem to be accurately reported. See Appendix C.

II. *The Bohemian Revolt*

Cavendish's relation of Wolsey's deathbed speech contains several historical errors that are just as marked as those which occur in his account of the Battle of Pavia. In this case, however, we know that neither Cavendish nor Wolsey is speaking of events which took place in his own lifetime. The Bohemian Revolt had occurred a hundred years before Wolsey's death and it is quite possible that the cardinal himself was misinformed about some of its central happenings. In any event we cannot place the sole responsibility for this narrative upon Cavendish; he may very well have forgotten some of the words which Wolsey uttered, but it is nevertheless possible that the substance of the narrative stems from Wolsey's own misinterpretation of events rather than from Cavendish's desire to drive his point home by a wilful perversion of history.[1]

The principal errors in Cavendish's narrative[2] concern his statement that 'the King of Bohemia' was at first inclined to favour the reformers but later was forced 'to put harness on his back' and campaign against them. According to Cavendish (or Wolsey), the king was killed in the ensuing battle; since his death, Bohemia has been a lawless and disorderly country. In point of fact, Wenceslaus IV (1361–1419), to whom Cavendish ostensibly refers here, was favourable to the cause of the reformers until 1419, when he ordered the clergy who had been expelled by the Hussites to be restored. He died in the same year, apparently of a stroke that was brought on by the shock he sustained when the Hussites revolted against his decrees. His brother Sigismund (1368–1437) succeeded him and waged a long series of campaigns against the reformers, who would not accept him as king. He finally won them over in 1435, two years before his death. Although it is quite true that some of the nobles did unite with the Hussites against crown and clergy in both reigns (and it is doubtful whether Cavendish refers to Wenceslaus or to Sigismund), there is no historical support whatsoever for Cavendish's statement that the king was killed in battle against them.

Furthermore, if these words are actually Wolsey's, it is extremely difficult to believe that the Cardinal of York, famed diplomat that

---

[1] It should be noted that Bishop Fisher had also cited the revolt in Bohemia as a precedent for the Protestant uprisings in the sixteenth century. See Pollard (p. 301, note 1).

[2] These are noticed by Professor René Wellek in his article 'Bohemia in Early English Literature', *The Slavonic and East European Review*, xxi (1943), pp. 121–2. I am indebted to Professor Wellek for his help in the elucidation of several obscure points in Cavendish's account.

he was, could have thought that anarchy still existed in Bohemia in 1530—four years after Ferdinand I, Charles V's brother, had ascended the throne in that country. Wolsey, it is true, may have deliberately slanted his words so as to paint the most terrible warning possible for Henry VIII; but one would scarcely think that he would have perverted contemporary history to such a degree.

As a matter of fact, Cavendish's whole speech is remarkably similar in tone and, at times, in actual detail, to the decidedly anti-Protestant history of Bohemia written by Aeneas Sylvius, the great fifteenth-century humanist scholar who had spent some time in Bohemia and had later become Pope.[1] Aeneas, though he seldom perverts actual fact and does not say that a Bohemian king was killed in battle against the Hussites, nevertheless devotes considerable space to virulent attacks on the reformers. Here is his description of their attack on a monastery after Wenceslaus' death:

Neque hoc modo contenti, apud Sclauoniam, [*the Hussites*] nobile monasterium fratrum praedicatorum extra moenia oppidi situm, a fundamentis deijciunt: Eaque prima ecclesiarum ruina in Hussitarum nouitate facta decurritur in ecclesias, monasteriaque passim: nobilissima superis dicata templa ferro atque igne uastantur nullum ergo regnum aetate nostra in tota Europa, tam frequentibus, tam augustis, tam ornatis templis dicatum fuisse, quam Bohemicum reor. (Sigs. E_5v–E_6)

All this was due to the 'rabies Hussitarum'. Later (Sigs. F_3–F_3v) Aeneas describes the sect of the Adamites, those early Protestants who had everything in common and who were, no doubt, the original for Cavendish's lines (180/20–22) about the reformers who 'lyved all in Comen lyke wyld bestes/ abhorred of all Cristyan nacions'.

Thus it appears that Cavendish's version of the Bohemian Revolt derives its tone and some of its details from the most popular account of the Hussites then available to Catholic Western Europe. As Professor Wellek has pointed out in his article, it was not until the reign of Edward VI that a less biased version of Bohemian history was made available to the general public in England. Both Cavendish and Wolsey undoubtedly saw the revolt as a bitterly chaotic anticipation of events that could well take place in England

---

[1] *Aeneae Silvii Senensis de Bohemorum origine*, Coloniae, 1524, the edition I use here. There were of course earlier editions, e.g. the quarto of *ca.* 1489 [Basel? Michael Furter?].

268   *Appendices*

and either of them might have been willing to distort the facts further in their effort to devise a convincing exemplum for Henry VIII.

APPENDIX C

The Speeches at the Divorce Trial

Since Hall's account of the divorce proceedings and the speeches of Catherine and Henry VIII often agrees quite closely with the details and sometimes with the actual phrasing of Cavendish's narrative, I reproduce the relevant passages here for the convenience of the reader. They are offered as partial confirmation of the suggestion made in the Introduction (above, p. xxxi) that Cavendish may have used Hall's book to refresh his memory when he began the Life.

I. *Catherine's Speech at the Divorce Trial*

Hall does not report the Queen's words at Blackfriars[1] but he does tell of a visit paid to her by Wolsey and Campeggio some time late in 1528, at which time she addressed the two legates as follows:

> Alas my lordes is it now a question whether I be the kynges lawful wife or no? When I haue been maried to him *almost xx. yeres* & in the meane season neuer question was made before? Dyuers prelates yet beyng aliue & lordes also & *priuie counsailors* with the kyng at that tyme, then adiudged our mariage lawful and honest, and now to say it is detestible and abhominable, I thynke it greate maruell: and in especiall when I consider, *what a wise prince the kynges father was*, and also the loue and natural affeccion, that Kyng Fernando my father bare vnto me: I thynke in my self that neither of our fathers, were so vncercumspect, so vnwise, and of so small imaginacion, but they forsawe what might folowe of our mariage, and in especiall the Kyng my father, sent to the Courte of Rome, and there after long suite, with great cost and charge obteigned a licence and dispensacion....
>
> (p. 755; cf. the *Life*, 80/17–82/6, especially 81/11–23. I have italicized the words and phrases which Cavendish may be echoing.)

[1] He says only that Catherine protested against the jurisdiction of the court and appealed to Rome at the first session on 18 June. Henry's speech on the 21st (reproduced below) is said to have occurred while the Queen was in the court, not, as Cavendish correctly has it, after she departed.

Catherine, in Hall's account, then goes on to attack Wolsey for having instigated the divorce as a means of revenging himself on Charles V.

II. *Henry's Speech at the Divorce Trial*

Hall reports how, on 21 June, the king 'saied these wordes in effect folowyng':

> My lordes, Legates of the Sea Appostolike, whiche be deputied Iudges, in this great and waightie matter, I most hartely beseche you, to ponder my mynde and entent, which only is to haue a final ende, *for the discharge of my conscience*: for euery good christen man knoweth what pain, & what vnquietnes he suffreth, which hath his conscience greued, for I assure you on myne honour, that this matter hath so vexed my mind, & troubled my spirites, that I can scantely study any thyng, whiche should be proffitable for my Realme and people. And for to haue *a quietnes* in body and soule, is my desire and request, *and not for any grudge that I bear to her that I haue maried for I dare saie that for her womanhode, wisedom, nobilitie, and gentlenes, neuer Prince had suche another, and therfore if I would willyngly chaunge I wer not wise*: wherfore my suite is to you my Lordes at this tyme to haue a spedy ende, accordyng to right, for the quietnes of my mynde and conscience onely, and for no other cause as God knoweth.
>
> (p. 757; cf. the *Life*, 82/23–84/5)

But even closer to Cavendish's version of Henry's speech at the trial is Hall's report of the king's words to the 'nobility, judges, and counsellors' at Bridewell on 8 November 1528 when he endeavoured to quiet the fears of the London citizens, who were very much on Catherine's side. After telling the false story of how the divorce question first arose during the negotiations for a French marriage for his daughter Mary, the king continued as follows:

> Thinke you my lordes that these wordes [i.e. those of the French ambassador to the effect that Mary might be a bastard] touche not my body & soule, thinke you y^t these doynges do not daily & hourly trouble my conscience & vexe my spirites, yes we doubt not but & if it wer your owne cause euery man would seke remedy when the peril of your soul & the losse of your inheritaunce is openly layde to you. For this only cause I protest before God & in the worde of a prince, I haue asked counsail of the greatest clerkes in Christendome, and for this cause I haue sent for this legate [Campeggio] as a man indifferent only to know the truth and to settle my conscience and

for none other cause as God can iudge. And touching the quene, if it be adiudged by yᵉ law of God that she is my lawfull wife, there was neuer thyng more pleasuaunt nor more acceptable to me in my life *bothe for the discharge & cleryng of my conscience & also for the good qualities and condicions the which I know to be in her.* For I assure you all, that beside her noble parentage of the whiche she is discended (as all you know) *she is a woman of moste gentlenes*, of moste humilite and buxumnes, yea and of al good qualities appertainyng to nobilitie, she is without comparison, *as I this xx. yeres* almoste haue had the true experiment, so that if I were to mary againe if the mariage might be good I would surely chose her aboue all other women: But if it be determined by iudgement that our mariage was against Goddes law and clerely voyde, then I shall not onely sorowe the departing from so good a Lady and louyng companion, but muche more lament and bewaile my infortunate chaunce that I haue so long liued in adultry to Goddes great displeasure, and haue no true heyre of my body to inherite this realme. These be the sores that vexe my mynde, these be *the panges that trouble my conscience*, & for these greues I seke a remedy.

(pp. 754–5)

APPENDIX D

Some Notes on the Later History of the Life

The only modern study of the influence which the *Life of Wolsey* had on later writers is contained in a long and informative article by P. L. Wiley, who traces the various uses to which Elizabethan and Stuart historians put Cavendish's work.[1] Wiley's account, which does not make use of any manuscript materials, extends down to the time of the Puritan revolution and concludes with a description of the atmosphere in which the 1641 edition was produced. The following notes, which should be considered as supplementary to his researches, are offered in the hope that they may help to elucidate some of the more puzzling aspects of what one might venture to call 'the Cavendish tradition'.[2]

As Wiley notes, the first historian to make use of Cavendish's narrative was John Stowe who, in his *Chronicles of England* (1580)

[1] P. L. Wiley, 'Renaissance Exploitation of Cavendish's *Life of Wolsey*', *Studies in Philology*, xliii (1946), pp. 121–46. Prior to this article, the best discussion of Cavendish's posthumous fame was the Rev. Joseph Hunter's pamphlet, 'Who Wrote Cavendish's *Life of Wolsey*?'

[2] Appendix E, on the secondary manuscripts of the *Life,* also contains a great deal of incidental information about its later fortunes.

printed large portions of it from manuscript. In order that his history might not meet with official censure, the tailor-historian showed himself to be quite adept at drawing a fine seam through the pages of Cavendish's story. Every time Cavendish mentions Anne Boleyn or manifests his dislike for the Protestant cause Stowe very carefully deletes the passage. The result is a somewhat tatterdemalion version of the *Life*, a story with its core gone and its tragic motif suppressed. In the sparse pages of Stowe's narrative, the *Life of Wolsey* stands out like a series of purple patches, its richly detailed descriptions contrasting sharply with the mere chronicle of events that precedes and follows it. In 1592 Stowe included even more of Cavendish in his *Annals of England*, still being careful, however, to omit anything that might be construed as casting doubt on the good *mores* of the queen's ancestors.

From Stowe, the *Life* passed to Holinshed's *Chronicle*, whence perhaps it first caught the imagination of Shakespeare and whoever may have been associated with him in the composition of *Henry VIII*.[1] Meanwhile, Thomas Churchyard, picking up some details from Cavendish, had included his 'Tragedy of Cardinal Wolsey' in the 1587 edition of the *Mirror for Magistrates*,[2] and Thomas Storer, himself a pupil of Wolsey's Oxford college, had made a quite imaginative use of the *Life* in his poem (1599) on the cardinal. After the succession of James historians no longer had to worry about offending the reigning house and Cavendish's narrative appears, with all the references to Anne Boleyn, in John Speed's *History of Great Britain* (1611, 1623), Francis Godwin's *Annals* (1616), and Lord Herbert of Cherbury's *Life and Reign of Henry VIII* (1649).[3]

[1] The *Life* first appeared in the second edition of Holinshed (1587). Thomas Woodcock, one of the printers who collaborated on this folio, was also the scribe who copied out MS. Jones 14. See Appendix E, no. 6, below.

I have not attempted here to enter into the much-vexed question of the authorship of *Henry VIII*, but it might be suggested that a closer examination of the uses to which the play's author[s] put the *Life* (a subject which to my knowledge has never been fully investigated) might cast additional light on the composition of the play itself.

[2] Churchyard perhaps worked from Stowe, but his poem contains many phrases that are direct from the *Life*. Thus he speaks of Wolsey's father as 'a plain poor honest man' and makes the lamenting cardinal speak of the time when 'degree of school I had/And Bachelor was, and I a little lad.' See the reprint of his poem in the Temple Classics edition of the *Life of Wolsey*, pp. 265–6 *et passim*.

[3] For these writers and their use of Cavendish, see Wiley, op. cit., pp. 132–8. To their works may be added Sir Richard Baker's *Chronicle of the Kings of England* (1643), a seventeenth-century imitation of Suetonius which draws upon Cavendish quite heavily in its summary of Wolsey's career (Sigs. Bbb2^v-Eee^v).

Lord Herbert, whose four folio volumes of collections for his *Life* are now the property of Jesus College, Oxford,[1] possessed a manuscript of Cavendish's work which he used with considerable discrimination. But by 1649 there were printed copies of the *Life of Wolsey* available to the general reader.

The edition of Cavendish which was issued from the press of William Sheares in 1641 has occasioned a good deal of comment from critics and historians.[2] Sheares's quarto volume, which appeared with the title, *The Negotiations of Thomas Woolsey, The great Cardinal of England, Containing his life and Death*, etc., was undoubtedly issued as a propaganda piece in the Puritan campaign against Archbishop Laud which had been raging openly since the suppression of the Star Chamber in 1640. It is a drastically foreshortened version of Cavendish's narrative, though it does not, as Marie Schütt (p. 143) notes, disturb the major outlines of his *Life*. One can scarcely help sympathizing with those early editors like Wordsworth and Singer, who, comparing the manuscripts with the printed copies, were often led to express their scorn for whoever was responsible for that first edition.[3]

The surprising thing about this controversy over the merits of the 1641 edition is that no one seems to have noticed that there were in fact *two* editions of the *Life* in the early 1640s, one of them (Sheares's) published with its printer's name and the date '1641' and another, with a different title page and no date, issued 'for the good of the Commonwealth'.[4] This second quarto edition, which is an entire resetting of Sheares's volume, has the following title page in the British Museum copy (Press Mark, 275. g. 27):

The/ Negotiations/ of/ Thomas Woolsey,/ The great Cardinall of England, Containing his life and death, Viz./ 1. The Originall of his Promotion./ 2. The continuance in his Magnificence./ 3. His Fall, Death, and Buriall./ [Rule, broken] Composed by One of his owne Servants, being his Gentleman-Vsher./ [Rule, broken] With many Errours Corrected, and some/ Additions Inlarged./ [Rule, broken]

[1] On deposit at the Bodleian Library.
[2] Their opinions and judgements are neatly summarized in Marie Schütt's 'Die englische Biographik der Tudor Zeit', *Britannica*, i (Hamburg, 1930), 142. She finds them all guilty of 'ein merkwürdiges Fehlurteil'.
[3] Wiley conjectures that William Prynne had a hand in the preparation of the book, a suggestion that need not conflict with Miss Schütt's attempt to prove that the manuscript upon which it is based was once in Bacon's possession.
[4] Sheares's edition is *Wing*, C 1619, but Wing did not record the other edition.

Whereunto Is added a Parallell between *Thomas* Lord Arch-Bishop of Canterbury./ [Rule, broken] London:/ Printed for the good of the Commonwealth.

Where Sheares's edition stops with the end of the *Life* this copy adds a verse epitaph on Wolsey (Sigs. O_4–O_4v) and one paragraph (O_4v) entitled 'A true Description or rather a Parallel betweene Cardinall *Woolsey*, Arch-Bishop of York; and *William Laud*, Arch-Bishop of Canterbury, etc.'

This concluding paragraph is evidently a summary of the Puritan tract entitled *A True Description or rather a Parallel betweene Cardinall Wolsey*, etc.[1] which, in some copies of the 'for the good of the Commonwealth' edition, was appended to the *Life* itself after the verse epitaph.[2] It would thus seem that the 'for the good of the Commonwealth' edition represents a clandestine (and perhaps pirated) version of Sheares's original publication in which no specific parallels had been drawn between Wolsey and Laud. Since the verse epitaph on Wolsey in this second edition has not, to my knowledge, been previously reprinted, I give it here in full:

> What State Geometry can take or find
> The large dimensions of great Woolsies mind?
> Whose Cedar-honours growing tall and straite,
> Aspir'd to over-top the King and State;
> While his ambition did in Oxford reare
> A Colledge, on whose Gates he did not feare
> To mount above the power of Soveraignty;
> And to create himselfe an upstart thing,
> Whose Clergy-greatnesse should transcend a King.
> While that he forged in his working braine
> Such cunning plots, whereby he did obtaine
> Possessions of the Kings heart, by whose Grace
> He freely was invested in the place
> Of Yorks Arch-Bishopricke, and made Counsellour
> Of State, then rais'd to be high Chancellour
> Of the great Seale of England; and withall
> The Pope advanced him a Cardinall.
>   Thus did he sit a while to be Times wonder
> Secure in honour, fearing not Joves Thunder,
> Nor dreading that his honours could bee broke;
> And rent asunder by Fates raging stroke;

[1] Reprinted by Singer (1825 ed., II, 230–43).
[2] For example, in the Bodleian copy (Gough Oxon. 147). Another copy in that library (4° B. 64 Jur.) does not contain the 'True Description' although the last page of the epitaph has the catchwords 'a Parallel'.

> Raigning in height of glory from low Birth
> To rivall Heaven, and affright the Earth:
> For wheresoever Woolsies name was heard
> In England, it was both ador'd and fear'd.
> But angry Fortune that exhal'd and rais'd
> By her owne power this Meteor, which long blazed
> Bright as a Comet, cloath'd now with a frowne
> Her threatning brow, and quickly cast him downe.
> The King tooke off some honours, that he might
> Both know his greatnesse, and affright
> His growing pride; which fledg'd with a strong wing
> Did strive to fly a pitch above the King.
> And being summond now to meete the danger,
> Of making Answer to the Kings just anger;
> His guilty Conscience made his Judge, did cause
> Poyson to execute the power of Lawes:
> And though from this great Clergy Phenix spring
> Many great Bishops, Heaven down can bring
> Their usurp'd Titles, and can make them have
> Before their death an undeplored Grave:
> For though this Cardinall did in greatnesse trust,
> His Fame doth now lye buried with his dust.

Sheares's 1641 edition was reprinted in 1667,[1] 1706,[2] and 1708[3] without any change in the text and it was not until the nineteenth century that a better text was offered to the public. Since the time of Wordsworth and Singer there have been numerous popular editions, none of them with any final textual authority.

APPENDIX E

The Secondary Manuscripts

The following catalogue of the extant secondary manuscripts of the *Life of Wolsey* should not be considered exhaustive, but it will

---

[1] *The Life and Death of Thomas Woolsey*, etc., London, for Dorman Newman.

[2] *The Memoirs of that Great Favourite, Cardinal Woolsey*, London, for B. Bragg. The Bodleian copy is Gough Oxon. 132.

[3] Really a re-issue, with a new title page attributing the work to Sir William Cavendish, of Bragg's 1706 edition. Bragg had probably been influenced by White Kennet's sermon on the death of the Duke of Devonshire in which the *Life* was ascribed to George's brother for the first time. For a full discussion of this edition see Hunter's article (in Singer, 1825 ed., II, lxvi–lxvii). There is no copy of the 1708 issue in the British Museum; the Bodleian copy, the only one I have seen, is Gough Oxon. 12.

Appendices 275

perhaps serve as a fairly comprehensive check-list for future students of the strange fortunes which overtook Cavendish's work.[1] I have included a description of all the secondary manuscripts which I have been able to discover or which have been brought to my notice by the helpful investigations of others. More extensive researches than I have been able to undertake might well reveal additional copies which have been preserved in the collections of private individuals or in the continental libraries;[2] the present list should, however, furnish a nearly complete guide to the manuscripts in the principal libraries of Great Britain and the United States.

The thirty-one[3] manuscripts my investigations have brought to light range in date from the 1570s to the eighteenth century. The latest of them (Christ Church, CLV) was transcribed, as its frontispiece tells us, 'by the care and at the expense of the Rev. Mr. John Blackbourn, M.A., of Trinity College, Cambridge', and was presented to Wolsey's Oxford College by his widow on 10 December 1741. The earliest[4] takes us back to a date not long after Cavendish completed his autograph copy (1558). Several of the manuscripts[5] were transcribed after the *Life* had appeared in print in 1641 for the first time, a fact that is not at all remarkable in view of the omissions and corruptions in that edition. Most copies, however, date from Elizabethan and early Stuart times, those years in which Cavendish's *Life* was not available at all in printed form, except for the extracts made from it in the chronicles of the period.

To the student who makes a more minute examination of the

[1] The Rev. Joseph Hunter remarked in 1815 that 'Scarcely any work of this magnitude, composed after the invention of printing, has been so often transcribed' ('Who Wrote Cavendish's *Life of Wolsey*', in Singer, 1825 ed., II, xxvii). At the time in which he wrote, Hunter knew of some fifteen manuscripts of the *Life*, not counting the autograph manuscript, which did not come to Singer's attention until 1821.

[2] It might have seemed likely that the Elizabethan Recusants, attracted by Cavendish's pro-Catholic interpretation of the reign of Henry VIII, would have made use of his work in their own accounts of the period. But I have not been able to find any evidence of Cavendish's influence on either Harpsfield's *Historia Anglicana Ecclesiastica* or Campion's *Brevis Narratio de Divortio Henrici VIII*, which were printed together at Douai in 1622. It may be noted, however, that Cavendish's sympathetic attitude towards Wolsey would not have appealed to the Catholic apologists any more than it did to their Protestant opponents.

[3] Thirty-two if Arundel 152 is included in the total. See below, no. 14a.

[4] Either Douce 363 or the York Minster manuscript. See below, nos. 2 and 26.

[5] Christ Church (CLV) and the Folger manuscript (below, nos. 16 and 27). Possibly too one of the Trinity College, Dublin, manuscripts (below, no. 22).

relationships between these secondary manuscripts than I have been able to do, a good deal of valuable information about Elizabethan scribes and scriptoria will inevitably be revealed. The very possession of one of these copies (for almost all of them contain in full Cavendish's attacks on Anne Boleyn) must have been tantamount to treasonable conduct during Elizabeth's reign.[1] Yet the manuscripts continued to be transcribed, several of them, as the anti-Catholic glosses show, by or for men who were ardently sympathetic to the Protestant establishment. Lord Burghley, Elizabeth's High Treasurer, possessed one of the manuscripts (British Museum Add. MS. 48066) and Archbishop Laud was later to present his copy to the Bodleian Library. There is no better contemporary testimony to the esteem in which Cavendish's work was held than this large group of manuscripts that has come down to us.

Yet none of the secondary manuscripts[2] goes back directly to the autograph itself. All of them omit a long section of the *Life* (61/20–62/30 in the present edition) which describes the boar hunt in France and the 'book' published there against the cardinal. Occasionally a scribe will try to bridge the gap in his original by filling in a few details of his own, but in most cases the lacuna in the original is quite openly acknowledged and a page or two left blank in the copy. It thus appears that all of these manuscripts go back ultimately to a lost original which did not contain the missing lines. Until this manuscript comes to light, we can do no more than conjecture about its contents. The missing lines, which would occupy approximately two pages, or both sides of one leaf in a manuscript of average size, do not contain any material that might have been considered 'superstitious' or 'papistical' and there seems to be no other obvious reason why a scribe should have chosen to exclude them.[3] I can only

---

[1] Did the search that was made of John Stowe's house on 21 February 1569 turn up a copy of Cavendish among the antiquary's books and papers? Stowe certainly owned a copy of the *Life* at some time before 1598 (below, no. 19) and he must have had access to one before 1580 when he printed extracts from Cavendish in his *Chronicles of England*. The account of the search in 1569 is preserved in British Museum MS. Lansdowne 27, art. 37, fol. 36 (printed by Arber, *Stationers' Register*, I, 484). See also A. C. Southern, *Elizabethan Recusant Prose*, p. 39.

[2] Dugdale 28 (below, no. 3), the only secondary manuscript that contains Cavendish's poems, is a possible exception.

[3] There are several compressions and omissions in the secondary manuscripts that can be ascribed to this cause. Thus Cavendish's account of the French king healing his subjects who were diseased with the king's evil (53/28–54/20) is reduced in the secondary manuscripts to something like the following (from the Cambridge manuscript, below, no. 23): 'Thus continued my Lo: and the King in Aymens, the space of two weekes and

Appendices

suggest that, by some means or other, the page which contained the passage was accidentally torn or lost from the manuscript and that it was this missing manuscript which formed the basic copy for all the extant secondary versions.

But even if these manuscripts had preserved the boar-hunt passage it would not be difficult to demonstrate that the text they offer must stand at a considerable remove from that of the autograph itself. In addition to this major omission, and many minor ones of less significance, the scribes of the secondary manuscripts for the most part treat their original quite freely. Grammar and spelling are, as might be expected, progressively modernized, but many changes in phrasing and occasionally entirely new readings are also introduced into the text. I have not attempted a collation of the thirty manuscripts—which would be necessary if any final certainty about their relationships is to be achieved—but it appears that the transcribers, most of whom, judging by the unevenness of their hands and the mistakes they make, were not professional scribes, did not greatly concern themselves with verbal accuracy as long as the sense of the original could be ascertained. Since this bibliography does not attempt to discuss in detail the variants in the manuscripts, I should like to cite the following passage as a typical instance of the corruption that has overtaken their texts. The reader may compare this version of Cavendish's account of England after the divorce with that in the autograph manuscript (above, 78/14–79/7).

> ffor soothe it is a world to consider the desirous will of wilfull princes when they be set and earnestly bent to have their willes fulfilled wherein no reasonable persuasions will suffice and how litle they regarde the daungerous sequele that maye ensue aswell to them selves, as to all their subiectes And aboue all thinges, there is nothinge that makith them more wilfull then carnall love and sensuall affection of voluptuous desire and pleasure of their bodies as was in dede in this ⟨s⟩ case wherein nothinge could be of greater experience then to see what inuentions were surmised, what lawes were enacted what costlye edifications of noble and aunciente monasteries were ouerthrowen what diuersitie of opinions then rose, what executions were then comytted, howe manie noble Clerkes and good men were then for the same put to deathe And what alteration of good aunciente and wholsome lawes customes, and charitable more, consulting and ffeasting each others [sic] diue*rs* tymes in Aymens, then was my Lo: and the King at Masse, the w^h receaved both the Sacram^t and vpon our Lady day the assumpc*i*on My Lord said Masse before the Regent and the Queene of Navarre, and gaue them the Sacram^t & there the King dressed a number of sicke folkes, etc.' (f. 26).

foundations were turned from the releife of the poore, to utter destruction and desolation almoste to the subuersion of this noble realme/ It is sure to muche pitie to heare or vnderstand the thinges that have since that tyme chaunced and happened to this region the proufe thereof hathe taught vs all inglishe men the experience so lamentable of all good men to be considered. If eyes be not blinde men may see, if eares be not stopped they maye heare and if pitie be not exiled the inward man may lament The Sequele of this pernitious and inordinate love although it lasted but a whyle, the plague thereof is not yet ceassed which our lord quenche and take his indignation from vs.

(British Museum Add. MS. 4233, ff. 62ᵛ–3, *ca.* 1600)

I. *Manuscripts in the Bodleian Library, Oxford*[1]

1. MS. Bodley 966 (Sum. Cat. 3033)

Large folio, paper, $17'' \times 11\frac{1}{2}''$, bound in red morocco and gold, *ca.* 1610. A collection of various items from the reign of Elizabeth. The folio runs to xxiv plus 684 pages, all of which are numbered. The *Life* occupies pp. 93–193, with the break in the text coming on p. 125. Roper's *Life of More* follows Cavendish's *Life* on pp. 193–220. This manuscript was presented to the Bodleian in 1620 by Sir Peter Manwood (for whom see below, no. 19).

2. MS. Douce 363 (Sum. Cat. 21938)

Folio, paper, $12\frac{7}{8}'' \times 8\frac{3}{8}''$, with seven illustrations (ff. 52ᵛ [2], 57, 58, 71, 76, and 91), two of which were reproduced by Singer (1825 ed., I, 181 and 221). The manuscript is a collection of various items, many of them conjectured by Douce in a frontispiece note to have been written by Dr. John Dee. All of it, however, seems to be in one hand, that of Stephen Batman (d. 1584), who signed his transcription of the *Life of Wolsey* (ff. 48–93) on 1 September 1578. The break in the text is on f. 62. Batman's marginalia express patriotic Protestant views, for example (f. 60), on Francis I curing the king's evil, 'The kinges of England doth cure the same dizease: and therefore no less christian'. This is one of the earliest[2], if not the earliest, of the

---

[1] The manuscripts are numbered individually and consecutively from 1 to 30 throughout the catalogue, but I have arranged them in groups according to their present location. It may be noted that the Bodleian, which in addition to its eight secondary manuscripts, also possesses a photostatic copy of the autograph manuscript (MS. Facs. d. 82), is the best single library in which the student may investigate the peregrinations of Cavendish's *Life*.

[2] The York Minster manuscript may be earlier. See the note on no. 26, below.

secondary manuscripts. The first page of the text, f. 48, is used in the present edition to replace the missing page in Egerton 2402.

3. MS. Dugdale 28 (Sum. Cat. 6518)

Folio, paper, $11\frac{1}{2}''\times 8\frac{3}{4}''$, *ca.* 1550–1660, a collection of items in various hands. The eighth item is an abridgement (ff. 220–8) of Cavendish's *Life* and this is followed (ff. 228ᵛ–64) by his poems, the only extant copy of them outside of the autograph manuscript. The whole manuscirpt has iv plus 370 leaves. The index in Dugdale's hand (f. 219) assigns the *Life* and poems to a 'Thomas Cavendish'. Two of the poems are signed 'qᵈ E.C.'

This interesting manuscript poses many problems that I have not been able to solve. It would seem that the scribe, whose handwriting can be dated fairly early, had access either to the autograph or to a copy of it which also contained Cavendish's poems. A long and garbled prose passage from the *Life* is inserted in the poems immediately following the legend of Cromwell (f. 239). In addition, the manuscript contains a stanza (from the poem on the Duke of Suffolk) which is not in the autograph. It runs as follows (f. 260ᵛ):

> To the great sclaundʳ & blot of his name,
> his credyt ys lost and so ys his estymac*i*on,
> and he confused, alas he was to blame
> hymselfe to overthrowe, and all his generac*i*on
> against god nowe howe ca*n* he make purgac*i*on
> yᵗ so against nature vnnaturally hath wrought,
> destroying all his bloud & brought hy*m*selfe to naught/

On the other hand, the scribe omits, from the final epitaph on Queen Mary, four stanzas which refer directly to Rome and to 'Popish practices'. These are the stanzas beginning 'Hyghe prieste of Rome', 'Which late restored', 'Whan sacred aulters', and 'O Virgin Mary' (Singer, 1825 ed., II, 166–9).

4. Gough Oxon. 22[1]

This is actually a copy of the 1667 edition (London, for Dorman Newman, 8vo) which has been entirely revised and corrected in a fine italic hand. The fly leaf tells us that it was in 1676 the property of a 'Mary Coney' and that it came into the hands of the collector William Herbert in 1773. In addition, the fly leaf

[1] See below, p. 288.

contains a list of previous editions and a short account of some of the extant manuscripts which had come to Herbert's notice.

The scribe who made the long series of corrections worked from a manuscript which, as his marginal notations tell us, contained seventy-four folios. An examination of the secondary manuscripts shows that the copy from which he took his revisions was in all probability Harley 428 (below, no 12), a manuscript of seventy-four folios that, like Gough Oxon. 22, marks the break in the text on ff. 24ᵛ–5. To illustrate the meticulousness with which the corrections in the printed copy were made, I quote the opening lines of the text: 1667 edition: 'It seemeth no wisdom to credit every light tale, blazed about in the mouthe of vulgars, for we dayly, etc.' Gough Oxon. 22 corrects this to: 'Mee seemes it weare no wisdom to credytt every light tale, blaised about by the blasphemous mouthe of the rude commonaltie, for we dayly, etc.'

5. MS. Jones 12 (Sum. Cat. 8919)

Folio, paper, $11\frac{1}{8}'' \times 7\frac{1}{8}''$, 194 ff., *ca.* 1650, contains only the *Life*. A good scribe's copy. The break in the text occurs on f. 68, where the scribe has noted 'Here was something left out of the originall'.

6. MS. Jones 14 (Sum. Cat. 8921)

Folio, paper, $12\frac{1}{2}'' \times 8''$, iii plus 365 ff., contains five items, of which the *Life* is number one (ff. 1–97). The manuscript, which contains many marginal comments and attempts to bridge the gap in the text on f. 33ᵛ, was transcribed by Thomas Woodcock, as his signature on f. 97 attests. Woodcock, an Elizabethan printer, was one of the men who joined together to produce the great Holinshed folio of 1587, a work that makes use of Cavendish's *Life* in considerable detail. He died (Arber, *Stationers' Register*, II, 267) 'about the xxii[th] of Aprill last past' (1593).

7. MS. Laud misc. 591.

Folio, paper, $11\frac{5}{8}'' \times 8''$, 128 ff., contains only the *Life*. The break in the text, which the scribe has attempted to fill in, occurs on f. 84. A frontispiece picture of Wolsey is an engraving by Elstrack, the same as that which appears in the 1667 edition. There are many marginal glosses and underlined passages in the text. This manuscript was once the property of Archbishop Laud, who presented it to the Bodleian in 1636. In November 1951 an endleaf was raised to reveal the name 'William Langham' and the date 1613. This is

Appendices

undoubtedly the same Langham who transcribed the manuscript and left the following inscription on f. 128^v:

> Ex manuscripto Rogeri Manwood olim/
> capitalis baronis de Scaccario dominæ
> Elizabethæ nuper Reginæ Angliæ
> fideliter extract.
> Per me Guilielmum Langham
> Notarium publicum.

Sir Roger Manwood (1525–92) was made Lord Chief Baron of the Exchequer on 17 November 1578 and held that office until he was arraigned for bribery in April 1592. He died on 14 December of that year. His eldest son, Sir Peter Manwood, possessed at least two copies of the *Life* in manuscript. See above, no. 1, and below, no. 19.

8. MS. Rawlinson D.104

Quarto, paper, $8\frac{5}{8}'' \times 6\frac{5}{8}''$, 118 ff., contains only the *Life* with William Marshall's engraving of Wolsey as a frontispiece on f. 1. The handwriting is *ca.* 1600 and the manuscript, according to a frontispiece inscription, 'erat ex libris Georgii Berkley'. The gap in the text occurs between ff. 71 and 78 and a later hand has transcribed the table of contents and other material from the 1641 edition into the blank pages. There are a few marginal glosses.

II. *Manuscripts in the British Museum*

9. Additional MS. 4233

Folio, paper, $11\frac{7}{8}'' \times 7\frac{1}{2}''$, 186 ff., *ca.* 1600–50. F. 2 contains a short life of the author, 'William Cavendish', written by Dr. Thomas Birch in 1759. This ascription of the *Life* to William is contradicted by the title of the work itself (f. 4^v), which assigns it to George. The manuscript contains only the *Life*, with the break in the text coming on ff. 49^v–50. A later hand has tried to fill up the gap by summarizing. This manuscript is described in Ayscough's Catalogue of the British Museum Manuscripts (1782), I, 86.

10. Additional MS. 48066.[1]

Folio, paper, vellum wrapper, $12'' \times 8''$, contains a series of tracts, *ca.* 1600, with many of the headings in Burghley's hand. The *Life*

[1] Formerly MS. Yelverton 72, in the collection of the Calthorpe family. For a further description, see Harpsfield's *More* (ed. Chambers, E.E.T.S., o.s., 186), p. xvii.

occupies ff. 90–165, with the break in the text on f. 114. Harpsfield's *Life of More* is also included in this manuscript (ff. 319–73). The contents of the manuscript are described in the Appendix to the Second Report of the Royal Commission on Historical MSS. (1870), p. 43.

11. MS. Harley 35

Folio, paper, $12\frac{1}{4}'' \times 7\frac{1}{2}''$, *ca.* 1600. The manuscript contains some 48 items, of which the *Life* is number 32 (ff. 342–51). The text is fairly good as far as it goes, but it breaks off on f. 351 with the words 'well was that nobleman and gent' that could preferre a tall yeoman to his seruice. Now . . .' (18/23–6 in the present edition). This manuscript is described in the 1808 Catalogue of the Harleian Collection, I, 5.

12. MS. Harley 428

Folio, paper, $13\frac{1}{2}'' \times 8\frac{3}{4}''$, late sixteenth century, 74 ff., contains only the *Life*, followed by a number of blank leaves. The break in the text occurs on ff. 24v–5, there is another short gap on f. 13. It was apparently from this manuscript that the corrections and revisions in Gough Oxon. 22 were taken (see above, no. 4). Harley acquired this manuscript from John Strype (Harleian Catalogue 1808, I, 251) who had obtained it from a 'Mr. Woodward' (Harleian Miscellany, 1810 edition, V, 126).

13. MS. Lansdowne 904

Folio, paper, $11\frac{5}{8}'' \times 6\frac{7}{8}''$, *ca.* 1600, in very poor condition, 111 ff. Some of the text has been lost at both the beginning and the end in this manuscript. It begins (f. 1) with the words 'Bed*es*, The master of the wardropp and .10. p*er*sons in the Landery, etc.' and ends (f. 111v) with 'soe I would quoth the Lord Percie but in this matter I have gon. . . .' But the last two leaves actually belong to an early part of the *Life* and the text really ends on f. 109v with the words 'Sir quoth My Lord I trowe that Mr Kingston is Constable of the Tower Yea what. . . .' (172/4–5 in the present edition). The break in the text at the boar-hunt passage occurs on f. 43. This manuscript is described in the 1819 Catalogue of the Lansdowne Collection, Part II, p. 226.

14. MS. Sloane 848

Quarto, paper, $7\frac{1}{2}'' \times 5\frac{3}{4}''$, apparently an early seventeenth-century commonplace book, which, on ff. 14–14v, contains a series of notes taken from Cavendish's *Life*. Evidently the compiler never completed his memoranda, for the last entry reads 'The k. came in a Maske like Sheapards'. The manuscript contains a wide variety of notes and jottings including extracts from 'the life of Iohn Picus Erle of Mirandula out of Sr Tho. Moore' and a series of skeleton plots for plays.

14a. MS. Arundel 152

Folio, paper, $15\frac{1}{8}''\times 6\frac{3}{4}''$, a collection of materials for a life of Bishop Fisher. The latest date that can be assigned to this manuscript is 8 December 1575 (see Chambers's *Harpsfield*, p. ccxiii). Although not strictly a copy of Cavendish's *Life* this manuscript contains long extracts taken from it; I mention it here because it may well be the earliest instance of Cavendish's influence on other writers. The passages from Cavendish that were ultimately used in the *Life of Bishop Fisher* are carefully noted in Van Ortroy's edition of the latter work, *Analecta Bollandiana*, x (1891), 121–365, and xii (1893), 97–281. The compiler of the collection or one of his informants certainly knew someone who was closely associated with the cardinal in the last months of his life. The following note, it would seem, could have come only from Cavendish's book, from the gentleman-usher himself, or, possibly, from someone who, like him, had been present at Wolsey's death:

And yet (god be thanked) I haue credibly byn infourmed by sundry good & [wise] 'credible' personages that weare abowt him & knewe m^{ch} of his secretes, [doynges], that after he once espyed the sequele of his doynges, he lyved in great sorrow & repentance for t⟨h⟩e same all his lyfe after. And being at Yorke a yeare & more before his death in the kinges heavy displeasure, he there lamented all the whole that euer he flatered so m^{ch} wth the kynge and neglected the displeasure of all mighty god. and to that effect he also sent a message to the kinge a little before his death by Sr Wyllm Kyngstone then constable of the tower. desyring him for goddes sake to procede no further in this busynes of his dyvorce what so euer he had said to him before, but rather to arme & prepare him self against those horrible heresies duly entring into his realme, lesse by overm^{ch} negligence in repressing them at the first, he should en⟨d⟩aunger him self & his wholl realme so farre, that at last the sore might be growen incurable. where of he shewed the example to be yet fresh in the realmes of Boheme & hungary. Many other like wordes he vttered to that effect wherein his repentance largely appeared.

(f. 25, cancellations in angular brackets)

It is extremely unfortunate that this very valuable manuscript was damaged in a fire at the binder's on 10 July 1865. Of the original 332 leaves only 313 remain, many of these, in Van Ortroy's words, 'dans un pitoyable état'.

III. *Manuscripts in the Library of Christ Church, Oxford*

15. MS. CLIV

Folio, paper, $11\frac{1}{8}'' \times 7''$, *ca.* 1600, 172 ff. The break in the text occurs on f. 57, where the scribe has written 'heere was some thing left out in the originall'.

16. MS. CLV

Folio, paper, $13'' \times 8''$, 115 ff., early eighteenth century, presented to Christ Church, according to its inscription, on 10 December 1741, by the widow of the Rev. Mr. John Blackbourn, M.A., of Trinity College, Cambridge, at whose care and expense it was transcribed. The break in the text occurs on f. 20^v and on f. 52^v the scribe has interpolated a long passage from the 1667 edition.

IV. *Manuscripts preserved at Delapre Abbey, Northampton*

17. MS. Finch Hatton 135[1]

Folio, paper, $11\frac{1}{4}'' \times 8''$, *ca.* 1600. The text is incomplete, ending with the words 'between whom was like to ensue great murther unless some mean might be used to redress the inconvenience that was like to endure and daily grow' (145/3-6, in the present edition). There is the usual break at the boar-hunt passage. The manuscript contains a few notes in the hand of Christopher, Lord Hatton (1632-1706).

18. MS. Fitzwilliam (Milton) Misc. Vol. 51

Folio, paper, $12'' \times 8\frac{1}{2}''$, *ca.* 1600. This manuscript also has the gap at the boar-hunt passage. The beginning of the text is missing and a good deal of the first quire, so Mr. King informs me, 'has been well chewed by mice in the right-hand margin'. The first words now surviving are 'in crimson velvet with a saddle of the same and gilt stirrups' (23/32-3 in the present edition). The text of the *Life* is followed by seven documents which relate to Wolsey and to the divorce trial.

[1] I am indebted to Mr. P. I. King, Archivist of the Northamptonshire Record Office, for the description of this and the following manuscript.

V. *Manuscripts in Lambeth Palace Library*

19. MS. Lambeth 179

Folio, partly parchment and partly paper, $11\frac{5}{8}'' \times 7\frac{3}{8}''$, 313 ff., a collection of various items. The *Life* occupies ff. 246–313ᵛ. The *Life of More* by Ro: Ba: is on ff. 199–243. The handwriting of the Cavendish *Life* is *ca.* 1575–1600. The break in the text occurs on ff. 266ᵛ–68. On f. 313ᵛ is the following inscription:

> My book. Anº: [16] 1598./ Pe: Manwood.
> Wrytten by my man Rich. I.
> borrowed yᵉ originall of Mʳ Iohn
>   Burrowes/ Iohn Stow/.

Thus this manuscript belonged both to Stowe and to Sir Peter Manwood (d. 1625), the son of Sir Roger Manwood who, it will be recalled, was the owner of the manuscript from which William Langham copied MS. Laud 591 (above, no. 7). Sir Peter Manwood also possessed MS. Bodley 966 (above no. 1) which he gave to the Bodleian in 1620. I have not been able to identify the 'John Burrowes' to whom Stowe refers. Lambeth 179 was adopted as a basic text by Wordsworth in his edition of the *Life* (*Ecclesiastical Biography*, 4th ed., 1853, I, 461–672). It is described in the 1930 Lambeth Catalogue, p. 282.

20. MS. Lambeth 250

Folio, paper, $11\frac{5}{8}'' \times 7\frac{3}{8}''$, 475 ff., a collection of 31 items, of which Cavendish's *Life* is no. 4 (ff. 73–154ᵛ). The break in the text occurs on f. 100. Several of the items that precede and follow the *Life* are dated 1586 and were transcribed by the same hand. It is thus likely that the Cavendish manuscript is also of this date. On f. 1 of this manuscript is written 'This boke ys myn/ Iohn fford'. This manuscript was also used by Wordsworth in his edition. Its contents are described on p. 35 of the 1812 Lambeth catalogue.

VI. *Manuscripts in the Library of Trinity College, Dublin*[1]

21. Trinity College MS. No. 180 (Press Mark B. 2. 12)

Folio, paper, $11\frac{5}{8}'' \times 7\frac{3}{8}''$, a composite volume of works, mainly theological, copied about 1600. The *Life* occupies ff. 284–321 and omits the whole of the boar-hunt passage from the words 'Then the

[1] I am indebted to Mr. H. W. Parke, Librarian of Trinity College, for the description of this and the following manuscript.

king returned, etc.' to 'They be matters so slanderous' inclusive (60/12–63/24 in the present edition). The manuscript seems to have come to the library from Archbishop Ussher (1581–1656).

22. Trinity College MS. No. 731 (Press Mark G. 4. 9)

Folio, paper, $11\frac{3}{4}'' \times 7\frac{1}{8}''$, a collection of five items, all of them written in a neat hand of the middle seventeenth century. The *Life* runs from f. 55 to f. 174 and, like the edition of 1641, is divided into twenty chapters. Mr. Parke was not able to compare the text with that of the 1641 edition, but it appears likely that the manuscript was copied after that date, even if it is not a direct transcript of the edition itself. The manuscript was presented to the library by Hieronymous Alexander in 1674.

VII. *Other Manuscripts in Great Britain*

23. Cambridge University Library MS. Mm. III. 6

Folio, paper, $12\frac{3}{4}'' \times 8''$, early seventeenth century, 86 ff., contains only the *Life*, with the break in the text on f. 29^v. This manuscript has many corrupt readings, giving, for example, the astounding figure of '1800' for the number of persons in Wolsey's household. On the fly leaf is written 'From the library of Richard Holdsworth, D.D., Master of Emmanuel College. 1664' and on fol. 1 the name 'Tho: Nott'.

24. College of Arms MS. Arundel 51

Quarto, paper, $8\frac{1}{2}'' \times 5\frac{5}{8}''$, a collection of miscellaneous items. The Cavendish *Life* is separately numbered and occupies 92 folios with the break in the text coming on f. 32. There are a few marginal glosses and one cancelled folio (92) which repeats part of f. 85. The manuscript was given by Henry Duke of Norfolk in 1678.

25. The Duke of Northumberland's MS. (at Alnwick Castle, Northumberland) No. 466[1]

Folio, paper, $11'' \times 6\frac{3}{8}''$, 134 ff., contains only the *Life*, with the break in the text occurring on f. 43^v. The handwriting is *ca.* 1600 and there are a few marginal glosses which refer the reader to passages in the 1641 edition. A prefatory note in the hand of Bishop Percy compares the manuscript with the seventeenth-century printed copies.

[1] With the Duke's permission, this manuscript has been examined from the microfilm deposited in the Library of Congress.

26. York Minster Library MS. XVI D. 1ª.

Folio, paper, $12\frac{1}{4}'' \times 8\frac{3}{8}''$, 70 ff., contains the *Life* only with the break on f. 20. This manuscript was formerly the property of Toby Matthew (d. 1628), Archbishop of York, whose signature appears on the first page of the text. Miss Brunskill, Assistant Librarian at York Minster, tells me that this signature is almost certainly in Matthew's youthful handwriting, i.e. it corresponds to the signature he used before 1570. If her characterization of the signature is correct, this manuscript is almost certainly the earliest of the extant secondary manuscripts. There are a few marginal glosses and Matthew has again signed his name at the end of the *Life* on f. 70ᵛ. Wordsworth took some readings from this manuscript for his edition of Cavendish.

VIII. *Manuscripts in the United States*

27. Folger MS. (Folger Shakespeare Library, Washington, D.C.) No. 759.1[1]

Folio, paper, $11\frac{3}{4}'' \times 7\frac{7}{8}''$, 53 ff., contains the *Life* only with the break on f. 17ᵛ. This manuscript bears the inscription 'Roger Bradshaigh' and the date 1659 (erroneously given in De Ricci's catalogue as '1569').

28. Harvard MS. (Library of Harvard University, Cambridge, Mass.) MS. Eng. 764

Folio, paper, $11\frac{1}{4}'' \times 7\frac{1}{4}''$, 109 ff., contains the *Life* only with the break on ff. 35–6ᵛ. The handwriting is *ca.* 1600. This manuscript was formerly MS. 6930 in the collection of Sir Thomas Phillipps and was acquired by the Harvard Library on 3 May 1946.

29. Huntington MS. (H. E. Huntington Library, San Marino, California) HM 182

Folio, paper, $11'' \times 7\frac{1}{8}''$, 123 ff., contains the *Life* only and marks the break at the boar-hunt passage with a blank page. The script is *ca.* 1600. The name 'Henrie Farleigh' is stamped on each cover. the According to De Ricci, Farleigh is presumably to be identified with writer connected with St. Paul's from 1616 to 1622. This manuscript was in Singer's possession at the time when he prepared his edition of the *Life*. Prior to his acquisition of it, it was among the duplicates in the Duke of Norfolk's library (see Singer's description, 1825 ed., I, xv, note).

[1] I am indebted to Dr. Giles E. Dawson, Curator of Manuscripts at the Folger Library, for the description of this manuscript.

30. Yale MS. (Yale University Library, New Haven, Conn.) MS. Vault Shelves Cavendish

Quarto, paper, 7¾"×6", 119 ff., *ca.* 1600–50. The *Life* runs from f. 1 to f. 90 with the break on f. 31^v. Ff. 91–119^v contain the last three chapters of Cresacre More's *Life of More*, first published in 1626.[1]

[Additional Note on Gough Oxon. 22. (See p. 279)

Mr. N. R. Ker has drawn my attention to the alterations and insertions in this book. They are undoubtedly in the hand of Humfrey Wanley, who, as is shown by the following extract from one of his letters to Dr. Arthur Charlett, Master of University College, Oxford, once proposed to write a life of Wolsey:

> As to your conferring with Mr. Dean of Christ-church about my Intention of publishing an account of the Life of Cardinal Wolsey, I return you many thanks. But if my intentions shall have the Honor of his Approbation. I shall go much farther than the setting of Cavendish in his own true light. For that Author was not made privy to very many important Affairs which concern'd his Master, or pass'd through his hands; and which have not been fully set forth (for ought that I have yet found) to this day. When the Parliament sitts, I will not fail to wait on Mr. Dean with my book, and have the benefit of his Advice thereon. . . . Mr Bagford at his return from Oxford, told me that he [Dr. Hudson, Bodley's librarian] has an MS relating to Cardinal Wolsey, but what it was he could not say, only that the Doctor was pleas'd to show an Inclination of lending it to me if there should be occasion. I would gladly know what it contains, and then I can easily guess whether it will afford any fresh matter. . .[2]

J. A. W. B.]

[1] Since this appendix was written I have learned of the existence of another manuscript of the *Life*, although I have not been able to discover its present whereabouts. On 30 March 1936 the '*Life of Cardinal Wolsey*' was sold at Sotheby's from the collection of Major Q. E. Gurney, D.L., of Bawdeswell Hall, Norfolk. The catalogue, in which the manuscript is Item 90, describes it as a 'Manuscript on paper. 194 leaves. Not quite perfect at end. Unbound. From the collection of Sir H. Spelman.' This description does not tally with that of any of the thirty manuscripts listed above. It was bought by L. Chubb.

[2] Bodl. MS. Ballard 13, f. 119 (10 Nov., 1708).

GLOSSARY

The glossary is not a complete concordance, but contains words occurring in the *Life* the forms or meanings of which are not easily recognizable. No attempt has been made to record such normal Elizabethan variants as *y* for *i*, *s* for *c* or *c* for *s*, *c* for *t* in *-cion*, *en-* for *in-*, *the* for *thee*, *than* for *then* or *then* for *than*, etc. The reduced definite article *th-*, which is often combined in the text with a following noun or pronoun beginning with a vowel (as *thexpectacion*, *theon* 'the one') is ignored in the glossary except in *thether* 'the other'.

Entries marked with an asterisk indicate a form or sense not recorded in the *Oxford English Dictionary*.

abate *v.* bring down, reduce 29/2, etc.
abhomynable *adj.* abominable 86/14, etc.
abiecte *n.* outcast, degraded person 172/24.
accompte *v.* account, reckon up 22/26, etc.
accordyng *adv.* accordingly 148/13.
accustumably *adv.* customarily 151/10.
accustumed *ppl. a.* customary 167/9.
actes *n. pl.* saintly deeds 35/22.
admonysshed (of) *pp.* warned against errors 48/14.
aduauncyng *pr. p.* moving forward 121/16.
aduertised *pp.* notified, informed 23/6, etc.
adustum *adj.* 173/34. *See n.*
advysement *n.* observation 27/28; discretion 33/2.
affecte *n.* passion, lust 75/5.
affiaunce *n.* trust, reliance 96/3, etc.
Agnus *n.* Agnus Dei 67/2.
alhalouday, alhaloutyd *n.* feast of All Saints, 1 November 104/26, 25, etc.
alie *n.* alley 127/27.
allewer *v.* allure, win over 149/27.
allowed *ppl. a.* approved 75/18.
allowyng *pr. p.* accepting as true 48/11.

almery, almosory *n.* almonry 19/23, 162/6.
almosyner *n.* almoner 12/14.
alternatly *adv.* in alternate order 64/29.
ambassette *n.* embassy 7/23, etc.
*****ambassitorie** *n.* ambassador 77/12.
annele *v.* anneal, anoint 181/27.
anowghe *adv.* enough 130/28.
apertly *adv.* manifestly, clearly 128/6.
apon *prep.* upon 150/26.
apparitor *n.* officer of an ecclesiastical court 17/22, 79/17.
appoynt *v.* point out 27/26.
appoynted *v. pt.* decreed, granted 37/22, 122/22.
approved *ppl. a.* acknowledged, tested 88/26; proved by experience 107/29.
appurtenaunt *adj.* relating, pertinent 47/22, etc.
appurteynyng *pr. p.* pertaining, belonging 24/35, etc.
a ray *n.* array, order 52/17–18.
armonye *n.* harmony 25/20.
*****armyng shoos** *n. pl., appar.* shoes worn with armour 55/18.
arrogauncye *n.* arrogance 182/3.
assay *n.* tasting 168/13.
assignement *n.* allotment 125/6, 130/25.
asskyrmouche *n.* skirmish 15/10. *See* **escramoche**.

Glossary

assocyatted *ppl. a.* accompanied 66/34.
assoyll *v.* clear up, resolve 136/2.
assuraunce *n.* marriage engagement 34/9; security 117/19.
assured *pp.* made safe, secured 65/16.
astoned, astonyed *pp.* struck mute with amazement 93/4, 102/23.
attendure *n.* attainder 125/20.
*****auctory** *n.* authority 116/6, 157/1. See *n.* (on 116/6).
auctoryte *n.* authority 4/20, *etc.*
avauncement *n.* advance 38/4.
avauncyng *vbl. n.* promoting 10/3; moving forward 16/1.
avoyde *v.* make void 32/12, 86/5; belch 168/17; eject by excretion 173/33; *refl.* withdraw (myself) 32/3.
axe *v.* ask 84/9, *etc.*
ayenst *prep.* against, in preparation for 110/25.

bagges *n. pl.* badges 6/1.
bakhowsse *n.* bakehouse, bakery 19/15.
bankett *v. trans.* entertain at a banquet 67/29; *v. intr.* 72/26.
Bartholmewetyd *n.* feast of St. Bartholomew, 24 August 92/3.
barynes *n.* barrenness 181/16.
based *pp.* lowered, humbled 6/9; *****seated at a lower level 116/23.
basse *adj.* base, low-lying 49/28, 55/21.
basser *adj.* baser, lower 82/28.
bassnes *n.* baseness, lowness 16/19.
batere peces *n. pl.* battery pieces, siege guns 55/35.
baudkyn *n.* a rich embroidered stuff 99/8.
baylles *n. pl.* bulwarks 24/17.
be *prep.* by 125/6, *etc.*
beafes *n. pl.* beeves 66/5.
bedman *n.* beadsman 118/35.
bestowed *ppl. a.* placed, employed 108/33.
blanked *v. pt.* nonplussed 95/34.

blasphemous *adj.* abusive, slanderous 3/2.
blazed *ppl. a.* proclaimed (as with a trumpet) 3/2.
bokerham *n.* buckram 162/5.
bolle *n.* bowl 22/22.
bord *n.* table 21/3.
boted *v. pt.* booted, availed 157/14.
*****bottell chayn** *n., appar.* a chain used to fasten a bottle top or cork to a bottle 103/15.
bowelles *n. pl.* bowels 72/28.
*****boystors** *adj.* boisterous, of rough or stiff texture 151/15.
brake *v. pt.* broke 32/26.
brake *n.* snare, difficulty 44/2.
brond *n.* brand 29/32.
brotherne *n. pl.* brethren 147/20.
brute *n.* bruit, fame 73/8.
bryge, brygge *n.* bridge 26/16, *etc.*
bugett *n.* budget, bag 16/18.
bullyons *n. pl.* bullions, ornamental fringes 51/28.
burgious *n. pl.* burgesses 112/21.
busse *n.* bush 61/2.
butt lengthes *n. pl.* distance between two archery butts 52/20.
byen venewe *n.* welcome 51/20.

caffa *n.* a rich silk cloth 23/11, 99/1.
candyllmas *n.* Candlemas, 2 February 122/14, *etc.*
cast *n., a cast of brede* the quantity of bread made at one time 22/20, 133/15.
cators *n. pl.* caterers 68/7.
certyntie *n.* quantity 149/14.
chaffed *pp.* scolded 86/28.
Chaffer of waxe *n.* 20/24. See *n.*
chambers *n. pl.* small pieces of ordnance 25/32, *etc.*
chargeable *adj.* involving responsibility 7/3.
chaundrye *n.* chandlery 19/12.
cheete *adj., a cheete love of brede* wheaten loaf of the second quality 71/31.

Glossary

cheke *n.* rebuke 16/7, *etc.*; *n. pl.* reins (of bridle) 52/14.
chekked *v. pt.* rebuked 9/6.
chekker rolle *n.* check-roll, list of servants 21/18.
childern *n. pl.* pages, attendants 19/2.
choke *v.* stop the mouth (of a witness) 76/15.
choyes *n.* choice 33/29.
cisis *n. pl.* sizes 71/30.
Clarke of the Chekke *n.* 20/24–5. *See n.*
Clarke of the Crowne *n.* 20/23. *See n.*
Clarke of the Grean clothe *n.* 20/33. *See n.*
Clarke of the hamper *n.* 20/23–4. *See n.*
clean *adv.* properly, completely 71/26, *etc.*
cloos *n.* close, precinct 146/25.
cloose stoole *n.* chamber-pot 171/14.
closter *n.* cloister 54/13.
coblett *n.* goblet 71/28.
cofferer *n.* 18/32. *See n.*
cognysaunce *n.* crest, coat of arms 6/1, 128/20.
colas *n.* cullis, a strong broth 178/10.
collect *n.* collect 23/4.
colour *n.* show of reason, pretext 13/12, *etc.*
colored *ppl. a.* feigned, pretended 85/17.
colour (adustum) *n.* 173/34. *See n.*
comenwell *n.* commonweal, commonwealth 35/27. *See n.*
(in) Commendam 17/33–4. *See n.*
commendatory *n.* holder of a benefice in commendam 97/15.
commenyng, commonyng *pr. p.* communing, conversing 55/28, 94/21, *etc.*
commonalty *n.* the common people 3/2.
commyn *v.* converse 24/7, *etc.*
commynycacion *n.* conversation 94/30, *etc.*; by the way of com-mynycacion as a matter of conversation 16/15, *etc.*
commyssaryes *n. pl.* representatives of a bishop in his diocese 17/21.
compased *v. pt.* devised, plotted 37/7.
compasis *n. pl.* crafty contrivances 11/3.
compellatory *adj.* compulsory 78/11.
complayn (on) *v.* complain (of, about) 31/6.
conceyt *n.*, in my conceyt to my mind 105/19.
condempne *v.* condemn 81/28.
condicion *n.* respect, regard 6/14; *pl.* manners, morals 82/29.
condygn *adj.* merited, fitting 47/7, *etc.*
confeccion *n.* medicinal preparation 23/16, 168/12.
confirmable *adj.* conformable 80/27, 82/25.
confiscatt *pp.* confiscated 37/31.
confuse *n.* confusion 11/11.
connyng *adj.* cunning, learned 19/32, *etc.*
consistory *n.* bishop's court for ecclesiastical causes 79/12.
conspire *v. trans.* plot, devise 165/9.
constitute *pp.* set up, appointed 118/6.
contentacione *n.* satisfaction 9/9, 159/27.
convented *pp.* summoned 78/10.
convenyent *adj.* suitable, fitting 31/17, *etc.*
conveyed *pp.* conducted 31/11, *etc.*; managed (?) 136/28.
coopes *n. pl.* copes 16/33.
correspondent *adj.* accordant, consonant 21/33–4.
corrysife *n.* cause of annoyance 123/12.
costly *adv.* sumptuously, dearly 50/11.
costumably *adv.* customarily 148/33.

countenaunce *n.*, *make a countenaunce of* make a show of 126/25–6.
counterfeyt *ppl. a.* imitated, portrayed 120/27.
countervaylle *v.* make an equivalent return for 108/18.
covent *n.* convent 174/20, 183/3.
crosberers *n. pl.* attendants who bear an archbishop's cross 20/4, 23/33.
crosseer *n.* crosier 182/31.
crymmosyn *adj.* crimson 21/35, *etc.*
cure *n.* spiritual charge of parishioners 124/18; (medical) cure 120/20.
*****custument** *n.* custom 56/25. *See n.*
cytuat *ppl. a.* situated 98/5.

dampne *v.* condemn 90/11.
dampnefied *pp.* injured physically 152/5.
*****dasht (owt with)** *v. pt.* 28/3. *See n.*
daynger *n.* power 39/14.
declare (you) *v.* tell (you) 38/13.
deficyll *adj.* difficult 14/7, *etc.*
defray *v.* pay out, expend 18/10.
defuse *adj.* obscure 48/5.
delay *v.* check, restrain 13/33.
delyuerly *adv.* lightly, nimbly 61/22.
delyuerest *adj.* nimblest 40/22.
demaundyd *v. pt.* asked 120/14, *etc.*
demayns *n. pl.* demesnes, landed property 18/18, 137/1.
demerites *n. pl.* merits 108/3, *etc.*
departe *v.* part with, bestow 109/25, *etc.*
departure *n.* divergence, withdrawal, parting 75/23 (*see n.*); parting with 118/25.
depeche *n.* dispatch 8/3.
depeche, dispetche *v.* dispatch 9/8, *etc.*; kill 166/19.
dependyng *pr. p.* in suspense, pending 179/10.
deprave *v.* vilify, defame 44/14.
depresse *v.* repress, suppress 179/25.

depryved *pp.* divested, stripped (from) 159/13.
derevyed *pp.* derived 90/18.
deskes *n. pl.* shelves 69/28.
determynat *ppl. a.* conclusive, final 44/21.
devyse *n.* device, plan 67/22.
devyse *v.* devise; *pp.* **devysied** 73/10, *etc.*
diett *n.* diet 173/12.
diffyaunce *n.* defiance 146/2.
dirige *n.* dirge 183/9.
discharge *v.* unload 133/31; relieve 22/6.
discontentacion *n.* dissatisfaction 80/32.
disdaynously *adv.* disdainfully 140/26.
disgestion *n.* digestion 74/31.
dishonestie *n.* unchastity, lewdness 81/7.
dispeched *pp.* 25/4. *See* **depeche**.
dispend *v.* pay away, expend 106/21.
dispetche *v.*, *see* **depeche**.
dissent *n.* descent 31/25.
disseyved *v. pt.* deceived 23/4, *etc.*
dissimull, dissembell *v.* dissemble 4/10, *etc.*; *pt.* **dissymbled** 9/12.
distilled *v. pt.* flowed forth 107/16.
diswade *v.* dissuade 179/19.
doon *adj.* dun 128/17.
dowghtyng *pr. p.* doubting, fearing 37/5, *etc.*
drave *v. pt.* drove 83/23.
dromes *n. pl.* drums 25/28, 26/25.
dulce *adv.* sweetly 59/31.
dwn *adj.* dun 127/31.
dyaper *n.* a linen or cotton fabric 69/16.
dyssayved *pp.* deceived 94/7, *etc.*

effect *v. intr.* have an effect 75/1.
eftsons *adv.* afterwards 28/5.
elect *v.* choose 173/10.
embesell *v.* embezzle 176/17.
emposte *adv.* in haste (French *en poste*) 46/8.
emprynt *v.* impress 171/7.
enbandon *v.* abandon 132/24.

Glossary 293

enbrodered *pp.* embroidered 44/37, etc.
encounterd *v. pt. intr.* met 180/15.
endevour (me) *v. refl.* exert myself 169/20.
endured *v. pt.* continued 53/12.
endyght *v.* indict 113/15.
enfrynge *v.* break, frustrate 30/12, 34/10.
enheritrices *n. pl.* heiresses 59/16.
ensewe, enswe *v.* follow, imitate 115/30.
ensured *pp.* engaged by a promise of marriage 30/7, 33/7.
enswe *v.* 145/33. *See* **ensewe**.
entaylled *ppl. a.* carved, sculptured 127/32, 128/3.
entendement *n.* understanding 8/8, etc.; intention 11/9, etc.
entercours *n.* entrance 12/27.
entermeddell *v.* meddle, interfere 25/3.
entertaynment *n.* reception, manner of reception 93/30.
entired *pp.* interred, buried 183/11.
enveyed *v. pt.* inveighed 113/12.
eschaunce *n.* exchange 18/15.
escramoche *v.* skirmish 38/9.
estate *n.* person of estate 56/22, etc.; *pl.* degrees, ranks in society 26/19, etc.
Ester *n.* Easter 132/30.
euery *adj.* every one 67/24, etc.
evyll *adj.* evil, ill 167/31, 174/15.
evyn *adv., evyn at hand* close at hand 114/17–18.
ewrie *n.* ewery 19/11.
exclamed *v. trans. pt.* proclaimed loudly 13/19.
excorriacion *n.* excoriation 178/26.
exebicion *n.* exhibition, scholarship 121/32.
expected *pp.* waited for, awaited 44/3.

fact *n.* evil deed, crime 31/35, 33/15.
famely *n.* family, household 104/17.
fantazed *v. pt.* phantasied, fancied 29/20.
fantzy *n.* phantasy, fancy 13/8.

farre fetche *n.* deeply-laid or cunning stratagem 34/24.
fate *adj., ffate fed* overfed, fatly fed 136/10.
faynyng *pr. p.* feigning 182/34.
feacte *n.* feat 61/33.
feare *v. refl., I feare me* I am afraid 166/19.
ferced *ppl. a.* farced, stuffed 124/13.
ferder *adv.* farther 123/19.
ferme *n., in ferme* let at a fixed rent 18/3.
ferrour *n.* farrier 19/21.
filed *ppl. a.* polished, smooth 11/32.
fired *v. intr. pt.* became inflamed, showed anger 104/9.
fletyng *vbl. n.* fleeting, gliding away from (?) 188/2.
foode *n.* feud 145/15.
forme *n.* bench 32/29; kneeling bench, prie-Dieu 46/2.
forse *v.* foresee 139/6, etc.
foyell *n.* repulse, defeat 137/2.
foyned *v. pt.* made a thrust, lunged 61/11, 14.
fraccion *n.* breaking of the bread in the Eucharist 54/5.
framed *v. pt.* was contrived 35/16; contrived 178/34.
francye *n.* frenzy 178/26.
franke *adj.* free from restraint 113/30.
frequent *v.* busy oneself with 143/13.
freuctes *n. pl.* fruits 152/28.
frustrate *adj.* fruitless, unavailing 96/4.
fullfyll *v.* satisfy 78/15, etc.; *pp.* **fulfill, fulfilled** filled; fulfilled 74/31, 128/23, 28.
funeralles *n. pl.* funeral 11/5, etc.
furnyished *ppl. a.* furnished 24/17.
furnyture *n.* furnishing 9/12, etc.; complement of occupants 23/7; accoutrements, furnishings 48/28, etc.
fyll *v. pt.* fell 15/12.
fynforce *n., of fynforce* of absolute necessity 15/1, 38/1.
fynne *n., in fynne* to conclude 111/33.
fyves *n. pl.* fifes 26/25.

gagge *n.* gage 131/5.
galhowsse *n. pl.* gallows 63/21.
garded *ppl. a.* furnished with an ornamental border 22/3.
garderobbe *n.* wardrobe 19/13.
garner *n.* granary 19/17.
garter *n., abbreviation for* Garter King of Arms 66/21.
gasyng *pr. p.* gazing 60/35.
gathowsse *n.* gatehouse 5/35.
generall receyvour *n.* receiver-general 82/11. *See n.*
genett *n.* jennet, a Spanish horse 51/30, *etc.*
*****gentilman for the monthe** *n.* 19/12. *See n.*
gere *n.* substance 168/10; doings, goings-on 184/23.
gested *pp.* made a jest of 142/27.
gesture *n.* bearing, deportment 29/31, *etc.*
goddes *n., a goddes name* in God's name 129/12.
gospeller *n.* one who reads the Gospel 19/28.
gratitudes *n. pl.* graces, favours 134/33.
gratuytie *n.* favour, kindness 135/2.
grease tyme *n.* 141/1. *See* **grece season.**
grece season *n.* 92/16. *See n.*
gree *n., in gree* with goodwill or favour 103/21, 140/21.
gresis *n. pl.* steps 54/3.
greve *n.* grief 141/34.
grograyn *n.* a coarse fabric 99/2.
gross *adj.* dense, thick 174/3.
gwerdenythe *v. pr.* 3 *s.* rewards 129/20.
gyft *n.* power of giving 5/14.

haboundaunce abundance 187/30.
habytt *n.* garb, clothing 23/9.
halewater *n.* holy water 46/20.
halfe hakkes *n. pl.* halfhacks, small-size hackbuts 51/23.
halhalou day *n.* 151/3. *See* **al-halouday.**
hand *n., in hand with,* endeavouring to persuade, engaged with 84/24; *owt of hand* at once, immediately 112/32, 139/21.
handfull *n., an handfull brode* the width of a hand (conventionally 'four inches') 51/29.
harbergers *n. pl.* advance messengers 45/14.
hard *v. See* **here.**
hartilest *adv.* most heartily 133/30.
hault *adj.* haughty 13/33, 35/8; high 150/33.
haunted *v. pt.* frequented 63/9.
hauour *n.* behaviour 48/9, *etc.*
herd *adj.* hard 55/32.
here *v.* hear 12/28, *etc.*; *pt.* **hard** heard 10/13, *etc.*
hignes *n.* highness 77/19.
hild *v. pt.* held 42/31, 61/9.
historygraffers *n. pl.* historiographers 11/9.
hit *pron.* it 45/13, 185/13.
holand clothe *n.* a linen fabric 99/3.
holden *pp.* held 90/23.
hole *adj.* whole 59/21, *etc.*
holledayes *n. pl.* holy days 133/21.
holy, holly *adv.* wholly 31/34, 113/21, *etc.*
honestie *n.* reputation, credit 114/30.
honorous *adj.* honourable 3/30.
howghes *n. pl.* houghs, hocks 61/24.
huntes *n. pl.* hunters 60/31, 61/15.

ieopard *v. intr. for refl.* risk oneself, venture 137/6.
iesture *n.* 97/31. *See* **gesture.**
imagyn *v.* imagine, plot, devise 150/8, *etc.*
imagynacion *n.* scheming, devising 11/13, *etc.*
*****imedyally** *adv.* immediately 168/17 (*possibly an error by Cavendish*).
impedyment *n.* hindrance, obstruction 41/30.
imynent *adj.* 171/7. *See n.*
incontynent *adv.* immediately 8/21, *etc.*
inconvenyence *n.* harm, injury 145/5, 28.

Glossary

indenture *n.* list, inventory 99/29.
indewred *v. pt.* endured, lasted 64/4.
indifferencye *n.* impartiality 4/21, *etc.*
indifferent *adj.* unbiased, fair 136/7.
indifferently *adv.* moderately, tolerably 112/11.
induce *v.* introduce, bring forward 36/9.
ingrate *adj.* ungrateful 140/30.
inhabytid *v. pt.* took up one's abode, settled 121/31.
insaciat *adj.* never satisfied 29/3.
instaunce *n.* urgent entreaty 121/2.
instrument *n.* formal legal document 5/20, *etc.*
intelligence *n.* information, news 123/29, *etc.*
invencion *n.* discovery 10/3, *etc.*
invented *pp.* devised, plotted 22/1, *etc.*
iote *n.* jot 47/23.
ioyell *n.* jewel 16/21, *etc.*
ioyntly *adv.* together, at the same time 130/22.
ipocras *n.* cordial drink of spiced wine 71/11.
issue *n.* exit 143/21.
iubely *n.* jubilee 45/28.
iusticers *n. pl.* judges 101/19.

kankard *ppl. a.* cankered, malignant 114/14.
kayes *n. pl.* keys 152/30, 31.
keuerchefe *n.* covering for the head 59/1.

laft *pp.* left 159/12.
lagacion *n.* legation 77/22.
laske *n.* attack of diarrhoea 168/22.
laughed (owte) *pp.* dismissed by laughing 142/27.
launceknyghtes *n. pl.* lance-knights 46/7. *See n.*
lawyng *pr. p.* laughing 28/2.
layeng *pr. p.* putting forward, alleging 145/34.
laysor *n.* leisure 44/12.
leade *n., under leade* under a seal made of lead 77/8.

*leanyng stone *n.* stone forming the inner sill of a window 63/21.
lease *v.* lose 95/14.
legacye *n.* legateship 17/29, *etc.*
legantyn *adj.* legatine 45/31.
lenger *adj.* longer 28/36, *etc.*
lett *n.* let, hindrance 39/6, *etc.*
looke *n.* lock 140/6.
loope *n.* loophole 154/2.
love *n.* loaf 71/31.
love dayes *n. pl.* days appointed for the settling of disputes 144/5.
loves *n. pl., for all the loves* (phrase of strong entreaty) 80/17.
lowd *adj.* lewd, villainous 33/15.
luke *n.* luck 105/20.
lyfe *v.* live 174/5.
lyueres *n. pl.* liveries, provisions 22/18, *etc.*
lyvely *adj.* life-like 120/27; **lyvelyest** most life-like 127/32.

male *n.* bag, pack 140/4, 154/32.
malyng, malygne *v.* malign 33/16, 137/16.
manchett brede *n.* the finest wheaten bread 22/20, 71/31.
markes *n. pl.* marks (13s. 4d.) 69/32, *etc.*
mase *n.* mace 23/28.
*maskeresses *n. pl.* female maskers 73/24.
mastresse *n.* mistress 56/18.
maysters cerimoniarum *n. pl.* masters of ceremonies 17/26.
maystres *n. pl., to worke maystres* to perform wonderful feats 35/11.
meane *n.* mediator, go-between 166/14.
meate *adj.* meet, suitable 21/27, *etc.*
merely *adv.* merrily 26/21, 48/2.
messe *n.* group at a banquet 21/4, 167/17.
messwage *n., in messwage* carrying a communication 110/32, 114/16.
mete *adj. See* **meate**.
metropolytan *n.* head of an ecclesiastical province 84/12.
mewlytor *n.* muleteer 19/22.

Glossary

mo, moo *adj.* more, greater in number 144/16, *etc.*
mocion *n.*, *of his mere mocion* of his own accord 10/15.
molt *pp.* melted 176/18.
monycion *n.* admonition 33/19.
more *adj.* greater in degree or extent 29/16, *etc.*
most *adj.*, *the most persons of estymacion* the persons of greatest estimation 49/35.
mottons *n. pl.* sheep 66/5.
moysted *pp.* slaked one's thirst 160/12.
moytie *n.* moiety, half 59/18.
mume chaunce *n.* dicing game resembling hazard 27/2.
mumerreys *n. pl.* mummeries, maskings 25/16.
muse *v.* muse, wonder 25/35, *etc.*
mutuall *adj.* mutual 147/5.
myght *n.* mite 176/17.
***myhell** *n.* a medal depicting St. Michael 66/12.
myslyke *n.* dislike 83/31.
mystery *n.* trade guild, 134/22.
mystrustyng *pr. p.* suspecting 41/5.
mysused *pp.* misconducted 33/3.
mytigat *v.* mitigate 118/4.

naked *adj.*, *naked bed* 'denoting the removal of ordinary wearing apparel' (*O.E.D.*) 46/27, 86/30.
naturall *adj.* hereditary, legitimate 11/10.
ne *conj.* nor 22/13, *etc.*
necessary *adj.* commodious, convenient 50/19, 51/4 (?)
necessary *adv.* necessarily 12/18.
necessitie *n.* want, poverty 144/3.
nekke *n.* neck 23/12.
nett *adj.* neat 127/16.
newe *adj.*, *of newe* anew 15/24.
newelties *n. pl.* novelties 100/30.
newter *adj.* neuter, neutral 49/5.
nons *n.*, *for the nons* for the occasion 51/19.
***norwithstandyng** *conj.* notwithstanding 167/32 (*possibly an error by Cavendish*).

nother *conj.* neither 24/12, *etc.*
noyce *n.* melodious sound 70/14.
nyght crowe *n.* night-crow (a bird of ill omen) 137/19.

obedyencer *n.* obedientary, liegeman 114/3.
occasion *n.* person who brings about something 121/31.
occupied *pp.* made use of, used 19/35, *etc.*
ode *adj.* odd 133/16.
often *adj.* frequent 169/2, 170/6.
on *adj.* one 85/28.
oncouche *v.* drive animal out of lair 60/31.
onreuerently *adv.* irreverently 86/15.
onsavery *adj.* unsavoury 123/5.
onthryfte *adj.* prodigal, spendthrift 32/33.
or *conj.* ere, before 95/17, *etc.*
ordynarie *n.* ordinary 5/18. *See n.*
ordynaunce *n.* ordnance, artillery 40/32, *etc.*
ordynyth *v. pr. 3 s.* ordains, plans 86/1, *etc.*; *pp.* **ordened** 128/3, *etc.*
orisons *n. pl.* prayers 183/10.
other *conj.* either 23/9, *etc.*
ouerthwart *prep.* upon, across 167/26.
owgth *v. pt.* owed 28/30.
owther *conj.* either 43/29, *etc.*

pact *pp.* packed 7/20.
page *n.* page 63/9.
paiauntes *n. pl.* pageants 50/3, *etc.*
palle *n.* pall, pallium 182/32.
paned *ppl. a.* made of strips of coloured cloth 25/24.
parcell *n.* portion, piece 99/24, *etc.*
parcell *adj.*, *parcell gylt* partially gilded 56/11, *etc.*
parelles *n. pl.* perils; *vppon ther parelles* at their own risk 145/22, *etc.*
parentes *n. pl.* relatives, kinsmen 132/25.
particypant *adj.* participating 39/20.

Glossary

parties *n. pl.* parts 4/4, *etc.*
passenger *n.* passenger-vessel 8/18.
passyng *pr. p.* caring, recking 28/27, *etc.*
pastery *n.* pastry-kitchen 19/3.
pasture *n.* pastor 84/1, *etc.*
paynfull *adj.* diligent, assiduous 10/25.
perceuered *v. pt.* persevered 130/17, *etc.*
perceueraunce *n.* perception, understanding 89/34.
perke *n.* perch 55/26.
personally *adv.* in person 182/20.
pervsed *v. pt.* handled one by one 54/15; read 45/34, *etc.*
pesterd *pp.* clogged, entangled 23/19.
peusaunt *adj. See* **pieusaunt.**
pevysshe *adj.* peevish 30/18.
pieusaunt, peusaunt *adj.* powerful 13/32, 42/33, *etc.*
pild *pp.*, **pild & pold** ruined by depradations or extortions 101/10.
pillers berers *n. pl.* 20/4. *See n.*
pirld *ppl. a.* purled, edged 52/12.
pitched *v. pt.*, **pitched a feld** arranged a battle 180/14.
plantyd *v. pt.* established 40/15, *etc.*
plate *n.* confection, sweetmeat 71/4.
pollaxes *n. pl.* pole-axes 24/3.
pollecy *n.* political cunning 13/3, *etc.*
poomen *n. pl.* poor men 133/12 (*perhaps erroneous form*).
port *n.* bearing 29/2, *etc.*
pottecarye *n.* apothecary 20/29, *etc.*
practised *v. pt.* plotted, conspired 34/17.
prease, prece, prese *n.* crowd, throng 23/18, *etc.*
precontracte *n.* pre-existing contract of marriage 30/12.
preferre *v.* advance in status, promote 115/7, *etc.*
premedytate *adj.* premeditated 149/32.
premunire *n.* 113/15, *etc. See n.*
prese *n. See* **prease.**

present *n.*, **at that present** at that time 7/24.
preserued *pp.* reserved 164/14.
prest *n.* payment in advance 131/22.
presumcyons *n. pl.* presumptive evidence 86/3, 10.
pretenced *ppl. a.* pretended, false 36/9.
prevencyon *n.* prevention 17/24, *etc. See n. to* 17/19–20.
preventyd *pp.* forestalled, baulked 159/12.
prevy *adj. See* **privye.**
price *n.* prize 59/35.
privye, prevy, pryvy *adj.* secret, hidden 35/1, *etc.*
probacions *n. pl.* proofs 166/12.
processe *n.* narration, relation 182/9; **in processe** in process of time 34/25.
proface *int.* formula of welcome 70/21 [< obs. F. *prou fasse*, in full *bon prou vous fasse* 'may it do you good'.]
prophicier *n.* prophet 128/31.
propone *v.* propose 36/18.
prour *n.* prior 45/26.
prove *n.* proof 33/33.
prove *v.* test 7/34, *etc.*; **prove to** become, grow to 95/24.
provoked *pp.* called upon 75/3; *pt.* urged to action 143/10.
pryvy *adj. See* **privye.**
purseuaunt *n.* pursuivant 9/14.
purvyours *n. pl.* purveyors 19/15.
pyllion *n.* priest's hat 23/12.
pystoler *n.* one who reads the Epistle 19/28.

qualefie *v.* moderate, mitigate 63/2, 146/3.
quyer *n.* choir 45/33.

race *n.* run 52/29.
raced *v. pt.* razed, scratched 151/20.
rathe *adv.* quickly, rapidly 130/34.
rathest *adj.*, **most rathest** most of all 114/8.
raylyng *pr. p.* 151/17. *See n.*
readopcion *n.* re-adoption 119/22.

recepte *n.* recipe, prescription 168/19.
recognysaunce *n.* recognition, acknowledgement 117/24.
reconsilment *n.* reconciliation 141/26.
reduce *v.* bring back, restore 58/18.
reedefied *v. pt.* rebuilt 5/35.
regally *n.* royalty, royal prerogative 181/12.
regard *n.* attention 28/22.
rehersyng *pr. p.* repeating 170/10, *etc.*
reiester *n.* register 147/32.
reioyce *v. trans.* feel joy on account of 65/26.
relented *pp.* melted 158/35.
remembred *pp.* recorded, mentioned 18/27.
remyssion *n.* forgiveness, pardon 9/24, 46/24 *See n.*
renommed *ppl. a.* renowned 75/18.
reparacion *n.* repair 138/10.
repayer *n.* repair, going 38/17.
repetor *n.* rehearser, trainer 19/27.
replenysshed *ppl. a.* fully stocked 69/21.
repugned *v. pt.* opposed, contended against 114/6.
requyer *v.* ask, request 27/4, *etc.*
respecte *n.* regard, consideration 130/2.
respeyght *n.* respite 92/2.
resumed *pp.* taken back 131/25.
resurreccion *n.* 133/17. *See n.*
retther *adv.* rather 73/22.
reuested *pp.* arrayed in vestments 58/31.
revelled *v. pt.* revealed 63/15, *etc.*
revestrie *n.* vestry 19/31.
revoke *v.* recall, summon back 34/35, 58/15.
reward *n.* gratuity 187/16.
ridyng clarke *n.* 20/23. *See n.*
robbyng *pr. p.* rubbing 54/16.
rochett *n.* linen vestment worn by bishops 107/11.
rome *n.* room, office, position 6/33, *etc.*
roodeloft *n.* rood-loft 54/10.

roundyng *pr. p.* whispering 27/23.
rownds *n. pl.* round marks (in archery) 183/24.
rowt *n.* retinue 162/9, *etc.*
rumour *n.* clamour, noise 57/13.
runnyng cootes *n. pl.* coats worn by footmen employed as runners 20/27.

sakbuttes *n. pl.* sackbuts 54/9.
saluegard *n.* safeguard 40/2.
sarcenet *n.* a fine silk material 99/2.
sault *n.* assault 40/32.
*****scripulositie** *n.* scrupulousness, scruple 83/3.
scripulous, scrypolous *adj.* scrupulous 14/5, 31/24, 83/14, *etc.*
scylence *n.* silence 80/4.
se *v.* see, ensure 107/2.
seased *pp.* seized 37/31.
season *n.* time 34/2, *etc.*
sedell *n.* 156/14. *See n.*
seen *ppl. a.* versed 122/1, 182/10.
semblable *adj., with the semblable* in the same manner 65/22, *etc.*
semblably *adv.* seemly, fittingly 49/19.
sentences *n. pl.* views 11/29.
*****seruauance** *n.* service 114/28.
seruyture *n.* attendant 30/1.
sewer *adj.* sure, certain 76/25, *etc.*
sewerly *adv.* surely 80/1.
sewers *n. pl.* servers 20/11.
sewartie *n.* surety 98/15, 162/33
sewger *n.* sugar 22/22.
sewgerd *ppl. a.* made sweet, agreeable 13/18.
shadowe *v.* shade, obscure 163/7.
shalme *n.* 60/6. *See n.*
shere *n.* shire 64/22.
shett *pp.* shut 161/16, *etc.*
shewe *v. pt.* showed 124/4.
shifte *n.* shift, expedient 52/7.
shyfted *v. pt.* changed 93/12.
sir *n.* sir (as term of address) 126/34, 127/24.
skaldyng howsse *n.* room in which utensils, etc., were scalded 19/8.
skantly *adv.* scarcely, hardly 9/15, *etc.*

skayn *n.* skein 87/29.
slaves *n. pl.* slaves (as term of contempt) 62/5.
slipe *n.* leash 60/25.
smell *v.* discern, suspect 41/30.
smoked *v. pt.* fumed, was angry at 34/21.
socours *n.* succour 6/29, 179/32. (O.F. *sucurs*)
soden, sodden *adj.* sudden 97/5, *etc.*
solomplest *adj.* most solemn 46/16.
solomply *adv.* solemnly 38/25, *etc.*
solompne *adj.* solemn 45/30, *etc.*
somme *n.* sum 8/27.
sompter man *n.* sumpterman 19/21.
sompter mewles *n. pl.* pack mules 45/2.
sonpmtyous *adj.* sumptuous 141/23.
sorte *n.* kind, manner; *with lyke sorte* in like manner 24/32; *vnder this sort* in this manner 26/1.
speres *n. pl.* pensioners, gentlemen-at-arms 48/23.
sprituall *adj.* spiritual 17/23.
spyall *n.* discovery, detection 63/14.
spyalles *n. pl.* spies 150/14.
stafe *n.* support, stay 6/29, *etc.*
staffe torche *n.* tall, thick candle 22/23, *etc.*
stale *v. pt.* stole 63/12.
stallacion *n.* installation 152/20.
stalle *v.* enthrone 66/10, 152/22.
stalled *v. pt.* came to a stand 60/35.
stand *v.* endure, bear 117/31; *stand in termes* take part in controversy 118/31.
standerdes *n. pl.* large chests 122/16.
standyng *n.* hunter's station 60/32.
standysshe *n.* standish, inkstand 63/6.
staye *n.* state 34/34.
stere *v.* stir up 37/10; *stere the coles* excite strife 95/35.
sterrechamber *n.* Star Chamber 24/12.
steyers *n. pl.* stairs 86/24.

stomake *n.* stomach 74/30; (as seat of lust) 35/7; temper, disposition 117/28.
stomaked *v. pt.* resented 58/6.
stopped *v. pt.* blocked 153/28.
stoutly *adv.* haughtily, proudly 58/7.
stowt *adj.* proud, haughty 35/8.
strak *v. pt.* struck 57/16.
strayngers *n. pl.* foreigners 25/8, *etc.*
*****strayntly** *adv.* straightly, strictly 145/21.
strenthe *n.* strength 40/29.
stroke *n.*, *bare the stroke* achieved a triumph 43/17.
stykke *v.* hesitate, scruple 108/17.
suerly *adv.* surely, steadfastly 116/19.
sumptioser *adj.* more sumptuous 72/14.
supportacion *n.* support, countenance 26/34, *etc.*
surmountythe *v. pr. 3 s.* surpasses 116/11; *pt.* **surmounted** prevailed over, overcame 102/28.
surveyour of the dressor *n.* 18/35. *See n.*
suspecte *adj.* suspected 173/3.
symple *adj.* humble 16/22.
symply *adv.* simply 131/6.
symplycyte *n.* plainness of life 148/31.

tablett *n.* flat ornament 121/7.
take *v.*, *take day* put off to another day 113/2.
taken *pp.* accepted by the mind 105/10. *See n.*
tappett *n.* cloth hanging 151/11.
tariaunce *n.* temporary residence 132/27.
tauny *n.* cloth of a tawny colour 44/36.
therfroo *adv.* therefrom 179/19.
thether the other 57/24, *etc.*
thrommed *ppl. a.* fringed 60/24.
*****thrust** (up) *pp.* trussed up, tied in a bundle 173/26 (*Suffolk dial.* 'thr' *for* 'tr').

Glossary

tippett *n.* fur scarf 23/13.
tonnes *n. pl.* tuns, large casks 97/20.
tornyng *pr. p.* tourneying 73/2.
tossed *pp.* ?set in motion; ?bandied about 78/30.
tother the other 57/30, *etc.*
towardnes *n.* compliance 65/27.
toyle *n.* net into which game is driven 60/15.
tract *v.* prolong, delay 175/35, *etc.*
trade *n.* course, path 123/20, 127/1.
trapped *ppl. a.* adorned with trappings 23/34.
trapper *n.* covering over a horse 52/11.
travell *n.* travail 6/31, *etc.*; *v.* 10/24, *etc.*
travelous *adj.* laborious 129/1.
travers *n.* compartment enclosed by a screen 54/1, *etc.*
treasorshipe *n.* treasurership 7/2.
tremlyng *pr. p.* trembling 155/15.
trompe *n.* trump, trumpet 3/3.
troppeters *n. pl.* trumpeters 54/10.
truppettes *n. pl.* trumpets 70/8.
trussyng chest *n.* chest used for packing 169/36.
trust *v. pt.* trusted 121/29.
turkkas *n.* turquoise 111/18.
tykkyll *adj.* tickle, uncertain 187/32.

valaunce *n.* valise, cloak bag 45/10.
vamppes *n. pl.* bottom part of stockings 148/26.
vanqiesshed *pp.* vanquished 115/26.
varyaunce *n.* discord, quarrel 145/1.
vaughtyng *pr. p.* vaulting 70/36.
vayn *n.* vein 12/10.
very *adj.* rightful, legitimate 147/4; *adv.* truly 154/3.
visonamy *n.* physiognomy, face 25/25.
vnreuerent *adj.* irreverent 86/14.

vsage *n.* usage, behaviour 4/4, *etc.*; custom 56/31, *etc.*
vse *v.* treat 65/22.

wade *v.* go 90/12, 149/28.
wafery *n.* wafer-kitchen 19/13.
waffetyng *pr. p.* sailing 100/24.
wane *v. pt.* won 27/15, *etc.*
ward *n.* first or outer court 55/5; custody 150/26.
wardens *n. pl.* baking pears 167/18.
ware *v. pt.* wore 130/16.
warfore *conj.* wherefore 150/9.
warne *v.* summon 70/8.
water *v.*, *water his eyes* shed tears 87/21.
way, *v.* weigh 166/34.
wele *n.* weal 6/8, *etc.*
wene *v.* think 186/33.
were *pron.* where 138/7.
wether *conj.* whether 137/32.
wexe *v.* wax, increase 29/1, *etc.*
whan *v. pt.* won 41/22.
where *v.* wear 103/21.
whether *n.* weather 143/31.
whether *adv.* whither 130/11.
wonder *adj.* wondrous 36/16.
wonderly *adv.* in a wonderful manner 24/28; to a wonderful extent 12/25.
wondersly *adv.* wondrously 34/27, 58/13.
wondyd *pp.* wounded 84/6.
world *n., ys it not a world* is it not a marvel 78/14.
wyhight *adj.* white 60/25.
wyllest *conj.* whilst 135/21, *etc.*
wyry *n.* wherry, light boat 77/30.
wysdomes *n. pl.* title of respect 145/14.
wytsontyd *n.* Whitsuntide 38/23, *etc.*

yerthe *n.* earth 159/30.
yerthely *adj.* earthly 73/13.
yewer *n.* ewer, pitcher 71/26.

INDEX OF NAMES

Abvyle Abbeville 50
Alyn, Sir Iohn 176
Amyens Amiens 50–1, 53–4
Arde Ardres 56
Argos Argus 150
Arthure, Prince 83, 85
Arundell, Sir Thomas 104
Assher Esher 98, 104, 112, 119, 121–3
Augusteyn, Doctor 151–2, 155, 157

Bathe 18
Bathe, Bysshope of 77
Bathe Place 77, 87
Baynbryge, Doctor 15
Beame, Kyng of King of Bohemia 179
Beddford, Erle of 37
Bees, Monsur de du Biez, Captain of Boulogne 46, 49
Bell, Doctor 79
Biean, Bysshope of Bishop of Bayonne 83
Blake ffriers Blackfriars (London) 78–9, 86, (Doncaster) 163
Blakhethe Blackheath 16, 77
Blythe Abbey 143
Bolayn (Bulloyn), Sir Thomas 29 etc., 128
Boleyn (Bolloyn), Anne 29–30, 34–5, 43–4, 74, 92, 120–1
Bolleyn, Bolloyn, Bulloyn Boulogne 46, 48–50
Bonner, Doctor 151–2
Bononye Bologna 76
Brandon, Charles 50
Breerton, Master 139
Brian, Le Countie 49
Bridewell (Bridwell) 11, 78, 86–7, 91
Brugges Bruges 22
Bryttayn, Duchy of Duchy of Brittany 59
Burbon, Duke of Duke of Bourbon 37–41, 43

Burgonyons Burgundians 51
Buttes, Doctor 120–1
Byllyngesgate Billingsgate 24

Calice Calais 6–8, 14, 46, 48, 64, 97
Cambryge 75–6
Campagious, Cardynall Cardinal Campeggio 77, 89, 92–3, 97
Carelyle (Carlylle), Bysshope of 86, 104
Castell Ayngell Castel Sant' Angelo, Rome 42–3
Caunterbure Canterbury 15 etc., 45
Caunterbure, Archebisshope of 15–17, 79, 84
Cawood 144 etc.
Cawood Castell 145, 151, 162
Charles the 5 21
Charterhowsse Chirche 130
Chastell de Crykkey Crecqui Castle 57
Chekker, The 46
Chichester, Bysshope of 79
Clement, Doctor 121
Clermount, Countie 15
Collett, Doctor 130
Compign (Compygne) Compiègne 54, 57, 60, 63
Cooke of Wynchester 79
Creekey, Monsur Monsieur Crecqui 55
Cromer, Doctor 121
Cromwell, Thomas 104–7, 109, 112, 115, 123–7, 129–32
Crystes Church, Abbey of 45

Dancaster Doncaster 163
Derby, Erle of 20
Dertford Dartford 45
Dolphyn, The The Dauphin 43
Dorsett, Lord Marques 5
Dover 8–9, 14, 64
Duresme, Bysshopryche of Bishopric of Durham 17–18

Index

Edward IV, King 50
Elis, Parson 177
Empson, Master 96
Emson, Sir Richard 11
Eston 96

Ferdynando, Kyng of Spayn 81
Feryebrigg Ferrybridge 144
Feuersham Faversham 45
Fissher, Doctor 79
Fitzwalter, Lord 61
Fitzwilliam, Sir William 133–5
Flaunders 7, 22
Flet Strett Fleet Street 11
Fountayn, Madame 59
Foxe, Doctor 7, 17
Fraunces I, King 59

Gagge, Sir Iohn 183–4
Garter the harold 66
Gascoyn, Sir William 100
Gonner (Gunner), Cristofer Sir Christopher Gunner 59, 63
Grafton 92, 96
Grantham 135
Graveshend Gravesend 8
Grenwyche Greenwich 24, 66–7, 72, 112
Gressham, Sir Richard 176
Griffithe, Master 82
Grysheld Griselda 35
Gwees, Monsur de Monsieur de Guise 52
Gwyldford, Sir Henry Sir Harry Guildford 26
Gwynnes (Gynnes) Guines 48, 63

Hall, Master 135
Hamnes Hammes 48
Hampton Court 67–9, 72, 98, 104, 123, 183
Hanworthe 69, 187
Hardwyke Hall 174
Hartwell Parke 97
Hastynges, Master Bryan 145
Hendon 132
Hereford 18
Herry V, King 181
Herry VII, King 6, 8, 10, 17–18
Herry VIII, King 11, 50, 80 *etc.*

Hikden, Doctor Doctor Higden, Dean of York 146, 177
Huntyngdon, Abbey of 133
Hykden, Doctor Doctor Higden, Dean of Cardinal College 176

Iokyn, Iohn Jean Joachim de Passano 38
Ipsewiche 4, 99, 113, 125
Iulius, Pope 15

Katheren, Queen 11, 29, 35, 80, 82, 179
Kent 45, 64
Kyngeston, Sir William 168–87

Lanterne Gate 46
Lasselles, Sir Roger 162
Lewyce, *see* Lowice
Leycester 185
Leycester Abbey 174
Leycester, Mayor of 182
London 8 *etc.*
London Bridge 44
Longvyle, Duke of 15
Lorrayn, Cardynall of 48, 52–3
Lorrayn, Duke of 52
Lovayn Louvain 76
Lovell, Sir Thomas 7, 9–10
Lowice, King 50, 55, 59
Lutarnaunce Lutherans 179
Lyncolne 10, 15
Lyncolne, Lord of 84

Madame Regent Louise, Regent of France 51, 53, 57–60
Magdaleyn Collage Magdalen College, Oxford 5
Marshall, Doctor 105
Mary, Lady Henry VIII's sister 50
Marye, Pryncess Henry VIII's daughter 62, 83
Maxymylian, Emperor 7, 14, 21
Middell Temple 5
Montdedyer Montdidier 57
More, The Wolsey's Palace (now Moor Park, Herts.) 92, 97
Muterell sur la mere Montreuil sur la mer 49–50

Index 303

Nanfant, Sir Iohn 6
Naver, Quene of Queen of Navarre 51, 53, 59
Naverne, King of King of Navarre 59
Neveyll, Sir Edward 27–8
Newarke 135
Newarke, Castell of 135, 138
Nicholas, Doctor 174
Norffolk 31
Norffolk, Duke of 94–5, 98, 114–16, 124, 127, 129–30, 184–6
Normandye, Duchye of 64
Norreys, Sir Herre Sir Harry Norris 93, 101–4, 184
Northamtonshere Northamptonshire 92
Northumberland, [fifth] Erle of 29, 32–3
Northumberland, [sixth] Erle of 150 etc.
Nothyngham Nottingham 174
Notre Dame Saynt Marye, Churche de 51, 53

OldCastell, Sir Iohn Sir John Oldcastle 181
Orlyaunce, Duke of Duke of Orleans 43, 62, 83
Orlyaunce, Vnyuersite of University of Orleans 76
Ormond, Erle of 31
Our Ladys Chappell (Peterborough) 133, (Leicester) 183
Oxford, College of (Cardinal College) 99, 113, 125, 133, 176
Oxford, Vnuyersitie of 4, 75–6

Padwaye Padua 76
Palmes, Doctor 175, 177–8
Paris 63, 76, 121
Parre, Lady 132
Pavya Pavia 38
Pawlett, Sir Amys 5–6
Percye (see also Northumberland [sixth] Earl) 29–32, 34–5
Peter, Doctor 79
Peterboroughe 133–4
Peterboroughe, Abbey of 133
Phillipe, King 21

Poumfrett (Pumfrett) Pontefract 161–2
Pountfrett (Pumfrett), Abbey of 151, 162
Powlles Chirche Yerd 66
Powlles, Cathederall Chirche of 66, 70
Pumfrett Castell 162
Putnethe Hethe Putney Heath 103
Putney (Putnethe) 100–1
Pykardy Picardy 49
Pynkney Picquigny 51
Pynkney Castell Picquigny Castle 50–1

Ratclyfe, Master (Henry) 61
Ratclyfe, Master (Robert) 186–7
Reigne, Madame Renée, Francis I's sister-in-law 59, 62
Rice John ap Rhys (?) 48
Richemond 7, 9–10, 38, 67, 123, 127, 132
Richemond, Erledome of 128
Richemond, Charterhowsse of 130
Rocheford, Viscount 29
Rochester 45
Rochester, Bisshope of 79, 84–5
Rofford Abbey 143
Rome (Roome) 15, 18, 42, 77, 90, 92, 96–7
Royston 132
Russell, Sir Iohn 37–8, 110–11
Russhe, Sir Thomas 112
Rycherd II, King 180
Rydley, Doctor 79–80, 86
Rye, The 132

Sadler, Sir Rafe 110
Salomon, Salamon Solomon 11, 81
Sampson, Doctor 79
Sandes, Lord 26, 63
Sandyngfeld Sandingfield 48
Savoye, Master of 176
Saynt Assaph, Bysshope of 79
Scottes Scots 51
Scrobye 141–4, 184
Seynt Albons, Abbey of 17, 125
Seynt Albons, Monastory of 97
Seynt Iames Chappell 148

Seynt Maris Churche 46
Seynt Oswaldes Abbeye 144
Seynt Thomas 45
Sheffeld Parke 163
Shelley, Master 116–19
Shrewesbury, Erle of 34, 140, 142–3, 163–4, 167, 170–1, 174
Smythe, Doctor 15
Somme 50
Souches Switzers 51
Southewell 135, 138, 140, 142
Stampford Stamford 135
Standysshe, Doctor 79
Stephens, Doctor 79, 92, 96
Strode 45
Suffolk 4
Suffolk, Duke of 50, 55, 57, 65, 90, 95, 97–8
Surrey 104
Sussex, Erle of 61

Tayllour, Doctor 48
Temmes Thames 26, 100
Temmes Strette 24
Tempest, Sir Richard 145
Temple Barre 77
Teurwyn Thérouanne 14
Tourney Tournai 14–15
Tower, The 100, 175, 181
Tower, Constable of the 169, 172
Tower Hyll 79
Tregonell, Doctor 79

Vademount, Monsur 52
Venus 29
Vyncent, Master 175, 184

Warham, Doctor 79
Welbeke Abbey 142
Welshe (Walshe), Sir Walter 152–3, 155–8, 168
Westminster 44, 64, 67, 72, 75, 86, 97, 117, 123
Westminster Abbey 16
Westminster, Abbot of 132
Westmynster Hall 22–4, 64
Wolsey, Thomas 3 *etc.*
Worcester 18
Worcetor, Bysshope of 79
Worsoppe Parke 142
Wotten, Doctor 121
Writhesley (Wrothesley), Master 139
Wyate, Sir Harre 64
Wycklyfe Wiclif 179–80
Wyltcher, Sir Richard 45
Wyltchere, Lord of 29, 66, 87
Wynchester 7, 94, 124–5
Wynchester, Bysshope of 7, 9, 17, 79, 92, 98
Wynchester, Bysshopriche of 18, 104, 124, 131
Wyndesore Windsor 67, 72, 98
Wyndesore, Castell of 50

Yorke 15–16, 94, 117, 124, 129, 138, 141, 146–7 *etc.*
Yorke, Archebysshope of 3–4, 15 *etc.*
Yorke Mynster 149
Yorke Place 117
Yorke, Treasorer of 177